GIFTS, FAVORS,
AND BANQUETS

THE WILDER HOUSE SERIES
IN POLITICS, HISTORY,
· AND CULTURE

The Wilder House Series is published in association with the
Wilder House Board of Editors and the University of Chicago.

A complete list of titles in the series
appears at the end of this book.

David Laitin and George Steinmetz, *Editors*

GIFTS, FAVORS, AND BANQUETS

THE ART OF SOCIAL RELATIONSHIPS IN CHINA

Mayfair Mei-hui Yang

CORNELL
UNIVERSITY
PRESS

Ithaca &
London

First published 1994 by Cornell University Press.
First printing, Cornell Paperbacks, 1994.

Printed in the United States of America

♾ The paper in this book meets the minimum requirements of the American National Standard for Information Sciences—Permanence of Paper for Printed Library Materials, ANSI Z39.48-1984.

Library of Congress Cataloging-in-Publication Data

Yang, Mayfair Mei-hui.
  Gifts, favors, and banquets: The art of social relationships in China / Mayfair Mei-hui Yang.
    p.   cm. — (The Wilder House Series in politics, history, and culture)
  Includes bibliographical references and index.
  ISBN 0-8014-2343-0 (alk. paper). — ISBN 0-8014-9592-X (pbk.: alk. paper)
  1. Social interaction—China. 2. Social networks—China. 3. Gifts—China.
4. Individualism—China. 5. Communism and individualism—China. 6. Civil society—China. 7. China—Politics and government. I. Title. II. Series.
HN733.5.Y366   1994
302.5'0951—dc20
                                                        94-2653

cloth printing   10 9 8 7 6 5 4 3 2 1

paperback printing   10 9 8 7 6 5 4 3

Contents

Acknowledgments

In the research and writing of this book, I have incurred countless personal debts to people and institutions in China and the United States. I am especially grateful to Eric C. White for moral support and intellectual inspiration throughout the research period and for reading through most of the manuscript. Two others who read the entire manuscript and gave copious and useful comments are David Laitin and my colleague Elvin Hatch.

I also thank my teachers: Jack Potter, who early on encouraged my academic aspirations and sparked a political flame; Paul Rabinow, who introduced me to French theory and inspired me to indulge in philosophical speculation; Cyril Birch, a gentle and generous influence in my education in modern Chinese literature; David Keightley, who nourished my interest in ancient Chinese thought and whose enthusiastic response gave me the confidence to retain Chapter 6; Frederic Wakeman, who has always been most supportive; and Burton Benedict, who gave useful comments on the earliest drafts. I also owe many thanks to friends and colleagues in China and the United States for their valuable assistance in providing and interpreting fieldwork data or in reading and commenting on different chapters of the book: Ann Anagnost, Tani Barlow, Deng Fang, Ken Dewoskin, Manthia Diawara, Prasenjit Duara, Ron Egan, Roger Friedland, Tamar Gordon, Abdul JanMohamed, Elliot Jurist, Benjamin Lee, Li Fan, Lydia Liu, Luo Xiaopeng, Aihwa Ong, David Ren, Lisa Rofel, Michael Schoenhals, Marilyn Strathern, Tang Ben, Wu Xiaoming, Yan Yunxiang, and Yang Xiaodong. For their help in the latter stage of the writing of this book, I also thank my research assistants Sun Hong, Julie Chuang, Kang Xiaofei, and Lu Mei-huan. Thanks also go to Li Weimin for help with the Index.

Without the financial and organizational assistance and encouragement of several grant agencies and research institutions, this book would not have been possible. I thank the following organizations and the people in them who supported my project. For research grants, I am grateful to the American Association of University Women; the Institute of East Asian Studies, University of California at Berkeley; the W. H. Mills Traveling Fellowship in International Relations, U.C. Berkeley; the University of California at Santa Barbara; the Faculty Career Development Award, U.C. Santa Barbara; the Interdisciplinary Humanities Center Fellowship, U.C. Santa Barbara; and the Presidential Young Investigator Award, National Science Foundation. For institutional affiliation, which facilitated my library research and the writing of the book, I thank the Center for Chinese Studies postdoctoral fellowship at the University of Michigan and the Fairbank Center for Chinese Studies, Harvard University. Thanks also go to the Center for Psychosocial Studies, Chicago, for inviting me to give presentations and interact with diverse scholars at their many conferences.

I am also grateful to the following Chinese institutions for hosting or approving my various visits to China: Beijing University, Chinese Academy of Sciences, and the Wenzhou City Government. Needless to say, the opinions expressed in this book are my own, and do not reflect those of these institutions.

All Chinese names used in this book are pseudonyms, except for those of famous people, or unless the person gave me permission to use his or her real name.

All translations from Chinese are my own unless otherwise indicated. Published English translations of Chinese texts which I have slightly modified are marked with an asterisk (*).

The exchange rate between Chinese currency (*renminbi* or *yuan*) and U.S. dollars has fluctuated from the official rate of about 4 yuan to a U.S. dollar in the early 1980s, to about 5.7 yuan in 1990, and to 8 yuan in 1993 in the streets.

Finally, I also thank two journals for giving me permission to publish here articles that originally appeared in them: *Comparative Studies in Society and History* (Yang 1989a; reprinted with permission of Cambridge University Press) and the French journal *Annales* (Yang 1991).

M. M. Y.

GIFTS, FAVORS,
AND BANQUETS

太上貴德，其次務施報. 禮尙往來.
往而不來，非禮也; 來而不往，亦非禮也.

In the highest antiquity they prized (simply conferring) good; in the time next to this, giving and repaying [*bao*] was the thing attended to. And what the rules of propriety [*li*] value is that reciprocity. If I give a gift and nothing comes in return, that is contrary to propriety; if the thing comes to me, and I give nothing in return, that also is contrary to propriety.

—*Li Ji* (Book of rites), "Qu Li,"
1987:7; Legge 1885:65

Fieldwork, Politics, and Modernity in China

The "Discovery" of Guanxixue

On a cold February night in Beijing in 1982, I set out by bicycle with my friend Du Ruoben, a graduate student in his thirties, to pay a visit to a worker he knew from his days in a factory during the Cultural Revolution (1966–76).[1] Ruoben and an old classmate of his periodically visited me at Beijing University to practice their English, and over the course of our few months' acquaintance, he had suggested several times that a social phenomenon called *guanxixue* (pronounced *guan-shee-shwe*) 关系学 was a facet of Chinese life worth examining. Tonight Ruoben was going to introduce me to his worker friend Ding Jian, who was not only adept at the practice of guanxixue but also fearless about speaking whatever was on his mind.

I had been an American exchange student at Beijing University since September 1981, and in the few months prior to visiting Ding Jian my anthropological interest in guanxixue had been aroused. The word *guanxi* (pronounced *guan-shee*) means literally "a relationship" between objects, forces, or persons. When it is used to refer to relationships between people, not only can it be applied to husband-wife, kinship, and friendship relations, it can also have the sense of "social connections," dyadic relationships that are based implicitly (rather than explicitly) on mutual interest and benefit. Once guanxi is established between two people, each can ask a favor of the other with the expectation that the debt incurred will be repaid sometime in the fu-

---

[1] The Cultural Revolution was a period of revolutionary zeal initiated by Chairman Mao. It saw the speeding up of economic collectivization and a radical leveling and flattening of social classes. This was achieved by instigating attacks on people in positions of authority (except Mao himself), and by sending city dwellers, intellectuals, and officials to the countryside to learn from peasants, and to the factories to do manual labor.

ture. Born in Taiwan of mainland Chinese parents, I was already cognizant of the cultural importance of gift-giving and maintenance of personal relationships in various Chinese milieus. What I started to discover that night was that in mainland China, these practices are quite elaborated and intensified, with interesting new twists of political and economic dimensions.

As we biked down some of Beijing's many narrow lanes (*hutong*), bordered on each side by high walls shielding residential courtyards, I asked Ruoben whether his friend would feel comfortable talking to someone from the United States for the first time. In 1982, China had just opened up to the outside world, and for Chinese in general, the cultural atmosphere was still one of wariness toward associating with "foreigners" or "overseas Chinese," lest they be accused of betraying their country.

"He'll really open up Chinese society to you. Don't tell him you're from abroad, that'll make him too nervous, and even someone like him won't talk. Just leave everything up to me, I'll do the explaining," he reassured me right before we knocked on his friend's door.

His friend opened the door and ushered us into chairs. He looked to be in his mid-thirties, a gregarious, talkative, and, to my mind, comical round-faced person who gesticulated freely with his hands to dramatize his points. Before I could utter a word, Ruoben had already introduced me as a Beijing University student studying in the new field of sociology, who because of an entire life spent as "a flower in the study" (*shufang li de hua*) protected from the outside world, now found it necessary in my studies of society to find out more about "the conditions at the lower levels" (*dixia de qingkuang*). In other words, without being explicit, Ruoben had managed to convey to Ding Jian certain impressions about my family background: first, that I was a native Chinese and, second, that I had been born to a privileged position, perhaps a daughter of a high cadre, someone whom it would be good for him to befriend.[2]

The unexpected introduction took me by surprise and caused me acute anxiety throughout the evening. At least I looked the part, and my Mandarin Chinese was fluent enough to be mistaken for a native's. That I lacked a Beijing accent could be attributed to a southern

---

[2] Later, after leaving Ding's house, I asked Ruoben how it was that after the great social dislocations of the Cultural Revolution, when elites were sent down to learn from the masses, there could still exist people of privilege who were sheltered from society and remained untouched by historical events. His response was to pronounce, in that cryptic and all-knowing fashion, words that I encountered many times in China, "There are still many things you need to know about China. Things in China are very complicated [*fuza*]."

Chinese origin. But I certainly did not feel or act like someone who had grown up all her life in socialist society, a society that for me was still filled with large expanses of the unknown. It was already hard enough for me to balance a schizophrenic split between a precarious identity as an "overseas Chinese" and an equally problematic identity as a "Chinese-American." Now I had to act the part of a native Chinese, born and raised under socialism. Under the circumstances, I felt compelled to go through with this deception of poor Ding Jian, and so made an effort to act as I thought a mainland Chinese woman born of influential parents might act, an undertaking made all the more difficult by the fact that I had as yet not knowingly met one, but had only seen a couple of portrayals in Chinese movies. Playing the part as well as I could, I hoped all the while that my shy and tentative demeanor and my glaring ignorance of Chinese society might perhaps be dismissed as due to my lack of exposure to the world. Ruoben, for his part, was totally unperturbed. After discussing various topics, he skillfully redirected the conversation.

"I haven't been keeping up much, but social relations [*ren yu ren de guanxi*] are really getting more and more complicated [*fuza*] these days. Tell us how guanxixue works," he prompted his friend on my behalf.

I present extracts of our conversation, a reconstruction of direct dialogue based on the notes I took afterward and my memory of that night. A reconstruction edits and smooths out the stutters and tangential detours of the actual flow of speech. In the course of my fieldwork, I learned to avoid taking notes directly in front of people, except those whom I had come to know well, for fear that the act would make them self-conscious, guarded, or even suspicious. Even more problematical was the use of a tape recorder in these casual encounters, although it proved a convenient method in interviews with officials, who usually spoke in a self-censored and formal official language for public consumption anyway.

Ding Jian leaned forward and explained patiently, "Guanxixue is doing favors for people. Everyone uses their guanxi network [*guanxiwang*]. You ask a friend for a favor, if he can't do it, he asks someone else. In this way the lower strata can connect up with the higher levels. You probably know already how high cadres get their information about society. Not through their secretaries' reports, but through their sons and daughters and their friends lower down."

"You mean lower and higher levels are connected up through doing favors for each other?" I asked, switching internally into the ethnographer's role.

"Well there're many levels in between. I mean, a need may arise from the lower level, and then pass through a lot of people and end up with a higher level doing the favor. Take me, for example, my birth was not good [*chusheng buhao*] [i.e., he was born into a family with a bad class background such as capitalist or landlord in the old society; as a result, his social and political status in the new society is low]. During the Cultural Revolution when work discipline in my factory was slack, I seldom went to work and fell in with some petty criminal elements—we sold stolen goods. After the downfall of the Gang of Four, I resolved to do better and managed to get into a night college program to study Chinese history. It will take five years to finish. I want to be a high school teacher; I don't want to be a worker anymore. In the night college, my guanxi network has broadened [*kuoda*], I have met all sorts of people coming from all different work units around the city, most of them at the middle levels of society. So between my Cultural Revolution contacts at the lower levels and my night-college contacts at the middle levels, my network covers a lot of ground, see?"

He proceeded then to recount with great relish and pride how he had recently managed to use guanxixue for his own purposes. One day a doctor he knew asked him for help in obtaining four pieces of an expensive and rare Chinese herbal medicine that could not be found in any hospital or pharmacy to which the doctor himself had guanxi access. The price of the medicine was 49 yuan per piece for B-grade quality and 80 yuan for A-grade.[3] He knew that this contact with the doctor was important to cultivate and was glad of an opportunity to put the doctor in his debt. So he "immediately mobilized [his] entire guanxi network" (*mashang fadongle wo zhengge guanxiwang*). He spent the whole morning pedaling tirelessly around town looking up various acquaintances and friends.

After feeling out a number of contacts to no avail, he dropped in on a friend who worked as a doctor's aide in a hospital in the Dongchen District in the eastern part of the city. The friend could not help directly because regulations for dispensing this kind of medicine are very strict, requiring a specialist doctor's prescription; however, Ding Jian's friend was able to refer him to another person who was on good terms with a specialist doctor who might be persuaded to write such a prescription. So Ding Jian went to see this friend's friend with a scribbled note of introduction from the doctor's aide. When Ding

---

[3] For exchange rates, see the Acknowledgements.

told this third person what he wanted, the latter stared at him and exclaimed, "Do you know what you are asking for? This stuff is for people who eat high-class food [*chi gaoji fan*] and shit high-class shit [*la gaoji shi*]!" But he agreed to take Ding Jian to the specialist doctor, who worked in a hospital in Haidian District in northwest Beijing. They managed to persuade the doctor there to sign and affix his seal to a prescription for one B-grade piece of the medicine. Ding Jian then rode all the way back to his friend in the hospital in east Beijing with the prescription and bought one piece of the medicine there.

The whole process took Ding Jian only one full day, which he considered a record in his experience. When he presented his hard-won trophy, the first doctor, who had made the request, was very happy and deeply grateful. Ding surmised that no doubt the medicine was not for this doctor's own personal use, but for an important patient or friend of the doctor's and that the doctor was engaging in a bit of guanxixue himself.

This particular guanxi transaction involved many steps. Between the doctor who made the original request and the person who actually granted it by signing a prescription stood three intermediaries who contributed their personal guanxi to the search for the medicine: Ding Jian, Ding's friend in east Beijing, and Ding's friend's friend who knew the herbal specialist personally. There was also the possibility that the first doctor was only an intermediary himself for another person. I asked Ding how far such chains of guanxi could extend. He replied that theoretically they could extend indefinitely, that in this way, one could start with a guanxi at the lower levels of society and find oneself indirectly relying on guanxi at the top levels of society. He admitted, however, that these cases were the exception rather than the rule. If there are too many go-betweens on the chain, it is difficult to keep track of the request, and the process will become so long and unwieldy that people will give up hope.

"What do you get out of all this work?" I prodded further.

"Well now the doctor owes me something [*qian wo yige*]. I can just put it [the debt] there [*fang zai nar*], for four or five years even, until I need something, and then I just go reclaim it. Actually, I've been thinking of going on a long vacation to travel around the country and see some sights. That would require a few months away from work. I'll probably have him write me a certificate of illness so I can get a long sick leave for my vacation."

It was not until the vivid descriptions given to me this night by Ruoben's friend, that I decided to devote my energies to understanding the dynamics of guanxixue. This area of inquiry promised to provide a crucial entry point into understanding certain lines of dynamism and tension within contemporary mainland society. Poised as this set of practices seemed, at an intersection between the "traditional" and the "socialist," it invited a closer examination. Guanxixue would serve as a window that would open up to me facets of a much larger and more complex cultural, social, and political formation.

Guanxixue as an Object of Study

Guanxixue involves the exchange of gifts, favors, and banquets; the cultivation of personal relationships and networks of mutual dependence; and the manufacturing of obligation and indebtedness. What informs these practices and their native descriptions is the conception of the primacy and binding power of personal relationships and their importance in meeting the needs and desires of everyday life.

Such a conception can be found as an underlying cultural assumption shared by Chinese everywhere, on the mainland before and after the Communist Revolution of 1949, in Taiwan, and among overseas Chinese in Southeast Asia. At the same time, however, in socialist China in the 1980s and 1990s, this corpus of assumptions and practices has been woven into a vociferous self-conscious discourse with both popular and official forms. It is a discourse that treats these personal gift-exchange practices as something new, a social phenomenon gaining strength in recent years.

What was remarkable for me was the sheer frequency with which the topic of guanxixue came up in conversation with Chinese of different walks of life, usually without any prompting on my part. Guanxixue is a ubiquitous theme; it appears in economic transactions; in political and social relationships; in literature, newspapers, academic journals, theater, and film; and in both popular and official discourse. Compared with other social practices, there also seems to be a greater cultural elaboration of vocabulary, jokes, proverbs, and etiquette surrounding guanxixue.

There are two ways to approach this discourse. One is to treat it as a description of social fact, a transparent medium for depicting the quality and conduct of interpersonal relations in socialist China. The other is to treat this discourse not merely as representation but as a social fact in and of itself (Rabinow 1986), whose history, conditions of formation, and specific contours provide information not only on its referent, guanxi practices, but also on the larger social forces that produced the discourse and gave it prominence.

I started out with only the first approach, with the assumption that guanxi discourse was perfectly coextensive with guanxi practice, but the complex nature of the field data made me realize the importance of the second approach. The same action of engaging in guanxixue could be described, interpreted, and evaluated in different ways by different people, or by the same person in different ways at different times. The question that occurred to me was, What prompted a significant number of people to recognize and comment on guanxixue at a certain time, or to form a rough consensus about when it was revived? It is this question, one prompted by recognizing guanxixue not only as social practice but also as discourse, which promises to extend a study of guanxixue into an inquiry into the kind of social formation that produces and recognizes it. This is the two-part task of this book: to describe and explicate, as much as possible in native terms, the logic and mechanics of guanxixue, and to explore the social and historical conditions that have led to its emergence (or reemergence).

Similar practices can certainly be found in non-Chinese contexts such as poor urban black communities in the United States (Stack 1974), the urban middle class of Chile (Lomnitz 1971), and the Nigerian bureaucracy (Eames 1992). It is especially interesting that the exchange of gifts and favors is a striking feature of the former state-socialist societies of Eastern Europe and the Soviet Union (Kenedi 1981; Wedel 1986; Sampson 1983, 1985; Berliner 1957). Personal gift relations also figured prominently in imperial and republican China, and still do in contemporary capitalist Taiwan (Yang 1957; Fei 1983; Fried 1953; Jacobs 1979; King 1991). These similarities notwithstanding, there are important features of the phenomenon under study peculiar to the historical situation of postrevolutionary China.

That very similar practices are found in Eastern Europe and the former Soviet Union suggests that this phenomenon cannot be reduced to a traditional Chinese resistance to change, but must be explored with a view to understanding its connections with a state-socialist political economy and culture. In this book I try to unravel the specific cultural, historical, political, and economic forces in socialist China which have come to mobilize and amplify guanxi practices and deploy an attendant multivocal discourse in the Chinese cultural repertoire. The information and arguments set forth in this book apply mainly to urban and not rural China.

Although "guanxi" exists in the lexicon of everyday language in Taiwan (see Jacobs 1979, 1980), its cognate term "guanxixue," which means literally "the study of connections," is hardly ever heard outside the new socialist society on the mainland. "Guanxixue" is worth examining because of the popular gloss given to its semantics, a gloss that brings out its satiric significance. *Xue* is the nominative suffix, which when appended to a word means "the study of" or "-ology," as in the words for "zoology" (*dongwuxue*), "biology" (*shengwuxue*), and "anthropology" (*renleixue*). Therefore, "guanxixue" can be translated "the study of guanxi" or "guanxiology." The satiric connotation of "guanxixue" lies in its elevation of the art of cultivating personal relationships into a full-fledged scholarly branch of knowledge equally valid and just as necessary as any other academic specialization. As the saying goes:

Xuehui shulihua, buru youge hao baba.

A command of mathematics, physics, and chemistry is not worth as much as having a good father [i.e., with connections].

The superiority of "guanxiology" over these respected branches of learning is implied ironically by the suggestion that guanxixue will get a person much further in the world than formal learning ever can. With this ironic resonance in mind, "guanxixue" would best be rendered in English as "the art of personal relationships," drawing on the sense of skill, subtlety, and cunning conveyed by the word "*artfulness.*"

Guanxixue or "art of guanxi" places an emphasis on the binding power and emotional and ethical qualities of personal relationships; "gift economy" highlights the components of gift, favor, and banquet exchange. "Gift economy" is a useful term because guanxixue's logic of operation shares many properties with the gift reciprocity that Marcel Mauss and other anthropologists found in systems of non-market exchange in a wide variety of societies (Mauss 1967; Sahlins 1972; Malinowski 1961). That is, in guanxixue can be found the elements of the "obligation to give, to receive, and to repay," a mixture of disinterested and instrumental generosity, of voluntary and coerced reciprocity. The term "gift economy" also suggests that whatever material benefit can be gained in this economy can only be won by the enactment of ritualized forms of such relationships.

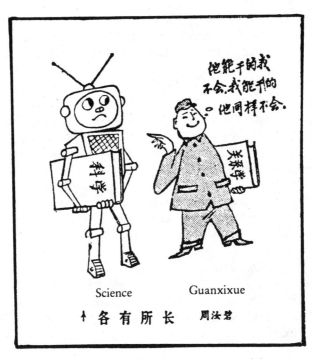

Science   Guanxixue

"Each has its own strengths," reads the caption of this newspaper cartoon (*ZGQNB*, 20 December 1984).

Besides the vivid description of guanxixue given to me by Ding Jian that memorable night, what also led me to the conclusion that guanxixue was worth thematizing in socialist society were my own frustrating experiences in Beijing as I attempted to carry out the kind of fieldwork I had originally envisioned back as a graduate student at Berkeley: a year-long holistic ethnography of factory life. The factory fulfilled my traditional anthropological conception of a field site as a bounded and delimited space; the fieldwork to be conducted there would take place in an identifiable community and consist of interviewing and interacting with people who all had long-standing relations with one another. In retrospect, two aspects of my less-than-satisfactory endeavors at factory fieldwork underscore the importance and, given the unique circumstances of fieldwork in a politicized urban China, the necessity of studying the art of guanxi.

First, the slow and painful process of obtaining permission to carry out fieldwork in a factory was a valuable, if excruciating, lesson in the thorough bureaucratization of urban China and in how and why such a system of power relations might preserve or produce the art of guanxi. The following excerpts from my notes on this extended process show how I attempted to engage different levels and sections of bureaucratic authority to obtain official permission. They sketch the outlines of the larger Chinese social structural context in which guanxixue operates: the complex edifice of bureaucratic power.

One may object that mine was a special case, that it involved a foreigner trying to pry into Chinese society, that it was not at all representative of the bureaucratic procedures that natives in their own society must go through. This line of argument says that I personally met with bureaucratic intransigence because officials were afraid of being called to account for my actions. Certainly my case was more politically sensitive than most, yet my experience of dealing with various state bureaucracies shares so many features with countless native tales of negotiating the bureaucratic maze, such as the experiences of a worker trying to get official permission to change residence recounted in Chapter 2. I learned that there are ways to deal with the bureaucracy which call for skill in the art of guanxi. These excerpts from my field diary illustrate the delicate and complex relationship between bureaucratic authority and guanxi power.

March 26, 1982

[At this point I had been petitioning (both verbally and in writing) for three months that the university arrange for me to visit a factory to study factory organization and interview workers about their daily lives.]

Each time I query them [university officials], they say they will look into it, but nothing happens. I have gotten to know Elder Sister Su, a woman accountant from the Number 1 Electric Fan Factory[4] in one of my university courses. She has said that she is ready to have me go to her factory to study. I have also gotten to know an older college student by the name of Fang Liping who has said she would use her guanxi to help me get permission to go to a factory.

Today Liping tells me that she has set up an appointment for us to meet with an official at the Light Industry Trade Union to discuss a field research site for me. Her mother, who works in the Ministry of Iron and Steel, has contacted a friend in the All-China Federation of Trade Unions (ACFTU) and asked him to help me. This friend has directed someone at the Light Industry Trade Union, a subordinate level of the Trade Union bureaucracy, to receive me this afternoon.

[So far we have two bureaucratic "systems" (*xitong*) here: (1) the Trade Union bureaucracy, at both the national level (ACFTU) and the

---

[4] I have changed the name of this factory.

specialized branch level (Light Industry Trade Union); and (2) the Iron and Steel bureaucracy.]

Liping asks me to prepare two items before we go: a letter of introduction from my unit, the university, and a research outline of what I intend to look at in the factory. She suggests that I delete the sections about living with factory workers (we will bring that up later); about wages and bonus systems, since this is currently a sensitive topic; and about Party activities within the factory, since the Party is, after all, a secret organization.

She says that in China, the formal or "public" (*gong*) contact such as the letter of introduction from my unit will not get me anywhere by itself. At the same time, "private relationships" (*siren guanxi*) alone, such as the personal introduction made by her mother, are not enough either. We need them both. Liping is also bringing a letter from her mother to the Trade Union official we are going to visit.

At the Light Industry Trade Union office, we are received by two officials whose manners are cordial, yet restrained. They take turns reading our two letters and the outline very scrupulously, their lips moving to pronounce the characters. Only when Liping finally mentions her mother's name, do they brighten up and start to relax a little. Liping, adopting her smooth and engaging persona, starts the conversation. I am an overseas Chinese (*huayi*) very interested in China. I learned Chinese in an American school out of enthusiasm for China and have already completed an M.A. degree. My unit in China stands ready to help me go to a factory, but they lack the direct contacts with factories. My factory study is motivated by friendship with China, and so on. And I even know a factory leader at the Number 1 Electric Fan Factory who says that their factory will receive me.

One of the Union officials picks up the phone to call the Municipal Trade Union to see if things can be arranged for me. "This case is sent down from above, so it's hard not to carry it out," he explains, referring to the fact that he has received a directive from both Liping's mother in the Iron and Steel Ministry and the ACFTU, both of which are levels that outrank him. All the while, Liping keeps up a smooth running commentary on how we do not wish to trouble them overmuch, how I will be responsible for all costs incurred, how I can adapt to any living condition, and so on. In the end, one of them says that it is their duty to undertake this responsibility for promoting friendship between two countries. He warns me that the state of Chinese industry is very "backward," that the standard of living is low in China, even though they do not have "exploitation." In the end, his final pronouncement is optimistic, "Going to the factory is not a big problem," and we leave in very good spirits.

April 1, 1982

Liping and I call up one of the Light Industry Union officials to see what action has been taken. He tells us that the Municipal Union has sent people twice to look up the Electric Fan Main Factory [the level with authority over the factory I wish to study]. Both times the person in charge at the main factory was not there. Liping asks him to deal with the matter urgently.

April 7, 1982

Liping calls again. The Light Industry Union official replies that according to the Municipal Union people, the main factory's Party Committee held a meeting about my research proposal and concluded that Number 1 was not a suitable site, but another electric fan factory could be arranged. In addition, they need to receive authorization from their direct superior administrative level, the Light Industry Bureau of the Beijing Municipal Government.

[Now a third bureaucratic system, the municipal government's industrial administrative hierarchy, has entered the application process. The Number 1 Electric Fan Factory I wished to go to lies at the bottom rung of a series of ascending administrative levels—it is controlled by the main factory above it, which in turn answers to the Light Industry Bureau (*ju*) of its municipal district (*qu*) government, which is under the guidance of the municipal government (*shi*).]

Liping's assessment of the situation is surprisingly bright. It is evident to her that now both national and municipal trade unions agree to my project. She believes that if we had just relied on my university to arrange a factory visit, it would not have worked because they would have had to go through their superior levels, the Ministry of Education and Beijing Education Bureau, all on a formal, "public" basis, whereas we have gotten this far because we have approached the project on both a public and "private" basis. However, the main factory's insistence that it get permission first from the Light Industry Bureau further complicates the process, as we do not have any personal guanxi in this bureaucracy. She had hoped the main factory would make a decision on its own.

April 15, 1982

Liping and I pay another visit to Light Industry Trade Union to inquire into our progress. They have still not received approval for this project from the Light Industry Bureau of the municipal government.

May 5, 1982

I've just come back from a field trip to Sichuan Province. The news is still not promising. The main factory has reluctantly agreed that I can study No. 1 Fan Factory after all, but they have still not heard from their superiors, the Beijing Municipal Light Industry Bureau. What is needed now is direct formal contact between my university officials and this bureau, to secure its approval of my project. My heart sinks because the whole point of my endeavors was to present my university with a fait accompli, so that, faced with the approval of the factory, the Trade Union, and the municipal government, they could only assent to my project. Now I must still go through them first, and they have already shown reluctance.

I take Elder Sister Su to visit one of these university officials at his home. Mr. Peng agrees to look into the matter, but warns that he will have to send up reports and requests to the Beijing Education Bureau and the Ministry of Education, both of which have jurisdiction over the university. My worst fears have been realized. These are very difficult bureaucracies to crack. [Now a fourth bureaucratic system has to get involved, the education bureaucracy at the national and municipal levels.]

May 17, 1982

Peng tells me he has contacted Beijing Industrial Bureau, who pronounced the fan factories "not open to foreigners" (bu duiwai kaifang). If I had kept my Taiwan citizenship, I would be exempt from this. Japanese businessmen are allowed to go, but they are not doing research. They suggest that my university now go through their higher level, the municipal government.

May 20, 1982

I'm at the end of my patience. No one can survive such ordeals. I'm convinced Peng is responsible for the negative response of the Light Industry Bureau. He doesn't really want me to go. I decided to make one last effort to convince Peng to help me, by appealing to his sentiments for a fellow Chinese. I asked whether the Soviets, when they were here in the 1950s, met with difficulties in research. Peng only laughed and said, "They understand us very well, and we understand them—they would never even think to ask to do fieldwork here, and we would not ask it of them in their country."

June 20, 1982

Peng has written to the Education Ministry about my research proposal, and he has even given it his own description and title: "A comparison between the material incentive system of capitalist enterprises and the socialist moral incentive system in order to discover the superiority of socialist methods." My first reaction is discomfort: This really misrepresents my whole scholarly enterprise to make it serve narrow political ends. On second thought, perhaps I'm much too naive. Peng knows how to work the system and speak its language. His approach will get much better results than my straightforwardness.

Since Peng is leaving town, he has turned the matter over to Guo, another university official. Guo is not impressed that I have already obtained the approval of the Trade Unions, the factory and the main factory.

"Let me tell you this," he says severely. "The thing Chinese people are most opposed to is individual effort outside of the organization [*zuzhi*][5] and one's unit. If you had come to us at the beginning, instead of seeking to make contacts here and there, this thing would have been pulled through much faster. You should realize that ours is an organized society with defined and ordered levels of command. Just because you know someone at a factory does not mean you can go there or try to get any place to give you permission. Everything has to pass through each level of decision-making bodies and get their approval. And you have first to apply through your own unit and get its approval. It's not really your fault because you still don't understand the correct procedures in our country."

I can't help showing some anger. "From the beginning I requested help from your office, but you did not show any signs of action. I'm used to the principle that if one path does not succeed, one makes all efforts to try other paths, instead of just sitting back."

"We admit that there is still some bureaucratism [*guanliao zhuyi*] in China and that it might cause your case to drag on a bit. But bureaucratism has been greatly reduced recently."

The lengthy and complicated process of obtaining permission is not surprising, given the number of bureaucratic systems (four) involved, and the number of administrative levels within each system (see figure 1). At each level and in each bureaucratic system stood one or more officials whose personal permission was required before officials at lower levels or in other systems were willing to consider my case further.

Eventually I was allowed to visit a factory in the fall of 1982 for a total of one month, but not to the factory where Elder Sister Su worked. Years later, through the good graces of a former official of the Beijing municipal government for whom I briefly served as interpreter when he visited Berkeley, it was also arranged for me to study a printing factory in Beijing for three months in 1984–85 (Yang 1989b). Because of this "private" (*si*) connection with an official of

[5] The word "organization" refers to the administrative structure in which every person is embedded, and to the local as well as higher levels of leadership to which each person is subjected in their units of work or residence.

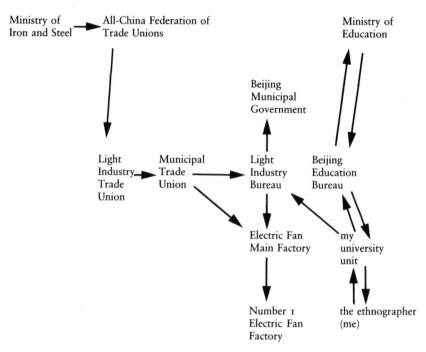

Figure 1. Bureaucratic systems and levels standing between the ethnographer (me) and the Number 1 Electric Fan Factory. Arrows show the paths of communication in the process of obtaining permission to study the factory.

some stature who was willing to assume responsibility for me, the bureaucratic process this time did not take half as long as the time required to gain entrance to the first factory. Thus the complicated process of obtaining official permission for a factory study gave me firsthand experience with the bureaucracy. This and other encounters with a multilayered bureaucratic power, whose officials and clerks are customarily indifferent or hostile toward the supplicants before them, suggested that I should turn my attention to sites of social tension surrounding bureaucratic intransigence. It began to dawn on me that guanxixue could in one sense be conceived of as a shortcut around, or a coping strategy for dealing with, bureaucratic power.

Fieldwork in a Culture of Fear

My ethnographic inquiries on the art of guanxi have spanned the 1980s and early 1990s, precisely the period of China's economic reform and opening up to the outside world. My fieldwork on guanxixue took place mainly during my two years of residence in Beijing (in 1981–83 and in 1984–85). Additional data were also collected in travels throughout China in those years, as well as on return trips in 1990, 1991, 1992, and 1993. During the first two visits, I assumed the roles of graduate student and teacher at Beijing University, as well as ethnographer in the capital city. In the 1990 visit, my role was elevated to that of an American scholar visiting Dezhou, Shandong Province, and a county in Hubei Province. In 1991, 1992, and 1993 I assumed the primary role of overseas Chinese visitor and a secondary role as overseas scholar in my visits with people in Shanghai and its suburbs, Hangzhou, Shaoxing, Wenzhou, and Xi'an. Back in the United States, I also conducted extensive interviews in the latter half of the 1980s and in the early 1990s with Chinese immigrants in Alhambra and Monterey Park in the Los Angeles area and with Chinese students and scholars at American universities where I have stayed: Berkeley, Colorado, Cornell, Santa Barbara, Michigan, and Harvard.

The modern urban conditions of fieldwork are quite comfortable compared with classical ethnographic settings of primitive or peasant societies; however, urban China presents difficulties and challenges of its own, such as the inevitable clashes with bureaucratic and official authority described above. Another difficulty I encountered in fieldwork, that posed by the culture of fear, also surfaced during my visit with Ding Jian, the astute guanxi practioner.

After Ding Jian had recounted his guanxi story that February night in 1982, our conversation wandered to the subject of marriage and divorce in China. Through an acquaintance at his night school, Ding had gotten hold of some statistics regarding the recent divorce rate in Beijing, in publications marked "internal classification" (*neibu*). Documents and publications stamped in this category are available only to a restricted audience of experts in the subject matter concerned. They are not intended for general dissemination, and are certainly not intended for foreigners or overseas Chinese. This classification pales in comparison with "strictly secret" (*jimi*), which is reserved for very secret Party and state documents and restricted to a readership of high levels of officialdom. The neibu classification is often not taken seriously, as I was later to realize from the number of occasions on which people offered to give me such publications, and from their contents, which usually did not reveal much more than the official media and were also couched in the same offical language. Not knowing I was from abroad, and wanting to extend certain courtesies to me, Ding insisted I take his copy home to read.

I accepted with great trepidation, torn by a temptation to acquire inaccessible information and also by the fear of doing something that might get both of us in trouble. Soon an inexplicable and paranoid suspicion descended upon me that Ding Jian had guessed that I was from abroad and planned to report me to the authorities for accepting this classified document. Mixed in with this fear was my guilty conscience: Was it ethical to deceive a person into talking freely by posing as a native? What if somehow I was caught with these documents and they were traced back to Ding? Then I would have gotten an innocent person into trouble. When Ding walked out of the room to get some more roasted watermelon seeds [eaten as a snack], I seized the opportunity to tell Ruoben that we had better reveal the truth of my identity. Ruoben saw no need for such foolish action, but when I insisted, shrugged his shoulders as if resigned to my folly. Ding's face was impassive and polite as I casually let drop where I was from and gave him back the publications. After a tactful lapse of time, Ruoben and I beat an awkward retreat.

Outside, Ruoben was furious with me, telling me in no uncertain terms that I had compromised both his and Ding's security and demanding to know how I thought he was to face Ding again. It was not so much what Ding had said about guanxixue, but other topics he had discussed with us (topics not recorded here), things of a direct political nature, which made matters delicate. My revelation would be certain to make Ding fearful of what he had said and suspicious of Ruoben in their future dealings, not to mention the possibility of Ding spreading tales about Ruoben's associations with people from abroad. These were indeed consequences I had not considered in the heat of the moment, consumed as I was with abstract questions of the ethics of fieldwork, questions that are ultimately based in a Western historical context. Finally, Ruoben consoled himself with the conviction that he knew Ding well enough to know that he was not the kind of person who would inform on him, especially since Ding himself had said politically forbidden things and, furthermore, did not have much credibility with his leaders at work.

Nothing came of this little incident, but this and several other examples of my clumsiness in delicate political situations quickly instilled in me the fieldwork habits of constant alertness to the dangers of getting people I knew into trouble with the authorities or into situations where they might be tempted to get one another into trouble. In my field notes of conversations with people, I never wrote down the names of those I had spoken to in Chinese characters, but only their initials in the Roman alphabet, just in case these notes should fall into the wrong hands. Care had to be taken to make my circle of acquaintances and friends a "low density" (Boissevain 1974:37) network of single-stranded relationships in which most of the people in the network were connected to one another only through me. To this end, I adopted a policy of not revealing to my informants which other Chinese I knew in Beijing, whom I had spoken with or visited, or what we had talked about. There was another rationale for the stress on single-stranded relationships. I encountered various versions of this common saying:

Liangren shuo zhenhua, sanren shuoxiaohua, siren shuo huhua, wuren shuo jiahua.

When there are two people, one tells the truth; when there are three people, one makes jokes; when there are four people, one talks nonsense; when there are five people, one tells lies.

It was explained to me that when talking with only one other person, one feels safe to say what one really thinks because if anything leaks out, one will know who did the leaking. Indeed, I often found that it was hard to collect good information when there were too many people present. People became instinctively on guard and their internal censors were activated in the presence of others.

Although I told almost everyone I interviewed or spent time with that I was from the United States, I was careful for their sake not to broadcast this fact in front of their neighbors, acquaintances, or colleagues. Instead, I tried to let them decide whether they wanted to make this information public. Since China's relationship with Taiwan was still on a precarious footing in the early 1980s, I was also initially careful as to whom I revealed my Taiwan origins, but by the mid-1980s this was no longer a concern.[6]

In the social structure of Chinese urban places, people are assigned to work in "work units" (gongzuo danwei) such as a factory, school, office, store, or hospital (Whyte and Parish 1984:25–26; Henderson and Cohen 1984; Walder 1986; Yang 1989b). Work units are not merely places of work, but total institutions in the sense that, to varying degrees, they provide a range of benefits (welfare, housing, some consumer goods) and serve as the basic cells of the state order. That is, almost every work unit contains Party, Youth League, and labor

---

[6] In 1988, the Taiwan government formally allowed its citizens to visit the mainland.

union organizations, which both help and control its members in matters of marriage, divorce, birth, and social mobility. Work units are also the sites for monitoring thought and conduct through the guidance of the leaders, peer surveillance (or "assistance"), and the compilation of an individual dossier (*dangan*) for each member. These personal files record each person's activities, wrongdoings, and character evaluations by peers and superiors.

The foreign population of Beijing was not exempt from this system. My work unit was Beijing University, which meant that the Foreign Students Office was responsible for my good conduct. I lived in a special dormitory for foreign students and became subject to the surveillance, real and imagined, exercised there. For an anthropologist, it was especially frustrating to be required to live segregated from the people among whom I was supposed to be a participant observer. For example, in visiting me at my dormitory, Chinese people had to register their names and work units with the doorkeeper downstairs. This written record of their contact with a foreign citizen was filed, and there is always the possibility that it will be dragged out again years hence, to be used to incriminate them in some unforseeable way. Therefore, throughout the period of fieldwork, I sought to overcome this major obstacle of a cultural and political logic that segregated foreigners from Chinese.

Not only did I have to break out of the physical and psychological barriers to contact with Chinese students at Beijing University, I also had to break out of the university itself. I did not wish to be restricted to the milieu of students and intellectuals there. Fieldwork required me to expand my social network outside of the university to people of other walks of life in the city. Through the introductions made by my university friends and acquaintances to their friends, neighbors, and relatives throughout the city, I was gradually able to learn about guanxixue and its larger social and historical context from workers, lower-level cadres, shop clerks, office workers, supply agents, and even people who belonged to the new category of individual enterprisers and entrepreneurs. I tried to visit people as much as possible in their homes or dormitories or to arrange meetings in parks, museums, or restaurants. Invitations to stay overnight in their homes were always gladly accepted, not only because of the extended contact they afforded me but also because of the problems of transportation in such a huge city. I lived with relatives in the south for over a month and saw my aging grandmother for the first time in my life, but not wishing to bring any political complications to their lives, I decided not to do fieldwork there.

The best way to arrive at peoples' homes without arousing the curiosity and suspicion of their neighbors was by bicycle, foot, or bus. In this way, I could take full advantage of my Chinese ancestry to blend in with other passersby. Although my Chinese clothes could not disguise my foreign posture and gait during my first six months in Beijing, by the end of the first year, I no longer attracted attention. Indeed, one morning in March 1983 I received final confirmation that my body language had finally lost its "foreign accent." Noticing that it had suddenly become fashionable to wear Western-style blue-jeans (even faded ones), I had screwed up the courage to wear my jeans for the first time in China. On the street, a bunch of young men, often called "hoods" (*liumang*) hooted and sneered after me, "Hey you 'sparetime overseas Chinese' [*yeyu huaqiao*]!" suggesting that I was "putting on airs" by pretending to be from overseas. I couldn't help triumphantly calling back to them, "Don't you know, I'm a real overseas Chinese?!" to which they just continued to jeer in contemptuous disbelief. This ability to pass as a native, if only a native trying to pass as an overseas Chinese, allowed me to move about without attracting the attention of individuals or the ever-vigilant neighborhood committees. The latter are organized as arms of state surveillance.[7] They can be found in every urban Chinese residential area, and since they are usually staffed by older women of a certain generation, they have sometimes received the epithet "bound-footed KGB" (*xiaojiao kegebo*). When it was more convenient or efficient to travel by taxi, I always asked the driver to stop a few blocks or lanes away from my actual destination and walked the rest of the way.

In the first half of the 1980s, the culture of fear was still a powerful force in constraining actions and speech in everyday life. To be sure, it was a milder form of the culture of terror that had reigned during the Cultural Revolution (1966–76),[8] but for me coming from another world, it was one of the main sources of culture shock. Michael Taussig is right in pointing out that much of the power of the State "with

[7] Neighborhood committees also take care of such things as sanitation, dispute mediation, and petty-crime and fire prevention (Frolic 1980:224–41).

[8] The literature in English on the Cultural Revolution is extensive, as befits the importance and complexity of this period in modern Chinese history. Cultural Revolution studies will no doubt be a major area of inquiry for several generations. For the time being, however, the following works provide a good introduction to this period: Thurston 1988, Liang 1983, Gao 1987, White 1976, Rosen 1982, and Chan, Madsen, and Unger 1984.

a capital S" derives from its very insubstantiality, from the fantasies of those who are kept outside its central and inner sanctum of knowledge (1992:113, 130). Although the state serves as an idea or totem for the expression and projection of social wholeness, it does so through a culture of fear which treats it as a sacred entity, as an entity with an awesome unity and a will of its own. Therefore, the presence of a culture of fear is a measure of the extent of state power and of the desire for an image of wholeness which is both reassuring and horrifying. To the extent that I became an active participant in the culture of fear, I also contributed to state power.

The political atmosphere in Beijing at that time was probably comparable to that of Poland in the 1970s, where even the absence of direct threats to one's personal security did not signal a dramatic change in the habits of wariness and self-protection (Nowak 1988). The atmosphere in Beijing became significantly more relaxed in the late 1980s until the trauma of June 4, 1989, which restored the climate of the early 1980s. Things started to relax again in the early 1990s.

As the political center of the nation, the axis of the symbolic and ideological power of the state order, Beijing is permeated with an especially heavy atmosphere of diffuse fear and danger. Beijing houses, on one hand, the vast bureaucracies of the central government. On the other hand, it is also the cultural and educational capital of the country, with the highest concentration of students and intellectuals in the nation. Locked in intense combat, both the state and the intellectuals are keenly interested in politics. Even workers and shop clerks are said to be more concerned with politics than in other places in China. So dense and oppressive did I find Beijing's political climate that at times I felt as if I could literally cut the overladen air with a knife. It seemed that every time I left Beijing on a train to go to other places in China, I always felt a physical sensation in my chest. As the train pulled out slowly from the Beijing Railway Station, and as it gathered speed in Beijing's outlying suburbs, I could feel my heart growing correspondingly lighter and freer, as the suffocating weight that it was under gradually lifted. Likewise, whenever I returned to Beijing, I always experienced a growing dread and heaviness of heart as the train pulled closer to the station.

I heard endless tales of the horrors and tragedies of the Cultural Revolution, a period of revolutionary idealism and purity, social turmoil, utopian-fascistic fervor, mass cruelty, and individual suffering. These tales were recounted to me, it always seemed, with an uncanny smile and even laughter (as if these were trivial amusing incidents), and they played no small role in inducting me into the early 1980s culture of fear. Soon the politicization of daily life became a palpable reality as I came to experience the disorienting and mind-numbing effects of a fear that was reinforced by the guardedness and reticence of many people with whom I came into contact. Had I been able to assess the situation with a cool head, I might have been able to resist the contagion of fear. After all, unlike my Chinese friends and acquaintances, I had a U.S. passport.

Newcomer and outsider or not, the fear was infectious. It affected my readiness to ask questions, for fear that they would make my interviewees suspicious of me, get them into trouble for telling me too much, or prompt someone to inform on me. Indeed, in a printing factory, I was told later by some workers I had interviewed that someone had reported to the office people what we had discussed. It did not matter that I was *not* trying to find out real state or military secrets, or what people thought about the leadership. The realm of secrets is a large one in this society, and there was often a vague sense that what people knew and had experienced in their personal lives, no matter how ordinary or common, was best kept a secret. In the culture of fear, people are always dogged by a feeling that they are guilty of something, even though they have done nothing overtly wrong, perhaps because life is so constrained that people end up commiting countless infractions of thought and deed, which leads to a general sense of wrongdoing. In the culture of fear, trivial infractions often become magnified into major transgressions against the state.

To my dismay, I was to find myself a trembling transgressor, when I unwittingly entered a military residential compound while visiting a friend at her home. The entrance gate to the compound did not bear any writing identifying the place as a military area. As it turned out, my friend's father-in-law happened to be high up in the propaganda wing of the People's Liberation Army. At that time he was a target for intense political criticism. Although we never met, he later found out that an overseas Chinese with U.S. citizenship had entered his house, which meant that he had violated the prohibition against foreigners entering into military areas in China. Already the target of criticism, he moved quickly to forestall any further trouble for himself and his family by making a full oral and written confession of my visit, with details of my identity, status, and work unit. My friend who invited me also had to give a full report to the authorities concerned.

The strange and, in hindsight, comical effect on me when I learned about this turn of events remains inexplicable. I present this anecdote to illustrate a powerful element I had absorbed in the ethos of the culture. I spent the next few weeks in a cold sweat, waiting for the authorities to come and interrogate me, to interrogate and punish those who had spoken with me, and deport me as a spy. That would be the end of my career in anthropology. I had to take measures to protect myself and the people I had spoken with. I resolved that when they come to search my room, they would find nothing. I took all my fieldnotes and cassette tapes to the apartment of an American family for safekeeping. But what about all those "internal classification" documents people had given me, and which I had been too bored to finish reading? The madness of the solution I came up with was matched only by my crazed state of mind.

Under the cover of darkness, I set out by bicycle with the troublesome publications and rode for about forty minutes into the countryside northwest of the campus. There in a dry irrigation ditch in a field, I proceeded to burn the "incriminating evidence." Two peasants stopped by and asked suspiciously what I was doing and to which work unit I was attached. I mumbled something about being from the city. A kindly concern came over one of them, and he bent down to whisper, "Comrade, you see that high wall behind us back there, and the searchlights mounted on the watchtower, roving around? We don't know what's in there, but it's probably a prison. This is perhaps not a good place for you to be." Indeed, in my preoccupied state I had not paid any attention to my surroundings. Chilled to the bone by these words, I managed to fight back the mounting delirium long enough to finish burning the papers and then fled back to the campus. No one ever came to question me about entering the military compound. Thus I gained another lesson in the course of the seasoning of a "flower-in-the-study" anthropologist.

The painful process of getting official permission to conduct fieldwork in a factory also led me to appreciate another significance of guanxixue besides its usefulness in dealing with bureaucratic intransigence. In this kind of social order, it was easier to conduct fieldwork through fluid social networks and relationships than at any fixed and contained factory site. When I was finally able to go to two factory sites (the Number 2 Electric Fan Factory and the printing factory), I found that at these sites, there was often a reticence on the part of some people to talk with me at length or to convey any substantive information about their lives and their thoughts. One reason was that they knew that other people at the factory would see them talking to me, suspect them of revealing too much, and even report on them to higher levels (*da xiao baogao*). Another reason was their wariness that what they told me might somehow reach the ears of their co-workers, with whom they also saw me talking every day. It did not matter that I was not interested in topics of a directly political nature; *any* conversation in the politicized milieu in which they lived could be construed or misconstrued by others in a way harmful to their political and economic security. Since guilt by association and collective responsibility for wrongdoing featured in the system of control, people were cautious about whom they were seen associating with. Thus I gradually realized that in a culture of fear, everyday social relationships are highly politicized, and identifiable organizations and communities such as work units and neighborhoods serve as basic units of social and political control and surveillance. In a system of power that relies on fixing subjects in place, the traditional approach to fieldwork which situates the ethnographer in a fixed site may not be the most realistic or effective strategy.

In terms of fieldwork methodology, I slowly came to realize that the best way to undertake a study of the art of guanxi was to adopt its very form as the method of fieldwork. That is to say, it was easier and more effective for me to gather information through networking with people across social groups and workplaces than to stay within a fixed fieldsite or organization. Therefore, both the *object* of inquiry and the *method* of inquiry came to consist in linking up with people through networks of relationships spread around the city of Beijing and elsewhere. Doing fieldwork by replicating the very network form of the art of guanxi, hovering always between fixed sites and locations, proved a much more resilient strategy in China because it enabled me to keep my network "connectedness" or "density" at a low level (Bott 1957:59). In other words, the degree to which "the members of [my] network [were] in touch with each other independently of [me]" (Boissevain 1974:37–40) was kept low to insure each person's security. Through personal introductions to a larger network of people, most of whom did not know of one another's existence, the element of trust produced by personal relationships and the feeling of security in anonymity combined to make my work much easier and more productive. Thus, a new fieldwork strategy arose out of the particular cultural and political conditions of the "field" that is contemporary China.

Since networks cross over and between bureaucratically defined work units, social groups, and geographic localities, the information and descriptions of guanxixue I gathered did not stem from Beijing alone but from wherever I met with Chinese people who were willing to talk about the subject matter. I was to discover something that has been pointed out elsewhere, that in a modern world of rapid transportation and communication, which blur the definitions of time and space, the notion of "field" is merely an ideal construct (Clifford 1990:64; Clifford 1992). Fieldwork by the network method could not be neatly restricted to the factory site, nor to the city of Beijing, nor even within the national borders of China. The network of Chinese acquaintances and friends who talked to me about the art of guanxi and other Chinese matters was initially developed in Beijing, but in the course of my travels, it spread to different places I visited in China, and among mainland Chinese working or studying in the United States. Although this kind of fieldwork lacks the sense of a geographically rooted and bounded community which is the hallmark of classical ethnography, my very methodology enabled me to comprehend an important facet of modern Chinese social life.

The Subject-Position of the Anthropologist

As the above accounts show, my Chinese ancestry was an important factor in the shape and outcome of my fieldwork. Therefore, the subject-position informing the orientation and perspective of the ethnographer needs to be clarified. One of the reasons why I was so susceptible to the culture of fear may have been my own split subjectivity as an "overseas Chinese" on the one hand, and as a "Chinese-American" on the other. The category "overseas Chinese" belongs firmly within a Chinese discourse that constructs it as people of Chinese ancestry who have maintained their language, culture, and kin ties with the "Motherland," who live in Chinese communities abroad, and who do not regard their current host countries as their primary point of orientation. The word *huaqiao* is the most frequently employed term for overseas Chinese, whereas *huayi* is sometimes used to refer to those who have become citizens of their host countries. In common usage, the first term often refers to overseas Chinese in Asia, whereas the second often designates those living in Europe or North America. The category "Chinese-American" designates an American of Chinese ancestry, and is also part of a new American discourse that affirms ethnic diversity (within certain implicit American cultural parameters) and that has come to replace an older discourse of the

Euro-American "melting pot." Besides these two subject-positions, the fact that in China I was so often mistaken for and treated as a native, meant that with the passing of time and the acquisition of more of the native habits of thought, feeling, and action, the moments when I came to adopt elements of native subjectivity gradually increased.

This triangular subject-composition made it all the easier for me to lose sense of any subject-grounding; this subjective freedom made me highly attuned to the culture of fear. Had I held more firmly to an American subjectivity, I would have had more faith in the protection that a U.S. passport provided and perhaps would not have felt as vulnerable. Instead, I became easily flustered, a state that perhaps did not trouble Europeans and other Americans in Beijing as much. That I could pass as a native meant that people were not put on their guard while conversing with me. This enriched my participant-observation experience, but it also made me prone to feel guilty of being an impostor or a spy, which further weakened my resistance to the culture of fear. At the same time, I was also not a real native and so did not possess a developed and sophisticated "immune system" to handle and contain either my fear, or the anger that welled up whenever I was thwarted by the bureaucratic system. Nor was I schooled in the everyday tactics of subverting and neutralizing this system. Thus I was triply vulnerable: first, as a semi-native, I came to share with other natives the subjective experience of living in a culture of fear. Second, having been brought up elsewhere, I also felt the fear that comes from not being versed in dealing with this society. I would probably never attain the level of stoic dignity, equanimity, or bravado and defiance that I have known in some natives. Finally, as an outsider who sometimes posed as an insider, I became susceptible to the fear of being unmasked, of having my true identity, whatever that was, revealed.

Although the traditional object of anthropological analysis, a culture as an essentialized and integrated unit, has been challenged in light of the sheer number and variety of border crossings in the modern world (Clifford 1992), the integrated Western subjectivity of anthropological texts is, for the most part, still intact. Even though in the field most anthropologists experience sharp ruptures in their sense of self, most textual reconstructions still depict the anthropologist as a firmly rooted Western subject. Of course, reflexive anthropology has challenged the Archimedean point of view in anthropology and has shown how the universal subject, which speaks as the omniscient narrator of traditional "objective" anthropology, is in the end merely a localized Western point of view. Still, reflexive anthropology has replaced the universal knowing subject with a Western subject, a self-critical one to be sure, but nevertheless still a subject, which has had the ironic effect of reinventing and reifying the West and thus bolstering its strength. It is perhaps time to fragment this integrated Western knowing subject, to show how not only "cultures" but also knowing "subjects" are subject to transcultural, transnational, and transgender border crossings. If anthropology is to be truly decentered, it cannot stay in the position of self-critical Western subject; it must engage with the non-Western subjectivities it studies and integrate native perspectives and concerns into its discourse.

Anthropology has in the past few decades experienced an influx of non-Western practioners, whether students from other lands who have come to study in the West or anthropology departments and programs set up in countries outside Europe and North America. Yet we have seen few of these developments translated into real changes in the construction of the knowing subject of anthropological discourse. A further pluralization of anthropological and ethnographic subject-positionings is in order. This pluralization must be broader than that of the gender, race, and class critique found in reflexive anthropology and cultural studies. At present, multiethnic discourse in the United States is limited to the construction of an "American" multiculturalism and is a project that seldom engages with the realities of trans*national* and trans*linguistic* border crossings. The kind of pluralization I am calling for will address issues stemming from these two border crossings of anthropological subjectivity.

In an insightful article on the writings of Edward Said, the literary critic Abdul JanMohamed outlined four types of modern border crossings between the Third World and the West: those of the exile, the immigrant, the colonialist,[9] and the scholar/anthropologist (1993). The subjectivity of the exile is marked by a sense of absence and loss of the home culture. This "structural nostalgia" is accompanied by a general "[indifference] to the values and characteristics of the host culture." At the same time, the enforced distance between the exile and his or her homeland can produce a renewed and profound linkage between the exile and the formative culture of birth. In contrast, the immigrant is propelled by a "desire to become a full-fledged sub-

[9] JanMohamed's category of colonialist can be stretched to include the modern Western businessman and woman of the postcolonial era.

ject of the new culture" and by a tendency to shed the habits and foci of the old subjectivity.

Both exile and immigrant are in turn differentiated from the colonialist and anthropologist, who "apprehend the new culture, not as a field of subjectivity, but rather as an object of/for their gaze." Whereas the exile and immigrant must confront the issue of "a rupture between and a re-suturing of individual and collective subjectivities," the colonialist and anthropologist are not troubled with a profound realignment or a threat to their subjectivity. Still, whereas the colonialist actively represses or lacks any desire to become a subject of the native culture, the anthropologist's approach to the problem of "going native" is much more complex. In order to understand the Other, the anthropologist must learn the native language and culture, which can often open up the borders of his or her subjectivity; however, the professional and epistemological strictures of anthropology have usually ensured that the anthropologist was able to reassert the detached stance of "objectivism" and maintain a clear borderline between the West and the Other.

The traditional strengths of anthropology (long-term immersion in another culture, openness to cultural difference, and understanding the natives' point of view) notwithstanding, when it comes to anthropological subjectivity, the border between the West and the Other has been clearly demarcated and maintained. The native point of view can be described and appreciated, as long as no one confuses knower and the known. JanMohamed's characterization of exiles and immigrants as border crossers who approach a host culture as a "field of subjectivity" and who experience a profound rupture and repositioning of their subjectivities suggests another course for the anthropological subject. What it suggests is that in both fieldwork and ethnographic writing, elements of native subjectivity be allowed to mingle with and reshape Western anthropological subjectivity. The anthropologist must seek to become not only like the exile who gains a certain perspective on his or her own culture while residing in another culture but also like an immigrant who starts to absorb a new subjectivity, interprets the world from its standpoints, and acts on its historical concerns as if she were a new member of that culture. Understanding and engaging with native self-interpretations of historical context and native self-critiques is a step toward dissolving the monolithic Western subject of knowledge, whether this subject is engaged in self-promotion or self-critique. In this way, anthropology will become more available and relevant as a discourse with which a wide variety of cultural and discursive subjectivities in the modern world can engage.

It is in this spirit that I have examined my own fragmented subjectivity as ethnographer. As a product of the Chinese "diaspora," I have approached anthropology not only as an immigrant to the West and an exile from China but also as an exile from the West and an immigrant to China. By recognizing both the "overseas Chinese" and the "Chinese-American" components of this ethnographic subject and by accepting rather than rejecting the process and the possibilities of "going native," I attempt to participate in a larger movement of decentering the Western knowing subject. I hope that the particular ethnographic interpretation of China that issues from this decentered subject of knowledge will provide a discourse that is useful and relevant to ongoing projects in native self-understanding, self-critique, and reform.

The question of a decentered anthropological subject-position from which to diagnose China's modern afflictions challenges not only Eurocentrism, but also the "center" of contemporary Chinese culture. At a time when the center of Chinese culture in the world (whether the political capital of Beijing or the heartland of China) is unable to articulate the concerns of a significant portion of the people who call themselves Chinese, it is on the "peripheries" of Chinese culture where dynamic cultural innovations and self-questioning will have to take place (Tu 1991; Lee 1991). This periphery is the product of waves of Chinese "diaspora" in the nineteenth and twentieth centuries, people fleeing warfare, impoverishment, and political persecution on the troubled mainland. It includes the Chinese societies of Taiwan, Hong Kong, and Singapore, as well as Chinese communities scattered in what Western anthropologists call the "core," that is to say, the societies of the West. The two latest waves of this diaspora occurred in the 1980s and 1990s as Chinese from Hong Kong,[10] Taiwan, and Southeast Asia and Chinese intellectuals escaping political repression on the mainland emigrated to North America, Europe, and Australia (Tu 1991:21–22). Therefore, it should be remembered that one society's core is another's periphery.

The notion of periphery implies the importance of distance, geographical or subjective, for diagnosis and cultural critique of the cen-

---

[10] Hong Kong Chinese, especially from the professional, middle, and upper classes, are leaving in order to escape the uncertainties of life after the Communist mainland takes over the territories in 1997.

ter. Just as the anthropologist of Western subjectivity gains an insight into the modern West by studying primitive and peasant societies on its periphery (Marcus and Fisher 1986), overseas Chinese immigrants and exiles can come to a new understanding of Chinese culture from a position peripheral to the mainland. Geographical distance produces subjective distance. For the immigrant and exile, long separation from the homeland means that part of the self is disengaged from identification with the homeland, so that the home culture becomes "objectified" to a certain extent. No longer is the home culture part of the new everyday reality in which the subject is now situated, rather the subject discovers within herself a habitus that does not fit in with the new surroundings. The contrast that the subject notices between the features of the host culture and those of the home culture relativizes the habitus of old as only one among many ways of dealing with the world. For the immigrant eager to embrace the subjectivity of the host culture, the objectified self becomes the target of criticism, repression, and efforts at self-transformation. For the exile, however, this objectified self becomes a focus for self-reflection and self-renewal as the subject reaffirms the ties that hold the self to the home culture.

Critique frequently arises among marginal people or on the peripheries of a culture. In the case of China, cultural diagnosis and critique from the periphery takes on added significance because the present political situation makes it impossible to speak at the center. This book can be viewed as part of an effort at cultural renewal coming from the periphery of China. The ethnographer is a product of the Chinese diaspora who came to the United States in the 1970s, fashioned herself as an immigrant, and became Americanized to a certain degree, only to reject the label "Chinese-American" because it sought to make her into an American minority subject. By studying China she recuperated the persona of "overseas Chinese," thus switching from the subjectivity of immigrant to that of Chinese exile. When she went to China as an anthropologist, one part of the experience was that of a culture-shocked Western subject of knowledge trying to understand an alien culture. The other part was that of an exile returning home after a long absence, sadly and unpleasantly reminded of all the reasons why she had left. The fieldwork became the mixed product of a Western subject emigrating to China and a Chinese subject returning from exile who, on the one hand, empathized with all the joys and sufferings of the mother culture, and on the other hand, objectified it as an afflicted part of herself that needed to be diagnosed and healed.

State Projects of Modernity in China and Native Critiques

The ethnographic process involves at least two dimensions of interpretation, which in this book appear as Parts 1 and 2. In the first dimension (Part 1), I observe, listen, investigate, describe, and transcribe, in order to understand and explicate the expressions and practices of a particular Other. The second dimension (Part 2) is a meta-realm of understanding, which incorporates or derives from native metainterpretive frameworks, native self-positioning, and native self-critiques of their own culture in a certain world-historical context. This dimension is not oriented to the anthropologist's own milieu in the West, but is the metainterpretation of the anthropologist's learning from and debating and engaging with native frameworks of understanding and critique. For the anthropologist, the work of this metainterpretive dimension involves not only talking to representative or average native practitioners and informants but also engaging with the thoughts of native critical thinkers, reformers, or persons who have reflected deeply on their own society and the experience of modernity. Only by engaging in the work of this metainterpretation can the anthropologist proceed to figure out how the cultural elements under study might fit into the natives' own larger historical context. This second level of interpretation and cultural analysis is perhaps the most challenging, problematical, and promising direction for anthropology to take at this juncture when the old assumptions of Western reason, modernity, and universal disinterested knowledge about the Other have been called into question (Clifford and Marcus 1986; Marcus and Fischer 1986; Said 1979).

The space opened up in recent years for self-reflexivity on anthropological representations of the Other has had a salutory effect of widening the possibilities and goals of anthropological inquiry. Calls for "thick description," for an ethnography of the "native's point of view" (Geertz 1973a; 1984), for dialogic and polyphonic representation (Clifford 1988b), and for "anthropology as cultural critique" (Marcus and Fischer 1986) are all part of an awareness of the historical specificity and relativity of the subject positions of observer and observed. They point out that the cultural forms found in many areas of the world are not the products of an essential native culture, but bear effects of Western imperialism and capitalism which must be subjected to critique. Although thankful for the creation of this "experimental [and self-critical] moment" in anthropology, I submit that the project of interpretive anthropology can be pushed much further, and that the promise of a decentered, polyphonic, and critical anthropology has yet to be realized.

The first dimension of interpretation of the Other has received much attention and refinement in recent anthropological discourse, but the second has seldom been thematized. The reason for this neglect is perhaps the assumption that there is only a single world-historical context in which all cultures are involved, which forgets that historical contexts are themselves interpreted and given diverse value inflections. The problem with the single-context approach in most anthropological writings is that the particular definition and interpretation of this world-historical context remains a Eurocentric one, tied up with a Western self-critique. A dominant model of existing anthropological critical inquiry, it seems to me, proceeds too unproblematically from the *second* dimension of Western intellectual self-critical discourse, directly to the *first* dimension of the Other under study. This ignores the metainterpretive and self-reflexive *second dimension within the culture of the Other*. Thus the understanding of the Other tends to become an exercise in finding solutions to problems and questions that issue from a Western milieu. The Other merely serves as a staging ground or experimental case for addressing and playing out issues of concern in the West. That is, the anthropologist travels thousands of miles to live in another culture in order to bring back material that will help the West better criticize itself. This renders anthropology insensitive to issues and concerns that arise out of native experience and native self-understanding.

This elevation of Western self-critique is in many ways just as Eurocentric as the old colonial attitudes of Western superiority because it continues to assign a central role to the West. Western self-critique, it is presumed, will also serve to improve conditions for the Other, since the Other's historical context is one of Western colonialism and therefore dependent on the West's self-critique. Even Edward Said, a major figure in the critique of the West, has expressed reservations about the basic assumption "that the whole of history in colonial territories was a function of the imperial. . . . [There] has been a tendency in anthropology, history, and cultural studies to treat the whole of world history as viewable by a Western meta-subject, whose historicizing and disciplinary rigor either took away or, in the post-colonial period, restored history to people and cultures 'without' history" (1986:59). Understanding the Other cannot be reduced to a cultural critique of the West. By merely reversing the terms of the old colonialist discourse so that now the Other is valorized while the West is criticized, much of reflexive anthropology still overprivileges the role of the West as the one needing and producing critique. If anthropology is to be more relevant to contemporary contexts outside the West, it cannot restrict itself to a critique of Western colonialism. A way must be found to accommodate and engage with different cultural critiques from the "natives' point of view": the new forms of power which have emerged in the postcolonial period.

After 1949, China closed its doors to a world that had thoroughly abused and wounded it and launched a project to revolutionize Chinese society to its very core. Thus began a process of relentless and collective self-laceration in mass-mobilization campaigns to transform society. Because China had suspended contact with the Western world, it is perhaps not surprising that three decades later, when China started to open up again, the native voices of critique were no longer aimed against the forces of imperialism or capitalism, but instead had taken the form of vociferous self-critiques of postrevolutionary mistakes. What prompted me to set the analysis of guanxixue within a general inquiry into the workings of power in socialist China were the native expressions of bitterness, pain, disillusionment, and anger directed against the new social order. These voices formed the backdrop of my investigations of guanxixue; thus my interpretations of this phenomenon can be understood as indirectly addressing these voices.

When I first arrived in Beijing in the fall of 1981, people from different urban walks of life with whom I came into contact were still haunted by what was often called the nightmare (e meng) of the Cultural Revolution, five years after it had officially ended. There was a deep sense that something had gone wrong with a revolution that most of them had enthusiastically and idealistically embraced. For some urban youth who had been sent down to the poorest areas of the countryside in different provinces, there was something deeply disturbing about the continued desperate poverty of the peasants and the despotisms of many local rural cadres. For some workers I met, the chronic housing shortage, low wages, and the authoritarian nature of rule in factories had over the many years since 1949 become cause for resentment. For intellectuals, for people designated as coming from "bad" class backgrounds (capitalist, landlord, rich peasant, counterrevolutionary, and "rightist"),[11] and for some cadres, the cru-

---

[11] The label of "rightist" was slapped onto a segment of the population, mainly intellectuals, during the Anti-Rightist Movement of 1957 for having spoken out critically against

elty and hatred to which they were subjected made them silent with fear, but in their hearts many came up with coping strategies of indifference, bitterness, and defiance. Others were totally crushed in spirit. For many who actively responded to Chairman Mao's call for continuous revolution out of resentment and concern that postrevolutionary China had lapsed into a new class structure, it was sobering to discover that there was a limit to how far the upper levels of the state would actually permit revolution. They realized too late that those on top who called for youthful rebellion and class struggle had an actual agenda quite different from their own. There was a general perception that human relationships had degenerated into mutual suspicion, cruelty, and self-interest, and that this posed a sharp contrast to the official rhetoric of socialist idealism and selflessness. The devastation of the Cultural Revolution caused many to reflect on and call into question other mass-mobilization movements, such as the Great Leap Forward (1958–60), which had resulted in a mass famine in the countryside, and the Anti-Rightist Movement of 1957, which had sent many intellectuals to labor camps. The Great Leap Forward led to an unprecedented number of deaths in human history (20–30 million), and the virtual absence of resistance among the people points to the totality of state power.

Having called for the incorporation of native critiques in anthropological endeavors, I am also aware of the difficulties and hazards of this enterprise. In addressing some problem areas in a social milieu not one's own, not only is there the old danger of imposing Western values on the natives, there is also the problem of uncritically adopting wholesale the self-critique of the natives. In the case of Chinese intellectuals in the current reform period in China, there is often a sentiment of rejection and condemnation of what is taken as Chinese culture, Confucian tradition, and "feudal thought," all of which are believed to be holding China back and preventing it from catching up with the West. Two books, *Chou lou de zhongguoren* (The ugly Chinese) by Taiwan author Bo Yang (1985), and *Zhongguo wenhua de shengcen jiegou* (The Deep Structure of Chinese Culture) by Sun Longji (1983), an American-trained scholar from Hong Kong, were extremely popular in the 1980s in urban and intellectual circles on the

---

the state and proving themselves to be unreliable elements of the new society. They had made the mistake of responding too sincerely to Mao's call to criticize the government ("letting a hundred flowers bloom"). Their punishment was political persecution, ostracism, and often imprisonment in the labor camps.

mainland. Both excoriated the Chinese people for a whole panoply of bad character traits. In the Chinese intellectuals' critique of an essentialized Chinese culture, the West is generally held up, implicitly or explicitly, as a paragon of progress, enlightenment, and virtue. The most vivid expression of this sentiment is in the 1988 TV serial *He Shang* (River elegy), in which the most sacred symbols of Chinese culture, the Yellow River, the dragon, and the Great Wall, are reinterpreted and denounced for representing violence against a helpless people, autocratic despotism, and conservative isolationism (Wakeman 1989). In the last scene, there is an airborne view of a muddy and sluggish Yellow River flowing out of the landmass of China to join and blend itself with the openness, dynamism, and liberation of the blue ocean, which stands for the modern West. Whether condemning Chinese culture or praising the West, these views share the assumption that culture is an essence that endures through time.

Faced with this native self-critique, the anthropologist from the West must resist the urge to label Chinese intellectuals "Orientalist," or exemplars of a colonized, "comprador" mentality. In these labels lie the Western insistence that the Other play a role for a West nostalgic for premodern times, a role of native "authenticity" and purity, a role no longer possible nor desirable, it seems, for much of the contemporary non-Western world. This Western self-critical perspective also implies that China's problems can all be attributed to the experience of colonialism and capitalism, to external imperialist forces. It does not account for the degree to which the forces of modernity introduced from without have over the course of the twentieth century not only destroyed some aspects of Chinese tradition but also appropriated and strengthened others, with the result that the arrangement of power in China today, however novel, still has a very familiar Chinese flavor.

When confronting this kind of essentialist self-critique by many Chinese intellectuals, my own inclination is to point out that although such self-criticism can serve as a galvanizing discourse for cultural renewal and innovation, it also suffers from its ahistorical perspective. To ascribe to Chinese culture an intrinsic timeless nature, and to blame this nature for various inadequacies in the modern world, overlooks what a perspective sensitive to historical context would recognize: much of what can be critiqued in China today are modern forms of power and control found elsewhere in the world in other experiences of modernity.

In examining the nature of power in contemporary China, one

would have to concur with Michel Foucault that the power of "administration over the ways people live" and the oppositional struggles it has engendered are "transversal" processes in the modern world. "That is, they are not limited to one country. Of course they develop more easily and to a greater extent in certain countries, but they are not confined to a particular political or economic form of government" (1983:211). Indeed, as I shall point out throughout this book, socialist China exemplifies many of the features of modern power-systems that Foucault discovered in the modern West.

I found, in constructing a historical framework for understanding state-socialist China, that neither Western reflexive self-critique nor Chinese essentialist self-critique was appropriate. They share the weakness of subscribing to a clear-cut and isomorphic set of binary oppositions: the West and the Other, the East and the West, the traditional and the modern and so on. In the modern world, the sheer number and variety of transnational, cross-cultural, and discursive border crossings accompanying human movements, communications media, and the circulation of commodities (Rosaldo 1989; Appadurai 1990) have together begun to affect the self-understanding and practice of anthropology. There is a recognition that the discipline can no longer remain wedded to a discourse of fixed borders between a Western knowing subject and a pure and culturally integral object of the Other (Clifford 1988a, 1988c). The very concept of "culture," so central in the history of anthropology, is now considered too constraining in its "highly localized, boundary-oriented, holistic, primordialist images" (Appadurai 1990:20). There are also suggestions that the outmoded organic-holistic model of culture might be replaced by a Foucaultian vision of modern transnational and translinguistic discursive formations (Clifford 1988c:274). Given these modern border crossings, it no longer seems adequate to mount a mutually exclusive critique either of the imperialist West or of Chinese tradition. Furthermore, once we recognize the "modernness" of forms of power in contemporary China, we will need to question the assumption made by both Chinese and some Western intellectuals that China represents a recalcitrant traditionalism that has resisted modernization.

In examining power formations in China, I propose instead a shift of focus to a diagnosis or critique of the disorders of modernity in China, a modernity that is the product of both native Chinese and transnational discourses and practices of power. Such a form of interpretation proceeds from a sense that something is wrong in a social body and is causing suffering. This sense of something wrong became increasingly evident to me as I listened to the voices of native self-critique and came to experience aspects of life as a partial native. A social diagnosis sets out to trace out the problematical conduits of power that have not only diminished life but actually threaten to extinguish it.

In deconstructing the notion of a unified and integral "West," Clifford writes: "When we speak today of the West, we are usually referring to a force—technological, economic, political—no longer radiating in any simple way from a discrete geographical or cultural center. This force, if it may be spoken of in the singular, is disseminated in a diversity of forms from multiple centers—now including Japan, Australia, the Soviet Union, and China" (1988c:272). In Clifford's terms, "force" appears in the singular, and its concrete manifestations in "multiple centers" comes "in a diversity of forms." This "force," I translate, is the transformative power of modernity, a global phenomenon and experience shared (to different degrees) by all cultures and linguistic-ethnic groupings, hence its singular nature.

Modernity can be defined in innumerable ways: (1) by the influence of the questioning scientific ethos; (2) by the rationalization and mechanization of production and economic exchange; (3) by growing urbanization, more efficient transportation, and the speeding up of the tempo of life; (4) by the establishment of new scientific and rational regimes of truth and knowledge, which launch and legitimate new social orders of power; (5) by the secularization or "disenchantment" of social and religious life (Weber 1968; Duara 1991); (6) by demographic changes and vast shifts of population; (7) by increasing bureaucratization to order this growing population (Weber 1968); (8) by mass social movements; (9) by the emergence of nation-states in a global political order; (10) by the increased scope and functions of the mass media (Berman 1982:16); (11) by more refined technologies of the self for self-transformation and individual surveillance (Foucault 1979b; Giddens 1990, 1991); or (12) by the discourse of a "new epoch," which sees "the present as a transition that is consumed in the consciousness of a speeding up and in the expectation of the differentness of the future" (Habermas 1987:6).

Modernity can be spoken of in the singular because it issues from the Western Enlightenment and Industrial Revolution. But when the force of modernity impinges on and interacts with hitherto more discreet cultural or political-economic zones, it produces not one form but many. It is interesting to note that out of the above list of modern features, Chinese state-socialist modernity did not exhibit much of the first three features, although in the post-Mao era, these are quickly beginning to shape a new order that can be called socialist state capitalism.

For a long time now, the West has ceased to be the only site of modernity or the only generator of the types of power found in modernity. Modernity in China was triggered by Western and Japanese imperialism in the nineteenth and twentieth centuries. Imperialism intruded on an already troubled social formation, producing traumas of its own. It gave rise to, and its direct impact was diffused and overtaken by, new social forces that were a complicated mixture of native and imported elements. The social formation that is contemporary China is a composite product of Chinese imperial and peasant forms of culture and power and Western Marxist discourse, as well as Soviet Marxist-Leninist and Stalinist institutions, which are themselves partially the products of the Enlightenment in the West. China's socialist modernity bears the marks of the international crossings of industry, nationalism, revolutionism, fascism, evolutionism, mass-media forms of persuasion, the discourse of progressive time (Lee 1990), and the rational Enlightenment project to reorder society totally.

At the same time, these external forces have summoned forth, shaped, and, most significant, been appropriated by indigenous forces from deep within the Chinese imperial past. The ancient native force of statism known as Legalism is addressed in Chapter 7. The Maoist interpretation of Marxism-Leninism was informed by Mao's considerable study of ancient Chinese texts of statecraft, such as the Song dynasty *Zizhi Tongjian* and the twenty-four-volume collection of dynastic histories. Modern China is the product of the conjoining of modernist discourses originating in the West and native institutions (such as the state), historical social conditions (for example, population increase and mass impoverishment),[12] and native reaction-formations such as peasant rebellions. Therefore, any diagnosis of power in contemporary China is a critique neither simply of the West nor of Chinese tradition, but of their offspring: Chinese modernity.

One definition of modernity has special resonance with the issues of modernity in China addressed in this book. In this definition, modernity is described as "an environment that promises us . . . transformation of ourselves and the world—and, at the same time, that threatens to destroy everything we have, everything we know, everything we are" (Berman 1982:15). As a reaction to the traumas of imperialism and impoverishment, China in the twentieth century has

[12] Between 1802 and 1834, it is recorded in the Chinese state census that the population of the empire increased an astounding 100 million to the figure of 400 million people (Gernet 1985:531), a 33 percent increase in thirty-two years.

embarked on a path of cultural self-transformation, accompanied in the socialist period by the rejection and destruction of practices deemed traditional and "feudal."

This will to total self-transformation can be seen as part of an international movement in the twentieth century toward modernization, which, as Foucault has pointed out, is based on a faith in the equation of rational knowledge with emancipation and progress. Proponents of the modern prison system and of modern mental institutions ("insane asylums") presumed that they were instituting a more "humane" and progressive system, even as they were extending and refining a new form of knowledge and power based on discipline rather than punishment (Foucault 1979b; 1973).

The Enlightenment belief in the powers of reason to reorder society can also be seen in the nineteenth- and early-twentieth-century French discourses of rational urban planning and public health, which were put into effect not only in France, but in its colonies (Rabinow 1989). Social projects of modernity can also be found in the international movement in modernist architecture, which subscribes to a utopian and totalistic vision for the rearrangement of life for a given population. The modernist urban planning of a city like Brasilia was likewise the emergence of a new form of power, a power that refused "any accommodation whatsoever to existing urban and social conditions [since] the break with the past must be absolute . . . the contrast between the new city and the old [was] one of total antagonism—a turning inside out" (Holston 1989:53). Like modernist architecture in Brasilia, revolutionary transformation in China also partakes of a transnational Enlightenment discourse of modernity which takes "society" as an object of knowledge and active human intervention. When combined with a state apparatus, this vision of total social transformation produces the idea of a center that has total knowledge of the needs of society and seeks to erase or to deny difference and division within the unified homogeneous and flattened social order (Lefort 1986:288).

Having situated this book in the field of critiques of modernity, I also find it necessary to incorporate into the analysis the specificity of modernity in China. Modernity has usually been understood in terms of one particular variant form, that of Western liberal capitalism. As a result, many critiques of modernity (such as the Marxist, or the Weberian, or that of the Frankfurt School) have targeted economic rationalization and utilitarianism (Sahlins 1976). Long before the breakup of state socialism in Eastern Europe and the former Soviet

Union in 1989, dissidents there pointed out that "actually existing socialism" is a social formation that is not so concerned with economic interests, but with political, and I may add, cultural ones (Feher, Heller, and Markus 1983). It is time to take a look at forms and projects of modernity found in noncapitalist and non-Western contexts and at the institutional and discursive forms of power that emerged in these places (Lefort 1986; Verdery 1991; Rofel 1992; Yang 1988).

In order to address the specificities of state-socialist versions of modernity, it is necessary to extricate the critique of socialist modernity from the critique of capitalism. That is to say, Western intellectual critiques of capitalism cannot address the problems of a cultural formation that combines modern state socialism with elements of the old imperial mode of power. The task of specifying and understanding the particular configurations of power in state-socialist versions of modernity has just begun. This book is one contribution to that effort.

Ironically, this work is undertaken just at a time when Chinese state socialism has begun to evolve in radically new directions, through the introduction of world-capitalist and market forces, toward a combination of statism and capitalism the world has perhaps never yet seen.[13] All the more reason, I believe, to analyze a fast-disappearing stage of Chinese modernity in the first three decades after the Revolution, when state power was still relatively independent and distinct from capitalism.

Although economic rationalization was actively suppressed in socialist China, what makes the Maoist era "modern" and different from other modernities is another kind of rationalization, a rationalization in the moral and political realms. Here the Maoist state version of "instrumental reason" in the moral-political domain has given a unique twist to the twelfth feature of modernity: the will to achieve total social transformation, to create a perfect society. The state's moral-political project, carried out with its particular brand of moral-instrumental reason, has justified the suffering and psychical dislocation of countless people in mass political campaigns, the purposive

---

[13] For a useful collection of essays dealing with changes in the economic institutions of socialism in China and Eastern Europe, see Nee and Stark 1989. On the penetration of capitalism into Guangdong Province, and the commoditization of female labor, see Ong 1994 and Siu 1993. On how statism in China has adapted to capitalism, see Anagnost 1992.

destruction of what is called "feudalism,"[14] and ultimately, even society and culture themselves.

This brand of modern Chinese moral-instrumental reason, in which the means to the end become the frightening ends themselves, is well illustrated in the essay "Between Idealism and Reality," by Hu Ping, a dissident Chinese intellectual (1990). Hu offers a refreshing approach to self-critique that does not essentialize or reify Chinese culture, but sets it in the developmental framework of a social order whose severe puritanist utopian (*wuduobang*) project turns into a dystopian (*fanmian wuduobang*) nightmare of self-destruction. The essay takes as its starting point a recent novel called *The Dream of the Land of Peach Blossoms* by Muo Yingfeng about a utopian community set in mythical-historical time and located outside civilization, much like the utopian "Land of Peach Blossoms" of traditional Chinese folklore and literature. The peaceful and rustic lives of its members disappear when a group of people decide that practicing strict vegetarianism is the highest attainment of virtue. They try to force everyone else to adhere to their strict code of moral behavior, through models of virtuous heroes, through intimidation, and through a system of rewards and punishments. For Hu, the analogy with the modern socialist experiment is clear: "How did a people who took virtue as their ideal turn into people of such ferocious cruelty?" (1990:21). With Nietzschean insight,[15] Hu points out the underlying hypocrisy of a moral-political absolutism that elevates the weak-willed and blind followers of a doctrine to the status of the most virtuous. Those who would be the most virtuous delude themselves and others by denying their own self-interested motivations for being virtuous and by hiding what Nietzsche called their secret "resentment" of the meat-eaters.

Hu Ping's article highlights as a dominant ethos of modernity in China utopian moral-political absolutism, but the social institution that crystallized and operationalized this ethos, the modern state, also needs to be put into focus. The modernist projects of social transformation in China have been inextricably tied in with the expansion of

---

[14] For a fascinating genealogy of the notion of "feudalism" in China, see Duara's "Provincial Narratives of the Nation: Centralism and Federalism in Republican China" (1993). In the 1920s and 1930s, "feudalism" (*fengjian*) for some Chinese political thinkers meant a decentralized system of provincial self-government, but this notion lost out to the forces of the centralized state, and to the new definition of "feudalism" entering from Japan, which equated it with "backwardness" (*luohou*) and oppressiveness.

[15] At the time he wrote his interpretation of this novel in 1986, Hu Ping had already read Nietzsche and Orwell's 1984 in Chinese translation (personal communication, Los Angeles, July 1992).

an interventionalist state that supervised and coordinated such projects. As noted by Prasenjit Duara, already in the late Qing dynasty and early republican period (1880s-1930s), the state was introducing modern schools, new administrative units, and a new class of state functionaries and brokers and was also coordinating local defense organizations in the countryside, all requiring heavy taxation of villages (Duara 1987, 1988a). State penetration through the village as the new territorial, administrative, and fiscal unit and through a new class of local state brokers served to displace the old system of indirect state rule through the "cultural nexus of power." The old system was formed by overlapping local organizations such as lineages, temple organizations, deity cults, water-control societies, and informal networks of affinal ties and patron-client and teacher-disciple relationships. With the Communist Revolution in 1949, the countryside was further integrated into the administrative apparatus of the new state order through such new organizational forms as mutual-aid teams, cooperatives, and later, the tri-level organs of commune, brigade, and production team (Potter and Potter 1990).

Twentieth-century Chinese urban areas also witnessed an increasing coordination of social activities by the modern state. In the Qing dynasty, policing activities were carried out by an assortment of different organizations: imperial troops, the staff of the local magistrate's office, the ancient *baojia* decimal system of mutual surveillance in neighborhoods, and the private militia of local gentry. In the 1920s and 1930s, a modern police force professionally trained in police academies with the latest scientific methods from Germany, Japan, and the United States systematized the state's policing functions and expanded them to deal with the realm of cultural habits and customs (dress codes, public conduct, and so on) (Wakeman 1988a). After 1949, through such measures as the nationalization of industries, the control of private service institutions such as hospitals and schools, the gathering of small enterprises, peddlers, and the unemployed into state-run collectives, and the new neighborhood organizations of social surveillance, urban life was also brought into the folds of state administration. With state ownership and control of the means of production, distribution, socialization, and communication, social structure came to be subsumed by state administrative structure, and the state became coextensive with society. Urban China, along with Eastern Europe and the Soviet Union, took the shape of the Stalinist "mono-organizational society," in which "most activities are directly managed by innumerable organizations or bureaucracies, all of which are linked up in a *single* organizational system" of the state (Rigby 1977:59; Yang 1989b:38).

In outlining the workings of state power, I do not simply seek to describe the state in terms of a narrow technical sense of the bureaucracy and its official class. The state is not its system of laws, rules, and regulations; nor is it a system of force based only on policing, punishment, and military action. What forms a point of departure for this inquiry into modern forms of social control and counter-control in contemporary China is Foucault's novel definition of power as a constitutive field and discourse of strategic action, rather than something possessed by a class or a group (1980:93–96). What is at issue in this book is not merely class or institutional control, but a modern technique and telos of power. Translated into anthropological terms, Foucault's approach to power is not to classify those who have it or do not have it, but to inflect the notion of culture (understood too often in the history of anthropology as "adaptation") with the notion of power.

His thesis on how knowledge and power feed into the modern project of increasing administration and "governmentalisation" (1979a) of life is an important one in the context of twentieth-century China. Neither the Mandate of Heaven nor alignment with the cosmic forces concerns the new configuration of power in China. Instead, the health, wealth, size, quality (*suzhi*), movement, and thoughts of the population are now the affairs of "bio-power" (1980), a governing order that is not external to, but immanent in society, and which seeks to plan and regulate it in its minutest aspects. Lisa Rofel points out that the panoptic arrangement of space for optimal surveillance, which is highlighted by Foucault for modern prisons, factories, and schools, does not operate in Chinese factories (1992). Instead, she finds that an older form of power, the "display of hierarchy," informs the architectural separation between management and workers. Nevertheless, I will show how surveillance is still very important in China, but it takes a form more linguistic than optical, a form that enables the state to monitor thoughts, speech, and writing.

Although the present critique of modernity and power in China is inspired by Foucault's analysis of the modern West, it is also clear that the historical trajectory and specific features of Chinese modernity are different in many ways from that of the West that Foucault described. For example, such elements as repressive force, punishment, and the personal power of the sovereign-cum-leader were important features of the imperialist and fascist phases of Western modernity that Foucault did not address. These same elements have also been prominent in modern China. Another important feature of Chinese modernity that does not figure in Foucault's analysis has been the dramatic eclipse of a long and deeply rooted kinship mode of power and discourse by the rapid expansion of the state and its discourse of nationalism. This very transformation provides the backdrop for the present book.

Whereas Foucault found a discourse of sexuality to be an important mode of power in the modern West, we see its significant absence in socialist China, and also the interesting Maoist tendency to erase gender difference or masculinize gender. What we find in modern China instead is that the state comes to define and appropriate any discourse of gender and sexuality into its own terms and according to its own agenda of creating loyal subjects. In Qing dynasty China (1644–1911), "Male and female, Confucian subjects always appeared as part of something else, defined not by essence but by context, marked by interdependency and reciprocal obligation rather than by autonomy and contradiction" (Barlow 1989:10). Persons were not shaped or defined by abstract categories, but were always caught up in paired and complementary relationships that "used kinship as the imaginary referent for a series of discourses that completely obscured socio-economic associations of extra-kin nature" (Barlow 1989:11). The May Fourth Movement of the 1920s was the first major movement of cultural self-transformation that helped inaugurate modernity in China (Chow 1960). May Fourth iconoclastic discourse attacked the Confucian family and kinship constructions of persons and substituted a Westernized individual essence of free will and biological nature; however, this individualism was from its modern inception, both in tension with and in collusion with nationalism, another powerful force that also came to define personhood as China was thrust into the modern global system of competing and encroaching nation-states. Through the waves of anti-imperial and civil wars, nationalist identity soon eclipsed individualism. The notion of being a loyal Chinese citizen came to override the other discourses of individual rights such as feminism, labor unionism, and the rights of the youth (Liu 1991; 1994). As Tani Barlow points out, in state socialism the resistance potentials of the new categories of "woman," "worker," and "youth" were diminished by their transformation into state classifications and administrative categories (Barlow 1991a).

Part 1 of this book presents a detailed ethnography of guanxixue, including its rich language, its diverse usages and contexts of operation, its logic and ethics, and the recent history of its decline and reemergence in socialist China. It is also an attempt to present the multiple native attitudes and interpretations of this phenomenon. Part 1 represents a dimension of interpretation that tries to stay as close to the "raw" ethnographic data as possible. Interpretation is found in the selection of features I deemed important to investigate and recount, in the kinds of questions I asked, and in the arrangement of the material into what seems to me the most effective narrative structure for describing guanxixue.

Whereas Part 1 shows both the pejorative and positive aspects of guanxixue in native discourse, Part 2 focuses on one particular historical significance of guanxixue's reemergence: its opposition to the lines of power comprising the "state" in the new formation of state socialism. The focus in Part 2 on the oppositional aspects of guanxixue is intended to counterbalance the way that it is usually interpreted by both natives and Westerners alike. Guanxixue is usually regarded as being in line with official and bureaucratic power, whether as official corruption or as patron-client ties wielded by officials to control their dependents (Walder 1986). Instead, the approach that will be taken in Part 2 is to see the art of guanxi working *against* state power, according to principles fundamentally at odds with state-building forces. Therefore, an analysis of one set of oppositional practices, guanxi gift relations, serves as a point of departure for a diagnosis and critique of state modernity and power in terms of political economy, social organization, and moral-political discourse.

PART I

AN ETHNOGRAPHY OF
MICROPOLITICS IN A
SOCIALIST SETTING

A society is . . . composed of certain foregrounded practices organizing its normative institutions *and* of innumerable other practices that
remain "minor," always there but not organizing discourses, and
preserving the *beginnings or remains of different (institutional, . . .)
hypotheses for that society.* . . . It is in this multifarious and silent
"reserve" of procedures that we should look for "consumer" practices.

—de Certeau 1984:48 (my emphasis)

In the chapters of Part 1 I undertake to describe and illustrate in
minute detail a body of everyday practices and discourses in urban
China which belong under the rubric of guanxixue. These practices
do not organize the dominant discourses of the society, which have to
do with such themes as "modernization," "economic reform," "socialism with Chinese characteristics," and so forth. They are not considered an important subject to be taught in schools or to be studied
much by serious scholarship. They do not form the major socially
recognized institutions of the society, such as factories, families,
schools, government organs, stores and markets, and so on. Yet they
are so common and pervasive in all aspects of daily life in China that
it might take an outsider or foreigner to take notice and attach social
significance to them.

Based on first-hand ethnographic inquiry, I lay out in Part 1 the
different inflections of meaning in the extensive vocabulary that goes
with the art of guanxi. I document the great diversity of situations

47

that call for the practice of guanxixue. I delve into the differences in its practice, such as rural-urban, gender, and occupational class differences. I attempt to convey the internal logic of guanxixue, by describing not only its tactics and methods, its system of personalistic ethics, but also its etiquettes or rules of performance. The art of guanxi is also compared and contrasted with another new field of social transactions in China: that of money and commodified relations. And finally, the recent historical trajectory of guanxixue's decline, reemergence, and development is also sketched out. Those readers already familiar with the workings of guanxixue in Chinese society can skip Part 1 and go directly to the theoretical formulations in Part 2.

This "minor" set of practices in contemporary China can be seen as the *beginnings*, or the rebirth, of a realm of social relations independent from state principles. At the same time, these practices are also the *remains* of a premodern kinship- and locality-oriented social system which placed importance on gift relations as ways of cementing relationships of mutual aid and obligation. And while de Certeau takes "consumer practices" to mean the creative uses made by consumers of modern mass media culture in the West, Part 1 shows how guanxixue is often a creative deployment of a "counter-ethics" which makes room for the personal and the private in a public sphere monopolized by the state.

CHAPTER ONE

Guanxi Dialects and Vocabulary

The term "guanxixue" does not appear in the 1947 edition of *The Sea of Words* (*Ci hai*), a Chinese dictionary (Shu 1947) similar to *The Oxford English Dictionary*, with its quotations from ancient and classical texts. Nor does it seem to be part of everyday speech in Taiwan. We can therefore surmise that "guanxixue" emerged in China in the socialist period. The word *guan*, however, has two definitions in *Ci hai* that are relevant to the phenomenon we are studying: "to connect" (*lianluo*) or "to make a linkage"; and "a pass or gate" that can be closed or guarded (Shu 1947:1412). These two dictionary definitions are directly relevant to modern guanxixue. A basic requirement of contemporary Chinese life is the ability to make social connections that enable a person to negotiate the countless "passes" or "gates" thrown in his or her way. To obtain the full flavor of the various social usages and attitudes toward guanxixue, we need to go beyond dictionary definitions to the thoughts and utterances of living people in everyday life.

Once I had settled on the art of guanxi as the focus of my research, I went around asking people to define the notion of guanxixue. The answers I received revealed that despite my attempts to uncover "the native's point of view" (Geertz 1984), there was no singular point of view regarding guanxixue. Instead, there were multiple points of view and native definitions. This indeterminacy indicates that guanxixue elicits a corpus of ambiguous and changeable cultural meanings and a correspondingly ambivalent social attitude toward its practices. Multiple and conflicting attitudes toward a social phenomenon suggest not only that there are different occupational, class, gender, or ethnic perspectives in any given society but also that a society is undergoing specific social changes or a historical shift from one worldview and set of habits and interpretations to another. At the same time, the direction of the change and the contours of the new order are still unclear in people's minds, and there is still no interpretive consensus on the new phenomenon of guanxixue. Therefore, in the midst of this process of open-ended change, when the question of the art of guanxi is raised, it is met with a multiplicity of contending discourses, all of which seek to fit the term into a particular interpretation of history.

This situation is similar to the state of "heteroglossia," which according to the Russian literary theorist Mikhail Bakhtin is the struggle among sociolinguistic points of view which gives rise to "the dialogic nature of language" (1981). These different points of view as expressed in language take the form of what he called "dialects," which in language are not restricted to the narrow, phonetic sense of the term but also include the socio-ideological languages of different social groups, generations, and interpretive viewpoints.

In the descriptions of guanxixue I have collected from both oral and written Chinese sources, four distinct "dialects" can be discerned, four sets of meanings and attitudes that are at times in conflict with each other. The first three belong to what can be called popular discourse, the forms of language and types of attitudes in everyday life which one finds expressed in localized and delimited spaces within the family; among friends, relatives, and neighbors; and between friendly but anonymous strangers on trains and buses. These popular forms of expression on guanxixue are usually found in spontaneous, everyday speech acts and seldom in writing, where a more orthodox attitude toward guanxixue is usually found. The three dialects found in popular discourse on guanxixue can be roughly distinguished by their attitudes: the pejorative, the mixed, and the morally neutral and pragmatic.

The fourth set of descriptions of guanxixue displays a certain coherence and a detectable agenda, meriting the label "official discourse." By "official discourse" I do not mean that its speakers and writers are only officials; rather, I mean the style of language which projects the authority and political correctness which plays a hegemonic role in unifying public discourse. Anyone, whether official, worker, or intellectual, woman, man, or child, can speak, write, or think in it. Indeed, people either feel constrained to do so in public contexts or fall into the habit of doing so. Official discourse also dominates the various forms of state-run media such as radio, television, newspapers, books, and even scholarly publications. Needless to say, even where official discourse replicates or coincides with certain elements of popular discourse, other aspects of its style, content, tone, and evaluative mode render it recognizably distinct.

Popular Discourse

First, guanxixue, as it is conceptualized in popular discourse, can have the pejorative connotation of an antisocial practice, an aberrant instrumental behavior based on self-interest, which should be morally rejected:

Guanxixue is using people [*liyong ren*]. (Woman factory labor union director)

Guanxixue is when you treat someone differently than you otherwise would because of how much that person is of use to you. Guanxixue is not upright [*bu zhen*]; it is crooked and sly. (Woman middle-school teacher)

Chen Zhongwang, a woman school teacher, had a slightly different reason for disapproving of the art of guanxi:

"I hate guanxixue because it's so demeaning. It's so obvious when you give someone a gift that you have a particular motivation in mind. So I never wanted to do it . . . but then, I had to win favor with the office in charge of giving out passports so I could go abroad. I had to wear a thick skin on my face [*daizhe hou lianpi*] and present a gift to the person in charge. Afterward I almost threw up [in disgust], but I did get the passport," she said, her face screwed up with distaste.

Also faulting guanxixue is Liang Xiaoming, part of a new breed of urban entrepreneurs involved in linking factory producers, distributors, and markets, who said, "Guanxixue is bad for society, because when you help your friends and relatives, they may benefit, but somewhere down the line, someone else without the guanxi will suffer. They won't get the thing that your friends got.

A woman factory worker surmised that guanxixue is part of the turn toward a general treacherousness in social relations. Her tracing of this turn to the period of the Cultural Revolution follows a common narrative motif in China in the 1980s, when the Cultural Revolution was regarded as a watershed or turning point for every conceivable aspect of the society. Before the Cultural Revolution, she reminisced, people were "honest" (*laoshi*), "simple" (*danchun*), and "straightforward" (*zhi*). Because of their experiences during the Cultural Revolution, people started "turning bad" (*bian huai*); and they came to harbor ill-will for one another, to use one another; they began to utter "falsehoods and deceptions" (*shuo jiahua*); and now they "do not speak from the heart" (*bu shuo xinlihua*). The woman lamented that she had especially suffered for being too frank and direct in speech in the past, so that many were the occasions when people took what she said out of context and used it against her. She resolved to learn guanxixue so that her words could not be distorted and she would be less vulnerable in the future.

Her association of guanxixue with a turn toward "badness," "deception," and the instrumental manipulation of relationships represents another explanation of guanxixue as a symptom of declining moral standards in society. There is something about guanxixue which makes it distasteful and morally objectionable to a lot of people. At the same time that she laments the moral decline, however, she also resolves to learn guanxixue herself. Guanxixue in this usage refers not to the substantive outcome or material benefit of a relationship of exchange, but to the very form, quality, and characteristic techniques of the relationship itself, to include the discernment, acuity, and cunning needed to get by in life. Thus the negative definitions of guanxixue in popular discourse can occasionally be found to contain a recognition and admiration of its style of operations and its potential benefits as a form of self-protection.

It is significant that four of the above five negative views of guanxixue came from women. I found that women, more than men, objected to the aggressive tactics sometimes found in guanxi dealings, to the use and manipulation of people. Men tended to have an accepting attitude toward guanxixue's instrumentalism, regarding it in a realistic light as something one had to do in order to accomplish certain tasks.

Another negative understanding of guanxixue in popular discourse in the economic reform period is the view that equates it with official corruption. A middle-aged relative of mine, who is an agricultural expert from the south, expressed a common anger and bitterness toward how officials engage in guanxixue to further their own political and economic positions. "Their guanxi network is very large, they exchange favors with one another, their children benefit from their fathers' position and use it to enrich themselves too." I asked innocently if officials were also acting responsibly since they were living up to their obligations to their kin and friends by helping them. With eyes flashing in indignation, he replied, "If they want to help their friends and relatives, they should find other ways, they should not turn their [official] positions into their private property [*siren cai-chan*]!"

Throughout the 1980s there was increasing popular resentment at the way officials employed their guanxi to secure "special privileges" (*tequan*) for themselves and their families. Indeed, during the spring of 1989, one of the most powerful rallying cries of the student movement in Beijing was the condemnation of official corruption. One "big-character poster" decried the art of guanxi among officials:

> Though I could see all the smaller spiders busily and carefully weaving exquisitely intricate, far-flung webs of relationships from which they would extract benefits, it never occurred to me that the . . . "high-level leaders" whom I so respected were also endowed with this instinct and talent for weaving webs, and indeed had, whether consciously or unconsciously, woven for themselves "magic webs." Our Party is becoming ensnared in these spiders' webs, its vision impaired, its ears stopped up, its throat strangled, its strength sapped. (Han and Hua 1990:37)

The passage duly notes the pervasiveness of guanxi networks among ordinary people ("smaller spiders"), but evinces surprise and disgust at guanxi among supposedly upright Party officials. The metaphor of becoming ensnared and put out of commission in spiders' webs presents guanxixue as a practice that harms the Party and society.

Wang Xiaobing, a male graduate student, also disparaged guanxi practices, but he focused not on the selfish and particularistic benefits guanxi networks can gain for a person, but on what they deny. He described guanxi networks as "suffocating" (*bu touqi*), a way of exerting social pressure on a person so that he cannot do what he really wants. For example, he has for many years tried to get a divorce from his wife, who only has a lower-middle-school (junior high) education. Although they are incompatible in education, personality, and style of life, she refuses to divorce him and is backed up by the community.[1] When he tried to apply for a divorce, the neighborhood committee where he lived mobilized his whole guanxi network of family, neighbors, and friends to take turns talking him out of it. So for Xiaobing, one's guanxi can put great pressure on a person to conform to social conventions and to accept the decisions of higher authorities. He

---

[1] In China, it is usually the case that a divorce can only be granted when both husband and wife agree to it. It is seldom granted if just the husband wants it, unless he can prove gross misconduct by the wife.

knows the power of this pressure firsthand and eventually gave in to guanxi pressure and stayed with his wife.

A second approach to explaining the art of guanxi takes the instrumental aspect of guanxi relations into account, but also stresses that guanxi operates according to a morality of its own and serves a necessary social function. Liu Fuqiang, a male factory worker, commented thoughtfully: "Guanxixue includes both ethical and unethical practices; both high moral principles and petty calculations. It's just like in mathematics, there are both positive and negative numbers." Amid the thundering roar of factory machinery one day in the winter of 1984, this worker explained the dual nature of guanxixue.

> For example, guanxixue does not only have to take place between two people who know each other very well. Say, one dark and rainy night you're riding your bicycle home and something on the bike breaks down and you don't know how to fix it. It's late and you really want to go home. A stranger rides by and for no reason, stops to help you fix it. You're so grateful to him, and you ask his name and work unit. Someday he may be in need of help which is ten times the kind of help he was able to give you that night, yet because of your gratitude, you'll do all in your power to repay him. That's the honorable part of guanxixue.
>
> However, guanxixue also has the petty behavior of the "inferior person" [xiao ren],[2] who does everything with a specific motive, who helps others and gives them gifts only in order to use them.

Echoing Liu Fuqiang's explanation of the positive and negative dimensions of guanxixue is an analysis by Lu Ming, a young Beijing intellectual and former worker, who undertook to respond to my queries in written form. I present a translation of part of his letter to me here:

> I believe that the notion of "guanxixue" must exhibit the following three features simultaneously:
> 1. It must possess a heavy coloring of emotional feeling [ganqing secai] and human sentiment [renqing secai]. It must always present itself in terms of "old friends," "old acquaintances," "old relationship," etc.
> 2. It must involve each side using the other and also mutual exchange— that is, have the coloring of an instrumental exchange of interests [liyi jiaohuan]. That is to say, one side offers a convenience to the

---

[2] It is noteworthy that much moral thought in China today is still couched in traditional Confucian terms. This worker's contrast between high principles and the petty calculations of the "mean" or "inferior person" replicates a passage in the Confucian classic text The Analects, "The mind of the superior man [junzi] is conversant with righteousness [yi]; the mind of the mean man [xiao ren] is conversant with gain [li]" (Legge 1961:vol.1:170).

other side, the other also in some way repays the first side. It has a reflexive, exchange, and mutuality principle. The kind of relationship that does not demand repayment and does not involve personal interest [*wu si*] does not exist in "guanxixue."

3. The most important feature of "guanxixue" is: objectively, it has an "oppositional character" [*duikangxing*]. That is to say, "guanxixue" in actuality is informal organization's method of opposing and resisting [*fankang*][3] formal organization. Of course, this kind of resistance is often unconsciously played out by the two sides involved in guanxi. For example: A gives B a present, and B helps A find a job. During this time, A is only thinking of a suitable career, earning some money, and not about resisting the government. B is the same way, only thinking of an old friend or how many gifts were given. If B doesn't help, he will feel guilty. He doesn't think about much more than this. But in actuality, this behavior posits as its goal, opposition to formal organization, opposition to authority and the law.

I believe that only if all three features (emotional feeling, exchange, resistance) are simultaneously present can it be called guanxixue.

This interpretation of the oppositional character of guanxixue in contemporary society is borne out by what Yuan Dahua, a male worker and entrepreneur in his spare time, told me, "Guanxixue is the people taking a deviant path in order to achieve a reasonable objective" ("Guanxixue jiu shi renmin zou wailu wei dadao heli de mudi"). What he meant was that the objectives that require the practice of guanxixue, such as getting permission to change jobs, are usually judged to be "reasonable" or "justifiable" (*heli*) in popular opinion, but may be against official laws or regulations. Ideally, a personal pursuit should be in accordance with three things: "in accordance with sentiment" (*heqing*) or the desires and feelings of the people involved; "in accordance with reason" (*heli*) or popular moral judgment; and "in accordance with the laws and regulations" of the state (*hefa*).[4] But since the state often makes laws and regulations that are "unreasonable" (*buheli*) or do not accord with the sentiments and feelings of the people, then the people have to take a crooked path around the law.

Indeed, I discovered that people like to tell and be told guanxi stories. During the course of several years of fieldwork in China as well

---

[3] I translate *duikang* as "oppositional" and *fankang*, a word connoting stronger and more active opposition, as "resistance."

[4] The Chinese notion of "law" (*fa*) must not be understood solely in the rationalistic, legislative, or procedural senses dominant in the Western legal tradition. Above all these, the Chinese understanding of "law" emphasizes the right and authority of officials and the state and the will of the leadership.

as back in the United States, I heard more guanxi stories than I could ever put in a book. In my understanding, through sharing guanxi stories, people construct an alternative reality in which their personal efforts and actions have an effect on the world around them. People enjoy tales of someone finding a way to beat the system. Guanxi stories provide narratives of people who can shape their own destinies and who can triumph even though they are weak. These stories also construct a sense of collective endeavor, of people relying on one another, to outwit the system.

Third, the morally neutral understanding of guanxixue is a position that either suspends judgment or finds it irrelevant to a realistic view of human limitations. Born of a world-weary and somewhat hardened stance toward life, this position favors a realistic assessment of "human nature" (ren xing), of social and political reality, and the constraints of everyday existence. Again, Yuan Dahua explains, "Guanxixue is a relationship of exchange [jiaohuan] between two people which is extremely subtle and delicate [wei miao] and difficult for a third person to perceive. It is a relationship entailing calculation and considerations of mutual benefit [huxiang liyi] which are necessary for people to get by in life." His is a description that does not seek to impose any moral evaluation of these practices, but accepts the need to engage in relations of exchange.

A similar sentiment is found in a middle-aged scientist's defense of people who practice guanxixue, "They are not 'bad people' [bu shi huairen], they just do it because they have no choice [mei banfa], it's a necessity of life." When two college students, one a former worker, the other a former peasant, were asked about people's attitudes toward guanxixue, they answered in the same vein, "Most people condemn it as a matter of principle, but when an opportunity arrives for them to engage in guanxixue, then they become realistic [shiji]."

This attitude of agnostic cynicism toward the human condition was quite common in urban China in the 1980s. For example, asked what he considered the more important concerns in his life, a factory electrician responded that there are three main tasks in life: to eat, to reproduce, and to protect oneself. By the last item he meant that one must be practical in human relations because people are not perfect like the idealized heroic characters of Chinese novels and movies.

"In other words," said the electrician, "I do not expect much or ask much from my friends. Merely that when I am enjoying prosperity and high position, they do not flatter [peng] me and act obsequious. And that when I am down and out in life, they do not step on me.

Those who are able to meet these standards can be considered good people [*haoren*]. One cannot ask for too much more."

A similar sober-minded construction of human nature was expressed by Liu Binyan, a dissident intellectual and writer I interviewed in Beijing in 1984. He recounted that back in the early 1950s, seeing the revolutionary idealism firing up everyone around him, he already had a premonition of things to come. All around him official exhortations to selflessness filled the air, echoed enthusiastically at the time by the people:

Hao bu li ji,
zhuanmen li ren.

Do nothing to benefit yourself;
devote yourself to benefiting others.

Liu remembers moments of doubt during those heady years after the Revolution when he asked himself how long the spirit of this popular slogan could last. Given human nature, he thought, its appeal did not seem very realistic.

Instead of that slogan, the popular saying that people in the 1980s were more likely to subscribe to is this:

Ren bu wei ji,
tian zhu di mie.

When people do not look out for themselves,
heaven will expel and earth will destroy them.

The electrician who recited this proverb to me asserted that he and most Chinese he knew abided by this wisdom.

This sentiment on the importance of guanxixue as a tool for everyday survival is further echoed by Yuan Dahua's philosophical reflections. When asked to explain why guanxixue is so important in Chinese life, he had this to say:

> There are two basic goals in human existence. First, a basic motivation of all humans is to improve their everyday life. People always want to live more comfortably, materially and spiritually, don't you think? That's why they must establish guanxi and rely on it to help them attain this goal. A second reason for guanxixue is the basic need in life for self-defense. If you don't want people to take advantage of you [*qifu ni*] or harm you [*hai ni*], then you'd better cultivate good guanxi [*gaohao*

guanxi] with everyone. You never know whether or not someone around you might turn out to be a calculating and ruthless person. He will not feel satisfied until he can eradicate anyone who happens to be in his path. So, take care not to offend anyone [*xiaoxin buyao dezui renhe ren*]. Instead, you should try to do people a good turn [*gei renjia haochu*] so they'll remember you.

Yuan ended his words of advice on life with this wise proverb:

Hai ren zhi xin bu ke you;
fang ren zhi xin bu ke wu.

A heart for harming others must not be harbored;
a heart for defending against others must not be lacking.

Official Discourse

Unlike popular discourse, what typifies official discourse is its monophonic character. This is found in its definition of the art of guanxi solely as a negative social phenomenon and in its moral and political condemnation of guanxixue for its corrupting influence on proper socialist ethics. A typical sample of the official perception of guanxixue reads something like this:

> The so-called guanxi network is the main manifestation of the deviant winds blowing within the Party and in society today. It is the remnants of traditional China's feudal and clan systems' way of thinking. It is also a product of the intermingling of [feudal thought] with radical bourgeois individualism and selfishness, which has occurred in the process of the reforms for "enlivening the domestic economy and opening up to the outside world." "Guanxi network" is found where, for narrow individual and small group interests, [people] connect together in mutual dependence and mutual utilization. (Yu 1987:103)

The word for "deviant" in the phrase "deviant winds" (*bu zheng zhi feng*) literally means "not upright," "irregular," or "crooked," in the sense of immoral or incorrect behavior. It suggests that guanxixue employs crooked and roundabout avenues to get things done instead of officially approved channels, implying that the moral character of guanxixue is not upright, but highly questionable. As soon as official discourse admits the play of moral obligations in guanxixue, this observation is suppressed in the condemnation that guanxi ethics are "backward" (*luohou*) and "feudal" (*fengjian*), counter to "modern" socialist ethics. On the one hand, guanxixue is said to stem from the persistence of a backward ethical system whose particularistic ethics of interpersonal relations hamper the development of universalistic loyalty to the country and the "socialist system." These "feudal remnants" (*fengjian canyu*) or "feudal poison" (*fengjian liudu*) are the products of a long tradition of the Chinese "clan system" (*zongfa zhidu*) or kinship morality (*lunli daode*), which arose out of necessity from a rural "natural economy" of subsistence (Yuan 1981; Ding 1983; Yu 1987). Despite the transformation of the relations of production under socialism, these traces of backwardness stubbornly persist in the new society and must be thoroughly swept away because they hinder equitable state distribution and now even threaten to corrupt socialist ethics.

On the other hand, official discourse also attributes the increasing practice of guanxixue to the recent introduction of polluting influences such as "bourgeois individualism" (*zichan jieji geren zhuyi*) from abroad, where human relations have been reduced by the cash nexus into impersonal instrumentality.

There is another way to distinguish between "popular" and "official" discourse than pointing out the different spatial and situational contexts of their utterances. There is also a power dimension involved in both the centripetal movement of official discourse and the centrifugal tendencies of popular discourse. This power dimension of discourses has been noted by Bakhtin who, writing on what he called "unitary language" in the midst of the Stalinist period in the Soviet Union, must have been fully aware of the political consequences of language and social discourse. He writes: "A common unitary language is a system of linguistic norms. . . . These norms . . . [are] forces that struggle to overcome the heteroglossia of language, forces that unite and centralize verbal-ideological thought, creating within a heteroglot national language the firm, stable linguistic nucleus of an officially recognized literary language, *or else defending an already formed language from the pressure of growing heteroglossia*" (1981:270–71; my emphasis). Thus, official discourse seizes on one "dialect" or point of view in popular discourse and attempts to fix and impose a single proper definition and attitude toward guanxixue. This process was also called "superscription" by Prasenjit Duara when chronicling how both the imperial and republican states sought to overlay their own interpretation of the popular god Guandi as a loyal warrior defending state authority, over the popular cult of Guandi as a god of wealth and protector of temples (1988b).

When faced with multiple dialects or discursive viewpoints on guanxixue, the reaction of official discourse is to seek to bring them back into a unified and correct moral-political stance, as two articles in the newspaper *Gongren Ribao* (Worker's Daily) attempt to do:

> Comrade Shi Kuiwu's argument for the dual nature of "guanxixue" precisely reflects the deviating and contradictory state of mind of a portion of the people. People intensely hate "guanxixue" and condemn it as deviant winds, but while they condemn it, many people also cannot help but bashfully study the mysterious secrets of "guanxixue." On the surface, what Comrade Shi says does make sense. During the chaotic period [Cultural Revolution], "guanxixue" did to greater or lesser degrees maintain the economic and productive activities and relations between enterprises and state offices. . . . [Recognizing the positive aspects of guanxixue] will undoubtedly allow some people whose thinking is unhealthy to fabricate a theoretical basis [for justifying guanxixue]. There are some people who really wish that "guanxixue" should have its own philosophical status. . . . However, in my opinion, "guanxixue" definitely does not have that "good" side which Comrade Shi recognizes. Its existence brings a negative impact on society; it subtly affects people's ways of thought and exerts an abominable influence. Its spread throughout society will only damage the normal conduct of interpersonal relations, damage the development of productive forces, and finally it will damage our country's socialist nature. (Wei Y. 1981:3)

> On the one hand, [guanxixue] poisons the social atmosphere, corrupts the spirit of the people. On the other hand, it will necessarily incite the hatred of the majority of the people, so that the people will employ all sorts of ways to struggle against it, and exterminate it. (Wei S. 1981:3)

In attributing a single negative character to guanxixue, official discourse often follows the strategy of overlooking the ethical principles through which the art of guanxi operates and focusing only on its instrumental and antisocial dimensions,

When it does recognize the important role of human feelings and ethical principles at work in the art of guanxi, official discourse relegates these elements to the realm of the "private" or the "selfish" (*si*), as opposed to the realm of the "public" (*gong*). Although the English word "private" is the closest to designating the Chinese word *si*, the Western notion of private does not quite capture the pejorative connotation of selfishness that is inextricably intertwined with the Chinese *si*. Furthermore, the Chinese *si* does not harbor the Western positive notion associated with the word "private," of the rights of an individual to be free from prying and intrusive eyes. Therefore, in

Chinese official discourse, the art of guanxi is regarded as a repository for sentiments harmful to the larger society, indifferent to the public good, and subversive to the principles of socialism. Here the notion "public" (*gong*) is a conflation of the idea of a public good for the larger community and that of government or officialdom, which is assumed to serve the public good. In official discourse, there is no conceptual distinction between the interests of the public realm and the interests of the state.[5]

The pejorative sense of guanxixue and the private realm in official discourse are highlighted in the newspaper article titled "A Person Who Does Not Submit to *Private Sentiments* [*siqing*]." A woman accountant at a military hospital in Wuhan is commended for adhering to formal "principles" (*yuanze*). That is, her courage in refusing to grant guanxi favors to superiors, friends, neighbors, relatives, a person from the same home town, and an old comrade-in-arms, all of whom wanted her to use her position to help them with some personal matter, won her official approval (*RMRB* 7 November 1983:2). In the interests of the public good and of Party principles, she successfully resisted giving in to the obligations and entreaties that issued from these private relationships.

The refrain of how a cadre was victorious over privatistic and nepotistic demands is repeated in one newspaper article after another criticizing "deviant winds" among cadres and their abuse of power: "A person outside [the home] is upright and honest, but when he reaches home, and the 'pillow wind' starts to blow, the ears become soft and pliable, and the heart and desires are activated. . . . In the past few years, 'irregular tendencies' in the society have often been mixed up with irregular family tendencies. Therefore, in rectifying social trends, it is very necessary to straighten out the family atmosphere" (*RMRB* 7 November 1983). The basic message is that, in carrying out the duties of one's office, one should always proceed according to the principle of "public matters should be conducted according to public procedures" (*gongshi gongban*), meaning that one should always follow impartial rules and instructions set by the state, instead of acting on the basis of personal obligations. It is a phrase always set in opposition to the practices of guanxi. Since one should

---

[5] This postrevolutionary conflation of "public" with "official" and "state" continues a long tradition in which the sense of "communal" or "collective" was eclipsed by the imperial state's appropriation of the term (Rowe 1990:317). The distinction between "official" (*guan*) and "public" (*gong*) as in "public sphere," which had emerged in late nineteenth-century China, virtually disappeared in the post-1949 period (Rowe 1990:318–25).

never give in to any demands or appeals to personal loyalties issuing from one's private relationships, then practicing the art of guanxi is to allow the private to take over the public.

Another feature of the treatment of the art of guanxi in official discourse is its tendency to portray guanxixue only in terms of official corruption and bribery. A common theme is the increasing prevalence of official corruption and how it threatens the purity of Party and state organizations and stirs up popular discontent. The following public speech locates guanxixue in the economic realm, where, as a result of the economic reforms of 1979, officials in charge of economic activities find increasing opportunities to use their office as a means for extracting benefits for themselves:

> As a result of the ten years of internal disruption, our fine tradition has been seriously damaged. Old practices and ways of thinking left over from the old society have been resurrected. Recently in the economic sphere of our society have appeared the abominable phenomena of banqueting and gift-giving, pulling guanxi, seeking "commissions," going through the back door, and engaging in extravagant and wasteful behavior. In a few economic units, economic management organizations and their responsible cadres are not only so familiar with this behavior that they do not bother to put a stop to it, but even go along with it and sink into the mire. This sort of phenomenon has already seriously corrupted the ranks of our cadres and workers and has given rise to intense discontent amongst the masses. (Zhao 1981:59)

This passage has a representative value in that it shows how in official discourse, the art of guanxi is predominantly understood as a negative phenomenon, the corruption of officialdom.

In popular discourse, there is often a distinction drawn between guanxixue and bribery (*shou hui*). In a hard-sleeper compartment of a train traveling from Beijing to Shandong, I initiated an animated discussion of this very subject among three male agricultural experts. They were all convinced there was a difference between guanxi and bribery, but I could see that they were struggling to articulate it. One distinction they came up with was couched in terms of motives for action. "Bribery is for selfish, individual-gain purposes, and it is not legal, . . . and it is bad for the country, or for the collective." Guanxixue, however, is often for small group purposes, for "reasonable" (*heli*) demands. It is the only way to accomplish something reasonable. Another distinction they drew was along the lines of the style and method of one's approach. In bribery, one's speech and action are somehow more obvious, so that people can immediately tell that you want something. Guanxixue is more subtle. Their third distinction pointed to the different nature of the relationship in guanxixue and bribery. In guanxi, the exchange relation cannot be separated from the ordinary or preexisting relationship between two persons, whereas in bribery, the relationship is established expressly for the purposes of bribing a person.

A woman graduate student studying in the United States expressed the culturally felt distinction between bribery/corruption and the art of guanxi perhaps most clearly. For her, bribery and corruption are pejorative, negative terms, whereas guanxixue connotes "human sentiments" (*renqing*), friendship, long-term personal relationships, and an image of people helping one another. "So there is a good side of guanxixue which bribery does not have. For example, if you and an official do not have a prior personal relationship already, such as shared native homes, kin relationship, and so on, and he is seen to help you, then other people will surmise that there is bribery going on between you."

Both official and popular discourse associate guanxixue with official corruption, but the former speaks of guanxixue almost solely in terms of corruption, whereas popular discourse harbors multiple strains and interpretations of guanxixue besides the theme of corruption. Furthermore, the condemnation of guanxixue by official discourse conveys an implicit message that the state does not tolerate the violation of Party principle by corrupt officials; that bad officials are being dealt with; and that the recent waves of "individualism" (*geren zhuyi*), selfishness, and "deviant winds" (*bu zheng zhi feng*) will not be allowed to flourish in society and despoil the socialist ethic. Yet when popular discourse castigates guanxixue as official corruption, a very different subtext sometimes develops. Popular discourse turns the critique of guanxixue into a process of questioning the legitimacy of the state itself, a state that accords special privileges to high cadres and their children.

Seldom in official discourse is the art of guanxi spoken of as also a practice of everyday life which often does not involve people holding positions of office. It follows that in the concern over the moral character of officialdom and in the unquestioned negative interpretation of guanxixue, official discourse has no room for a view of guanxixue as the only way for people to get anything done, to penetrate an impersonal and powerful bureaucracy, and to replace state institutional, bureaucratic, and political relationships with personal ones. That is to say, official discourse generally cannot or does not entertain the possibility that the art of guanxi is produced by certain socialist systemic conditions and that it serves to loosen state control over all aspects of society. Whereas popular discourse contains diverse, ambivalent, and contradictory understandings of guanxixue, official discourse only recognizes its negative, selfish, and antisocialist character.

Key Words and Concepts of Guanxixue in Popular Discourse

A review of the vocabulary associated with the art of guanxi illustrates further the multifaceted meanings and moral evaluations that it elicits in popular discourse, and the different dimensions of its practice. First, there are a few compound words and phrases incorporating the word *guanxi* (social relationship). *Guanxiwang* (guanxi network) refers to a person's web or network of social contacts and connections. Some people's networks can be "big" or "wide," which means that they have established guanxi with a large number of people, who may vary in social and occupational position as well as geographical location.

The strands of social relationships within a guanxi network link a person to two types of juncture points, the *guanxihu* (guanxi household) and the *shouren* (familiar person), depending on the direction of the flow of social exchange at a given time. In real life, these two terms may refer to one and the same person. *Guanxihu* or "guanxi households" are those persons or corporate groups to whom one *owes* guanxi favors, and to whom one has an obligation to exert one's influence to give assistance.

Shouren or "familiar person," however refers to a person in one's guanxi network of whom one can *ask* a favor. A "familiar person" is someone well placed in a position to influence the allocation of something desirable who, because of a preexisting relationship such as friendship, kinship, or guanxi indebtedness, can be relied on to help obtain that desirable object or to "get something done" (*banshi*). "In today's society one cannot get anywhere without *shouren*." Variations on this sentence can express irony, bitterness, amusement, or resignation. The speaker may be saying that he or she does not have the right kind of *shouren*, or does not have many in the right places at the right times, or does not relish the thought of going through a *shouren* to get something done.

To *la guanxi* means literally to "pull social relationships." This phrase is used to describe the active manipulation of social relationships, especially through gift-giving, with an end to obtaining a product or service not immediately or directly in reach. The English colloquialism "pull strings" is similar in meaning, but its narrower connotation and usage cannot fully convey the whole range of complex tactics, social rituals, gift-giving etiquette, and proper form encompassed by the Chinese phrase.

Very close in meaning to *la guanxi* is the phrase *zou houmen* or "going through the back door." The distinction between them, as I understand it, is that "going through the back door" is less a descriptive term concerning the actual *process* of utilizing social relationships than a classificatory label for a set of practices that are either semi-legal or irregular (such as not going through proper official channels of the front door, but stealthily through the back), or exclusivistic or particularistic ways of getting something, by using "channels" (*luzi*) not open to everyone, but only to a few who have the right guanxi. The difference between these two phrases was succinctly put to me by a woman on the office staff of a factory, "If you want to 'go through the back door' [*zou houmen*], then you must first 'pull social relationships' [*la guanxi*]."

The adjective *you*, "oily" or "greasy," is sometimes applied to people who are especially adept at guanxixue. It describes people who are sly and cunning, possessed of wily social skills, and versed in the arts and guiles of impression management and social persuasion. Such people are bound to have wide guanxi networks because they know how to negotiate their way in social relationships and also possess *shili yan*, an "eye for power." That is to say, they do not cultivate social relationships or friendships indiscriminately, but only after astutely gauging the other's social position and influence. The crowning skill of someone who is *you* is the ability to maintain harmony and smoothness of relationships with everyone. Having command of the rhetorical aspects of speech and possessing an acute sense of when, how, and with whom to exercise tact, apply flattery, or feign meekness and humility are essential to being *you*. Thus, favors are extracted from people without evoking resentment and sometimes even without the other being aware of being manipulated.

Two variants of the notion of *you* are *lao youtiao* (old oily dough strip) and *hua* (slippery). The first expression compares a person to a long deep-fried pastry that is a standard breakfast item in most parts of China. *Hua* is used in the same sense as *you*. One of my uncles visiting me from a southern province explained that *hua* refers to people who are like actors on stage. They can change their demeanor and behavior to suit each person they are dealing with, and they have a special knack for feeling out their target's predispositions and character: "People who are *hua* know how to talk in front of leaders [cadres in charge of their work units]. If a leader likes to be flattered, they'll 'pet the horse's ass' [*pai ma pi*]. If the leader is more of an upright cadre, then they'll act real honest and hard working, [like] people who say little, but get things done."

It is evident that this explanation harbors a negative moral evaluation of "oily" or "slippery" character traits as being self-serving and insincere. But this attitude is not the only or even the most common stance toward people who have wily social skills. A case in point is the remarks made by Chen Shaoxiong, a thirty-year-old carpenter who works in a polytechnical school.

A person can be *you*, but not "bad" [*huai*] or mean-spirited. There is a difference. In my work unit there are both *you* and "bad" people. There is one worker who was a terror during the Cultural Revolution. He beat up the intellectuals in the unit. Now his former victims are his superiors, but they are still afraid of him because he is "bad." A "bad" person, for no apparent reason, will try to make relations between other people very tense. For example, if you should complain about someone to a "bad" person, he will turn around and go tell that person what you said, just to foment bad feelings between you. In the meantime, both you and that person [you complained about] will be thinking that he's a good fellow, loyal only to you. A *you* person does not harm others on purpose. *You* just means that a person's actions have first passed through his brain. He uses his brain, therefore he is "smart" [*congming*]. Other people all admire and envy him. The opposite of *you* is "foolish" [*sha*]. Some people have the ability to get things done in a very smooth and complete way. They please everyone and offend no one.

Just as my uncle's and Chen's statements reflect two different approaches to a character trait commonly found in the practice of guanxixue, so also there is a social ambivalence in popular discourse toward the character trait known as *laoshi*, which is commonly contrasted with that of *you*. *Laoshi* can mean "honest," "upright," and "reliable," referring to people who do not cheat or deceive others, and who abide by moral principles. The word can also denote the personal qualities of ingenuousness and naïveté. Finally, *laoshi* is frequently employed in the pejorative sense of "simple-minded" and "obedient." Someone who is *laoshi* in this sense readily believes whatever his or her leaders or the government says, has no independent thoughts, and does not engage in critical reflection. Whereas *you* people are adept at guanxixue, *laoshi* people seldom practice guanxixue.

It would seem that the ambiguity of the notions of *you* and *laoshi* is a significant social fact. The negative connotations of *you* as manipulative is undercut by the other sense of *you* as "smartness," a quality distinct from being morally "bad." Similarly, the ostensibly positive meaning of *laoshi* as "honest" is subverted by the view that *laoshi* people are simply malleable, obedient, mindless tools of whatever power is above them. The moral ambiguity of these two character traits carries over in evaluations of the art of guanxi in popular discourse. On the one hand, the art of guanxi is morally suspect since it attracts *you* people. On the other hand, people who are good at guanxixue are not really morally bad, but simply smarter than others, whereas those who do not engage in guanxixue are fools, like those *laoshi* people who mindlessly do or believe whatever they are told.

Other terms associated with guanxixue can be found in an older discourse of "human feelings" (*renqing*). (pronounced "ren-ch'ing"). *Renqing* has a venerable history, as it can be found in ancient Confucian discourse, such as the Han dynasty (206 B.C.E.–220 C.E.) text *The Book of Rites* (*Li Ji*), in which renqing refers to the natural human feelings and emotions found in father-son relationships, family and kin relationships, and friendship. These feelings and sentiments were thought to be the source from which issued "ritual" (*li*), the proper conduct of social relationships and social events and affairs that made possible and preserved the whole social order (*Li Ji* 1987: 741). The Tang dynasty (618–907 C.E.) poet Du Fu wrote a passage: "Presenting fine rice cakes to create renqing" (Shu 1947:80). In the Qing dynasty (1644–1911), this term stood for the giving of gifts and the salutary sentiments accompanying such acts (Xu 1990:22).

In contemporary China, renqing shows another dimension of guanxixue, an ethical dimension that is unexpected, given the frequent condemnation of the art of guanxi's privatistic, selfish, and instrumental character. My fieldwork inquiries elicited three senses in which renqing is understood in contemporary China. First, there is the notion that renqing is part of the intrinsic character of human nature. Human nature here is understood not as individual, but in terms of social relationships and interaction, which are taken to be naturally infused with affect or *qing*. "Human feelings" toward other human beings are both ethical and emotional, and this is what distin-

guishes humans from animals. To accuse someone of "lacking human
feeling" (*meiyou renqing*) is tantamount to saying that he or she does
not exhibit the natural affect and feelings of attachments and obligations to other people. It questions whether a person is morally worthy
of being called human, whereas to behave according to renqing is to
be a virtuous human, or "to know how to act like a human" (*hui zuo
ren*).

Second, renqing is also the proper way of conducting oneself in
social relationships, treating each according to the behavior that their
specific status and relationship to oneself dictate. Here the stress is on
proper conduct, rather than natural predisposition. If someone has
done a favor, one should express thanks through a gift or other
means. When a close friend or relative is sick, one feels obliged to
visit him or her, bringing along some fruit or other present. "Not
understanding human feelings" (*budong renqing*) is to be poorly socialized in the proper and moral ways of relating to others, and to
lack social discernment and grace. The "network of human feelings"
(*renqingwang*) is composed of a circle of people who are deemed de-
pendable and trustworthy, and with whom one is emotionally attached, such as family, kin, and close friends. A *renqingwang* differs
from a guanxi network (*guanxiwang*) in its greater "degree of affective feeling" (*qingfen*) between persons, and in the lesser degree to
which instrumental interests are recognized or expressed.

Third, renqing also refers to the bond of reciprocity and mutual aid
between two people, based on emotional attachment or the sense of
obligation and indebtedness. The phrase *qian renqing zhai*, "to owe a
debt of human feeling," illustrates how ethical requirements of reciprocity preside over social relationships. When I visited my relative, a
middle-aged technician of a small factory in a southern provincial
town, he asked me to help a certain cadre in his town who was in fear
of his life because of recurrent stomach pains, which no local doctor
could diagnose. My relative asked if I had any special American medicines that could cure the official. The best I could do when I got back
to Beijing was to send him some packets of Alka Seltzer and a bag of
what was then hard-to-acquire powdered milk for what I thought
might soothe acid indigestion or ulcer. He wrote back gratefully,
"You have given me a renqing" ("Ni geile wo yige renqing"), meaning that through me, he had gained a bit of "human feeling" or sense
of obligation from the official, who is now bound by the principles of
renqing to repay him.

In the same vein, a person can "perform an act of renqing" (*zuo ge renqing*) by doing someone a favor, or "call on renqing" (*tuo ren-qing*) when it is his or her turn to extract a favor from someone else. In order to get another person's aid, it is sometimes enough merely to "speak the language of renqing" (*shuo renqinghua*) or couch things in terms of the moral discourse of "human feeling" to appeal to a sense of personal obligations. The "power of renqing" (*renqing shili*) or the pressure of its moral force is such that it is very difficult for a person to decline a request for help or fail to repay a debt of renqing.

Renqing expectations in the 1980s and 1990s are not much different from the following observation of Chinese ethics made by an American in China in the 1940s: "Failure to help with jobs and other concessions is to demonstrate a lack of *renqing*, human feelings. If he fails to help close relatives, he is even worse. He may be said to be unfilial or to demonstrate *pei de*, that is, not loving those whom one is bound by natural ties, both of which are extremes of inhumanity. His failure to be swayed may lead to his ostracism by friends and relatives alike. The pressure brought can be extreme" (Levy 1949: 355). In this passage, however, renqing is presented as a heavy burden, but for most people I spoke with in the 1980s and early 1990s, renqing more often had a positive connotation. It often seems to them as if, since the Cultural Revolution, there is not enough renqing in society, as if people have become hardened and insensitive to ties of affect. What many people like about films from Taiwan is their stronger "renqing flavor" (*renqingwei*), and their themes of interpersonal emotions that are not subsumed to the higher ends of political doctrines, as in most mainland films. In 1991, what many people appreciated about the popular TV serial *Ke Wang* (*Yearning*) and the film *Jiao Yulu* was not so much the deprecation of intellectuals in one and the propaganda about a selfless Party cadre in the other, but their "renqing flavor." For Chinese viewers I spoke with, these shows expressed authentic feelings and bonds of interpersonal relationships.

Queried about the meaning of the phrase "renqing flavor," Tian Meng, a middle-aged artist living in exile in the United States, answered that it referred to the natural capacity of people to have warmth (*wenqing*) and affection between kin, friends, and neighbors, without the "political distortion" (*zhengzhi waiqu*) that occurred in social relationships during the Cultural Revolution. Without renqing, people are cold and cruel to one another. He cited an example of how, even during the Cultural Revolution, some renqing could still be found. When he was being "struggled," that is, put up on a stage to be subjected to the wrathful criticism of the assembled masses, two old workers in his work unit were supposed to force him to assume the "airplane postion," a painful position with the body bent down at the waist and the arms pinned upward behind the back. The two old workers, with whom he had always been on good terms in the work unit, whispered to him to assume the position himself, so that they would not have to exert painful pressure on his arms. These two workers "did not forget renqing"; they did not allow political pressures to alienate the long-standing friendship they had with him.

It can be said that the moral discourse of renqing, so prevalent in contemporary Chinese societies in Taiwan and Hong Kong and on the mainland, derives from the Confucian stress on the ethics of human relationships (*lunli*) and the notion of *li* or ritual, which was the set of ancient customs governing social interaction and exchange (Jin 1982:70). Confucian social theory proceeds from neither the society nor the individual, but from interpersonal relations (Liang 1949). This point of departure leads logically to the emphasis on exchange behavior to concretize and nurture social relationships, and thus the notions of reciprocity and empathy also become important (Jin 1982: 71). With its concern for the proper and ethical conduct of social relationships and its stress on obligation and indebtedness, renqing discourse is the popularized version of the classical Confucian textual tradition.

Another key notion of guanxixue further bears out its connection with a popularized Confucian ethics. This is the concept of *li* 禮 or "ritual." *Li* is part of the word *liwu*, the modern Chinese term for "gift." Translated literally, *liwu* means "ritual object," in the sense that a "gift" is an "object" with which one enacts a "ritualized relationship." The classical Chinese meaning of this term, however, is much richer than the modern restricted sense of "gift." *Li* in the classical sense also meant the social "rituals" in which ritual objects were used, such as ancestral sacrifices, funerals, and banquets. It also had the sense of "ethics" and "etiquette" (proper comportment or style), which were the performance of the social roles of host and guest, official and subject, and so forth. The interrelatedness of "gift," "interpersonal ethics," and "etiquette" was captured in another classical sense of *li*: reciprocity in social intercourse. Gifts require reciprocity, and so do relationships; therefore the ethics of gift-giving are extended to all human relationships. These relationships in turn are guided by "rules of propriety" or etiquettes of behavior based on the relative statuses of high and low, near and far, old and young, inside and outside. In Chapter 3 I explore in detail the ethics and etiquettes of gift relations in contemporary guanxixue. Then in Chapter 6 I trace one line of guanxixue genealogy to the role of "ritual" in ancient China, before the rise of the first centralized state.

The tracing back of renqing, gift relations, and the art of guanxi to traditional Chinese kinship ethics also finds support in a scholarly treatment of guanxixue in a mainland article that departs from the usual official discourse on the subject. The art of guanxi is attributed to the Confucian and Mencian tradition of "personalized ethics," which eschews universal love in favor of obligations based on "distinctions between inside and outside, close and distant relations" (Zheng 1984:53–54). Thus the Confucian virtues of filial piety, brotherhood, loyalty, and trust, which place primary emphasis on the relations of kinship and friendship, are seen as the cultural roots of the art of guanxi.

Given that renqing discourse is an important feature of Chinese culture everywhere, care must also be taken not to essentialize either renqing or Confucian culture. It must be recognized that in different social and historical contexts, renqing discourse assumes variable contours and roles. In Hong Kong and Taiwan, it operates amid market relations, whereas on the mainland, it is situated in a very different type of political economy, a political economy in which the state is a dominant actor and discursive subject. It can be said that on the mainland, guanxi discourse has grown out of an older renqing discourse, so that although it retains many of the principles of renqing ethics, it also has developed new political and economic dimensions that were only latent and rudimentary before. Indeed, when asked to explain the difference between renqing and guanxi, a woman worker declared that guanxixue is the "distortion of renqing" (renqing zouyang), meaning that guanxi is a particular instrumentalized and corrupted form of renqing.

I take up the question of the embeddedness of the art of guanxi in traditional Chinese ethical discourse and in the principles of friendship and kinship again in Chapters 3 and 4. For now, the interrelationship between guanxi and renqing serves to make the point that the art of guanxi is a complex cultural phenomenon that combines instrumental motivations with a highly developed set of ethics rooted in aspects of a populist form of the Confucian tradition. This built-in contradiction within guanxixue between instrumentality and ethics helps to explain why guanxixue is commonly regarded as morally ambivalent.

The art of guanxi's renqing elements also explain another sort of cultural ambivalence toward it, one born in the conflict between a state-espoused "public" (*gong*) collectivist ethic and a "private" (*si*) ethics of personal relationships. Official discourse generally regards the ethics of renqing in a negative light, equating it with the selfish sphere of "private" individual or small-group interests. For example, a newspaper article praises an upright cadre in Shanxi for refusing to respond to the *"feelings and sensibilities"* (*qingmian*) of such people as his former leaders, his former subordinates, and a person of the same hometown who sought to persuade him not to expose their wrongdoings. Said he, "We are Communists, not *sworn outlaw brothers* [*jianghu dixiong*]![6] We must speak the truth, preserve Party character, and adhere to *principles* [*yuanze*]. We cannot consider '*feelings and sensibilities*' [*qingmian*]" (*RMRB* 10 December 1983:1).

Another newspaper commentary applauds a rural Party secretary for daring to offend his relatives and friends by holding a meeting with them immediately after he assumed office in their township to tell them he would not be able to help them while in office. Wrote the commentator,

> Who does not have three relatives and six kin or "seven buddies and eight friends'? Who does not need to have big or small affairs taken care of [with someone's help]? . . . Often one meets with [requests] that one should not help out with, but one finds it hard both to openly turn them down or to discreetly delay action. What should one do? The only way out is to *steel one's heart* [*tie renxin*] and charge the "pass" [*guan*] [of private relations] and smash the "network" [*wang*]. (*RMRB* 11 December 1983:1)

In the above examples, the notion of "sentiment" (*qing*), as in the "human sentiment" (renqing) of personal affective relationships with relatives, friends, former superiors, and subordinates, is set up in opposition to ideas of Party loyalty, collective or state interest, and abstract principles. According to official discourse, these kinds of sentiments should be actively countered by "steeling one's heart," which is the seat of feelings. As I discuss later, the suppression of "private sentiments" is an integral component of the cultivation of state universalistic ethics in postrevolutionary China.

A phrase often uttered in speech contexts involving the topic of

---

[6] "Sworn outlaw brothers" is an allusion to the classic fourteenth-century novel *Shuihuzhuan* (Water margin), which chronicles the adventures of a band of outlaws and their intense personal loyalty to one another.

guanxixue gives another indication of why the deployment of guanxi practices disturbs officialdom:

Xianguan bu ru xian guan.

A county official cannot compare with [a person] directly in charge.

Frequently recited to me with relish, this common saying shows a particularly ingenious feature of how guanxixue often engages the bureaucracy: one does not always have to depend on an official of the highest formal position. Sometimes, when the official overseeing an area of jurisdiction is inaccessible or unwilling to help, other people around the official can be persuaded to help.

This principle of cultivating a working relationship with a lower-ranking person instead of with the official formally in charge, was illustrated to me by the carpenter Chen Shaoxiong. He was very pleased one day about how he had recently helped his work unit by persuading the local municipal electricity bureau branch to increase electricity output to his workplace. His work-unit leaders, not willing to concede that favors are often only extracted by a recourse to the art of guanxi, had tried unsuccessfully for a whole year to petition the local electricity bureau for a larger supply of electricity for their buildings. The approach they took, of making formal requests to the electricity bureau, proved ineffectual. Finally in desperation, they turned over the task to my friend Chen. Chen chatted up a few of the cadres and staff of the electricity bureau branch office and invited them to a sumptuous banquet at a restaurant, paid for by his unit. Not long afterward, his work unit was able to receive the extra electricity they had requested.

Reflecting on how he had been successful in increasing electricity to his work unit, Chen recited the saying above to explain why he, a mere worker with no position of authority or status, could undertake such a task. On my request for explanation, he further elaborated:

An official such as a county magistrate may have a high position. Especially from the viewpoint of an ordinary peasant in his county, a county magistrate seems very powerful. However, he may not have authority over the area where you want something done, so he is useless to you. A lower-level official or even a clerk who is directly in charge of something is in a better position to help you. So, high social position, or [high] political position are not always necessary to get things done.

Often someone low like me may have lots of guanxi which are more effective.

Therefore, the people with whom Chen pulls guanxi at the local electricity office are not necessarily the top officials there, but they are the persons "in charge." At the same time, Chen's unit did better to send someone like him, who understands the art of guanxi, than a stiff and proper official of high position who could only appeal to formal regulations to demand the electricity their unit needed. In the illustration above can be seen how guanxixue exploits the discrepancy that exists between hierarchical authority in general and specific jurisdictional authority.

CHAPTER TWO

The Scope and
Use-Contexts of Guanxi

A survey of some of its typical use-contexts draws into sharper relief the contours and the scope of guanxixue and brings to light some
of the crucial social and historical factors that may have given rise to
this set of practices. In this chapter I discuss the various social contexts in which guanxixue comes into play and the multiple social uses
that it is made to serve. Since the practice of guanxixue is not univer-
sally or evenly distributed across society, I also attempt to deal with
the variable degrees to which different types of people and social
groups (divided according to gender and occupational classes) are associated with guanxixue. What is offered here are only my fieldwork
encounters with guanxi. They represent only a few threads plucked
out of a giant and complicated patchwork of social usages and functions. The examples of guanxi use-contexts and guanxi stories are
endless, and what is captured here cannot deal with the full range of
social occasions for guanxi practices. It does, I hope, give an indication of the enormous role guanxi practices play in everyday life in
contemporary China.

The City and the Countryside

Before I discuss the use-contexts of guanxixue in urban society, a
brief examination of the rural-urban scope of guanxixue is in order.
Chiao Chien (Qiao Jian), a Chinese anthropologist at the Chinese
University of Hong Kong, writes: "This 'guanxi network' has been in
existence for a long time, but in contemporary mainland China, it is
of unprecedented importance. Therefore it is the first subject which

one must understand in the study of mainland Chinese society, *especially in the cities*" (Qiao 1982:354; my emphasis). After noting that the art of guanxi is an especially important feature of mainland *urban* society, Chiao does not go on to explain why he chooses to stress the cities. Is it because guanxixue is not practiced in the countryside? Or is it because its pervasiveness in the cities is made more noteworthy by the fact that modern urban places are in general supposed to run on the basis of impersonal and rationalized norms of behavior?

The answer to the first of these questions must be negative, since there is ample evidence that the art of guanxi exists in the countryside as well as in urban society. Chinese newspaper articles have constantly exposed the phenomenon of "going through the back door" or nepotism in the countryside.[1] Interviews conducted in Hong Kong with peasant emigrants on life in a Guangdong village during and immediately after the Cultural Revolution confirm the importance of guanxixue (Chan, Madsen, and Unger 1984:276–81). Rural cadres, and procurement officers especially, rely on their guanxi networks outside their localities to obtain raw materials for village factories and extra fertilizer, bricks, and nails for their communities (Chan and Unger 1982).

Indeed, some urban Chinese I interviewed believe that guanxixue is even more pervasive in rural areas than in cities because its very "source" or "origin" (*fayuandi*) is rural culture where kinship ties and a tradition of labor exchange and mutual aid and obligation have always been dominant. The Beijing residents I interviewed who have lived in the countryside or who have relatives there have personally experienced the importance of guanxixue in the countryside. Most of them were "sent down" in various waves of the state-sponsored rustification programs of the 1960s and 1970s. As urban youth, cadres and intellectuals were sent down to labor in the countryside and learn from the peasants, they arrived when collectivized agriculture was still in force. They report that at that time, a peasant had to maintain good relations with rural brigade or production-team leaders through gift-giving, invitations to wedding feasts, and so forth, so that the peasant might be assigned lighter and easier work or receive better work evaluations. When from the mid-1970s through the early 1980s, the families of these "sent-down" urban youth tried to help them escape the harsh life of peasants and get back into the cities, they had to spend considerable energy and personal resources

---

[1] See, for example, the following newspaper articles: *RMRB* 13 December 1977; *ZGQNB* 22 May 1983; *RMRB* 4 November 1983; *GRRB* 20 April 1983.

in gift-giving and in guanxi-pulling with team leaders and higher local authorities in rural areas.

In the 1980s, with the dramatic rural economic reforms, there seemed to be even more opportunities and situations that called for engaging in the art of guanxi. With the economic responsibility system entrenched in the countryside, the commercialization of agriculture, and the growth of rural enterprises, peasant entrepreneurs had to work through guanxi to obtain raw materials and secure markets in other localities. On a visit to a rural county in Hubei Province in 1990, one of my areas of inquiry was the organization of "village and township enterprises" (*xiangzhen qiye*). I learned that a very important aspect of the work involved in setting up, maintaining, and running rural enterprises is the delicate yet difficult task of "developing good guanxi" (*gaohao guanxi*) with various offices and personages of local government. A rural enterprise must rely on rural government for a host of things: raw materials, electricity, labor transfers, transportation, distribution of products, and tax exemption. Obtaining these favors requires an adeptness in the art of guanxi.

The use of guanxi is not restricted to the economic and entrepreneurial function in the countryside. On the same trip in Hubei, I encountered another important arena for its practice in the countryside: the movement of a portion of the peasantry to settle in local urban places. In a county town I shall call Shanhu, most of the town residents are peasants from the surrounding countryside who moved into the town in the 1940s and 1950s, before the strict state controls on migration took effect. In the 1980s, under conditions of relative social mobility, peasants still living in the surrounding countryside began seeking the help of their relatives in town to leave the land and move to the county town. According to a townswoman named Ling Ping, one way that many young peasant women move into town is by first serving as housekeepers and nannies (*baomu*) for their town relatives. Since they are kin, their relatives in town do not pay them for their service but provide them with room and board, gifts, clothing, and sometimes their wedding dowries. Most important of all, after a few years the town relatives are often able to secure for these peasant women official permission to reside permanently in the town. Peasants wishing to gain a foothold in town also go through their guanxi network of kin in town to secure for them a job in an individual enterprise (*getihu*) restaurant or store, or to help them set up their own small enterprise in town. These examples show that the art of guanxi is practiced both in the countryside and in the cities.

Since I have spent most of my time in China in urban areas, most examples of guanxixue in this book have urban settings.[2] In the Conclusion, I bring in some examples of a renewal of peasant gift exchange in rural southeastern China in the Wenzhou area. This ritual and festival gift-giving that goes on among kin and friends, and between people of different villages contrasts with the more situational and purposive gift relations of the urban art of guanxi. Therefore, it can be said that in many rural areas, there exists both the art of guanxi and an elaborate ritual gift-economy, while in big-city life, guanxixue is more important than the gift-giving associated with births, weddings, and promotions.

From Chiao's Hong Kong perspective, when compared to modern overseas Chinese urban communities where it is relatively less prominent, the pervasiveness of guanxixue in mainland urban society today seems striking and in need of explanation. This is the very task that informs the writing of this chapter. By giving a sense of the types of people or occupational groups that are especially prone to practice guanxixue, and by laying out areas of everyday urban life that typically give rise to the art of guanxi, I will point in the direction of an interpretive, explanatory, and theoretical framework to account for the importance of this phenomenon in urban areas in mainland China.

The Gender Dimension

The distribution of guanxi practices can also be examined along gender lines. What was most noteworthy about this line of inquiry was that my questions relating to gender often stumped people. When asked about gender differences in the practice of guanxi, respondents, whether women or men, would usually pause and give the question some thought before they answered. More often than not, the answers were vague or tentative and lacking in conviction, as if this was the first time that they had pondered the question. I can only conclude that for most of the people I interviewed, gender was not a salient category in deliberations of guanxixue. It can be said that in urban guanxi discourse, whether popular or official, such distinctions as those of occupation, status, and class, of urban and rural contexts, and of past and present are foregrounded over gender distinctions.

[2] Two anthropologists have written Ph.D. dissertations about guanxi and gift-giving in rural places in China: Yan Yunxiang at Harvard University and Andrew Kipnis at the University of North Carolina.

Since gender did not seem to be a major component of guanxi discourse, I relied more on my own observations of guanxi practice to integrate the discussions of gender I could gather.

Although I found no general consensus as to whether the art of guanxi is practiced more often by men or by women, I was able to solicit perceptions of how gender distinctions affect the form and set of tactics employed in guanxixue. Fang Liping, a woman student who had used her guanxi to help me secure permission to study a factory, asserted that most women tend to use guanxixue for "small things." These include currying favor with their work-unit leader to get a few days off from work, buying foodstuffs that are not readily available in stores through friends, or trying to enter their child in a nursery with a good reputation. Those more complicated guanxi-pulling tasks, which require going out into the larger society and cultivating various relationships, such as obtaining a job, acquiring construction materials, or obtaining official permission to move to another city, are usually left to their brothers or husbands to handle, she thought.

Adding another twist to this view of a sexual division of labor in guanxixue in which women take care of tasks related to the domestic scene is the notion, shared by many men I talked to, that because guanxixue involves mixing with a wide assortment of people in society, it is not good for a woman's social reputation. For them, women are not suited to engage in guanxi because it often requires a great deal of running around outside the home to different work units, offices, and homes to cultivate relationships. A worker confided that he had his fiancée go to a hospital to have her virginity confirmed before he would marry her. So a concern with feminine chastity acts as an effective social deterrent to women who would stray too far away from home.

Chen Shaoxiong, a male carpenter, explained that few women can operate in the world of guanxixue for long because people will talk and they will gain a bad reputation. "Sooner or later someone will say: 'This woman sure runs around a lot. She knows too many men.'" This is especially the case for those lines of work which require making many social contacts to locate goods to do business, such as the position of a supply agent or individual enterpriser. "If it's an unmarried woman who's in this kind of work, her parents will soon be against it because they're afraid she'll have trouble finding a husband," Chen said. "If it's a married woman, her husband will be pretty uncomfortable when people start gossiping and laughing at him. So chances are, he'll have none of it [ta buhui gande]."

Likewise, for Wang Xiaobing, a male student and a former peasant, "smart women" or women who are more outgoing, ambitious and shrewd than the majority of their sex, will avoid work involving extensive use of guanxixue because "they will not come to a good end." According to him, men are more aggressive than women and will try to take advantage of them in social transactions and in the exchange of benefits. They will try to extract sexual favors in return for granting requests from women. That is why those women who are "smart" usually steer clear of these risks in the world of guanxixue and go to college or into a teaching or medical profession. Indeed, thought Wang, those few women who remain in work involving daily guanxi transactions are extraordinary individuals who must be twice as tough as the ordinary male and who are unmindful of their reputations.

It would seem then, that as in most male-dominated societies, there is still a tendency in urban China to consider it proper for women to stay close to the home. Although the entrance of urban women into the workforce in the late 1950s marked a significant departure from the traditional seclusion of women, I found that three decades later, women, especially working-class women, still tend to be more circumscribed than men in their daily lives to small circles of workmates on the job and family members, relatives, and neighbors at home.

In the Beijing printing factory where I did research for three months, I observed that the women workers conducted a great deal of exchange of store-buying favors. If one woman purchased a bargain household item at a store or free market near her home, other women would give her money to purchase the same item for them. Another day another woman would announce that she had access to buying a special shampoo because of a connection with a relative. She would then proceed to take orders. As a benefit to its workers, the factory would occasionally acquire a shipment of goods such as fruit, vegetables, or towels and sell it at wholesale prices. It was always the women in the factory who lined up to purchase these items, for their families, friends, and neighbors.

Han Sulan, a woman in her early fifties with a peasant and working-class background, lives with her husband, daughter, and mother-in-law in a modest three-room cement cottage (ping fang) belonging to her husband's factory. In Beijing it is often said that these old-fashioned one-story houses sharing common walled courtyards are more conducive to socializing with neighbors than the new multi-storied apartment buildings. Han's family shares an outdoor water faucet and toilet facilities with five neighboring families. Because of the proximity of the neighbors and the long time they have all lived there, these families have come to know each other well and feel comfortable calling on one another for help on a small scale. There is a steady mutual borrowing of vinegar, soy sauce, eggs, and so on, when home supplies run out. Often when one family acquires a hard-to-find item in a store or through guanxi, or when a family's out-of-town relatives bring them a delicacy not obtainable in Beijing, they will share with a few of the neighbors. Sharing is the best policy, says Han, because invariably neighbors find out what you have acquired, so failure to offer them something will cause resentment on their part and a loss of face for yourself. "Neighbors must share things among themselves [jiefang yao guo dongxi]," says Han.

Her mother-in-law once made a cotton-padded winter jacket for a neighbor who could not sew very well. Six months later when the mother-in-law was going to visit her other son in the countryside, the neighbor bought her some cakes to give to her son's family. "This is observing renqing," says Han. Another time her husband was away on a trip and she alone did not have enough strength to lift the heavy metal cooking-gas container onto a bicycle and get a new supply at the local gas supply outlet. Her neighbor sent her son to help. Once they had guests from out of town visit just before their next payday, so they were short of cash when they needed to put extra dishes on the table. A small loan from their kind neighbors saved them the time and effort of going to the bank. Han says that through these rounds of giving and helping, one maintains good relations with the neighbors and finds peace and security at home.

On the basis of these observations, we can posit that there exist two gender domains of guanxi activity, that of the domestic arena, in which women tend to be more active than men, and the public society-wide domain, in which men tend to be more active than women. The domestic domain of activity includes the exchange of favors and gifts among neighbors, kin, and family friends in everyday life or in such contexts as marriage introductions or matchmaking services, providing for children's education, the giving of Chinese New Year's presents of money for children, and rites of passage such as weddings, childbirth, and funerals.

These domestic contexts of exchange, in which women play an important role, can be distinguished from the public domain of guanxi-xue in two ways. First, the emphasis is on promoting sociality and maintaining a family's good relations within its network of relatives and friends, rather than on gaining material or political benefits. The comments in Chapter 1 show that many women I interviewed subscribe to negative evaluations of guanxixue. This is due to their perception of guanxixue in terms of crude instrumentalism and aggressive tactics, which is in contrast to the warmer social exchange relations of the domestic domain. Second, compared with the public domain, the domestic domain of guanxi exchange is less often engaged with the political sphere, with extracting benefits from officials and administrative offices and bureaucracies. In both these differences, it can be said that the domestic domain is closer to a prerevolutionary ethic of renqing, whereas the more male-oriented public domain of guanxixue adopts a more aggressive style in engaging with state institutions, where positions of influence are usually held by men.

There is yet another view which finds women to be full participants in the public domain of the art of guanxi and ascribes to them important roles in its repertory of tactics. For Hu Lan, a woman graduate student, the art of social relationships is not an officially approved way of doing things, therefore men often ask women to "show their face" (*chumian*) on their behalf. In other words, since guanxixue has the status of informal exchange or relationship, and since women are associated with informal or secondary social status, then it seems more appropriate that they engage in it. Furthermore, she believes that women possess more renqing or "human feelings" than men and therefore will do better at cultivating relationships and appealing to people's feelings of indebtedness. When queried about examples of women's limited social scope of operations, Hu Lan explained the discrepancy by pointing out that there is a certain class specificity to women's participation in the art of guanxi. Workers tend to be more conservative, so working-class women are less visible as guanxi transactors. Among the ranks of cadres and intellectuals, however, women are very much involved. Frequently, the wife is the person sent out to present the gift in a guanxi overture because it is generally thought that women have a better chance of getting results.

This point is borne out by a middle-aged male intellectual of peasant background who told me that it is a common tactic for husbands, after consultation with their wives, to send their wives to "pull guanxi" for them. In his view, since women are more gracious than men, men will be more receptive to a woman's request. In general, he thought, men are inclined to "look out for" (*zhaogu*) women. "Since men do not want to embarrass a woman, they will make sure that she can step down from the platform easily [*rangta hao xiatai*]." In other words, since a person loses face if a request is denied, men will tend not to reject a woman outright, but will at least promise to try to help her, so that she can retain her dignity.

A rule of thumb frequently pointed out to me was that if the guanxi target is a man, then it is best to send a woman to deal with him and get him to grant a favor. If the target is a woman, especially an older woman, then the most effective tactic is to send a younger man to soften her up and win her help in a matter. The following proverbial wisdom shows that in the art of guanxi, both sexes can play the game:

Tong xin xiang chi; yi xin xiang xi.

Same sexes repel; opposite sexes attract.

With this heterosexual principle in operation, there will always be an important role for women to play in guanxixue.

Indeed, women do seem to enjoy certain advantages in the public domain of the art of guanxi, since cadres are often guanxi targets, and most of them are men. A young female factory supply agent told me that when women, especially young women, practice the art of social relationships, they do not need to rely on material exchange as much as men, for the attraction of the opposite sex is often enough reason for men to come to the aid of a woman. And since most positions of control in the society are occupied by men, women can get quite far in practicing the art of guanxi. This does not mean that women must provide sexual services, but that they can go a long way with charm. Women, she noted, can save money in not having to buy gifts because women can use their personal charm as a substitute for gifts. Furthermore, many men feel obliged to take care of women, since they are considered more dependent in life. This proverb, which I collected from a male college student and former construction worker, reflects a widely held belief that women have certain advantages in the art of guanxi:

You mianzi bu ru you bianzi.

Having "face" is not as good as having braids.

"Face" here signifies the social standing and social connections of a man, whereas "braids" signify the social asset of being a charming woman. This college student has noticed that the pretty and vivacious women students in his experience tend to get better grades and job assignments than all the men students. These observations suggest that in a male-dominated society, there is still some leeway for women to get their way, albeit on terms that could be described as male-oriented. They also reveal that often the art of guanxi provides a staging area for the enactment of sexual politics and the contestation of the gendered status order.

I asked Liu Fuqiang, a male factory worker, if men are sometimes not satisfied with women's charming personalities, but also try to take sexual advantage of a woman in return for a favor. He was quick to emphasize that although there have been cases of sexual misconduct, the male obligation to "look out for" (zhaogu) women should not be construed as sexually motivated, for this reasoning is demeaning to women. That is, just because women can rely on their charming personal qualities to bend a man's will, that does not mean that they would also stoop to sleep with him, Liu thought. However, a woman who lived for seven years in the countryside as a sent-down youth during the Cultural Revolution told me that she remembers that some women she knew in those days were so desperate to get back to the cities that they slept with the local cadres.

Whether or not women offer their attractiveness, charm, or bodies to get something in return, they must give up more of themselves than men who engage in material gift exchange are required to. For women, offering personal qualities, which are intrinsic parts of a person, is a bigger prestation than material gifts. It can be argued that although women do participate in the public domain of guanxixue, they are disadvantaged in that they must play up to male expectations, since most guanxi targets in this domain are male cadres or office workers.

This point should be qualified. The domestic and public domains of guanxixue are not mutually exclusive; rather, they overlap. This is especially the case in socialist society, in which the state penetrates deeply into everyday domestic life. Neither the acquisition of basic foodstuffs and household necessities nor such "private" activities as marriage and childraising have escaped the organizing power of the state. Therefore, in maintaining the domestic domain, women often encounter the public domain. Furthermore, one's domestic or familial guanxi network of neighbors, kin, and close friends is often a resource for dealing with the public domain.

There is another way to look at gender in guanxixue besides asking whether it is women or men who practice guanxi art more, or analyzing the different contexts and methods with which they do so. We can also inquire into the very gender nature of guanxi relations themselves. That is to say, at a deeper level, what sort of gender does the practice of guanxixue produce? In psychoanalytic object-relations theory, it is posited that the personalities or the moral systems of the two genders differ: women tend to be more relational and attuned to the feelings and needs of people around them, their ego-identities more entangled with others, while men tend to be more independent and individualistic, their egos more clearly demarcated and separated from others (Chodorow 1974; 1978). Men subscribe to abstracted universal principles of morality centered on rights and rules, while women experience a moral persuasion defined by responsibilities and obligations in interpersonal relationships which provide specific contexts for morality (Gilligan 1982). Suspending for the time being the question of whether this portrayal applies only to modern Western culture, we can say that, if we were to adopt this psychoanalytic perspective and assign a gender to guanxixue, it would be more female than male, because of its relational and situational ethics. Therefore, what in the modern West is a female construction of subjects and a female version of moral thinking works in modern as well as traditional China, on both women and men. Western individualism, which is based on the radical separation of the subject not only from the mother, but also from all future objects in a person's life, is by this definition more of a male-gendered cultural construction. Guanxixue's discourse of interpersonal obligation and indebtedness runs counter to this individualism, and in this context, exerts a "feminizing" influence in Chinese culture which is not well developed in the West. This question of the gender of guanxixue is taken up again in the Conclusion in a discussion of the rural gift economy and its gender influence on the larger society.

Urban Occupational Strata

In the native classification of occupational and status groupings in the urban milieu before the economic reforms, the most common designations were those of "cadres" (*ganbu*), "workers" (*gongren*), and "intellectuals" (*zhishifenzi*). During the economic reforms of the 1980s, the social division of labor multiplied, so that these three categories have become less dominant as new and anomalous social positions have emerged. These new occupations include individual enterprisers (*getihu*), entrepreneurial managers (*qiyejia*), advertising agents, and "public relations misses" (*gongguan xiaojie*). Nevertheless, "cadres," "workers," and "intellectuals" continue to serve as broad overarching categories.[3]

Regardless of their highly differentiated levels of rank and authority, it is commonly believed that cadres are the most adept guanxi practitioners. The reasons given are twofold. First, cadres have at their disposal decision-making and resource-allocation powers that make them frequent targets of gift-giving and guanxi overtures. A middle-aged worker commented that the people who generally "pull guanxi" the most are cadres. They have the resources to engage in exchange, whereas workers do not have any goods or social position to practice guanxixue. Cadres are also generally believed to be the most frequent beneficiaries of guanxixue, receiving and sometimes even demanding gifts and banquets in return for granting favors to those whom they administer. A second reason why cadres are perceived as the social category most associated with the art of guanxi is that they are said to lead a relatively leisured and mobile life, with more opportunities for promotion or job changes, to travel on business, or attend regional meetings with other cadres. Cadres as leaders are less supervised during the workday and thus have more opportunities to engage in private guanxi transactions.

Two economists recited a folk saying they had picked up when they used to be factory workers:

Yideng ren songshang men; erdeng ren zou houmen;
sandeng ren yao tuo ren; sideng ren qisi ren.

First class people get gifts delivered to the door;
second class people go through the back door;
third class people rely upon others;
fourth class people can only fume.

They supposed that "first class" refers to some high cadres and local officials in leadership positions who just sit back and enjoy the flow of gifts arriving at their homes. Second-class people include doctors, drivers, lower-level cadres, and shop clerks who have no real political position, but do have resources to bargain with in guanxi transac-

---

[3] For a more detailed discussion of social stratification in China, see Watson 1984 and Yan 1992 on the new dual system of stratification (bureaucratic rank status and market economic class) in rural areas.

tions. Those in the third class must spend a lot of time seeking out guanxi to connect them up with people of influence. Fourth-class people are basically out of luck because they do not possess good guanxi connections, nor do they have resources with which to expand their guanxi network.

A former resident of Fuzhou, in Fujian Province, also pointed to the disparities between different levels of the practice of guanxi. He drew a distinction between the back door for extra meat or coal, which is really "an informal system for bartering and redistributing food and a few necessities of life" (in Frolic 1980:129) and another type of guanxi activity which serves to entrench and solidify official position:

> All this [using the ordinary back door] is common practice in China, and no-one gets excited, since everybody, somehow, sometime, uses the backdoor for personal needs. It reduces dissatisfaction and it gives ordinary people a chance of getting something. What makes the common people angry is the abuse of the Big Backdoor by higher level government, Party and army officials. This is the backdoor that really makes a difference, a backdoor based on one's political background; it determines one's social and economic position. Top cadres use the backdoor to keep their children from staying in the countryside. (Frolic 1980:130)

This perceived disparity between the ordinary back door and the "Big Backdoor" has led to a great deal of resentment toward cadres, especially high-level ones, by the common people.

Political office implies control over a particular resource. Almost every day the newspapers carry stories about how an official in charge of the administration, distribution, and assignment of such things as grain, electricity, housing, jobs and promotions, household registration, coal, lumber products, and so forth, has been brought to justice for his or her abuse of power. When an official position is treated as a personal possession and its particular resources are offered up in guanxi exchange in a trade of comparative advantage, then the collective power of officials, both as a social group or stratum and as the deputies of a state that would directly order and shape society, is thereby enhanced. In this way, the art of guanxi in the hands of officials can be seen as a mechanism that helps to extend state domination.

The term "workers" (gongren) refers to the manual or line workers in manufacturing, mining, or construction. It can also refer to "clerical staff" (zhiwuyuan), "service staff" (fuwuyuan) in the commercial sector, sanitation workers, and so on, since these people share the same culture as industrial workers, and often are their family members. Industrial workers do not occupy positions that give them formal decision-making powers and direct control over allocating social resources, therefore, they do not have leverage to help them in guanxi exchange. Nevertheless, this by no means excludes them from engaging in guanxixue, for resourceful persons always manage to use whatever material or social resources they are able to acquire as a basis for guanxi exchange. For instance, a worker with metal-soldering skills told me with some satisfaction and amusement how he occasionally absconds with some metal scraps and parts from his factory, and borrows factory tools to fashion metal smoking pipes for his friends. Construction workers are also said to be good guanxi contacts because they have access to precious building materials such as wood, bricks, and cement, which they can smuggle out of construction sites for their friends who want to add a new room to their tiny dwellings.

When factory workers are compared to clerical staff and service personnel such as shop clerks, restaurant workers, or ticket sellers, they are at a disadvantage. Clerical and service workers are believed to be better equipped to enter into guanxi exchange since they exercise direct control over the goods and services the public seeks to buy from them. This, I submit, may be the reason for their surly treatment of customers: they are equivalent to petty bureaucrats feared for their power to withhold valued items from the people, while at the same time, they are not subject to the types of control exercised in capitalist societies, such as the threat of being fired for poor performance or the incentive of higher wages and tips for good performance. Fang Liping's sister, a clerk in a university library, has no great decision-making power, but she has control over books. She often sets aside books with great public demand for her special friends or those who have done her guanxi favors, giving them priority over other readers. A waiter in a restaurant will bring out the best dishes only for his or her friends and guanxi connections. Therefore, although they do not possess the administrative power of formal office, clerical and service personnel are able to find things with which to enter into guanxi exchange and to overcome their relatively low formal positions in society.

Opinions differ on whether intellectuals (*zhishi fenzi*) as a group have fewer guanxi dealings than other occupational groups. The term "intellectuals" is usually employed in a very loose sense in everyday life, so that it can designate anyone with some education, including primary and secondary school teachers, doctors, engineers and scientists, university lecturers and professors, as well as artists and musicians. The terms "high-level intellectuals" (*gaoji zhishi fenzi*) and "little intellectuals" (*xiao zhishi fenzi*) distinguish the two subgroups within the occupation.

The difference in lifestyle between intellectuals and workers was described by a college student who had been a worker for many years. Intellectuals, he said, have to choose between "living" and "career." They do not have the means to pursue both because they are too busy and too poor. Those who opt for the career have little time to see to their material living standards and to keep up with housework; instead they have to spend most of their money buying books and supplies. Workers, he explained, need only put in an eight-hour day and then can devote the rest of their time and energy to improving their material living standards, which entails, among other strategies, practicing the time-consuming art of cultivating guanxi. A factory worker agreed that intellectuals are less prone to practice guanxixue because they are engaged in "spiritual" pursuits and have no time to seek material comforts. They prefer fame to wealth. A woman who used to work in a factory and is now married to an intellectual, said that her image of intellectuals is that they are usually too proper and too timid to engage in guanxi dealings. That is, since they were one of the main targets of the persecutions of the Anti-Rightist[4] campaign and the Cultural Revolution, they would not want to risk getting into trouble again by being caught in the act of pursuing personal ends.

Yet others, including many intellectuals themselves, believe there is no difference between intellectuals and other social groups in their capacity for the art of guanxi. Intellectuals also have to live, they also need the amenities of life, and therefore they have to learn guanxixue too. Since the Cultural Revolution, according to one worker, intellectuals are no longer so "ingenuous" (*laoshi*), but have become more "artful and cunning" (*you*). One Beijing college professor pointed out that two areas where he and his friends have to resort to guanxixue are getting their children into good schools and enabling themselves or their children to go abroad for study. Here guanxixue facilitates obtaining a passport, getting permission for a leave of absence from one's work unit, and reducing or waiving the education fees that the

[4] The Anti-Rightist campaign of 1957 was a concerted effort by the Party-state to cleanse its ranks of those who had criticized the Revolution and government policies during the Hundred Flowers Movement of the same year. Those labeled Rightists were deprived of certain rights or sent off to prison camps.

state charges for anyone leaving without adequately repaying the country through serving a term of work. Among intellectuals, guanxi-xue is also needed to get a manuscript published.

The following popular saying, which I collected in Beijing, illustrates the fact that formal office, such as the position held by a cadre or Party leader, is by no means the only guarantee of active engagement in guanxi exchange:

Yisheng siji laozike zhibu shuji shouhuoyuan

Doctor, driver, personnel and wage department, Party branch secretary, and shop clerk.

There is general agreement that these represent some key positions in urban society. The people who occupy these positions are the main targets as well as beneficiaries of guanxi overtures because they have discretion concerning who will receive the goods or crucial services and opportunities under their control. It is significant that only two of these positions involve cadres (personnel department, Party secretary), and the rest would fit into the broad categories of workers (driver, shop clerk) and intellectuals (doctor).

It would be wrong, however, to conclude that access to or control over some desirable is a prerequisite for engaging in the art of guanxi. Lack of direct access to goods for guanxi exchange can always be compensated for by individual social talents. Certain individuals in this social stratum can make themselves as powerful as those who hold high formal office just by developing refined skills of negotiating social relationships and acquiring an ability to form large social networks that can serve as a form of wealth and a resource-base in itself. It is a commonplace in popular discourse that the talent and propensity for guanxixue is unevenly distributed among individuals, regardless of their occupations.

This was explained to me by Liu Fuqiang, a factory worker, who divides society into three types of people: (1) those who are born with a talent for the art of guanxi, who do not need to learn it, but are just naturally skilled practitioners; (2) those who desperately want to "pull guanxi," but lack the ability to get it right, who are very clumsy at it and manage to offend guanxi targets rather than ingratiate themselves with them; and (3) those who have the capacity to engage in it, but do not wish to because they consider it distasteful and demeaning. In Chapter 3 I explore in detail the artful deployment of social skills, etiquette, and ethics which certain individuals can grasp better than others.

The Variety of Use-Contexts

The range of occasions in which guanxi is put to use covers all facets of everyday urban life. What follows are a mere sampling of different occasions for guanxi practice which I encountered randomly in fieldwork. This brief survey cannot hope to cover all guanxi usages, since the list is endless and constantly changing along with the rapid pace of the growing commodity economy.

Obtaining Goods in Short Supply, of Better Quality, or at Lower Prices

During the Cultural Revolution, the production of consumer goods was very low, and people were modest in their everyday material needs. In the first half of the 1980s, as the state fostered increased production and encouraged consumer desire, there arose a general perception that goods were scarce. In hindsight, this was probably due to the inability of the old centralized system of production and distribution to keep pace with new demand. It seemed as if almost everything people wanted was scarce, and so they had to resort to guanxi to acquire things not readily available in state stores and markets.

In most of the 1980s, there was a high demand for such industrial consumer products as famous-brand bicycles (*Fenghuang, Yongjiu,* and *Feige* brands), color televisions (especially imported ones), sewing machines, washing machines, and, later, refrigerators. One could get to the top of a long waiting list at one's work unit or even buy them at wholesale prices through the use of guanxi. Through formal official channels, these name-brand products could only be bought with special allocation slips, which were distributed by every work unit to selected employees each year. The slips authorizing purchase of a bicycle or sewing machine were usually very difficult to acquire, as it was common for a work unit of say, six hundred people, to receive only four or five allotment slips in a whole year for any one product. Very often in a work unit, these slips were distributed on the basis of guanxi, although some unit leaders conscientiously raffled them off. Food items such as lean cuts of meat, cooking oil, some kinds of fruit, and some alcoholic beverages were also obtained by having guanxi with a shop clerk in a state store. Many producer goods such as raw materials (for example, iron and steel, wood, or cement) and machinery were also in short supply. Factories often depend on guanxi with administrative superiors of producing units to procure enough raw materials to meet and surpass their production quotas. Individual entrepreneurs (*getihu*), usually small shopowners or street vendors, also rely on guanxi with people in factory sales outlets or state commercial organs to obtain wholesale items for their retail sales. At the beginning of the 1990s, there was an overproduction of electric household appliances, so that they became readily available in urban stores, and people no longer needed guanxi to acquire them.

Obtaining Employment, Job Transfers, and Promotions

Cadres in charge of personnel or "organization departments" (*zuzhi ke*) overseeing the assignment and discipline of cadres in a work unit, or of "labor departments" (*laodong ke*) in work units or in branches of the municipal government, are frequent objects of guanxi overtures, especially from "youth-awaiting-employment" (*daiye qingnian*), those youth who have graduated from middle school or who have returned to the city from serving in the countryside, but have not been assigned permanent jobs by their street committees or the labor bureau of the municipal government. For these youths, guanxi is often essential in getting a job. It is also important in getting assigned to a light office job or to a position that will provide some technical training or the possibility of advancement. Guanxi can also make the difference between being sent to a desirable work unit, such as a state enterprise with better work security and welfare benefits, or being sent to a small collective enterprise where wages and benefits tend to be lower and the work harder.

Transfer between work units and promotions also present difficulties that are often solved by recourse to "pulling guanxi." For example, two cadres, one a subordinate in charge of a factory, the other a superior, may exchange favors. The subordinate will write the name of his superior's son on a slip of paper and pass it on to the cadre in charge of hiring, who dutifully hires the son over others. This practice of "passing down name slips" (*di tiaozi*) is well established and has been an object of attention in the press (*RMRB* 6 November 1983; *RMRB* 8 November 1983:3). In return for getting his son a new job, the superior may recommend his subordinate for promotion at the appropriate opportunity.

Enabling Geographical Mobility

Domestic migration is subject to even stricter administrative control than work-unit transfers. To curb urban population growth, official policy since 1959 virtually forbids anyone moving from a smaller town or the countryside to a larger town or city (Potter and Potter 1990). Many married couples and families have been permanently separated as a result, although in the 1980s there were some attempts to remedy this situation. Migration is restricted by the elaborate "household registration" (hukou) system for every citizen established in 1958 under which every single urban or rural household had to register all its members with the local public security station (Tien 1973: Appendix L). Their registration at birth gives them the right to live in that village or that particular district of their town or city. No household member can move to another district, town, or province without filing for a change in household registration, a long, arduous, and usually unsuccessful bureaucratic procedure. Short visits to another town or city, however, are usually permitted by applying for a "temporary household registration" (lingshi hukou). Changing one's residence to a less desirable place or smaller town than the current residence is always permitted and even encouraged.

A further complication in changing residence is the fact that the hukou system is backed up by the system of monthly grain and other foodstuff rations, which are issued only in the specific urban district or neighborhood in which one is registered to live. This means that even when a person has managed to change household registration, he or she must still practice the art of guanxi with the grain bureau of the new place in order to receive basic monthly rations. By the early 1990s, grain rations were made meaningless by the fact that they were readily available in the free markets.

In the aftermath of the Cultural Revolution when so many urban youth sent down to live with and learn from the peasants in the countryside (Bernstein 1977) desperately wanted to return to the cities, the pressures to change household registration to a more desirable town or city was intensified. As a result of rural economic reforms instituted in 1979, which freed many peasants from the land, large numbers of people currently living in the countryside have been trying to move to the cities and towns. Since the 1970s, the art of guanxi has emerged as an important way of getting around the tight controls on geographical mobility.

Since getting permission to change one's residence is one of the most important yet most difficult things a person might have occasion to attempt in a lifetime, the gifts and banquets that are given as part of one's repertoire of guanxi tactics can cost several years of savings. Yuan Dahua, a worker, told me that his friend who was trying to get into Beijing from the city of Taiyuan had told him that the going rate for entering a place like Beijing (in 1982) was about 2,500 yuan worth of gifts. This means that if a person is earning an average wage of 60 yuan a month and saving about 15 yuan each month, then it would take a single person more than thirteen years to save up the money. Usually, however, a person can draw from the generous help of one's friends and relatives. A Beijing worker trying to get his brother into the city in 1983 from the surrounding suburban country-side reported that it would take at least 1,500 yuan worth of gifts. Often luxury goods such as stereos and TVs are involved as part of the payment.

It would seem that at the provincial level, the cost can be considerably lower. A worker in Jiangxi Province informed me that in 1983 it cost 300 to 400 yuan in gifts to move from his regional district-level (*diqu*) town to the higher-level city of the provincial capital, Nanchang. He described the process through which he himself was hoping to move to Nanchang. First, he had to secure permission in writing from his work-unit leaders to leave his work unit. Next, he also had to obtain approval to leave from the labor bureau of his town. At the same time, he was also trying to find a work unit in Nanchang that was willing to accept him. Next, he needed the approval of the Nanchang City Labor Bureau for his entry, and also its public security bureau had to agree to establish his household registration there. Somewhere in the process, he also had to get the approval of the provincial-level labor bureau. At each step and at each administrative office, he would have to *la guanxi*, so the whole process could take many years. Even with guanxi speeding up this bureaucratic process, he said, people may still spend half a lifetime trying to change their place of work or residence.

Going abroad, whether to visit, to study, or to emigrate, is also extremely difficult. Guanxi comes in handy in getting permission from one's work unit to leave, or in getting to the top of a waiting list for a passport. A college student, who was planning to use guanxi with his municipal public security bureau to gain permission to visit some relatives in Hong Kong, said that the formal waiting list in the mid-1980s for personal travel to Hong Kong was three to five years long.

Maintaining Good Health

In urban China, those who have a job in a work unit generally have access to low-cost health care provided by the state. For minor ailments, people who are employed can go to the clinic run by almost every work unit, and for serious illnesses or surgery, they go to their "contract hospital," a hospital with which their work unit has an agreement to send their employees. Yet there are still many occasions when the art of guanxi is needed to maintain one's health (Zhong 1982). Getting into a good hospital, a hospital already filled to capacity, or the hospital with the right specialization for one's illness requires guanxi. Often one's contract hospital is not the best hospital around or does not specialize in the particular type of illness being treated. For example, a friend of mine was stricken with cancer and was admitted into a high-level military hospital with a good reputation for dealing with his form of cancer only because a friend of his father was an administrator there. I myself was able to see a well-known Chinese herbal-medicine doctor only because a friend personally arranged the appointment to fit me into his busy schedule. To this day, the lasting effectiveness of his prescription attests to why he is in so much demand.

Doctors are important people with whom to cultivate guanxi because, in addition to providing access to hospital beds, guanxi with a doctor can sometimes make the difference between whether he or she seriously listens to a patient and gives a good diagnosis during a visit or only half-heartedly deals with the patient in a pro forma way. Furthermore, doctors are also a potential source for rare and potent medicines that are generally hard to obtain, and they can also write sick leave permission slips so that one can take some days off from work. That guanxixue is often a feature of the practice of medicine has been noted by the official press: "Some people in the medical profession lack professional ethics. They indulge in feasting and accepting bribes. Toward relatives and friends, 'familiar people' [shouren] or 'guanxi households' [guanxihu], they turn on the green light, giving out good medicine and sick leave permits at will" (BJRB 25 August 1983:1). The line between doctors cold-bloodedly accepting bribes from desperate people and harried doctors predisposed to pay more attention to patients with whom they have personal relationships of obligation is difficult to draw. Since doctors have a powerful role in an overburdened system of state medicine, a role in stark disproportion to their working-class-level wages, they are both besieged by guanxi overtures from anxious patients as well as predisposed to becoming participants in the art of guanxi in the medical sphere.

Obtaining Housing

Most urban housing in China is allocated by either the municipal government or one's work unit. Through state subsidies, rents are kept very low (only 2 to 6 yuan per month in the mid-1980s), so that rents are a relatively minor proportion of a household's monthly income. Since housing construction came to a virtual halt during the Cultural Revolution, housing in Beijing in the mid-1980s was in short supply. Even though new apartment buildings have sprung up throughout the city since 1979, many young couples still cannot get married for lack of an apartment to move into. In the economic reform period, many of these young urban couples turn to the growing market sphere of the economy for a solution to their housing problems. At the Beijing printing factory I studied for three months in 1984–1985, there were about ten young couples who rented living quarters from suburban peasants on the outskirts of the city. They had to pay exorbitant rates of 15 to 30 yuan per month as rent, about one half a worker's wages. This indicates that despite the frustrations and waiting involved, obtaining housing through state allocation is still the more desirable and cheaper way.

Regardless of whether one obtains an apartment from one's work unit or from the municipal government's housing management bureau (*fang guan ju*), the practice of the art of guanxi may enable one to attain success in a shorter time. For house repairs, one must also establish and maintain good guanxi with people from the powerful housing bureau, taking care never to offend them in any way. Thus, housing-bureau officials and clerks as well as work-unit leaders become frequent targets of guanxi overtures.

Promoting Political Security and Advancement

Occasionally, guanxixue is also useful in developing some political security for oneself, in stemming any potential criticism of one's political behavior, or in preventing oneself from being betrayed by either a peer or a superior. People are less likely to report on someone who has done them a lot of favors. The postrevolutionary society has witnessed wave after wave of political movements incited by the central government, during which demands for ideological purity, behavioral conformity, and the cooperation of the masses in denouncing and turning in the "enemies of the people" among them have reached fever-pitch intensity. During such political campaigns, especially the last big one, the Cultural Revolution, fear of denunciation and hatred of class enemies were so powerful that when it came to protecting a person who was a likely target of the revolutionary masses, ethics of personal obligation and indebtedness carried little weight. Therefore, it would seem that during these times of intensity, guanxixue was not a reliable form of political security.

But in periods of political relaxation when mutual denunciations and political tensions in everyday social relationships are muted, guanxixue can have more of an effect on political status. My interviews and interactions with people in the 1980s, a period of relaxation, indicate that people are still always suspicious of informants or those who "make small reports" (da xiaobaogao) to get them into trouble, and they are still alert not to offend anyone around them. Such considerations lead people to cultivate good guanxi with anyone who could potentially do them harm, establishing relationships of debt as a form of political security.

Guanxixue is even said to be a factor in gaining Party membership and making advancements in a political career. A middle-aged intellectual has seen how in his scientific research institute, gifts and favors to influential members of the Party committee have resulted in a few people becoming Party members. But since inquiry into matters of internal Party activities, even at the local levels, was a sensitive undertaking, I was not able to get a clearer picture of how frequent or influential a role guanxixue played in Party dynamics.

Facilitating Transportation

Drivers are always popular people. In the first half of the 1980s when automobiles were relatively rare, drivers enjoyed more social prestige than factory workers because of their specialized skills. Moreover, they often managed to use their work unit's car to fulfill guanxi obligations. This may take the form of helping their friends by giving them a ride, both during and after work hours, or by hauling heavy items for them which cannot be fitted onto a bicycle or public bus. The respect with which drivers are treated was graphically illustrated to me one Sunday in 1984 when I took a taxi to the home of a worker to attend his wedding banquet. The worker's family would not let me send the taxi driver back, but insisted that he, a man they had never met before, also partake of the banquet and their hospitality. As we departed, the worker's family members hovered around the driver and invited him back to their homes as a friend.

In Beijing, third-class hard-seat train tickets are generally easy to buy, but they involve long uncomfortable hours of travel, often in standing-room-only conditions on an overnight trip. There is always a shortage of second-class hard-sleeper tickets, because these do not cost much more, but include for each ticket-holder a reserved bunk to sit and sleep on. Needless to say, purchasing these tickets often requires guanxi.

A friend in Beijing described how he was able to buy a hard-sleeper ticket for a business trip. First, he approached his mother, who because she works in a hospital serving railroad workers, is the one person of all his acquaintants who has any contact with the world of trains and railroads. She made a request to someone she knew at the Beijing train station office, who then wrote down her son's name on a slip of paper and also personally made a telephone call to a ticket seller at the station. The son then obtained this slip through his mother and took it to the train station where in 1984 they actually had a special window booth just to sell tickets to *guanxihu* or people with guanxi. He got in line and bought his ticket by presenting the slip with his name on it. Airplane and boat or ferry tickets are also often bought through guanxi.

Obtaining Better Education

Since 1978, when education became officially and socially recognized as important to the country, an avenue to upward mobility, and prestigious (during the Cultural Revolution, being educated incurred suspicion and contempt), guanxixue has also played a role in obtaining a good education. At the same time, however, guanxi activities in education are curtailed by the institutionalization of formal examination procedures. Since 1978–79, when the government reinstituted objective and universal college-entrance examinations, similar examinations to get into better-ranked high schools, junior middle schools, and even the best elementary schools were also established. Having guanxi, which was so important in selecting the "worker-peasant-soldier" brand of college student during the latter half of the Cultural Revolution is now less effective for getting into college, but may still make a difference in a choice between two students who score the same on tests. Guanxixue can also be useful in getting a child into a nursery, especially into one with well-trained nannies and better facilities. In a factory, guanxi may sometimes influence the selection of a limited number of privileged workers to attend technical training classes offered by the factory or the municipal district government.

Enjoying Recreational Activities

The art of guanxi is also employed in buying tickets or gaining admission to recreational and cultural events such as movies, plays, sporting events, and music shows that are highly popular or available only to a restricted audience. In 1982, just a few years after China opened up to the outside world, I was amazed to hear from a worker that he had seen such "internal distribution" (*neibu*) foreign films as: *Star Wars, Superman, Streetcar Named Desire, The Godfather,* and *Apocalypse Now* (whose showing to some cadres at one unit was justified with the explanation that the film revealed U.S. military strategy). Certain research units in large cities such as Beijing can show such films to a very limited audience of people who study the outside world. This worker did not belong to the research unit that showed these films, but through guanxi, was able to gain entrance. A factory labor union director whom I interviewed told me how he carefully cultivates guanxi with the ticket seller of a nearby movie-house so that he will always reserve group tickets to good movies for the workers at the factory. Without guanxi, a person wanting to attend a popular show or sporting event would have to stand in line for hours, with little chance of actually buying a ticket.

A Society of Gatekeepers

In a newspaper poem, a satiric jab is made at all the gatekeepers in society who not only hinder one's passage but extract rewards for their services.

ROADBLOCK
(not a satire of traffic policemen)

Ensconced in the traffic directing booth,
in charge of traffic lights.
Vehicles come from all four directions,
sounding their horns to pass through.
Whether or not you get to pass through
depends on how sharp you are;
Simply present a gift,
and at once the green light shines;

> To anyone with nothing to present,
> the red light has no mercy.
> Even fire engines on their missions
> must pay a bribe or be stopped.
> Though the horn blasts shake the heavens,
> the powers that be feign deafness.
> If you don't pay the toll,
> forget about getting past the booth!
> (Chen Xianrong, *Wenhui Bao* 15 April 1983)

The metaphor of toll booths blocking and restricting the flow of traffic suggests a society layered and honeycombed by offices of all sizes administering all aspects of daily life and staffed by as gatekeepers who have the authority to grant or deny access to the general public. Anyone who has lived in a large city in China, and especially in Beijing, will probably remark on the number of *literal* gatekeepers who guard entrances to all major work units, government offices, factories, and academic institutions. These gatekeepers suspiciously look each person wishing to enter up and down, ask to see their identification or work cards with the inevitable surly and peremptory question, "Where are you from?" ("ni nar de?"), which implies not only "Which unit are you from?" but also "What business do you have here?" A newspaper article's complaint under the title *Men Liao* (Gate bureaucracy) bears out my point:

> I often meet a steely-faced person on duty who scrutinizes the faces and "passes" of each person approaching [the gate] for any faults. Sometimes because a person's show of respect is insufficient or for some other small reason, he will be severely lectured and berated, and waved out the gate again. . . . Gate security is a government office's "window" [to the world]. When a person enters for the first time and meets with such cold treatment at the door, he will very naturally think that it will prove to be even "colder" inside. (*ZGONB* 13 December 1984)

In this gatekeeping model, society is punctuated by a series of posts guarding innumerable boundaries between the inside and the outside. Gatekeepers in everyday life include posts of all types: shop clerks, office clerks, housing-bureau cadres, labor-allocation cadres, ticket sellers, nurses and doctors, electricians, librarians, and public-security officials. All of these people may exercise certain discretions, based on personal loyalties, obligations, and interests, in the dispensing of resources or services under their charge. Often these gatekeepers turn out to be "tolltakers" who need to be prodded with personal favors or outright fees in exchange for granting safe passage.

Given the plethora of guardians at the gate in this society, often the best policy is to show generosity to anyone who might be in a position to open a door someday, and especially if one needs to "accomplish a task" (*banshi*) at the moment. Accomplishing a task usually involves skillful maneuvering to win numerous official letters of introduction, official seals of approval, and personal permission from various levels of administration in more than one bureaucratic department. This has already been illustrated by my own experience in obtaining permission to study a factory. A middle-aged Beijing intellectual employed this proverb to describe how one must placate the authorities and influential persons to secure official seals of approval for anything from a work transfer to a housing assignment:

Meige pusa dou yao shao dao.

[Incense] must be burned before every bodhisattva.

The presentation of offerings to officials and influential persons is reminiscent of the rather practical attitude toward the gods or immortals in traditional Chinese popular religion. Peasants pray and make offerings to gods or immortals for help in saving a sick family member, giving birth to a son, or ensuring a bountiful harvest. The choice of which god or bodhisattva to target depends to a great extent on the god's proven efficacy in the past, or on another person's recommendation. If requests or pleas are granted, the god receives endless offerings of gratitude; if the god fails, prayers and offerings might be withdrawn for another god (Ahern 1981; Wolf 1974).

The gatekeeper model of Chinese society provides a useful representation of a social system with two outstanding features: the multiplicity of officials and bureaucrats directly engaged in supervising, regulating, dispensing, and guarding material goods, persons, and opportunities; and the importance of personal relationships as well as material inducements to unlocking the innumerable gates under such people's charge.

Corporate and Administrative Uses

Guanxixue is not restricted to the social exchange between individuals, it is also found in relations between corporate organizations and administrative levels of the state. Work units such as factories, commercial enterprises, schools, and offices must also practice this complex art as part of its tactics of survival and improvement of the lives of its members. Shops and stores practice guanxixue with state distribution outlets so that they may receive goods of high quality and assorted varieties and colors to sell to their customers. Schools and offices sometimes resort to cultivating guanxi with the local electrical power and coal-supply stations to ensure a steady supply of electricity for lighting and coal for heating. Factories also practice the art of guanxi in order to acquire raw materials, technical assistance, and other essentials for production. General goodwill must be maintained not only with other units and enterprises, but also with offices at superior administrative levels above the factory, and even with organizations ranked administratively lower. Both horizontal and vertical relations can affect an organization's well-being.

How the small printing factory I studied in Beijing distributed the calendars it printed at the end of 1984 illustrates just how important the art of guanxi is to a factory. That year the factory printed a total of five thousand calendars containing color pictures of pretty Chinese women in traditional and modern dress for each month. After giving out over three hundred calendars to each of its workers as year-end gifts, three thousand were sold at 4.20 yuan each, with profits going back to the factory. That left seventeen hundred or so calendars, some of which were distributed to different heads of department offices and workshops in the factory to be given by them as gifts to *guanxihu* outside the factory.

The Supply and Marketing Department gave out over three hundred calendars to important customers of the factory, such as big publishing corporations in Beijing and other units who contract with the factory to print books, journals and miscellaneous paper receipts, account forms, and the like. In the absence of assured state purchase of their products because it is a collective, and therefore lower on the administrative ladder than a state enterprise, the factory has to *la guanxi* to maintain its small market of buyers. Calendars were also sent by this department to enterprises that supply them with paper, ink, and lead bars for lead character-printing blocks, including a new paper-supply source in Inner Mongolia and one high-grade ink supplier in the city of Tianjin.

About thirty calendars were personally delivered by the factory's electricians to two electricity supply stations in the city, with key persons there receiving as many as six calendars each. Experience has taught the electricians that if only one calendar is given to a person who has a very inflated sense of his own importance, he will think the factory too cheap and decline to accept it at all. Electricity officials must be carefully appeased and flattered because once offended, they may find an excuse to reduce or even turn off a work unit's electricity supply or refuse a future request for electrical power equipment repairs.

Calendars were also given out to various other friendly connections of the factory. The labor union gave two calendars to the ticket agent at a local movie house where the labor union periodically buys tickets for workers to see a movie during worktime. The youth league gave calendars to the library where the factory borrows books for some of its workers, and to a friend at the magazine kiosk who keeps them supplied with periodicals. The medicine-dispensing station where the factory is authorized to obtain medical supplies also received a few calendars from the factory clinic. Calendars also went to the local municipal traffic corps in whose jurisdiction the factory lies, so that the factory may continue to receive permits allowing its delivery trucks to pass through certain congested streets. The local automobile-repair station was taken care of because the factory will often need them to repair its trucks and van. The bookbinding workshop gave eighteen calendars to contacts in another, larger printing factory where they can buy a good quality brand of glue and also occasionally ask for technical help to fix their paper-cutting machine. I was not able to account for the rest of the calendars.

Although guanxi between corporate entities usually benefits all or most of its members, actual guanxi transactions are carried out on a personal rather than a formal, unit-to-unit basis. In matters of guanxi exchange, units do favors for each other mainly as a result of personal ties between their staff members or representatives. That is to say, it is through face-to-face dyadic relationships that much of corporate business is transacted.

One occupation predicated on the cultivation of personal guanxi ties for corporate ends has become a specialized profession: the industrial-supply agent (*caigouyuan*). Like their counterparts in the command economy of the old Soviet Union, the *tolkachi* (Berliner 1957: 207–30), Chinese supply agents are also assigned to the procurement of supplies for their factories and enterprises. And just as *tolkachi* possessed the talent for *blat* (use of personal influence), *caigouyuan* must also be adept at cementing guanxi with significant persons in units that are potential suppliers and also find ways to induce suppliers to sell to *them* instead of other competing buyers. A skillful supply agent can also ensure that supplies are of good quality and that they will be shipped on time. Because this lifestyle entails frequent travel and sleeping in strange places, *caigouyuan* are usually men.

From piecing together various interviews with economist friends and factory supply directors, I assembled the following picture of the importance of guanxixue in the industrial sphere. In the early 1980s, the procurement of raw materials and equipment was an important item on the agenda of most factories. Type One producer goods such as steel, cement, lumber, glass, coal, and gasoline were in theory tightly rationed, centrally allocated, and guaranteed to each factory. In fact, smaller factories at lower administrative levels were at a disadvantage because they never got adequate allocations and so often had to rely on teams of supply agents who combed the country to find supplemental, out-of-plan sources of these materials. Even large factories, which received official allocation slips and signed contracts with a supplier, sometimes found it difficult to get hold of enough materials because their authorized suppliers would rather take care of their own *guanxihu* first.

Type Two producer goods included machinery and high-wattage electrical equipment. Some of these products were allocated by regional governments, and some could also be sought on the market. Type Three materials, such as work tools, light bulbs, window screens, and low-wattage electrical equipment, were less controlled. Their sale was in general directly negotiated with state wholesalers or the producing factory. Whether materials and equipment were allocated or acquired outside state plans, the art of social relationships was an indispensable mechanism in their acquisition. By the late 1980s, most of these building materials were no longer state-controlled, but were found in a growing market economy.

The following discussion with a gregarious head of the supply and marketing department (*gongxiaoke*) of a medium-sized light-industry factory in Beijing in 1982 illustrates the importance of guanxi exchange between corporate organizations in industry. With very little prompting, he explained at great length how public business relationships between a factory and its suppliers and buyers are mediated through the private and semiprivate guanxi of its supply agents:

Q: "Could you tell me how your department deals with other units when you have to buy or sell products? How do you go about the work of interpersonal relations [*ren yu ren de guanxi*]?"
A: "I've been in the supply and marketing business for over ten years now. . . . Of course the quality of your factory's products is important, but

probably the most important is the 'relationship between factories' [*chang yu chang de guanxi*]. And this relationship consists of the personal relationship between the representatives of each factory. This relationship in foreign countries is probably pretty straightforward, but in our country, it includes the realm of 'irregular winds' [*bu zheng zhi feng*], so our work is not easy [i.e., the line between giving personal favors in return for supplies and outright bribery/corruption is a fine one; supply agents must therefore be cautious of illegalities, but at the same time cannot rigidly follow every letter of the law]. When the personal relationship between representatives of two units deteriorates, then it's generally the case that if the units don't replace these people, then the two units can no longer have anything to do with each other."

Q: "How do you establish relations with customers or suppliers you have never had anything to do with?"

A: "In our line of business, even if two agents have never met, we all have historical backgrounds [i.e., we know *about* each other]. From the day when we first started working, we've been cultivating long-term relationships and making contacts . . . we generally all know each other or about each other; everyone knows which factory has which people. Our socializing is quite extensive—I know you, and so your friends all know me—it's like a spider web [of relations]. . . . So at our National Light Industry Meeting for Ordering Goods [a state-directed meeting for the exchange and allocation of producer goods], held once a year for over ten years now, we have seldom had a change of personnel. Only in recent years have some new people entered because a batch of older people retired. When new people are introduced, it's generally after the older men have already taken them around a bit to familiarize them with the scene and enable them to get to know other agents. Why is it that agents are seldom changed? Because when you introduce a newcomer, no one wants to deal with him. If they don't know you, they'll just fend you off with 'official talk' [*guan hua*]: 'Yes, yes, times are indeed difficult for getting this material. I sympathize entirely, but I'm afraid I can't help you.' . . . For example, a few years back there was a shortage of coal. We sent a new young agent down to the Beijing Coal Corporation. They asked him, 'Where're you from [*ni nar de*]? Let's see your letter of introduction.' They wouldn't give him a release for coal, even though he had a [state] allocation slip. They called me up at the factory and asked me if he was one of my men. They weren't satisfied with me just telling them on the phone, they still wanted me to go down there in person. So I went and got the coal. Both of us were agents from the same factory, but they only wanted to do business with me, whom they *know*. . . . So in China, supply and marketing work relies on your factory's good planning and allocation from above, and also on human relations [*ren shi guanxi*]. In our line of work, public and private business are really intermingled; can't have one without the other. So long as you don't go too far, private relations are still permitted by the government."

Q: "What do you mean by 'private relations' in your work?"

A: "With regard to 'private relations' [*siren guanxi*], it's more or less the same as 'public business' [*gongshi*]. We [in the supply and marketing business] are all friends in different units, we help each other out. For example, in our country there's the problem of uneven supply of goods. Beijing is an exception—it's almost like heaven here, you know, because it's the capital and we get everything. For a period there was a great shortage of pork in the Northeast [Manchuria]. So we in this office each carry up a few catties [*jin*] of pork to give out whenever we go up there on business trips. Southerners have a taste for sugar, and sometimes they don't get enough down there, so we make a point of bringing some along when we go. If we can't buy enough [sugar is rationed: two *jin* per household per month in Beijing in 1982], then we go through friends and relatives to get more from their rations. All this is not really 'irregular winds.' Relations between agents are like friendship—you go visit each other's homes on your trips, treat each other to meals, and so on. These activities don't involve the use of the state's money. The state doesn't try to limit them, and it would be unable to limit them. If you want to use the state's money, then you have to write it up on an expense account. But now the state really opposes supply agents using up state money on these activities. This practice of 'you eat mine, I eat yours' can escalate out of proportion, and really cut into our private pockets. . . . Another thing, personal relations must be based on trust [*xin yong*]. For example, when a certain raw material is in real short supply, I will still spare some to give to another unit to help its production along. Similarly, in hard times when you can't sell your products, they will remember that you helped them once when they were in need, so they will buy some of your stuff. This is showing the 'spirit of righteousness' [*yiqi*] or loyalty to friends. So our work is predicated on 'emotional feeling' [*ganqing*]. . . . But there is one exception to all this. If the commodity supply is abundant, then it doesn't matter how good private relations are. If you're selling at two yuan and five mao a piece, and someone else is selling at two yuan and four mao, [I will buy from them because] I have to look to my unit's interest first, just like any capitalist abroad."

Besides maintaining corporate relations in the industrial and economic sectors of Chinese society, guanxixue also plays an important role in the conduct of business between different administrative levels in the state bureaucracy. A university professor of political science told me that when he went down to visit some county-level officials, they told him of an ingenious method they had of giving gifts to their superior-level officials. When provincial-level officials come down to inspect the county, the county officials say to them, "Here are bags of high-grade local products [gaoji tutechan] [in this case, dried mushrooms and red dates], won't you take some home?" The provincial authorities refuse, "No, no. We cannot accept gifts." The county officials then reply, "Oh, but we are not giving them to you, they are for sale. Won't you buy some, you can't find these anywhere else." So the county officials "sell" the items, but at an extremely low price, about one-fourth or one-fifth of what they are really worth. According to the county officials, not a single official from their superior levels has refused this courtesy, even though they know in their hearts that these local products are gifts in disguise.

Very disappointed in the provincial officials, the professor confronted them with this story. They explained their behavior by showing him how complicated the situation actually is in relations between administrative levels, "If you accept this 'red packet' [hongbao; gift], then the lower level will be 'put at ease' [fangxin], then your working relations will be good [gongzuo guanxi hao]. They will feel that they have forged a good link with their superiors, that their superiors will 'look after' [zhaogu] them. If you refuse to accept, you not only offend [dezui] them, you will also create tension in the relationship. They will always be anxious that you won't look after their local needs." The professor came away from his talk with the provincial authorities with the realization that gift relations between superior and subordinate levels of government could not be reduced to a matter of personal greed and corruption.

A woman scientist studying in the United States has a father who used to be an official of a bureau of the Shandong provincial government. She described the situation of gift-giving between different administrative levels in Shandong. The township (xiang) [formerly commune] gives to the county (xian); the county gives to the regional district (diqu); then the regional district gives to the province (shen); and the province gives to the central government (zhongyang). She remembers many Chinese New Year's festivals when the trucks that pulled up in front of her home bearing gifts from various county authorities to her father numbered above ten. Then when he retired, they stopped coming. "All this has become an unwritten law," she said, "a common way of doing things, and it feels quite natural."

Tian Meng, a middle-aged artist whose father had served first as a county, then as a regional-district Party secretary of a certain province, remembers that their home was always full of gifts and they hardly ever had to buy liquor themselves. He recounts that around 1988, his province was so strapped for money to pay the peasants for the grain they sold to the state, that the province sent a special delegation led by a vice-governor to Beijing. Bearing gifts of special local products from their province worth 10,000 yuan, they hoped to get the central government to return 100 million yuan of the tax money the provincial government had had to deliver to the central authorities. Despite their effort of spending over a week in the capital, "pulling guanxi," and delivering gifts to various ministerial and other central-government officials, their request was eventually denied. That year, said Tian, the province had to pay their peasants with "white strips of paper" (*bai tiaozi*; IOUs] instead of money, causing more peasants to refuse to sell their grain to the state, but to sell at higher prices in the "free market" (*ziyou shichang*). Such guanxi and gift-relations between vertical administrative levels of the state bureaucracy have been referred to as "the locality pays tribute [to the court]" (*difang jinggong*), a phrase suggesting continuity with the past or a strategic resurgence of an aspect of imperial China.

Whether it is horizontal guanxi between industrial corporate bodies or vertical ties between administrative levels and regions, this dimension of guanxixue shows that the effects of the work of guanxi benefit not only individual persons, but whole groups and social categories of people. Since relations between groups are always negotiated through particular, strategically positioned persons, and these persons often stand to benefit from their positions as representatives of groups, the line between guanxixue and bureaucratic corruption is often a fine one. Nevertheless, the art of guanxi cannot be reduced to a modern western notion of corruption because the personalistic qualities of obligation, indebtedness, and reciprocity are just as important as transactions in material benefit.

CHAPTER THREE

The "Art" in Guanxixue:
Ethics, Tactics, and Etiquette

In the "art" of guanxi three elements—ethics, tactics, and etiquette—intertwine with and merge into one another in the course of practice. That is to say, the decorum required in the conduct of guanxixue—deferential acts, comportment of generosity, and modest speech—is also part of its ethics and arsenal of tactics. Similarly, the tactics deployed in guanxixue must remain within the parameters of its ethics and are even performed in order to satisfy its ethical prerogatives. At the same time, the instrumental logic of tactics may at times overpower the logic of ethics and etiquette, pressing them into its service.

These three interacting yet distinct components of the art of guanxi can be understood as its ethical, instrumental, and aesthetic values. They are guanxixue's internal forces. Sometimes they coexist, peacefully complementing one another; at other times they contend with or temporarily eclipse one another. Moments of eclipse or overshadowing of one force by another give rise to different "dialects" of discourse on guanxi. Each "dialect" seizes on one aspect of guanxixue in order to define it as a social phenomenon with a single nature or function.

I discussed the renqing ethical dimension of guanxixue in Chapter 1. I will start here with guanxi tactics. Like renqing, guanxi tactics also draw on a venerable cultural repertoire of strategic acts of cunning, which can be found in oral popular culture or codified in old manuals of military strategy and statecraft (Qiao 1988). The guanxi tactics I encountered in fieldwork bear a strange resemblance to many of those described in the book *Houheixue* (Thick and black learning), by an unorthodox native scholar, Li Zongwu (Li 1990). First written in 1917, but banned on the mainland until 1934 and again from 1949 to 1990, *Houheixue* satirically exposes the artful and cynical techniques people employed to negotiate their way into and up the ranks of officialdom. "Thick" refers to having a thick skin, being immune to such weaknesses as shame, guilt, and embarrassment for the tactics one employs. "Black" refers to having a black heart that has no qualms about employing cunning tactics and hurting others to get ahead.

Li located "thick and black learning" in a three-fold, quasi-historical scheme. The first period is the ancient past of the sages Yao and Shun and the philosophers Confucius and Mencius, who represent the reign of the pure and simple goodness of humanity. The second period is the ugly period of "thick and black learning," epitomized by the mythohistorical characters of Cao Cao and Liu Bei of the Three Kingdoms period (220–80 C.E.). The third period is one in which "thick and black learning" continues to be important for survival, but it must be practiced according to, or in the language of, the principles of Confucian-Mencian ethics. Li argued that in the third period, it is as if history has returned to the first period of pure ethics, but actually, the course of "evolution" is not cyclical, but spiral. Therefore, the third period is a mixture of the first and second; one cannot get by with just "thick and black learning," but if one were to rely solely on Confucian-Mencian ethics, one would be destroyed. Li saw himself as living at the end of the second period and the beginning of the third, in which people increasingly "harbor the heart of Confucius and Mencius while employing the techniques of Cao and Liu" (*yi kongmeng zhixin, xing caoliu zhishu*). Often the means may be distasteful, but the aims can be redeeming.

Li's schema helps explain the conflicted nature of the art of guanxi in the 1980s. In guanxixue, ethics and tactics coexist in tension and harmony, a coexistence expressed in the choreography of guanxi etiquette. In guanxixue can be found the interplay of the first and second periods of Li's scheme. Adopting Li's schema, guanxixue is very much a product of the third period, a period in which some of the traditional ethics of interpersonal relations have started to resurface, after a period of eclipse when state ethics reigned, and during the terror of the Cultural Revolution when impersonal cruelty and indifference were the order of the day and cunning and instrumental tactics were required for survival. Yet in the third period, neither ethics nor tactics have yet clearly established themselves as the stronger force, and so they coexist in an uneasy tension.

Cynical tactics not only continue to be necessary, but also remain as an obsessive "bad habit," so to speak, whereas the reappearance of interpersonal ethics answers to a social yearning for more warmth and cooperation in social relations. Guanxixue can be viewed as both a symptom of and a reaction against the politicization of interpersonal relationships in the larger social order.

Guanxi Bases: Kinship, Friendship, and Other Personal Relations

Guanxi exchange can only be carried out between two parties who have established in one way or another, a basis of familiarity. I recall seeing a cartoon that played on the double entendre of the word *shou*, which can mean "ripe" or "cooked" when referring to fruit or food and "familiar" when referring to people. In the cartoon, a booth where watermelons are being sold to a line of waiting people displays a sign reading, "Ripeness of melons not guaranteed." One lucky person, however, does not have to wait in line and is sold a very ripe and red melon. The caption explains, "When the person is *shou* [familiar], the melon will also be *shou* [ripe]" (*FCYYM* 20 February 1982).

Elements of mutual trust and obligation, which are part of the notion of familiarity, pave the way for guanxi by ensuring a sympathetic ear to guanxi proposals. This emphasis on familiarity as a prerequisite for guanxixue can be found in the importance attached to relationships in which there is a shared identity or in which there are shared personal experiences. The word *tong*, meaning "same" or "shared," is used to designate a whole set of close personal relationships which serve as guanxi bases: "person from the same native place" (*tongxiang*), "classmate" (*tongxue*), and "coworker or colleague" (*tongshi*) (Jacobs 1980:41).

It is important to point out that these relationships cannot be reduced to guanxi relationships, for in some respects their spirit is also opposed to guanxixue. Friendship, kinship, classmates, and so forth are not coextensive with guanxi, but serve as bases or potential sites for guanxi practice. Kinship and friendship, of which all the *tong* or "shared" relationships above are offshoots, are understood in popular discourse as being more disinterested, less instrumental, and ethically purer than guanxi relationships. They act as spheres of potential guanxi operations, as reservoirs of binding ties and ethical obligations on which guanxixue draws to fulfill its own ends.

The range of guanxi bases in urban society may be subsumed under the following categories: family and kinship, neighbors and native-place ties, non-kin relations of equivalent status, and non-kin superior-subordinate relations.

Family and Kinship Ties

One's immediate natal and nuclear family is the strongest kinship tie, followed by the extended family and consanguineal relations, and then the more distant set of affinal relatives. In Beijing I did not find any evidence of lineage or clan organization, but I did find that kinship relations served as a model for guanxi exchange. Kinship still remains a common idiom of social relations in that general principles of kinship loyalty are applied to both actual kin and fictive kin. The transformation of kinship ethics into guanxi ethics will be discussed after a brief foray into some kinship examples in Beijing.

Kinship bonds are maintained by acts of giving and sharing. In this respect, Chinese culture can be compared with American inner-city African-American culture, in which resources are pooled among kin and neighbors (Stack 1974). Indeed, a Chinese friend studying at the University of Chicago noted this similarity after observing black service workers taking home food and other items from cafeteria kitchens and hotels to distribute among their networks. A forty-year-old woman worker recounted how when her three children were very young and her wages low, her four older brothers, who all lived in the vicinity, would buy clothes for her children. Once when she had to go visit her husband's parents in a small town in Hebei Province, without being asked, her brothers gave her between 10 and 20 yuan each, about a third or a fourth of their monthly wages, so that she would have money to spend on the trip.

A close kinship can entail deep "emotional feelings" (ganqing) of attachment, as expressed in this proverb in rhymed verse recited by a worker:

Gubiao qin beibei qin;
zasui gutou lianzhe jin.

Cousins are close, close through generations;
Smash their bones, but they're still attached by tendons.

At the same time, there can also be considerable indifference, even hostility in kinship. Nevertheless, the proper form of ethical kinship conduct must still be observed, and that entails mutual giving and receiving.

A woman worker with a three-year-old daughter said that ganqing between her widowed mother and herself is not very "deep" because her mother always favored her younger sister when they were growing up. Nevertheless, she feels she must still live up to her filial obligations, so she occasionally visits her mother who lives near her sister. At each Chinese New Year holiday her husband receives a duck or a chicken from his factory, a year-end bonus for all the workers at the relatively well off military factory where he works. This she always gives to her mother. She prefers, however, to spend most of her leisure time with her in-laws. During the Lunar New Year festival of 1985, her little daughter received the traditional gifts of pocket money to children (*ya sui qian*) worth a total of 50 yuan from her grandparents, aunts, and uncles.

Wen Shifu, a fifty-year-old woman cadre, first left her home in the North Hebei countryside to come settle in Beijing in 1959 when the Great Leap Forward called for more peasants to participate in industrial labor in the cities. Since then she has only returned to her rural home twice to visit relatives. She would like to visit her hometown, poor as it is, more often, for she misses the fresh air, the open spaces, and the warmth of her relatives; but she cannot afford the gifts that would be required for such a visit. Besides gifts for her relatives, she would also have to throw banquets to thank them for the banquets they would certainly lay out to welcome her. To fail to meet these obligations would be to "lose propriety" (*shi li*), or "fail to observe proper form."

The last time she went back with her husband, who is from the same village, was in 1978. In the ten days there, they were invited to relatives' homes for dinner and lunch every day, so that they ate only three meals at her own sister's home where they were staying. The round after round of feasting tired them out, but they could not refuse some invitations and accept others, for that would have offended people greatly. If they had declined someone's dinner, that person would have thought that now that she and her husband live in the city, they have put on airs (*bai jiazi*) and look down on country folk. All in all, a total of 300 yuan was spent on the trip, equivalent to five months of Wen Shifu's wages at the small collective factory where she works.

Kinship is one base from which guanxi overtures may be made, but in large cities it is no longer the main basis for two people entering into guanxi exchange. The urban people I met considered kinship as something more confining than guanxixue, which for them is more enabling. Two workers in Beijing observed that they tend to spend more time socializing with friends than with relatives, whom they only see at holidays. They complained that dealing with kin is "too complicated" (*tai fuza*). Relatives can be very demanding and tend to expect you to help them just because they are related to you, they said.

Where no actual kinship tie exists, fictive kinship ties are expressed by employing such kinship addresses as *shushu* (father's younger brother), *bobo* (father's elder brother), *a-yi* (mother's sister), *bomu* or *dama* (wife of father's elder brother), *dajie* (elder sister), *xiaomei* (younger sister), *dage* or *laoxiong* (elder brother), *di* (younger brother), and so on for friends of the family, neighbors, and personal friends. These fictive kinship extensions bring people outside the family group into the circle of familiar and trusted relationships.

It can be said that in large cities like Beijing, guanxi ties based on the familiarity principle have come to supplant the centrality of agnatic and affinal kinship ties described by so many ethnographies of rural Chinese life (Yang 1945; Hsu 1967; Fei 1983; Cohen 1976; Baker 1979). Guanxi connections today are more important than the "nepotistic ties" in Chinese cities observed by Olga Lang (1946) and Marion Levy (1949) in the 1930s and 1940s. In contemporary Chinese urban life, what is now important is the extension of such kinship principles ("familiarity," obligation, mutual aid, sharing, and the gauging of relational or affective distance) to guanxixue.

A point worth noting in the reproduction of kinship in urban contexts is that guanxixue replicates or emphasizes one aspect of traditional kinship organization and not another. Guanxixue commonly adopts the fluid, expanding network structures of kinship organization, not the hierarchical, rigid, and boundary-maintaining corporate-group aspect of traditional kinship, as found in clan and lineage formations. This is probably because the bureaucratic state has monopolized the organization of urban life, replacing kinship and other forms of group formation with the social cells of work units. Therefore, guanxixue evolved horizontally to bridge these rigid state boundaries and cut through the vertical links of administrative levels. The relationship between kinship and guanxixue will be further explored in Chapters 6 and 8 and in the Conclusion.

Neighbors and Native-Place Ties

In the city, non-kin relationships often become more important than kinship, as illustrated by the common saying:

Yuan qin bu ru jin lin.

Distant relatives are not as dear as close neighbors.

Distance can weaken the kinship bond of "familiarity" and obligation. Neighbors become an important guanxi resource, and there is a great deal of mutual obligation between neighbors.

An older worker I interviewed was thoroughly proud of his urban origins, having spent his youth as a street vendor of deep-fried breakfast pastry (*youtiao*) on the streets of Beijing in the "old society." He drew a line of separation between urban workers in his factory like himself and the peasant "temporary workers" (*lingshi gong*) who also worked in the factory. He could not understand how, for these peasants, a mindless kind of unquestioning kinship loyalty could provide the sole basis for building up powerful and exclusive interest factions and for giving mutual assistance. For him, social relationships among the urban workers in his factory do not rely on blind kinship loyalty, but are based on diverse bonds of affect.

Besides neighborly relations, there is another important, spatially defined sphere of relationships, which provides a basis for guanxi operations. This is the native-place (*tongxiang*) tie. People who come from the same village, town, county, or province, or speak in the same dialect have an affinity for one another and can be counted on to do a favor or open a back door.

Gong zhang bu ru laoxiang.

An official seal is not as good as a fellow from the same hometown.

Indeed, when I visited a county in Hubei Province with a researcher who was born and raised there, I was more warmly received and people were more open to my questions and willing to help me, than they were in places I visited without an insider accompanying me.

In the 1980s, some urban places witnessed the reemergence of "native-place associations" (*tongxianghui*), or regional "offices" (*ban shi chu*), through which people from the same county or province meet periodically to discuss events in their native homes, to share information about jobs and ways to make money to benefit themselves or their hometowns, and to introduce guanxi connections to each other.

Non-Kin Relations of Equivalent Status: Classmates, Coworkers, and Friends

Most of the young workers I knew continue to maintain close ties with their favorite elementary and middle-school classmates, even years after they have been assigned to different work units in the city. Workers in their thirties and forties remember their adolescence, spent mostly during the Cultural Revolution, when classroom discipline had broken down, as a carefree time in which strong impressions were made and binding friendships forged, in contrast to the factory discipline and marriage and family responsibilities of their adulthood.

Middle-aged people also maintain ties with former classmates. One middle-aged cadre who had graduated from a technical two-year college stated that most of his and his wife's close friends are from their high school and technical college years. They feel vulnerable in relations with colleagues at work because they are directly subject to the same authority relations in their own work unit, whereas their classmates do not share the same work unit or local authority relations and therefore pose no personal political security risks.

The importance of having a classmate basis for guanxi was graphically illustrated to me once when I went to have dinner at the home of my friend the carpenter, Chen Shaoxiong. Since the number of the month and day (24 April) were both even, and the day fell on a Sunday in the spring of 1982, it was a propitious and popular day for weddings throughout the city. My host had tried to buy beer everywhere, but because of the number of weddings being held, all of Beijing's beer seemed to have been sold out. According to his wife, the rest was probably being withheld by store clerks to sell to their own friends. Then Chen Shaoxiong remembered that he had heard from mutual friends that a former elementary-school classmate was now working in a small individual enterprise restaurant and might have access to some beer. The fact that he had not seen the classmate for nearly six years did not deter him because he was sure the other would remember him and acknowledge their past acquaintance.

When we arrived at the restaurant, unfortunately his old classmate was out. Another clerk, not knowing him, was, in the manner of shop clerks, neither helpful nor friendly. He demanded that we drink the two bottles of beer on the premises because it was a restaurant, not a store. My friend indignantly invoked his old classmate's name, declaring, "Wait a minute, you just go find Zhang Xueming and tell him to come here. He was my classmate in elementary school and then during the Cultural Revolution we worked on the same state farm in the Northeast [Manchuria]; he was in Number 3 Brigade and I was in Number 5 Brigade, very close to one another!" The clerk immediately changed his tune and said that if this was the case then there was no problem in his buying *three* bottles of beer and taking them home. By invoking the guanxi bases of classmate and coworker, Chen Shao-xiong was able to assert the rights of familiarity and deploy guanxi tactics.

Friendship is another sphere of personal relationships which is frequently appropriated by guanxixue; however, it is also friendship that is most often set up in contrast to guanxi in popular discourse. Notions of friendship are expressed in the different categories of "heart-to-heart friends" (*zhixin pengyou*) and friends who use each other (*huxiang liyong*), a contrast that follows the distinction between expressive or emotional friendship and instrumental friendship (Wolf 1966:11–12). "Heart-to-heart friends" are good for confiding with and for depending on when one needs help. One cannot use them for gain, that is, as an instrument to acquire resources, because in real friendship, one gives without thinking of a return. "Heart-to-heart friendships" are said to be rare because they take so long to establish, and real trust can only be proven over time. Furthermore, there are many perils in life which give rise to the betrayal of friendship. Therefore, most people tend to have more "ordinary friends" (*yiban peng-you*) or more guanxi contacts than "heart-to-heart friends." "Ordinary friends" are people with whom one can share a good time. Among young male workers, these are called "liquor and meat friends" (*jiurou pengyou*), drinking buddies who come together when there are good times and food to enjoy, but who are not always reliable during hard times.

Non-Kin Superior-Subordinate Relations: Teacher-Student, Master-Apprentice, and Others

Among these guanxi bases are the relationship between teacher and student, master and apprentice in a factory, work-unit or section leader and subordinate, and so on. In the first two relationships, it is generally recognized that there is an element of "emotional affection" (*ganqing*) between superior and subordinate, which is weak in the third relationship because it is a "political relationship" (*zhengzhi guanxi*). A middle-school teacher recounted how one day he was waiting in line to buy meat at his local state butcher store. When his turn in line came up, the youthful meat-seller behind the counter recognized him as his former middle-school teacher and went out of his way to cut out the best lean cuts of pork available on the chopping block for him, leaving out the fat that would otherwise have been an obligatory part of the purchase. The other people waiting in line resented but were resigned to this common practice.

Despite the Cultural Revolution, I found teachers still greatly respected by their students. At least three university lecturers have told me on separate occasions, with a confidence I can only now envy as a professor, that their students would think nothing of rendering them a service because they feel they owe a personal debt in learning from them. A young musician informed me that he still visits his aging teacher at home regularly even though the teacher is too feeble to practice with him as they used to do. The reason, says the musician, is that "our *ganqing* is very deep. He taught me almost everything I know about Chinese music. It is the least I can do to visit him now that his health is not good."

The relationship between master (*shifu*) and apprentice (*xuetu*) in a factory is often a deep, lifetime relationship involving both emotional bonding as well as guanxi exchange. Older workers who can remember their days as young apprentices in "the old society" and in the early years after Liberation point to the fact that today the relationship between master and apprentice is much more egalitarian than the harsh authoritarian relationships of old, when masters sometimes beat their cringing apprentices. Nevertheless, a young woman worker reports that a distinct status difference persists between master and apprentice. It is common for the latter to treat their masters with great deference and to keep their thermos bottles filled with boiled water every day at work. In turn, masters treat their apprentices sternly, but also with almost parental regard. Since women entered the workforce in the 1960s, women can be masters too, but there are still fewer women than men who have learned a skill to pass down.

Often in factories, factions (*bangpai*) run along lines of successive generations of masters, their apprentices, and the apprentices of these apprentices. For example, a master may set up his child as the apprentice of his own former apprentice so that the latter, out of a sense of obligation and indebtedness to his or her former master, can "look out for" (*zhaogu*) the master's child. The first, second, and third generations of apprentices will all be tied by guanxi and belong to the same faction as the original master.

The guanxi between work-unit leader and subordinate is less sel-dom suffused with affective elements as strong as those found in teacher-student or master-apprentice relationships. In the relationship between manager and workers, between workshop directors and workers in a factory, or between the leader and work-unit members in an office, the state disciplinary component is generally more promi-nent than affective or paternal warmth. Therefore, guanxi exchanges in these relationships tend to be motivated by more instrumental and politicized considerations.

Affective Sentiments: Yiqi, Ganqing, and Renqing

In the popular discourse of urban people, the notion of *yiqi* ("loy-alty" or "ethic of righteousness") is an important concept attached to friendship. Yiqi is the unswerving loyalty that cements friends as if they were blood siblings. It is a term that describes the affective senti-ment found in non-kin peer relations and especially same-sex bond-ing. For example, it is called yiqi when a person has been promoted to higher office and enters different social circles, but does not forget old friends. The Chinese dictionary explains yiqi as "referring to the will-ingness to risk danger and to sacrifice personal benefits for a personal relationship" (Zhongguo 1982:1356).

A young male factory worker explained the concept of yiqi by com-paring the character of Zhu Yuanzhang (1328–98 C.E.), the ruthless founder of the Ming dynasty, with that of Zhao Kuangyin (927–76 C.E.), the founder of the earlier Song dynasty. Zhu was a man without yiqi because after he ascended to the throne, he had all his generals assassinated, for fear that they would plot against him. In contrast, upon establishing the Song dynasty, Zhao remembered the contribu-tions of his generals and enfeoffed them. This example sums up the cultural distinction between impersonal, cynical political power and the personalism of friendship loyalties.

A middle-aged cadre who has weathered many political storms and vicissitudes in his career recalled during the years 1966–68 he did not dare let his guard down and talk frankly even with his closest friends. The unprecedented ferocity of the Cultural Revolution caused him to lose his political bearings so that at the time he could not fathom the social and political situation. He feared that the political storm might be strong enough to prevail against the bonds of friendship and lead to personal betrayals. As the Cultural Revolution wore on he gradually came to realize which of his friends had a true sense of yiqi. There were friends who when interrogated about him would put up a pretense of criticizing him on minor points, but actually withold from his persecutors more serious accusations that would have really brought him trouble. Thus on the surface yiqi would not be evident to outsiders, but in actuality it was there, but hidden.

The phrase *gemenr yiqi*, "ethic of brotherhood," is especially common among younger people in the cities of North China. It refers to the tight bonds of mutual aid, trust, and loyalty linking the members of a friendship network at a workplace, in a neighborhood, or spread out over the city. When a person says, "They are all my *gemenr*," it means that they are all his or her "bosom buddies." Although the term "brothers" suggests males, it can also be applied to women friends and mixed-sex friends. When, in preparation for a wedding, good friends get together to whitewash and fix up the apartment or room that one of them will share with his bride, it is called *gemenr yiqi*. "Brothers" will share both good times and personal tragedies because they have the desire and the obligation to help one another in times of need. On a number of occasions, people have said to me that the "ethic of brotherhood" can at times prove stronger than the bonds between husband and wife or child and parents.

When an all-female circle of close friends is involved, the phrase "ethic of sisterhood" (*jiemenr yiqi*) is sometimes employed, although this phrase is heard less frequently than the other. When a network of friends includes both men and women, often the women will also be referred to by the men, as well as by each other, as *gemenr*. A college-educated woman informed me that the "ethic of sisterhood" is a phrase found more among working-class women than college or professional women. A Beijing woman worker said that *jiemenr yiqi* is important among women she knew, but that these bonds of friendship were weaker among women than among men because she thought that women as a rule are more divided than men, and their friendships are more fragile.

Like the difference between guanxixue and friendship, both *gemenr yiqi* and *jiemenr yiqi* are also often distinguished from guanxixue. There is *ganqing* or "emotional feeling" between "brothers" (*gemenr*) or "sisters" (*jiemenr*), but no keeping of accounts or any stress on balancing debts as in the material exchange of guanxi. In fact, Chen Shaoxiong, the carpenter, remarked that he tends not to go to his *gemenr* for certain kinds of help resulting in personal material gain because it might jeopardize the relationship and move it to a lower order. In addition, even though he knows his friend will be eager to help him, he would not want to make him feel bad should the latter be unable to. The "ethic of brotherhood" still preserves the principles of enduring inconvenience, risk, and hardship for a friend. This was exemplified by Chen's close friend who, on a business trip to the northeast, willingly lugged a large and heavy ceramic sink all the way back to Beijing by train for Chen. When asked to explain *gemenr yiqi*, a young woman worker remembered how in high school a boy confessed to a theft actually committed by his best friend and went to jail for it. Although this is an extreme and unrepresentative example, she explained, it still expresses the spirit of this ethic.

The presence, absence, or the amount of a certain quality of "emotional feeling" (*ganqing*) in a relationship is frequently considered. *Ganqing* stands for the emotional commitment in such long-standing and intimate social bonds as those found between a parent and child, husband and wife, close friends, teacher and student, and certain favorite relatives. When a husband and wife's ganqing is said to be ruptured (*ganqing polie*), it means that the only thing holding their marriage together is the difficulty of obtaining a divorce or financial considerations in separating. Ganqing applies to a broader range of social relationships than yiqi and tends to emphasize affective and emotional identification rather than duty, loyalty, or obligation.

Ganqing can also be understood by looking at relationships that lack it. A general consensus seems to exist in China that human relations "abroad" (*zai guowai*), a vague zone usually understood as "the West," are impersonal, detached, mechanistic, and devoid of ganqing. From foreign films and second- or third-hand accounts from people who have gone abroad, many in China infer that friendship in the West is neither deep nor enduring, and that no strong ganqing exists between close blood relations such as parents and children. It is said that even between friends and family members there is an open and unabashed economic relationship. For example, one topic of frequent comment when I lived in Beijing in the early 1980s was the fact that in the West, when friends go out to eat, each person has to pay for their own portion. This is unthinkable in China, where eating together is in order to be indebted to the host. Other stories about the West were recounted with wonder: that in the United States, when grandchildren go to their grandparents' home and cut the grass or pull out weeds, the grandparents have to pay them, or that parents have to pay for their own meals when they have dinner at their married son and daughter-in-law's home. What is significant here about

these perceptions of Western and capitalist society as lacking in ganqing is the notion that ganqing and the meticulous settling of economic
accounts are mutually exclusive. Ganqing should involve an element
of sacrifice in giving. Overt repayment and material compensation
detract from or deny the emotional commitment in the relationship.

Not all personal relationships are imbued with deep ganqing. In
such cases, these ties are best characterized by *renqing*, the observance
of proper social form, which involves lesser degrees of affection.
Whereas emotional sentiments are central to the notion of ganqing,
the discourse of renqing articulates the moral and decorous character
of social conduct. Asked to explain the difference between ganqing
and renqing, Tian Meng explained, "Renqing is when you [meaning
me as an anthropologist] go to a county town for social research and
you bring some gifts for the local officials. This is not called ganqing
because your relationship with them is not deep." In other words,
giving gifts to the local officials is a matter of courtesy and observance of proper social form and etiquette. It will lead to the establishment of a good relationship, but not to ganqing.

An important feature of renqing principles is the notion of the necessity of reciprocity, obligation, and indebtedness in human relations. What activates reciprocal relations, what imbues relationships
with a sense of obligation and indebtedness are the work of relational
sentiments and ethics. Concrete expressions of renqing are found especially in the gift-giving that goes on at special occasions such as
births, deaths, weddings, and New Year's. Most of the gifts given at
these occasions are examples of what, in the case of Japan, has been
called "expressive gifts" rather than "instrumental gifts" (Befu 1967).
"Expressive gifts" reinforce the affective sentiments and feelings of
obligation that accompany kinship, friendship, and superior-subordinate ties.

How does the art of guanxi relate to such principles of affect, ethics, and etiquette as ganqing, yiqi, and renqing? Guanxixue can be
said to draw on elements from the first two discourses. From the
discourse of ganqing, guanxixue has incorporated into its repertoire
of forms, the mechanisms of affective sentiment, and a certain degree
of emotional identification. From the discourse of friendship and yiqi,
guanxixue borrows another ingredient, the ethic of loyalty, duty, obligation, and trust. Guanxixue, however, does not borrow from renqing discourse; rather, it is embedded in it, and at the same time, extends and reconstitutes renqing practice. Guanxixue is embedded in
the renqing formulation of human relations as an endless flow of interpersonal exchanges and reciprocal commitments.

The tactical and instrumental dimension of guanxixue d<
ist in ganqing and yiqi, and exists only as a potentiality in
This instrumental dimension of guanxixue links it with tw\
types of exchange relations in which affect and ethics do not ,
role: impersonal money relations and bribery.

Another way to address the embeddedness of guanxi in this array
of cultural discourses is by thinking in terms of four inflections on the
conduct of social relationships. *Emotional affect* is the first inflection
on a social relationship. Money/bribery relations are the weakest in
terms of emotional affect, followed by guanxi, renqing, yiqi, and
ganqing as the most filled with emotional content. The second inflection is that of feelings of *diffuse obligation and indebtedness.* Measured along this scale, the money/bribery register is very low here,
because it is based not on diffuse obligation, but on the narrow return
on a payment for specific services. Guanxi possesses diffuse obligation, but not as much as renqing, ganqing, or yiqi. The degree of
etiquette and propriety of conduct gives a third inflection, in which
bribery and yiqi have the weakest requirements for observing etiquette, followed by ganqing, guanxi, and renqing, which has the
strongest. The fourth inflection on social relationships is the degree of
gain-and-loss calculation. Whereas yiqi and ganqing possess very low
levels of instrumental calculation, the level rises with renqing, then
guanxi, and ends up with money and bribery relations, which have
the strongest measure of instrumentalism.

Guanxixue certainly possesses a heavy dose of gain-and-loss calculation and means-ends concerns for material gain, but these concerns
can only be expressed and satisfied *through* various social bonds of
affect, obligation, and propriety. Guanxi can only be activated by employing or playing on the idiom of friendship and kinship as well as
by adopting the language and decorum of renqing, yiqi, and ganqing.
The intersection of guanxixue with the discourses and practices of
yiqi, ganqing, and renqing are what make it distinct from impersonal
money and bribe relations.

Enlarging a Guanxi Network

It is a rule that the larger one's guanxi network, and the more diverse one's guanxi connections with people of different occupations
and positions, the better becomes one's general maneuverability in
society and with officialdom to obtain resources and opportunities.
There is a certain cumulative effect in extending a guanxi network.

The more guanxi one has, the more it is possible to increase one's guanxi network because through one's guanxi contacts, one can reach people in different social spheres. Merely invoking the name of a mutual friend, whether or not he or she is present, provides both parties with a basis for familiarity and for "establishing guanxi" (*jianli guanxi*).

One incident especially impressed on me how social networks may be extended through the skillful and conscious use of existing guanxi. Lin, an electrical repair worker in his thirties, and I arrived at a museum just after it had closed for the day. The gatekeeper came out to tell us that we could not enter, but had to come back another day. Lin suddenly recognized him and asked if he knew his uncle, who during the Cultural Revolution worked in that museum as a groundsman. The gatekeeper's face lighted up, and he graciously ushered us into the museum. Since we had established ourselves as "familiar people" (*shouren*), we were no longer subject to the regular closing time for the public and were even extended the courtesy of not having to pay for our tickets.

After our tour, Lin wanted to chat with the gatekeeper and make a new contact. They exchanged information on each other's working conditions, wages, and raises. Lin asked how he acquired such an ideally light job as gatekeeper and added with some calculation, "You must have some good channels [*luzi*]." The other grinned and replied that it is always helpful to have some guanxi in these matters, thereby implicitly admitting that he had gained his post through guanxi. Before parting, Lin asked to exchange addresses and invited the other to visit him sometime, especially if he needed help in some matter. Outside, Lin expressed how pleased he was to have made another contact that day. I asked why he bothered to get to know such a person and what benefits a mere museum gatekeeper could possibly bring. Lin replied that even though this person may not have direct access to certain opportunities, the fact that he was able to land this job indicates that he probably has access to friends in various influential positions, who could be approached through him.

The work of broadening one's guanxi network frequently depends on a go-between or intermediary (*zhongjianren*) to make an introduction to a stranger. The intermediary is often a friend who is familiar with the other person, and who implicitly vouches for one's virtue and reliability to the other person. Since guanxixue has to work through channels of familiarity, introductions by an intermediary are often much more effective than self-initiated acquaintance. The role of intermediaries also shows that the art of guanxi is not restricted to ascribed relationships, but also depends on what can be called "achieved familiarity." This injects a dynamic element into the art of guanxi and adapts it to the fluid and heterogeneous context of urban life relative to the more stable social pattern of rural life.

In a social context in which everyday social relations are often politicized, trust is an important consideration. The logic behind "achieved familiarity" is illustrated in what one factory deputy Party secretary said in response to my request for an interview with him: "Old Liao and I have been close friends for a long time. Since it was Old Liao who introduced you to me, it must mean that he trusts you, so I trust you too. Besides, since you are his friend, helping you is helping him too." Although in this particular case it was a mutual friendship tie with Old Liao which linked the deputy Party secretary and myself, any other guanxi base would also have served as a bridge.

An intermediary may also act as a scout for his or her friend in cases in which the guanxi between two potential guanxi transactors is not sufficiently strong or secure. A go-between who has better personal ties with the guanxi target, say a cadre, may inquire into how responsive the cadre might be to guanxi overtures from his friend, what kind of gifts are most likely to win him over, or whether the position and jurisdiction of the cadre would enable him to fulfill the particular request.

A general principle in long chains of guanxi transactions involving go-betweens is that such chains are composed of a series of dyadic relations in which each person will help the next person in the chain on account of their direct personal relationship and not necessarily with the intention of helping the stranger who made the original request. In many cases the person who performs the last favor in the chain of favors will not know and will never meet the originator of the request. Indeed, intermediaries are often unaware that they are merely links in a chain of personally transferred requests. They think that they are simply helping the person who approaches them when in fact their kindness will ultimately benefit a stranger.

In these guanxi chains, indebtedness is embedded within each specific link or dyadic relationship, not diffused all along the chain. That is to say, each person in the chain will only be indebted to the next person to whom she or he made a request. In this way a person may, through the guanxi of guanxi, transcend his or her own limited social network and cross over into several others without incurring an exorbitant debt to everyone involved. Although the art of guanxi involves the principle of "familiarity," which implies not assisting strangers, through the reliance on intermediaries and dyadic obligations in a long chain of guanxi, one can also come to rely indirectly on the assistance of strangers. This flexible and enabling aspect of the art of guanxi must be recognized in order to avoid conceiving of it as just an exclusionistic, static, and tradition-bound system of exchange.

Another way to enlarge a social network is to use one's existing guanxi as a resource to attract and maintain more guanxi. The ability to help others is enhanced considerably if one grants a favor to one person by asking the same favor of another who is in a better position to obtain the necessary service. In this way, guanxi itself becomes a social resource in addition to one's occupation, social position, and material possessions, hence the constant efforts made to expand this resource. If in capitalist systems "the rich get richer," it can be said that in China today, the more guanxi one has, the more one can maneuver in society. It would seem that in Chinese urban life today, in deploying guanxixue as the "weapons of the weak" (Scott 1985), one's independence in everyday affairs is gained paradoxically through a dependence on social relations.

The Tactic, Obligation, and Form of Giving and Receiving

Exchange is a fundamental and inalienable part of the nature and process of guanxixue. In the art of guanxi three things are exchanged: gifts, banquets, and favors. Since I have already described the variety of favors and services exchanged through guanxi, I focus here on the gift and the banquet.

Virtually every person I spoke with in the 1980s and early 1990s, as well as the official press, said that in recent years there has been a rising "gift-giving wind" (songli feng) in all spheres of social relations. Despite official concern and disapproval, social pressures to give more gifts and more expensive gifts have mounted. In 1982 a taxi driver related to me how his friend, also in the same occupation, spent a lot of money on gifts for the occasion of his first meeting with his future father-in-law. He bought a bottle of Maotai spirits, then a bottle of Wuliang spirits, then a few cartons of cigarettes, and, on top of that, a Western-style cream cake in a large box. His friend spent practically his whole month's basic wage (at that time 40 yuan) just because he wanted to make a good impression and cement good relations with his future father-in-law. The taxi driver shook his head, muttering,

"This gift-giving wind is getting out of hand. I told my friend he gave too much, but he didn't think so."

Along with concern about pressures for gift-giving in the social sphere, especially in the context of weddings, people also remark frequently on the escalation of gift-giving as a tactic in the art of guanxi. Although gift-giving in the art of guanxi has much in common with the type of gift-giving practiced among relatives and friends as a social etiquette and expression of respect, affection, and social prestige, it also displays its own unique features. The instrumental nature of gift-giving in the art of guanxi distinguishes it from gift-giving according to renqing principles, such as wedding gifts, New Year's gifts, courtesy visit gifts, and funeral gifts. This distinction between two realms of gift-giving can often be found in popular representations. A satiric cartoon shows a frustrated man whose monthly wage is being eaten up by the obligation to give presents of alcoholic beverages at such social occasions as weddings, births, retirements, on the one hand, and in order to get a job, a promotion in wage-grade, a work transfer, and entry into school, on the other hand (FCYYM 20 February 1982). Although one shades off into another, renqing gift-giving is mainly prompted by diffuse social obligations and is an expression of affection, while guanxi gift-giving is more specific and purposive.

The distinctive tactics and etiquette of guanxixue can be discerned in the following areas: (1) in the kinds of gifts given, (2) in the initiation of guanxi exchange, (3) in the occasion and form of gift-giving, and (4) in the dissimulation of objectives.

The Kinds of Gifts Given in the Art of Guanxi

Depending on the magnitude of a request and the social position of the recipient, the kinds of gifts given in anticipation of or in return for favors range from a simple bag of fruit or a chicken to an expensive stereo, color TV, or refrigerator. According to a middle-aged worker in a provincial town in the south, a gift of chinaware or textiles worth thirty to forty yuan given to the head of the factory labor department in the hopes of switching from a schedule of three-shift rotation to a fixed day shift was considered reasonable in his factory in the early 1980s. In same period, a request for transferring one's household registration from a rural administrative area to an urban one, or from a small town to a larger town was considered a major request since the transaction would be very risky and more seriously illegal than other guanxi exchanges. It would most likely involve major gifts such as a black-and-white TV worth over 600 yuan or a color TV worth over 1200 yuan.

Often where the guanxi is more formal between two people who do not know each other very well, or where the gift recipient is in some sort of official capacity, the gift may consist of bottles of wine and cartons of cigarettes. There is a common saying that male officials, when requested to help out in a certain affair over which they have jurisdiction, are always given to declaring that the matter needs more "study" (*yanjiu yanjiu*) on their part. In Chinese the words *yanjiu* for "study" also happens to be a homonym to the words for "cigarettes and liquor." Therefore, the suggestion is that officials are essentially asking for an inducement to render the service. In the early 1980s, prestige brand domestic cigarettes such as Phoenix (*Fenghuang*) and Peony (*Mudan*) from Shanghai or Double Happiness (*Shuangxi*) from Beijing or the even more difficult to obtain brands of Red Pagoda Mountain (*Hongta Shan*) and Double Nine (*Da Chong Jiu*) from Yunnan Province were the more suitable for these occasions. Filterless local brands, at a fraction of the cost of prestige brands, were bought only for personal consumption and were not suitable as gifts. In the late 1980s and 1990s, American and British cigarettes became readily available to Chinese without foreign currency, and they also entered the guanxi circuits. Alcoholic spirits are often given in conjunction with cigarettes for "pulling guanxi." The following saying confirms the special importance of cigarettes and alcholic spirits:

Shou liu dan, zhayao bao, ershi xiang bo ke qiang

Hand grenades, a satchel of dynamite, twenty rounds from a Mauser pistol

The analogies made here are to bottles of spirits or beer, a box of cakes and pastries, and packs of twenty cigarettes, enough ammunition to storm any fortress by way of the "back door." In a similar vein, a supply agent from Guizhou Province on a train heading for Xinjiang Province to make a purchase order of gasoline for his factory, was confident he could win a major purchase. Pointing to the several cases of famous Guizhou Maotai spirits he had brought along, he said, "We have prepared all the artillery shells. These things are very effective" ("Women paodan dou zhunbei haole. Zhexie dongxi hen youxiao").

From the early 1980s to the early 1990s, there has been a price inflation as well as a gift inflation in China. A bottle of Maotai liquor cost only 11 yuan in 1982 before any price increases, but 140 yuan by 1992. Favors, which used to require just a dinner in payment, ten years later required much more in compensation. Money was seldom given, for it would deprive the relationship of a personal basis and insult or scare off the recipient. Large sums of money were considered an escalation of guanxi exchange from the socially and legally tolerable to the more dangerous and unambiguously illegal realm of bribery and corruption. In the ten years from 1982 to 1992, however, money gifts in certain contexts became more acceptable socially and more popular, their legal status having been assured by increasing market forces which sanction payment for services rendered.

A railroad supply agent named Chen Minglu remembered that back in 1978 when he first started working, simply opening up a new pack of cigarettes, offering a few to a potential guanxi, and then discreetly leaving the box of remaining cigarettes behind when he left, was enough to cement relations. In 1990, I picked up a lot of conversation on how drivers have become more and more arrogant, to the point that if you give them a pack of cigarettes, they will consider such a paltry gift an insult and throw it aside and ignore it right in front of you. Indeed, this was exactly my own experience on one occasion. Drivers in the 1990s now frequently refuse to be thanked for their labors with a home-cooked meal, but request to be paid in money.

With the inflationary spiraling of gifts and the changing types of gifts considered appropriate for different kinds of occasions, needs, and social ranking of persons, the question emerges of how a social consensus is formed on what is an appropriate gift to give. I put this question to two middle-aged technical advisers who frequently travel around the country: given that guanxixue gifts are secret and not aboveboard, how do they or others know how much or what to give? They explained that there are two ways of finding out. First, among close friends a lot of information is exchanged. Friends will tell you what they did to get something and how much they spent on a gift to la guanxi. Of course the recipients of gifts seldom reveal how much they received, but the givers will usually tell. Second, among anonymous strangers, especially on trains, people will talk in casual conversation. You might ask, "How much did you give? 100 or 200 yuan?" His or her response might be to laugh and say, "That's hardly enough at all." You'll then ask, "400 or 500 yuan?" He'll say with scornful amusement, "How can you think that's really presentable?" ("Na hai nade chulai?"). Then you'll ask, "800 to 900 yuan?" And finally he'll say, "That's closer to the mark." Then you will know how much to give for a specific purpose, they said with grins on their faces.

Initiation of Guanxi Exchange

Part of the "art" involved in guanxixue is in knowing that one gets one's way not by observing formal and bureaucratic regulations or by going through proper channels, but by creatively seeking out unofficial routes, detours, and shortcuts to get around the officially recognized ways of doing things. Chen Minglu, the railroad supply agent, remembers how when he first started his job in 1978, he was ignorant of guanxixue and very "ingenuous" (laoshi). On his business trips to see potential suppliers of materials, he presented himself to them by dutifully showing a formal letter of introduction from his work unit and requesting to buy supplies. With such a formal introduction, no one paid any attention to him. They would always tell him to come back in a few days because the person in charge was not there. He wasted a lot of time sitting around in hotels and waiting to be called. Gradually he realized that a letter with an official seal on it was useless without the careful work of establishing personal relationships.

The first step in the successful initiation of guanxi exchange is finding the appropriate guanxi target person. If the target person is unable to help, then no matter how many gifts or banquets, the task will not be accomplished. If the target person is an official, one must ascertain that he or she is still in a decision-making position, and not retired or without jurisdiction over the matter at hand.

Once the correct person for guanxi overtures has been selected, and the familiarity base has been presented, the next concern is to find the most skillful and diplomatic way of signaling to the other party the intention of engaging in exchange. One needs to find out if the person is amenable to granting aid in return for gifts, and what he or she would most appreciate in a gift. These questions must be presented in a subtle and tactful manner so that one receives answers without appearing to ask questions.

According to a middle-aged cadre, this information may be obtained secondhand from the target person's friends, family members, or colleagues. Through the mediation of an intermediary, one can also arrange to go to the other's home to feel the person out about the receptivity to a potential request or what might be a desirable gift. This cadre described a characteristic scene. A person wishing to establish guanxi goes to the home of an official who he believes can help him, and after some polite bantering, casually suggests to him, "Your wristwatch is an old one, would you perhaps like to change it for a new digital one? I have a way of getting a good one." At some point before or after the offer, this person may in the course of conversation make the request, or the request may be made long after the gift has been delivered. If the other replies something to the effect, "Come to think of it, I wouldn't mind a change, but haven't had the opportunity to buy a new watch myself," then the deal is pretty much sealed. A skilled transaction is carried out through suggestion and innuendo; direct or outright requests are avoided.

In the art of guanxi the burden is on the recipient to accept the gift proffered. Guanxixue shares with Marcel Mauss's tripartite formula for "total prestation" "the obligation to give, the obligation to receive, and the obligation to repay" (1967:10–11). The middle part of the formula is reflected in the culturally imposed difficulty and embarrassment of refusing a gift overture. Most Chinese accept gifts even though they would rather not go through the trouble involved in repaying for at least three reasons. First, it would be a loss of face to refuse, as it is an admission of an inability to repay. Second, declining to accept sends antisocial signals to the giver that one does not want to establish a relationship of mutual aid with that person. Third, most people welcome the opportunity to expand their guanxi network and are aware that it involves both going into debt and putting others in debt. Should the recipient find it impossible to gratify the giver's specific request, an alternative countergift serves as a discreet message to the original giver that the debt has been paid off.

The task of initiating guanxi exchange is a delicate one, especially since one must couch a request in such a way that a refusal will not jeopardize the whole relationship. For example, on a visit to his home village in Hubei Province, Guo Lanrui, a social science researcher from Beijing who accompanied me, was besieged by the adult children of his peasant sister to exercise his guanxi with his old classmate, now the county town magistrate, to get them transferred into the town. They no longer wanted to "cultivate the fields" (zhongtian), that is, they did not want to remain peasants: agricultural work was too tiring, there was no money in it, and they had a hard time selling their rice. Guo was put into a difficult dilemma between his obligations to his kin and his reluctance to embarrass himself and compromise his relationship with the county magistrate by making a personal request. "This matter is really difficult to broach [with the magistrate]" ("Zhe shi zhen buhao kaikou"), complained Guo to a friend in the bus we were riding. His friend advised that the most diplomatic solution would be to put his request for his kin in writing, instead of approaching the magistrate directly. That way, the magistrate would not be put on the spot, but "would be given some leeway" (*geita yidian yudi*) to quietly ignore the letter if he could not, or did not want to help. This would save the magistrate the embarrassment of rejecting Guo's request directly, and Guo the embarrassment of receiving a direct rejection. Thus, no matter what the outcome of this guanxi overture, the long-standing classmate and native-place relationships would not be jeopardized.

The Occasion and Form of Gift-Giving: Discreetness and Coercion

A third tactic in the art of gift-giving is the attention to the occasion or context for giving gifts and the discreet way in which a gift is given. One socially astute factory worker put it this way: "The most important rule is that you take the gift straight to a person's home [*song shang men*], or give it when no one else is around. Otherwise you will embarrass the person in front of others and he'll hit you with a barrage of formulaic official language [*da guanqiang*]. He'll act really upright and proper and utter with indignation, 'This is irregular wind' [*bu zheng zhi feng*], 'I don't engage in such dealings!'" Therefore understanding the correct context and form in which to give gifts avoids embarrassment and rejection. Gifts are often delivered to people's homes under cover of night.

Pulling guanxi through gift-giving is such a recognized feature of the society that stories and jokes about the practice circulate. Two accounts illustrate the importance of tact and the appropriate context for gift-giving. Chen Minglu, the railroad supply agent, told an amusing story of how a neighbor's family, simple working-class people, were initiated into the art of guanxi. A member of their family had died at the hospital. The hospital had a temporary interment room for the deceased, but if the body had not been claimed by relatives and family after two days, a daily fee was charged. The family wished to avoid paying the fee while they waited a few extra days for relatives from out-of-town to arrive in Beijing for a proper funeral service before cremation. Through friends, they found out that the doorkeeper of the interment room had a soft spot for gifts and might be persuaded to waive their fees to the hospital. Lacking proper finesse in the art of gift-giving, the family tried to shove a bottle of spirits and a carton of cigarettes at the doorkeeper right in the presence of many other people. The latter had no choice but to draw himself upright and vehemently refuse to accept. That night, acting upon the advice of a friend, the family went to the doorkeeper's home and presented him with the gifts again and made their request. Accepting the gifts this time, he admonished them for having put him in an embarrassing position in front of so many people at the hospital, but also agreed to allow the body to stay there longer free of charge.

Another example given to me of the pitfalls of staging gift-giving in public occurred in a provincial town in the south and drew the attention of neighbors in an apartment compound. A local cadre had a reputation for always accepting gifts. He became the guanxi target of a woman who planned to persuade him to help her son secure employment by giving him a live chicken, but she very indiscreetly went about telling everybody her plan. Of course word of her intentions reached the ears of this official, and he was disturbed to find out that most of the community knew the woman's plan. So when she came bearing the gift, he was resolved to make a public and dramatic refusal in the hopes of brightening his tarnished public image. He took the chicken onto the fourth floor balcony of his apartment and, before onlookers in the compound, soundly berated the woman for trying to buy him. Then with a dramatic flourish to show the indignation suffered by his upright character, he threw the poor chicken, strident squawks, fluttering feathers and all, off the balcony to the ground below. After this event, the word was that although the community was thoroughly entertained by his performance, it was still not persuaded of his upright character.

Besides the importance of discreetness in the occasion and the means by which one presents a gift, there is another element frequently found in guanxi overtures. This is the element of coerciveness, aggressiveness, and threat. Sometimes the art of guanxi involves the exercise of aggressive humility and coercive generosity. The following vignette, which I would describe as a hostile gift overture, was told to me by a worker who had witnessed the incident and knew the subject personally.

A worker wanted to get a few authorized days off from work to attend to some personal business. He first tried to give presents in private to the factory manager, but the latter declined. So he cunningly worked out a way to make the manager accept. He waited for an opportunity when the manager was in the presence of many other workers to give the gift to him. This time he offered the gift in a different way. He said to the manager, "Here is the gift which my father, your old comrade-in-arms [*zhan you*], asked me to deliver to you. Please accept it so his feelings are not hurt." Both the worker and the manager knew that the story about his father being an old friend of his was made up, so the real aim of the gift was apparent to the manager. In front of so many people, however, the manager was in danger of losing face if he refused to accept the gift unless he could immediately come up with a good reason. He could not say in public that the reason why he cannot accept is because he does not want to help the worker, since he would then appear ungenerous. Nor could he call the worker a liar, since he was not ready to have the worker lose that much face. Perhaps caught by surprise by the ingenius way the gift was thrust upon him, the manager was not quick enough to extricate himself from the situation tactfully. So all he could do was to accept. Later when the resourceful worker made the inevitable re-quest for authorized days off from work, the manager would have to honor it because so many people had seen him accept the gift. Should he refuse the request, the worker could tell all those people that the manager had accepted a gift without feeling any compunction to re-pay, then all over the factory people would be talking about how the manager lacked renqing.

This guanxi transaction involved a cadre who makes decisions af-fecting people's lives, being coaxed, tricked, or coerced into a position of indebtedness where he would have to make concessions to the giver of the gift. It represents how the skillful deployment of guanxi tactics can reverse the power relations between officials and those whom they rule. It shows how, without resorting to revolution, guan-xixue provides a leverage for control by those in weak social posi-tions. Much like the Malaysian peasants described by James Scott (1985), who appeal to the precapitalist noblesse oblige or notions of virtuous charity to manipulate their employers, guanxi tacticians also make use of ethics, rather than just conform to them.

At the same time, the benefits that guanxixue can bring may also be merely transitory. Another person who was present at this scene thought that the worker's action was too shortsighted. He may have gained the upper hand for now by obligating the manager to grant him the request, but he is bound to suffer in the future. Eventually the manager will find some excuse to get even with him and make him "wear small shoes" (*chuan xiao xie*), that is, make his life difficult.

The tactics of coercive generosity and veiled threat displayed in the example of the hostile gift overture are reminiscent of the "thick and black learning" described by Li Zongwu, writing in the early twentieth century (1990:17–19). Li outlined six types of "thick and black learning" which can help in a man's quest for official position. First, a man must have "empty time" (*kong*), that is, he must make time and devote himself solely to this enterprise, and he must also have patience and perseverance. Second, he must know how to "drill" (*zuan*), that is, to create an opening for himself or seize any opportunity to further his own interests. Third, a person must know how to "brag" and "boast" (*chong*), and have rhetorical skills of persuasion. Fourth, a person cannot do without the ability to "flatter" (*peng*), especially superiors. Fifth, if flattery fails, an office-seeker can try "threatening" (*kong*), or a mild form of blackmailing. Sixth, "giving" presents (*song*) are also effective, and one must discriminate between those occasions calling for "big giving" (cash) and those calling for "small giving" (tea, ham, or a restaurant banquet).

In discussing Li's category of "threat" with Wang Haifeng, a woman student studying in the United States, I asked her if this was still relevant in the contemporary art of guanxi. She was convinced that it was, and thought up a hypothetical situation to illustrate its relevance today. Jia is an entrepreneur who wants to obtain some bricks from Yi, an official of a brick factory. Jia knows that Yi once used the back door to get his son a job. So Jia hints subtly to Yi that he possesses this knowledge, and if Yi does not do him the favor, Jia might spread this information around, embarrassing Yi. Jia might say casually to Yi: "Bricks are really hard to come by, I know. I really don't want to trouble you, but it's not as big a request as some others I know who have gotten their daughters jobs through the back door." The word "daughter" is substited for the word "son," so that the threat is carefully veiled and not too direct. This subtle way of threatening means that Yi cannot be sure that Jia really meant it as a threat or if it was just coincidence. Yi would still want to play it safe, so the bricks are granted to Jia to keep him quiet. A veiled and indirect threat is better than an open and confrontational threat, because the latter could very well backfire on Jia. If Jia should incur Yi's anger and hostility, then Yi would think of endless ways to use his position to beat him down.

Etiquette and Dissimulation

The phrase "throwing banquets and giving gifts" (*qingke songli*) signify two very important social activities in Chinese culture, activities laden with the symbolism of social solidarity. When these two activities are incorporated into the art of guanxi, they impart an aura of renqing to an otherwise instrumental relationship. Since there is an unwritten social convention that guanxixue must accord with proper renqing principles and etiquette, care is often taken not to allow the instrumental nature of the relationship to become too obvious. For example, in order to obtain a favor, a person may consider the timing of the presentation of the gift. To present a gift out of the blue is socially awkward, since the instrumental nature of the gift becomes all too obvious. If a person can afford to wait longer for the relationship to firm up, then it is best to give at suitable occasions such as weddings and the lunar New Year. These occasions are usually the sites for the circulation of renqing or "expressive gifts," which cement relations of kinship, friendship, and superior-subordinate sentiments without a clear objective of tactical advantage in mind. For this very reason, that is, their renqing associations, these occasions are especially suitable for deploying guanxi gift-giving because the instrumental nature of the gifts will be submerged with the renqing features, and appealing to "sentiments" (qing) is often a much more effective way of indebting someone.

Gift- or banquet-giving both involve much etiquette and polite rituals, which serve to mask or mute the instrumental nature of the gift and to save face for both sides. Efforts are made by the gift-giver or dinner host to leave the impression that he or she does not regard the gift or dinner as a crude bribe or mere payment for services rendered, but as a social occasion for establishing good relations. Consequently, it is considered hopelessly indelicate and in bad form to make a request at the exact time or occasion that the gift or banquet is given.

Instead, one should give a gift well in advance of making a request. Such occasions as Chinese New Year's, the birth of a child, weddings, and so on provide good opportunities to "lay the groundwork" (da dizi) for future requests with gifts. One must also take care not to give one's guest a feeling that behind the dishes laid out before him or her, lies some ulterior motives (you mudi). This is difficult to do since most people are sensitive to others' motivations. This saying reminds people that being cautious and patient in cultivating social relations will often reap big rewards:

Fang chang xian diao da yu.

Let the line out far and one catches big fish.

As with reaching out into deeper waters, drawing out the time between giving and requesting, between receiving and repaying, improves the chances that the target will agree to help. As a result, the art of guanxi requires much shrewdness and considerable time and patience on the part of its practitioners.

Sometimes the very discreet way in which a gift is presented may result in some embarrassing misunderstandings. A middle-aged cadre told me a story about a man who wanted to retire a few years ahead of the legal retirement age. At New Year's, he instructed his wife to deliver a basket of pears and a carton of cigarettes to the home of the cadre in charge of making the decision about him, leaving only his name in the basket. She did not remember the cadre's apartment number correctly and delivered the gift to his puzzled neighbor instead. Due to the reticence in the art of guanxi to make explicit the real purpose of a gift, the mistake was not recognized on the spot. The unfortunate couple not only lost their gift investment, but also lost face as other parties soon figured out their intentions.

Ritualized patterns of conduct exhibited at the moment of presentation further illustrate the etiquette of dissembling crude instrumentality in guanxi transactions. In typical gift-giving sessions, the gift-giver presents the gift with self-deprecatory remarks on the meanness of the gift. The recipient declines the gift with a flourish, usually more than once, protesting, "We're old friends, you need not go to this trouble," or "This is too much, I really don't need this." The gift-giver will persist and finally the other accepts, saying, "You are much too polite," or "It's really embarrassing that you went to such trouble." Sometimes this ritual can be very vehement and intense, turning into a culturally rehearsed choreography of push and shove, the giver pressing the gift on a vociferously reluctant recipient. In my own experience, it seemed that working-class people are more insistent and take more physical measures than intellectuals to assure acceptance of a gift or dinner. These insistent movements of the body forcefully express the exaggerated modesty and generosity of actors in the art of guanxi.

As with gift-giving, banqueting in Chinese culture is not merely a tactic in the art of guanxi, but is also an important ritual in the social sphere. Weddings are occasions not only for gift-giving between the families of the bride and groom and on the part of the wedding guests, but also for the throwing of lavish banquets for relatives, neighbors, and friends. Banquets of several tables serving ten people each bring much social prestige to the hosts, even if they must go into debt for years to afford them. Other social occasions for inviting persons to a special dinner are the visit of out-of-town relatives or friends, the departure of a friend or relative for a distant place, a promotion at work or the winning of prize money for being voted model worker, the celebration of Chinese New Year's, and so on.

Banquets and dinners subject both host and guest to a similar set of cultural etiquettes as entailed in gift-giving. Out of either a consideration for polite form, the desire not to burden their would-be host, or the reluctance to owe a debt to their host, guests usually demur at the invitation to dinner. The hosts for their part usually respond by insisting more vigorously, sometimes to the point of physically dragging their guests into their home or to a restaurant, as the case may be. In my first days in China, my husband and I were riding in a car in the company of a Chinese friend who pointed out a strange scene on the side of the road. A small group of people were gathered around two men and a woman outside a house. One of the men was shouting at the other man and woman, and trying to drag them both toward the house, despite their loud protests and resistance. Several times, amid a flurry of dirt kicked up by the latter's dragging feet, the man almost succeeded in getting them into the house, only to have them wriggle out of his grasp. With a twinkle in his eyes, our friend asked if we knew what they were doing. Surmising what seemed to me the obvious, I replied that the scene must be a domestic quarrel between husband and wife, with someone trying to protect the wife. Our friend gave a hearty laugh and explained that, on the contrary, one family was trying to persuade another family, probably friends or relatives, to stay for dinner.

Such exaggerated hospitality continues once the guests are inside the house. When it is time to be seated, there is often a minor ritual struggle over who is to occupy the seats of honor, with everyone determined not to sit at the center of the table. Round tables are no deterrent to observing the protocol of seating, as guests of honor always sit farthest away from the door. During the course of the dinner, hosts do their utmost to keep their guests' bowls or plates perpetually heaped with food, and for men, to fill their glasses to the brim each time they take a sip of beer, wine, or spirits. There is a constant chatter by hosts of how modest and simple the meal is, and by guests of how sumptuous is the repast laid out before them.

When banqueting is employed as a tactic of the art of guanxi, it remains embedded in the larger symbolic tradition of the rituals and etiquettes of banqueting in general. What distinguishes banqueting in the art of guanxi from other kinds of banqueting is its role as a medium of not only social, but especially economic and political exchange and its stronger binding power on the guest to repay. Although guanxi banqueting has more narrowly defined objectives and interests than the diffuse social-solidarity and social-prestige goals of banqueting in general, it retains the other's basic form, language, and etiquette.

Since most Chinese urban families already spend about 70 percent or more of their total family income on daily food alone, being invited by someone to dinner is not taken lightly. Dinners require extensive preparation in scouting out different markets to buy various kinds of meat and vegetables, and in cutting and cooking. Often the whole family must get involved in what is a major project. One can generally tell from the tone of the host and the occasion and context in which the dinner is given whether there are any hidden "motives" (*mudi*) behind the invitation. From the host's point of view, treating someone to a dinner with the intention of "pulling guanxi," whether at home or in a restaurant where it is even more costly, is therefore reserved for larger favors. For example, the desire for a job transfer or to get one's child into a good nursery with a long waiting list might call for throwing a banquet, whereas a request for a day off at work would rely merely on a small gift or just on general good relations with one's superior.

A large amount of banqueting is also done in guanxi transactions in official business, surreptitiously paid for with public funds. When officials from a higher administrative level go down periodically to lower-level units to conduct investigations on productivity, sanitation, birth-control-policy implementation, and so forth, they are often treated to lavish banquets by units eager to please them so that they will write good reports. Factory supply agents can draw from a special fund in their factory budget set aside for such purposes when they engage in intricate guanxi dealings to secure raw material shipments for their factories.

The Obligation to Repay

In the art of social relationships the principle of social obligation complements the principle of "familiarity" and the orientation toward relying on others. The obligation to help out one's personal circle of family, relatives, and friends is experienced both as an internalized social norm and as an external social sanction. A number of people all gave the same two basic reasons why they felt compelled to help their "guanxi households" on request. First, one has to take into consideration one's standing in "public opinion" (*shehui yulun*) and to avoid losing face in the eyes of others. People also do not "feel" right if they let someone down or if they do not live up to obligations. Especially among workers, the sense of "righteous code of brotherhood" (*gemenr yiqi*) is strong, and one would be apprehensive of being called "lacking in brotherhood" (*bugou gemenr*). Second, one may feel obliged to help others with a certain sense of self-interest and material benefit in mind. That is to say, the obligation to help can arise merely from not wishing to jeopardize a relationship in case someday one may need to rely on that guanxi. So one should avoid "dismantling the bridge after crossing the river" (*guo he chai qiao*). According to the worker who quoted this saying, people live in a more or less finite circle of social acquaintances and run around and around on the same tracks. If one does not repay guanxi debts and spend some effort to keep up good relations with people, a day is bound to come when one needs to cross the same river again, but will find no bridge left.

The Chinese notion of "face" is an important mechanism through which both obligation and reciprocity operate. Although many different cultures have a notion of face, perhaps few of them have as much cultural elaboration on face as the Chinese. In a classic work on the subject, Hu Hsien Chin distinguishes between two Chinese conceptions of face corresponding to two different words representing "face" (Hu 1944). *Lian* (*lien* in the original) refers to the public recognition of the ego's moral integrity, the result of a deep internalization of society's fundamental code of ethics. Violation or loss of lian results in social ostracism and the collapse of ego as a whole. Not being primarily linked to evaluations of ultimate moral worth, *mianzi* (*mien-tzu* in the original) is gained or lost in the jockeying for social prestige and social advantage. One accumulates mianzi by showing oneself capable, wealthy, generous, and possessed of a wide network of social relationships (1944:61). I found that mianzi is a more common factor constraining guanxi reciprocity than lian. In conversations regarding the art of guanxi, I seldom heard the word lian. This greater importance of mianzi in the art of guanxi indicates that as a pragmatic set of tactical maneuvers, the art of guanxi eschews the universalistic and transcendental morality associated with lian and instead is guided by a set of situational and relational ethics. The flexibility of situational ethics allows a person to press for social and personal advantages without jeopardizing self-esteem and social standing and without prescribing fixed social roles and expectations.

Mianzi is a combination of a sense of moral imperatives, social honor, and self-respect. A friend in Beijing who used to work as a factory staff member in the city of Loyang offered her help to me, saying that should I have trouble obtaining train tickets in that city, I should simply look up her friend who works in the Loyang train station ticket office. People who work there always keep a few extra tickets unsold in their pockets or desk drawers, even though they may tell customers that they are all sold out. In reply to my query as to the reason behind this practice, she patiently explained: "People feel obliged to keep tickets for their friends, just in case their friends make requests. It is very embarrassing not being able to help one's friends; one would not have face [*meiyou mianzi*]. People cannot raise their heads up in front of friends again after letting them down." When a person lets a friend down and is said not to have mianzi, it is not so much that he or she has violated some fundamental ethics, but that the person has lost social standing.

My informant Chen Xiaoxiong confessed that the common saying *si yao mianzi, huo shou zui* (Wanting face so bad; willing to suffer alive for it) applies to himself. When a friend asks him for a favor, though he knows that the task is difficult and will involve a lot of time and effort, he will still try his best to help his friend because it is a matter of mianzi. On the one hand, his sense of self-respect as well as the friendship are at stake. On the other hand, he does not want the word to get around that he is unreliable. In short said he, "Mianzi is what keeps the relationship together."

Chinese may go to great and comic lengths to establish face as illustrated by a middle-aged skilled worker:

Very often, if a family is poor, it tries to hide it. In daily meals they scrimp and scrape, but when guests come, they will buy the best foods, which are way beyond their means. You often hear of stories where a young man without a regular job and from a poor family will impress his girlfriend by dressing up, borrowing someone's nice apartment, and inviting her "home" to a fancy meal. It's after marriage that the girlfriend sees his true [economic] circumstances, and wants a divorce, but it's too late then. We Chinese love face [*ai mianzi*] because face gives you social status, others will respect you and be willing to enter into social relationships with you.

Indeed, the saying "His mianzi is greater than others" means that this person has won social prestige for helping many people and a reputation for having the social skills and social connections to do so. This person stands in a superior position over those indebted to his or her magnanimity.

The principle of indebtedness or reciprocity acts as a sort of safeguard against guanxi abuses. Whenever a gift, banquet, or favor is accepted, there is the obligation to reciprocate. Indeed, it can be said that implicit in the very act of accepting is an agreement in trust to repay in another form at a later date. Mauss's observation that in archaic exchange the thing given "is at the same time property and a possession, a pledge and a loan, an object sold and an object bought, a deposit, a mandate, a trust" (Mauss 1967:22) applies to Chinese guanxi exchange. The thing given in the art of guanxi is not an inert, objectified commodity such as is exchanged in a pure monetary transaction, but is imprinted with social and moral imperatives of the relationship between donor and recipient. The constraining principle of reciprocity endows guanxi exchange with the character of a "total prestation" because the exchange is at one and the same time an economic, legal, and moral act.

I asked a Beijing worker what would happen if a person reneged on his or her repayment; when a gift bestowed in anticipation of a return favor does not meet with the expected service promised implicitly with the receipt of the gift? He replied:

> Usually this does not happen because people are not so stupid. They know that if they make a practice of not repaying their debts, sooner or later they will gain a bad reputation, lose friends, and be ostracized. Also, they may need you again in the future to help them on something. So people seldom look on renqing so lightly. Of course, if you do something for someone and nothing comes of your efforts for your own benefit, then the whole thing is a failure. But my attitude is that one can't measure and calculate everything so precisely.

The principle of reciprocity, often translated in terms of considerations of face, takes on a role in guanxi exchange similar to the role of codified law in monetary transactions.

The same Beijing worker responded to my next question: How does one measure the value of the good or service being exchanged, in order to repay appropriately?

It's hard to fix an exact value on something [an object of exchange]. It is often very subjective. Generally, value is determined by the timeliness and rarity of what is given. Say a person needs something done urgently, and you are able to help him, right when he most needs it. He will be filled with gratitude and forever indebted to you. Sometimes it is good to do a lot for someone, more that he can pay back, so that you have the upper hand over him. Since he is so obliged to you, you are at leisure to call on him any time for help.

In guanxi exchange, there are no objective or universal exchange rates. The monetary worth of what is given, although important, is not the sole consideration in deciding how much to repay. The timeliness of the gift, the rarity of the gift or service, the status of the person giving the gift, the extent of the recipient's indebtedness to the donor, as well as the closeness or intensity of the relationship between donor and recipient, are all factors in establishing the total value of the gift. Since there is no fixed value for each gift, but a value arising out of the context of each gift-giving situation and contingent on the particular persons involved, repayment often causes anxiety and lengthy deliberations over how and how much to repay.

The indeterminancy of value may cause Chinese to agonize over what to give, but the concern to prolong social relationships constrain them always to give generously. This orientation as to how one should conduct one's social relations is evident in these common sayings:

Ni jing wo yi chi, wo jing ni yi zhang.

You honor me with a foot; I honor you with a yard.

Shou ren dian shui zhi en, dang yi yong quan xiang bao.

Receive a droplet of generosity; repay like a gushing spring.

A repayment of merely equivalent value tends to end an ongoing guanxi, since the other person is not indebted anymore to respond to a future request. Therefore in order to maintain one's moral superiority, the best policy is always to keep the other indebted. It can be said that built into guanxixue is a propensity for escalation.

The value of what a person gives or does in repayment is a factor in perpetuating an exchange relationship, but the interval of time before repayment is also a consideration. Speaking from a donor's viewpoint, Ding Jian, the worker at the beginning of the book who mobilized his guanxi network to perform a great favor to the doctor, said with a trace of self-satisfaction, "Once you have done someone a favor, you don't have to reclaim it right away, you can just leave it there for a while. It can lie there unreclaimed for as long as four or five years even, before you look up your debtor and ask him for help. It is better to be in this position where the other person owes you something, the longer the better, because you are in a superior position in future dealings."

From the debtor's perspective, there are also practical and social constraints against immediate repayment. According to Chen the carpenter, when a person is granted a favor and repays it immediately, "it is the worst and most foolish kind of social relationship." Even though one may be in the disadvantageous position of the debtor, the extension of a debt is what one should aim for in the art of guanxi, because a debt keeps a relationship open. It is true that the person with higher social position might want to quickly repay a person of lower status and opportunities who has been of service to him so that the latter will not have occasion to make any requests in the future, but in general, leaving a debt unpaid encourages the other to call in his or her debt with a request for help, thus rendering that person dependent on and indebted to you. In other words, an unpaid debt provides opportunities for further cultivating the relationship. According to Chen, the common saying "business transaction in one hammer blow" (*yi chuizi mai mai*) succinctly describes the short-sightedness and social awkwardness of rushing to neutralize a debt. By repaying immediately and ending the relationship so soon, one not only gives up a chance to cultivate a long-term guanxi, but the relationship is also demeaned into an overt instrumentality of "buying and selling" (*mai mai*). As in the case of gift-giving in which the instrumental nature of the gift must be masked, the extension of the time before repayment emphasizes the strength and continuity of the personal tie rather than the objects or favors exchanged through this tie.

The indeterminancy of exchange value and the prolonging of the interval before repayment are assumptions reflected in the conduct of this worker who refused monetary payment for his service. Jiang had taken up the hobby of carving stone seals in various styles of classical script. He would stay up into the middle of the night practicing and refining his art. One day the leaders of his unit approached him and asked if he would carve a pair of large seals bearing the name of his work unit to be used in stamping contracts and documents. On completion of the job, the leaders were pleased and wanted to pay him for his materials, time, and labor. Jiang declined graciously, but adamantly, declaring that he enjoyed carving and that it was his duty to contribute to the collective. Privately he explained to me: "What good is money? I take it, spend it and it's gone. By offering the service free, I create a lasting relationship with the leaders. They will remember what I did and will always treat me well in the future—they will give me days off when I ask, and give me special consideration. To be paid is to be shortsighted, it is just 'business transaction in one hammer blow.'" For Jiang, to accept money in payment is to close off his chances of establishing a long-term give-and-take relationship with his unit leaders. Money, then, is perceived as less of a gain and less secure than the social investment of incurring obligation and producing indebtedness, an action that will bear fruit for a longer time.

The complex tactics and etiquettes of the art of guanxi suggest that although it is instrumentally motivated, it is not an amoral or totally rationalized pattern of conduct. Its practice is embedded in a system of situational and relational ethics which promote personalistic loyalty and mutual obligation. That is to say, the art of guanxi does possess an ethics, albeit one that is different from, and often at odds with, the universalistic ethics of socialist nationalism and the formal impersonal procedures espoused by the state. At the same time, guanxixue is also different from the rationalized and impersonal exchange relations of capitalism.

On the Recent Past of Guanxixue: Traditional Forms and Historical (Re-)Emergence

What are the precursors or the roots of guanxixue in the traditional cultural repertoire? How did the art of guanxi come to assume new life despite the fundamental transformations (economic, political, and ideological) brought by the Communist Revolution? What sort of trajectory has the development of guanxixue followed in state-socialist culture? To what do people in urban China attribute the emergence or reemergence of guanxixue?

Three Official Histories

In accounting for the reemergence of guanxixue, official discourse generally attributes its recent vigor to three causes. First, as I pointed out in Chapter 1, contemporary guanxixue is said to be based on "traditional guanxixue" (*chuantong guanxixue*), which comes from China's thousands of years of "feudalism" and its "natural" or subsistence economy, which produced a reliance on "blood ties" (*xueyuan guanxi*) and a "clan system" (*zongfa zhidu*) (Yuan 1981; Yu 1987: 103).

Second, the blame for contemporary guanxixue is laid at the doorstep of the Cultural Revolution. The 1950s are nostalgically recalled as a period when social order reigned and people acted properly according to regulations:

Remembering back to the first years after Liberation, we see that interpersonal relations were normal. When people wanted to get something done, they generally went through organizational guanxi [i.e., observed proper bureaucratic procedure] and mutual-aid guanxi to accomplish their tasks. At that time, if people wanted to employ improper [*bu zhengdang*] guanxi to obtain personal goals, they would be subject to the condemnation of public opinion. Furthermore, they themselves would feel embarrassed. (Yuan 1981:3)

Regrettably, according to this official view, this state of affairs was greatly harmed by the "Gang of Four" and their Cultural Revolution. Damage to socialist morals by factional struggles during the Cultural Revolution unleashed "feudal remnants" of thought. Furthermore, the breakdown of social order and loss of organizational discipline created by the Cultural Revolution forced everyone to rely not on state and Party organization but on personalistic relationships to secure everyday survival (Yuan 1981).

This official view implies that once the state restores social order and discipline through a reinstitutionalization of state power as it existed before the Cultural Revolution, guanxi practice will diminish significantly. My fieldwork evidence suggests quite the opposite, that in the aftermath of the Cultural Revolution, guanxi practices and guanxi awareness have both increased at an accelerated rate.

A third official reason for the prevalence of the art of guanxi is that with the economic reforms and the opening up of the country to the world, especially the capitalist West, "bourgeois individualism" (*zichan jieji geren zhuyi*) and its ethic of self-gain have infiltrated China (Yu 1987:104–5). According to this view of the cause of guanxixue, the "deviant winds" (*bu zheng zhi feng*) that plague officialdom are examples of how officials have turned to narrow self-interest without regard for the good of the larger whole. Similarly, in official eyes, the "bad" turn that the "social climate" (*shehui fengqi*) has taken among the people reflects the same individualism and selfishness that a concern with material benefits and the abandonment of socialist ideals have engendered.

This third official explanation, that guanxixue arises out of the "bourgeois individualism" brought into the country since the opening up to the West, coincides with the first appearances of the phrases "guanxixue" and "guanxiwang" in China's official newspapers and journals. In a random survey of the newspaper *Renmin Ribao* (People's Daily) from 1957 to 1987, my research assistant Sun Hong, reports that discussions of guanxixue first appeared in the newspaper around 1978, when guanxi practices were condemned as harmful to the country. This date cannot be taken as an objective indication of when the art of guanxi started to emerge in socialist society, because under the conditions of a state-controlled media, it cannot be assumed that the media at any time is a direct reflection of ongoing social processes. It merely shows at what point the state starts to become concerned about guanxixue and decides to take concrete measures against it.

My fieldwork inquiries also show that popular discourse roughly parallels official discourse in the construction of a threefold history for the emergence of the gift economy in socialist society, but also adds significant interpretations of its own. The notion that guanxixue emerged sometime during the Cultural Revolution seemed to be the most common response. Some who did not subscribe to this genealogy of guanxixue insisted guanxixue has always been part of Chinese culture. Others believe that guanxixue started around 1978–79 with the economic reform period and opening up to the outside world.

Guanxixue and Chinese Culture

Those who gave the second type of history for guanxixue assert that reliance on established social relationships to get things done has had a long tradition in China. Old folk sayings that bear the marks of the bygone imperial era were frequently recited to me to show the venerableness of guanxixue:

Chufang you ren hao chi fan;
chaoli you ren hao zuo guan.

If you know someone in the kitchen, it's easier to eat; if you know someone in the court, it's easier to become an official.

Yiren de dao, jiquan sheng tian.

When a person attains the Way, his chickens and dogs will also ascend to Heaven. (When a person gets to the top [or gains office], his friends and relatives will also benefit.)

Older people remember that in the old society, such things as giving gifts and banquets in order to curry favor did exist, only these were not referred to as guanxixue, but conceived of as appeals to "human sentiments" (renqing). Before the 1949 Revolution, some say, these appeals were especially important in finding a job in the cities, as practically all jobs were the result of personal introductions by a friend or relative. Using renqing could even get a person out of jail in the old days.

These memories of renqing in the period before the 1949 Revolution are borne out by a study of 316 persons living in the cities of
Shanghai, Tianjin, Wuxi, and Beijing in the 1940s conducted by Olga
Lang. Lang found examples of "nepotism" in four contexts: (1)
employment in government offices, stores, and factories; (2) free
transportation on streetcars and trains; (3) free public utilities, especially electricity; and (4) student scholarships (1946:182–84). Officials and professionals were often helped by kin in their education
who "considered the money given an investment and expected repayment in the form of positions. The refusal to comply was considered a
breach of good faith" (1946:187). Workers, servants, shop assistants,
and coolies were also prone to "nepotism." Although businessmen
tended to favor impersonal hiring on the basis of ability, honesty, and
devotion to work, even this group sometimes gave in to the pressures
of kin obligation.

Much of the literature by Western and Chinese observers and historians of Chinese culture in prerevolutionary and imperial times describe what we could call the "precursors" of socialist guanxixue.
Historian Yang Lien-sheng traces the concept of "reciprocity" (bao)
as a continuous thread running from ancient to late imperial times
(1957). Three sources of the concept of reciprocity, he argues, can be
found in (1) Confucian ethics and philosophy, (2) the knight-errantry
tradition, and (3) Buddhist notions of retribution.

The Confucian stress on affective interpersonal relations and ethics
(lunli), and the notion of ritual propriety (li) in conducting relationships in terms of graded degrees of kinship distance and levels of obligation, have found popular expression in the conduct of renqing principles (Jin 1982; Liang 1949; Fei 1983). "The ethically graded order
[renlun zhixu] of the Way of Confucius and Mencius [followed the
principles of] distinguishing between inside and outside, and between
relationships of closeness and distance. [This order] was opposed to a
universalized humaneness and love" (Zheng 1984:54). In Confucian
ethics, renqing principles were not merely sentiments but also concrete social expressions such as the offering of congratulations or con-
dolences, the giving of gifts on appropriate occasions, and the fulfillment of obligations (Yang 1957:292). Furthermore, the Confucian
emphasis on personal justice in the sense of repaying a kindness and
avenging a wrong done to oneself or a family member (Wen 1982)
played an important role in defining the proper conduct of human
relations.

The Chinese "knight-errant" (youxia) tradition emerged in the Warring States period (403–221 B.C.E.) when displaced warriors and

knights wandered the land looking for patrons (Ch'u 1972:186). These knights-errant cultivated an ethical code of loyalty, commitment, generosity, and self-sacrifice in male friendships (*yiqi*). In subsequent dynasties down to the present, this code was preserved and renewed through popular martial-arts (*wuxia*) literature of male bonds of friendship and sworn brotherhood between knights or martial-arts fighters, who always repaid their social debts (Yang 1957: 296; Liu 1967). Two of the most famous classical novels in which sworn brotherhood and yiqi are displayed are *San Guo Yanyi* (The romance of the three kingdoms) and *Shui Hu Zhuan* (Water margin). In China today the popular sentiment of *germenr yiqi* ("ethical code of brotherhood") can be said to be a modern variant of the ancient knight-errantry tradition.

There is ample scholarship tracing the importance of personalistic and fictive kinship relations in the basic organizational framework of late imperial China. Since kinship was "a dominant element in thought, it manifested itself as a model in various other areas of social life" (Baker 1979:162). These "other areas" included Buddhist monasteries and nunneries, secret societies, and overseas Chinese surname associations.

Even the imperial bureaucracy was threaded through with kinship-like relations of obligation and indebtedness between officials and the people and among officials themselves. The sociologist C. K. Yang found that officialdom in imperial China was always torn between the conflicting ethics of "universalistic value-orientation" derived from bureaucratic impersonalism on the one hand, and Confucian "particularism" and "nepotism" on the other (Yang 1959). Indeed, it has been pointed out that officials were often able to shield their lineages and local communities from imperial taxation and conscriptions for labor or war, as the following folk saying suggests:

Yiba san zhe yixiang ren.

One umbrella serves to shield the people of a whole village. (In Quan 1949:116)

It was for reasons such as these that the imperial bureaucratic system, at least since the Qing dynasty (1644–1911), made it a policy to avoid assigning officials to serve in their native places and to rotate official posts throughout the empire every three years.

In order to provide assistance to his kin and local people, however, an official did not have to rely on the direct power of his own office, but could also count on his good relations with fellow officials (Fei 1968:134). One type of personalistic relationship produced by the imperial examination system, was that between an examiner and the successful candidates who passed the exams supervised by him. The case of Cui Chun, an examiner in the ninth century C.E., illustrates the operation of personal networks in the imperial bureaucracy. One day Cui's wife suggested that he buy some land to bequeath to his descendants. With a smile, he replied, "I have thirty excellent manor houses with rich fields spreading all over the empire. Why should you worry about real estate?" When his wife asked him what he meant, he answered, "You remember the year before last I served as examiner and passed thirty candidates. Are they not excellent estates?" (Quoted in Yang 1957 and Folsom 1968:25).

Another kind of personalistic relationship which operated in late imperial bureaucracy can be found in the *mu-fu* system, a practice of privately hiring provincial consultants who worked for local officials at the county and district levels (Folsom 1968:33–57). The system arose out of a need by local officials, trained only to be amateur Confucian scholars for technical and legal expertise to deal with the practical affairs of local administration. The relationship between an official and the members of his *mu-fu* was not the impersonal relationship of employer and employee, but conceived as the affectively charged one of "host" and "guest," or student and teacher, with the official assuming the courtesy or ritually lower position in the relationship. The imperial government often tried to diminish the close personal ties between the official and his *mu-fu*, as it tried to pry official loyalties away from family, lineage and clan, and native place.

Besides facilitating the conduct of the bureaucracy, personalistic relationships also operated in everyday life among the people. These relationships could be based on kinship ties or other principles of social bonding. In late imperial urban life, native-place ties, much like kinship ties, were an important principle of social organization and cooperation. Sojourners and merchants in a strange city relied on the help provided by a network of people from the same county or region of the empire who spoke a common native dialect (Skinner 1977a). These networks often assumed the forms of guild associations (*huiguan*) or native-place associations (*tongxianghui*).

The high degree of commercialization in late imperial China was not made possible by a set of systematic commercial laws regulating business transactions, since the Chinese legal system was primarily concerned with penal law (Bodde 1981), but by the institution of the "intermediary-guarantor" (van der Sprenkel 1977). Two merchants entering into a contract did so through the introduction and mediation of an intermediary of good reputation who assumed personal responsibility for ensuring that each side kept their word. What gave business agreements security was not a legal system of sanctions, but the personal authority of the intermediary.

So important a role do personalistic relations seem to play in Chinese culture that fieldwork in a county seat in the 1940s led Morton Fried to thematize *kan-ch'ing* (*ganqing*), which he defined as the good or bad quality of a relationship between persons of different social status unrelated by kinship which is cemented with gifts (1953). The quality of *kan-ch'ing* determined how such relationships as those between landlord and tenant, shopowner and shop assistants, merchants and guild members, and gentry and government officers were conducted and what opportunities they produced. For gentry and merchants, cultivating *kan-ch'ing* with officials and bureaucrats could spare them the payment of extra taxes and the duty to quarter government soldiers. For tenants, good *kan-ch'ing* with the landlord meant the possibility of reasonable rents and even loans to tide their families over to another year.

Taken together, this body of literature dealing with imperial and modern China easily leads to the conclusion that Chinese culture is in its essence a personalistic, kinship-oriented one. One problem with this conclusion, it seems to me, is not that it is false or misleading, but that it is simply a truism that fails to situate this aspect of the culture in a dynamic with other changing cultural and social structural features. It is a generalization that "flattens" Chinese culture and makes it uniform, posing an all too symmetrical dichotomy with the West and with a construction of industrial society as rationalized and universalistic. The other problem with this conclusion is that it represents an ahistorical approach to Chinese culture which fails to take into account the historical waxing and waning of personalism and neglects the examination of the changing and variable forms in which personalism is historically constructed and reconstructed. The essentialist conclusion cannot answer the question of why the socialist art of guanxi, given that it bears so many timeless features of Chinese culture, burst forth with such vigor and self-conscious discourse at a certain historical moment in the socialist order. These reservations lead me to turn to those responses obtained through fieldwork, which indicate a historicity for guanxixue.

The Postrevolutionary Decline and Rise of Guanxixue

The great upheaval of the Revolution in 1949 produced a dramatic transformation, palpably felt, in social relationships. People I spoke with were almost unanimous in recalling that in the 1950s, human relations were very simple and straightforward (*danchun*), and guanxi was seldom practiced. One explanation for this holds that after the Revolution, everyone was generally too idealistic about building a new socialist society to think about using guanxi to improve their own lives. Spirits were high, and people genuinely embodied the socialist ethic of working hard and helping each other for its own sake. There was very little crime, and people did not tend to think of how they could get ahead and acquire things that were difficult to obtain. It is remembered that there were few scheming and manipulative minds then, for people still had few reasons to distrust one another.

This description of the relative absence of personalistic exchange relationships in the 1950s accords with Ezra Vogel's conclusion,[1] that after the Communist Revolution, the universalistic ethic of "comradeship" came to displace the personalistic ethics of friendship and kinship. "Comradeship" decreed that a person should treat all social relationships equally, so that there is an "absence of a private ethic to supplement the public ethic and support the commitment of the individual to his friend" (Vogel 1965:59; Gold 1985). "Nepotism" and the use of personal influence to help a friend were negatively sanctioned, since having a special relationship with one person was seen as interfering with one's obligations to others. At the same time, the trust and mutual confiding that friendship requires came to carry with them certain risks such as the intentional or unintentional leakage of confidences.

There were, however, a few people who told me that throughout the fifties, especially the late fifties, people did have the desire to use guanxi to improve their lot, but they had learned to be afraid to do so. They did not dare to approach people for favors, fearing someone might inform on them for lacking collective spirit. An economist remembers that he first heard of the phrase "going through the back door" (*zou houmen*) when he was about thirteen or fourteen years old during the "Three Years of Hardship" (1959–61). This economically harsh period followed the Great Leap Forward's zealous drive

---

[1] Vogel's article is based on interviews conducted in the early 1960s with mainland emigrants to Hong Kong.

toward total collectivization of agriculture and rapid industrialization. Food was very scarce in those years, and he remembers that a woman waiting in line to buy food asked someone, "Comrade, can you tell me where the 'back door' of this store is around here? They say that there's a better chance of getting things through some 'back door.'" Others in line laughed at her innocence. Obviously the term was new at the time, since she did not know what it meant, but understood it in its literal sense. This suggests that elements of guanxixue were already beginning to emerge before the Cultural Revolution.

Among people interviewed in the 1980s about when they first noticed the importance of the art of guanxi, the majority located its revival in the period of the Cultural Revolution (1966–76). This time of intense social chaos, revolutionary zeal, and terror brought pressure on everyday social relationships among family and kin members, among friends, and among coworkers. Personal relationships were frequently transformed into what is called "political relationships" (zhengzhi guanxi). For example, two friends in a workplace would suddenly find themselves in two different factions based on whether or not they supported attacking the work-unit leader. Under such political pressures, countless personal friendships collapsed under the strain as one or both parties betrayed the other. Within the home, husbands and wives sometimes ended up in opposite political factions, and occasions arose when they might even publically condemn each other or inform on each other. Care was taken not to say very much in front of children, since there was always the danger that in their naïveté, they would either blurt out in public whatever incriminating things one had said or worse, feel duty-bound to report it to the authorities. The following examples of two personal experiences illustrate the politicization of countless personal relationships during this period, and how they were adversely affected by the change from an interpersonal ethics to a state-oriented universalistic ethics.

Wang Haifeng, a woman graduate student at the time of my interview, was in middle school during the Cultural Revolution. She remembers that there were frequent "criticism and struggle" (pidouhui) meetings held, with mandatory attendance. These meetings, she said, were also called "living a democratic life" (guo minzhu shenghuo) because of the active participation of the attendees. Participation involved "criticism and self-criticism" (piping yu ziwo piping), in which the attendees criticized both themselves and others for not living up to a certain standard of socialist political consciousness. Faults ranged from trivial things like having selfish thoughts and cutting in line to more serious inadequacies such as failure to "draw a clear line" (*huaqing jiexian*) between oneself and one's "backward" parent who has been branded a counterrevolutionary. Toward friends or classmates who needed help to recognize their political failings, one had to adopt "a steel face without private feelings" (*tiemian wusi*). This attitude toward your friends is similar to the attitude "public affairs should be conducted in a public manner" (*gongshi gongban*) which a public official who does not make exceptions for his friends and relatives adopts. In this way, one shows that one "has principles" (*you yuanze*). That is, one does not allow private loyalties to get in the way of upholding principles.[2]

As a Red Guard, Wang Haifeng and her classmates would march to the homes of people suspected of "old thinking" (*jiu sixiang*), including the homes of her school leaders and teachers, and harrass them, sometimes beat them, ransack their homes, and destroy any "old" possessions they could find. They dragged them out of their homes and demanded that they confess their guilt to the people. They would make their victims run up and down long flights of stairs repeatedly. They would make them wear heavy placards declaring themselves enemies of the people and march them around on the streets. Even though she never hit anyone, but only stood by and cheered her fellow Red Guards on, she remembers having second thoughts about these activities. She would sometimes think that what they did was "not humane" (*bu rendao*), but each time her faith in Chairman Mao and the correctness of the Party always triumphed, and she chided herself for not being as "progressive" (*jinbu*) as others.

There was one occasion that especially troubled her. This was the night her Red Guard unit went to "ransack" (*chaojia*) the home of her "homeroom teacher" (*banzhang*). "Struggling" (*dou*) her homeroom teacher was different from doing it to other teachers at her school. This was her own teacher whom they were humiliating, a person whom she genuinely liked and who had helped her out a number of times. As the others dragged him out and roughed him up, "the feeling in my heart was very uncomfortable—it is hard to describe," said Wang Haifeng with pain in her voice. "I could not bear to look at his face or to meet his eyes." Even years later, when she ran into

[2] For a detailed account of how during one mass campaign in the Cultural Revolution, state-politicized relationships came to attack and replace kinship ethics and notions of "human feelings" (renqing) in a Guangdong village, see Madsen 1984:177–98, and chap. 6.

him on the street, she would avert her eyes and run away because she felt ashamed.

Whereas Wang's account of a hardening of the teacher-student relationship is from a persecutor's point of view, Tian Meng's memory of how his family was ostracized during the Cultural Revolution is from the victim's point of view. Tian Meng's father had impeccable revolutionary credentials. He came from a poor peasant background and joined the Communist guerrilla movement in the 1940s. In the new society, he served as a cadre leader at the regional-district (*diqu*) level of government. These credentials, however, did not spare him from being locked up for two years during the Cultural Revolution when someone accused him of expressing discontent with certain Party policies. Tian remembers that before his father went to prison, their home was always filled with friends, neighbors, and people who had come to ask his father to help them in his capacity as a local official. After his father was locked up, no one came to visit, not even their closest friends and relatives. No one even asked how his family was doing, except for one person, who once asked him in a whisper when no one was watching. Even though they knew that with the man of the house away, Tian's family could do with some help in household chores, they were all afraid to be seen associating with someone who was politically condemned. They did not wish to get into trouble for harboring sympathies for a class enemy. For Tian, this was the most painful thing to bear: to be deserted and ostracized by all the people he thought he could count on.

Explanations of how and why the Cultural Revolution brought on the complicated art of guanxi are wide ranging. Hu Lan, a woman student studying in the United States, believes that guanxixue, along with its renqing principles, were responses to the total lack of renqing during the Cultural Revolution when people were so callous toward one another. Even family members betrayed one another, and friends could not be trusted, she said. As the Cultural Revolution was drawing to a close, people discovered a need to bring some "humanism" [or "humaneness"] (*rendao zhuyi*) into social relations. What was needed was an introjection of some morality and ethics.

A very different explanation closely follows official discourse, or coincides with it. It subscribes to the view that the excesses of the Cultural Revolution made people so cynical and mutually distrustful that they lost their capacity for moral judgments, gave up their socialist ethics of brotherhood and respect for the state and the collective, and retreated into small private circles. People became selfish, lost their sense of law and morality, and started using whatever opportunities their positions provided to help only those who were useful to them.

Wang Haifeng, a woman student studying in the United States, gave three commonly cited reasons for the emergence of guanxixue during the Cultural Revolution. In the 1950s guanxixue was not a feature of everyday life because everything in the society was under rigid control. "It was like a neat orderly bookshelf; everything had its specific designated slot. Then all this order was smashed during the Cultural Revolution, so then getting things done was difficult. It was hard to find who was in charge, what the chain of command was. So people had to devise their own ways to get things." Another reason she cited was the growing scarcity of goods and the material needs of the people. Much production was stopped and curtailed during the Cultural Revolution because of the many political campaigns, ceremonies, and struggles that went on. A slowdown in production meant that the people did not have enough basic necessities, and so they had to resort to guanxixue to feed, clothe, and shelter themselves. Third, the policy of sending youth down to the countryside also gave rise to guanxixue. According to Wang Haifeng, urban parents were willing to do almost anything to ensure that their children would not have to go to poor rural areas. They were even willing to become thick-skinned (*lianpi hou*) and to embarrass themselves by stooping to give gifts.

Indeed, her third reason for the emergence of guanxixue was a common theme in the explanations I received in Beijing. A number of people thought that guanxixue started in 1968–69, two or three years into the Cultural Revolution, with the policy to send urban youth down to the countryside in the poorest and remotest areas of such provinces as Shanxi, Shaanxi, Anhui, and Inner Mongolia, to live like poor peasants. Those in high positions such as high cadres and military officials used all their connections to save their children from the hardships they would experience from being sent down. The resentment thus harbored by ordinary people, they said, fueled the spreading of the practice of gift-giving, banqueting, and "pulling" of connections to prevent their own children from leaving the city. Three to four years later (1971–72), as some sent-down youth were starting to trickle back into the cities, another massive round of gift-giving was initiated as urban youth from all over the country desperately tried to get back to the cities and, once back, tried to find jobs.

An analysis given by Du Ruoben, the graduate student who originally urged me to make guanxixue the object of my fieldwork, sees the very pressure of the state in the people's lives as the force that propelled them to seek respite from it by engaging in the art of guanxi. Summarizing his main points, in the 1950s the traditional forms of social organization and social relationships were smashed to make way for a new society. At the time, people did not need to rely on personal relationships to acquire things because the state provided for all their needs. It was also for this reason that people did not feel threatened by the loss of the old prerevolutionary institutions and relationships they had been familiar with. The Cultural Revolution destroyed this sense of security. The formal institutions of the state may have been reduced to shreds and tatters during the Cultural Revolution, but a different form of state power emerged during this period which proved much more overpowering than its formal institutions. The elements and features of the Cultural Revolution (individual and family persecutions by the crowd, struggle and confession sessions, Mao-worship rituals, work-unit political factions, the military presence, and so on) all served to introduce the spirit of extreme state control over all aspects of society down into the family. The pressure for conformity they exerted was so great, and the intrusion of politics so deep into personal lives, thought Du, that the people went back to thinking that they needed a larger "private sphere" (*si-ren quanzi*) of friendship, kinship, and guanxi network around them to serve as a sort of buffer zone against the state.

This view is similar to an observation made by a Pole about the situation in 1970s Poland: "The reliance on family and friends bears witness to the system's powerful pressure. It is a means of defense that allows the preservation of a given society's culture, be it only in its customs, conversation, mentality, personality and character traits, when that becomes impossible in public or institutional life." (Wojcicki 1981:102–3). In the face of the extreme politicization of culture and the penetration of every aspect of life by state power, kinship and friendship ethics serves as a refuge for people.

So, following Du Ruoben, we can explain the emergence or reemergence of the art of guanxi during the Cultural Revolution as a defense against the saturation of the social order by political forces. Practitioners of the art of guanxi weave self-sufficient circles of reciprocity and obligation to protect themselves from state control and reduce their dependency on the state for material resources and social sustenance. In hindsight, the 1970s can be regarded as a transition period: the invasive state was retreating, and non-state social forces were gathering strength. The result is the partially reconstructed social realm of the 1980s.

From "Use-Value" to "Exchange-Value": The Entrance of Market Forces

A number of people also wanted to make a distinction between the guanxixue of the Cultural Revolution and that of the economic reform period of the 1980s. "During the Cultural Revolution people were not into material interest [*wuzhi liyi*]," said Yao Dongya, a graduate student and former soldier. "Back then it was mostly 'political exchange' [*zhengzhi jiaohuan*], not gifts for their 'use-values' [*shiyong jiazhi*] like today. It was: 'You give me permission to go back to live in the city and I get somebody I know to give you a promotion' or something like that. . . . Nowadays, guanxixue is mainly for economic uses, for obtaining goods which are scarce."

This distinction explains perhaps why some people I interviewed traced the origins of guanxixue to the economic reform period. Unlike official discourse, which blames the guanxi wind of the 1980s on the penetration of Western bourgeois influences, popular discourse here takes up the theme of economic need and scarcity. In exploring the historical development of guanxixue during the period of economic reform, I will trace not only how guanxixue has developed from what Yao calls the "political exchange" of opportunities to a materialist exchange of usable goods but also how it has developed from this exchange for direct use and consumption to one with an independent "exchange-value." That is to say, with the introduction of elements of a market economy, oftentimes, it is not direct use and consumption that is at stake in each guanxi exchange, but guanxi's transmutation into further wealth and opportunities. The means are now often the end.

The economic reforms were launched in 1978 at the Third Plenary of the Eleventh Party Congress. In the cities, the introduction of market elements and transnational linkages to a global capitalist economy abroad have brought a string of changes, not only in the organization and activities of production, distribution, and consumption but also in how people think about the morality of work, money, and relationships. At "free markets" (*ziyou shichang*) dotting every city, peasants from the surrounding countryside and middlemen sell rural produce of better quality and variety than can be found in the state-run grocery stores. These rural produce dealers are known as "second-time dealers" (*erdao fan*), a general term for middlemen, a group generally regarded in the popular, Marxist-derived discourse as people who extract wealth for themselves without creating real labor value by doing productive work.

In workplaces, the evaluation of work came to rely mainly on monetary incentives and penalties and less on the political criteria of earlier decades. Most collective and state-run enterprises adopted profit-oriented principles of operation, shedding some of their former roles as basic units of state control (Yang 1989b). The rapidly expanding field of private economic activities has spawned a trend beginning in the mid-1980s of workers and cadres with secure state jobs leaving their work units (while preserving their affiliations in order to keep their health and retirement benefits) to work in the private sector. Others simply take on a second job (*di er zhiye*) after official work hours.

As a direct result of the economic reforms, two new social categories have emerged: the "individual enterpriser" or "individual household" (*getihu*), and the "entrepreneurial manager" (*qiyejia*). Individual enterprises have mushroomed in urban areas across the country and have started to compete with collectives and state-run enterprises.[3] These small operations are usually owned and run by youths who have not been assigned a state job, by retired workers, and by families. They offer a gamut of goods and services ranging from clothing, beauty salons, restaurants, bicycle and shoe repair, and herbal remedies to English-language classes. They can also be large commercial "corporations" (*gongsi*) dealing in interprovincial trade, sometimes hiring as many as twenty to thirty people.

Individual enterprisers are people who do not have formal positions at any state-or collective-owned work unit, but make their living solely from the market. In the early 1980s, most people I spoke with were ambivalent toward individual enterprisers. Most people believed that individual enterprisers are wealthy but that they have not really earned their wealth. The Marxist view still held sway that people who did not work with their hands were the exploiting class because they dealt not in "use-values" but took advantage of fluctuations in "exchange-values." Several people told me that few women would want to marry such people because, first, they had no welfare benefits from

---

[3] See Gold 1989 for a useful overview of the development of small urban private enterprises in the 1980s.

a work unit and, second, if the state policy changes again, these people will be condemned as "exploiters" and "capitalist roaders." This group is generally considered to be adept at guanxixue because their economic survival depends on it. They must practice guanxi with such entities as the bureaucrat who grants them a license of operation; with the battalions of tax collectors, traffic guards, and policemen who plague them; and with various wholesale enterprises who supply them with goods to sell. By 1990 when I returned to China, it seemed that fewer people looked upon them with suspicion, although there were many who envied them for their reputed wealth.

Most entrepreneurial managers work as managers for state- or collective-owned enterprises and factories; however, because of the "economic management contract system" (*jingji guanli chengbaozhi*), these people, who contract with the state to run an enterprise for a specific period, are becoming a class more and more independent of the state. In many cases the bureaucracy dares not fire them because they are economically effective and because they have earned the respect of the workers, whose bonuses depend on good group performance. Among themselves, there is a lot of guanxi as they do favors for each other not only in economic matters (exchanging goods, raw materials, market information, and so on) but also in political matters. When one among their network is being pressured or threatened by the state, they often rally to help each other stay in their positions or rise up. This is the emergence of a new managerial class in a system in which market forces are becoming more and more important.

Along with the economic reforms, popular sayings recognizing money as a basic human motivation and satirizing official socialist ethics have surfaced. These sayings utilize the abundant homonyms in the Chinese language to construct new meanings from old words. For example, "ideals" (*li xiang*) is construed to mean "If there is profit to be gained, then I want it" (*you li jiu xiang*). The word "future" (*qiantu*) is broken down and transformed into "If there is money in it, go for it" (*you qian jiu tu*). The archetypal socialist slogan "Serve the people" (*wei renmin fuwu*) has been turned into "Serve the people's currency" (*wei reminbi fuwu*). Finally, the exhortation for progress, "Look to the future" (*xiang qian kan*), can be taken to mean "Look toward money," pronounced in the same way. These parodies of standard official phrases and slogans circulate widely, expressing a tongue-in-cheek cynicism and irreverence toward official moral-political dogmas.

Around the mid-1980s, the private sector and market elements in urban areas were further expanded from their beginnings in small individual enterprises and "free markets." "Supply and marketing corporations" (*gongxiao gongsi*), which act as intermediaries between producing units and distribution and retail outlets blossomed across the country. Many of these "corporations" have distribution networks across provincial and city boundaries. Although most of them are devoted to pure commerce, some are also engaged in manufacturing, technical consulting, or moneylending (*RMRB* 13 July 1985:5; *CNA* 1 April 1985; *JSND*, April 1985:19).

By the late 1980s and early 1990s, further developments in the economy were such that the private sector started to encroach on the public (Wank 1991). In 1991, a Chinese friend in the United States who had just come back from a visit to Beijing, reported the astonishing fact that in the famous Wang Fu Jing State department store, more than half of the counter space was now rented out to private sellers. He added that it was quite obvious which counters were private and which ones were still state-run because the former were stocked full of goods and more people flocked to them because of the better selection and better "service attitudes" (*fuwu taidu*). He also estimated that the people he knew in Beijing were purchasing over 70 percent of their groceries in free markets as opposed to state markets.

In my 1991 and 1992 visits to the cities of Wenzhou, Hangzhou, Suzhou, and Xi'an, I was struck by the proliferation of economic enterprises whose ownership, property, and management status straddled the division between public and private. Through the practice of "contracting" (*chengbao*), many collective and state-owned factories and commercial units are actually run by private persons with special managerial and economic skills who often are not part of the bureaucracy of cadres or even Party members. Many new enterprises, which are actually privately financed and managed, masquerade as state-owned enterprises through a practice known as "hanging and leaning on" (*guakao*). By attaching themselves to state-owned enterprises and agreeing to pay a portion of their profits to them, these private organizations are allowed to hide within the folds of a legitimate state enterprise. This enables them to avoid extra taxation and official interference and restrictions in their activities. Other privately owned and managed enterprises pass themselves off as collective enterprises for the same reasons, and also in order to reassure their clients and customers of their official legitimacy and reliability. A new label has been coined for such operations: "fake collectives" (*jia jiti*). So fast are market forces moving that along the Eastern seaboard, such things as the sale of urban real estate for fifty- or seventy-year contracts, privately owned banks, and the sale and exchange of stocks in industrial enterprises are no longer things of the past.

Along with the development of a commodity- and profit-oriented economy, monetary transactions are increasingly encroaching on the space of the art of guanxi. Relationships concerned mainly with monetary gain and loss are of a different order from relationships based on guanxixue. They do not involve renqing and its offshoots. Indeed, they are often characterized by the expression, "not talking renqing" (*bujiang renqing*), which means to treat someone on an impersonal basis. The bestowal of money, however, does not in and of itself comprise an impersonal monetary relationship. Money may be given instead of gifts to fulfill renqing obligations, as when adult children give money to aging parents. Money must appear in conjunction with the primary calculation of gain and loss, means and ends, as well as with some social distance between persons in the exchange. Furthermore, the tendency toward short-term relationships is also considered an impersonal monetary relationship operating independent of the scope of renqing.

Among many people I spoke with, I found a common attitude that giving or paying money for a service is much simpler and more efficient. Relying on personal relations to get a task done involves thinking out how a certain person could be persuaded to help, figuring out the most appropriate gift, buying the gift, planning how best to present the gift, and waiting for the target person to perform the favor. When or whether that person will oblige you cannot always be determined, since in guanxixue, one would feel uncomfortable insisting on a deadline, as that would painfully lay bare the reason for the gift.

"It used to be that if you had a 'familiar' person [*shouren*] who was a driver and had access to a [work] unit's vehicle," said Wu Rong, a woman workshop director, "you could call on him to haul something for you. In return you could just invite him to dinner or just chalk it up to a renqing debt." "In the past one or two years [this conversation occurred in January 1985]" she and her friends noticed a change. Many drivers now prefer to be paid cash for their services. How much one offers to the driver depends on the circumstance and the person, but if one offers too little, the driver might find an excuse not to help you. Often there will be no explicit talk of money at the beginning, but since nowadays many people already know what is expected, there is the understanding that the driver will receive some money. Should a person not be abreast of changes in the society and merely thank the driver with a small gift or invite them to dinner afterwards, they may meet with an embarrassing decline of the gift or dinner. The driver will shake his or her head, eye the gift contemptuously perhaps, give a chuckle or a sigh, and say dismissively, "Ah . . . forget about it [*suanle ba*]." "This will then be a loss of face for you [*geini mei mianzi*]," said Wu Rong.

The introduction of money greatly alters the nature of this exchange, but at the same time, certain elements of the art of guanxi are not fully eclipsed. According to Wu Rong, one cannot go up to just any driver and offer to pay them for their services. There must be some prior personal connection or "familiarity" with the driver, perhaps an introduction through a mutual friend, or even a debt owed, for the encounter to be successful. Drivers are generally afraid or reluctant to use their work unit's car for someone they do not know. This is because they cannot be sure that the person requesting help will not tell others that the driver accepted money for the private use of public property. The element of trust that comes from a gradually cultivated relationship, as is found in the art of guanxi, remains important, even as the relations between the two transactors is somewhat distanced by immediate cash payment. What has changed is that once cash payment has been made, neither side will have a claim on the other and may probably not have any future dealings; however, if the driver happens to be a good friend, the whole question of money would still not arise.

When Lan Hong, a woman worker at the small printing factory I studied in Beijing, was asked by her workshop director to help find outside technical assistance to fix one of their machines, she remembered her old master at a larger factory under whom she had learned her trade. Her present factory, being very small and very low on the state administrative ladder, did not have its own technicians and engineers, and so always had to call on larger factories for help. The factory had until then relied on the personal guanxi networks of its own staff and workers to find outside assistance, and on appeals to renqing and face to persuade them to come. Until recently, said Lan Hong, it was enough to thank those who came to give technical assistance with a free lunch and perhaps small items printed by the factory because the task was not regarded as a paid job, but a fulfillment of personal obligations or an exchange of guanxi favors. In recent years it has been difficult to find help because those technicians and skilled workers had become reluctant to leave their work posts for an unpaid task when they could spend the same time making extra bonus points by surpassing their quotas. Indeed, Lan Hong went to visit her former master whom she had not seen for four years and had to spend a long time cajoling and begging him to come. He finally consented. There was no mention of money, the whole job being couched in terms of a personal favor. When her former master arrived at the factory, they brought him tea. After almost half a day of work, he had the machine running again. Lan Hong and her workshop director thanked the old worker profusely. They then slipped 15 yuan and a pack of cigarettes the factory had prepared into his pocket despite his ritual protests.

On a bitterly cold and windy day in December 1984, I sat huddled with five workers in a tiny room located in the back lot of the printing factory, lighted dimly by a bare light bulb. Between shoveling fresh supplies of coal every twenty minutes into two large coal ovens kept glowing around the clock, the factory coal workers rest in this room. The coal ovens keep the factory buildings' central heating system going. We were talking about the increasing importance of "money relationships" (jinqian guanxi). They confirmed that recently it had become acceptable to give money without any embarrassment, to a person for a favor. Money was becoming more desirable than any other kind of gift, they said, it is more "substantial" (shi hui) and practical. One coal shoveler put it hypothetically:

> Say you helped me through your various "channels" [luzi] to [locate and] buy a color TV [which could not be found on the market those days]. I give you a small sum of money in gratitude. You will not be insulted or angry, but happy. Money is more convenient [fangbian]. If I give you alcoholic spirits and cigarettes or something, you may not need them, they may be of no use to you. But with money, you can use it any way you want. Also, this type of payment and favor is totally legal, so you have nothing to fear.

One of the coal workers hinted that he would be happy to compensate me for my services if next time I came into China, I brought in a Japanese motorcycle and sold it to him. Chinese customs would not charge high duties for only one motorcycle for personal use, and motorcycles are so much cheaper abroad.

The rationale cited by many people for preferring money over gifts is that money is a more easily convertible form of wealth. In order for a person to extract the value of a gift that has no personal use, that person must give the gift again to another person with whom he or she is "pulling guanxi." Money, however, enables the person to convert the gift's value directly into anything he or she desires without the long and involved process of negotiating guanxi. In addition, although people had been reluctant in the past to accept money because it made the illegal nature of the transaction too overt, now money is preferred because it is actually easier to hide than expensive gifts such as TVs and other items, which are displayed at home where visitors can see them.

The infiltration of money as an alternative medium of exchange has occurred in both legal and illegal spheres of guanxi exchange. The language of friendship, mutual obligation and assistance, and sharing, which constituted the practice of guanxi in the mid-1980s, has (in many cases) been transformed into the new terms of monetary compensation for labor and other services rendered. Although "familiarity" was and still is a component in the initiation of exchange, in many cases money payment has lifted the veil of the language of friendship and made explicit the exchange of material interests. Although guanxi exchange was predicated on long-term relationships, implied in money relationships is the notion that after an exchange, there is no remaining debt on either side.

The Art of Guanxi Does Not Retreat

Although money relationships have increasingly impinged on guanxi operations, oddly enough, this movement has not been accompanied by any significant reduction of the scope of guanxixue. On a research visit to Xi'an in 1992, I went with my friend Fang Lei to an arts and handicrafts store, where her friend worked in the sales department. Fang Lei had worked there three years earlier, and she could get me a discount there from her friend. Sure enough, her friend came down from the upstairs office and told the sales clerks to give me a 50 percent discount on everything I purchased in her sales area. Fang Lei and I both protested that this discount was too generous, that her friend could not even recover the original wholesale cost, but her friend insisted. Later I asked Fang Lei if we might have gotten her friend into trouble with the store manager. Maybe the clerks would report her for giving discounts without authorization. Fang reassured me that there was no danger about that—her friend had "contracted" (*chengbao*) with the store to take care of several booths, so she could sell at any price she wanted, as long as she delivered a certain amount each month to the store. Her friend makes a lot of money each season from foreign tourists, so she did not mind this favor. "Besides," said

Fang, "we are very good friends." Here is an example of how the emergence of a profit-driven market economy does not always lead to the waning of the gift economy. According to the logic of commodity economy, her friend, having "contracted," should have disdained the tiresome ethics of renqing because it would cut into her profits. On the contrary, her friend still observed the long-term debt logic of renqing ethics.

Another reason for the coexistence of gift and commodity economies is that guanxixue has found new territory to colonize. Far from fading into irrelevance in the rapidly commercializing society, the art of guanxi plays a new and important role in all types of commercial transactions which have emerged with the economic reforms. Money still cannot buy everything, and guanxi still provides a better access to goods. Guanxi and gifts have also come to be used explicitly to save money and to earn money in the new commercial context where they are frequently employed as money equivalents. An important consequence of the encounter between guanxixue and commodity/money relationships is the effect that each has on the other. On the one hand, when money and guanxi are mixed together, the art of guanxi personalizes an otherwise impersonal money transaction. On the other hand, the art of guanxi is also altered in its basic raison d'être as its very structure and form become commoditized into a shadow of money exchange.

Attached to the small printing factory I studied in Beijing, is a side-line enterprise called a new corporation (gongsi). In the mid-1980s, its young entrepreneurial force planned to enter the retail business selling clothes, household items, and electric appliances, such as electric fans and stereo cassette recorders. The preparations were extensive. Aside from hiring a construction crew from a suburban commune to knock down part of the factory wall to build a store opening out to the street, the young corporation managers spent months laying down a guanxi network to facilitate all aspects of their business. Their supply sources (huo yuan) were their lifeline, so they cultivated relations with old acquaintances, old schoolmates, friends, and friends of friends, with anyone who was in any way connected with state distributing centers, wholesale corporations, or sales departments of factories. Consumer goods in high demand in the society brought in the biggest profits, but were very difficult to find, since distributors always save these for their guanxihu and "familiar persons." Buying directly from a factory was the most desired way of acquiring supplies because prices were at "factory price" (chu chang jia), lower than wholesale price. These channels were hard to open up because in most cases others had been there before them and had already made arrangements. So the work of finding good, steady supply sources was a big headache. As soon as they received their operating license and the official corporation seal was carved, the corporation managers and their superior, the manager of the factory, intended to invite all their suppliers to a big banquet to sow goodwill and to impress them with the idea that this corporation had enough financial resources to be generous.

The factory invested 17,000 yuan in this corporation, but that did not exhaust the funds at the corporation's disposal. The corporation's supplies were to be paid from another fund of 300,000 yuan, which was in the bank. They managed to borrow this sum from another, wealthier unit because of a personal guanxi with one of the heads of the unit. As the relationship was a close one, no interest would be charged on the loan. The young managers had great ambitions for their corporation. Initially their energy would focus on the storefront, but since this store could only bring in a limited income for both the corporation and its mother factory, they planned to expand operations across provincial borders. They hoped eventually to sell Beijing products in other provinces and to bring in outside products to sell in Beijing at retail prices. At this stage they would need to make their corporation known outside the neighborhood and outside Beijing. They were confident that they would be able to advertise themselves very cheaply because one of them had guanxi in a newspaper office who would give them a special price on ads in that newspaper.

At the printing factory, a factory-wide meeting was held in December of 1984. One of the items on the agenda was the manager's explanation why a great chance for the factory to be a middleman in color TVs and to make some quick money had been lost. Someone in the factory had a personal guanxi with suppliers who had access to a shipment of one thousand Japanese color televisions, which had just arrived at the docks in Tianjin. These suppliers were willing to sell the TVs to the factory at 1,300 yuan per set, which was 100 yuan below the going price. The factory happened to know people who were very interested in buying these televisions and who had offered to buy them all up at 1,600 yuan a set. In addition, under state regulations, the factory could also extract a 13 percent commission from the buyers for locating a rare supply source. The factory manager, however, always careful not to violate state regulations in these times of unpredictable government policy, discovered that the government document permitting this kind of activity had been withdrawn two months earlier (in October). The new regulations ruled that industrial enterprises were no longer allowed to be "second-time dealers." On the basis of this information, the manager decided not to go through with the deal, even though his factory had stood to make a large sum of money and his disappointed buyer called him some ugly names.

I asked the naive question of why the buyer could not go straight to the original suppliers and negotiate a sale without the factory. They patiently explained that the buyer could only obtain the TVs through their factory guanxi. Since the buyer himself did not have the direct personal guanxi with the suppliers, the suppliers would refuse to sell to him because they did not know him. Instead of selling to strangers, the suppliers would rather save the television sets for another "familiar person" (shouren).

The operations of another marketing corporation attached to a hotel for foreigners in Beijing were on a much larger scale than the small factory-attached corporation mentioned above. This corporation had a much bigger investment and capital-funds pool and even a certain amount of foreign currency at its disposal from its association with the hotel. It included both a retail section, which sold jewelry and handicrafts at high prices to foreigners, as well as a wholesale business for the domestic market, which dealt in anything from clothing manufactured in China originally for export, to expensive household appliances, including occasional batches of Japanese videocassette recorders. It had also established branch offices in several other cities.

In its commercial activities, this corporation relied a great deal on guanxixue. Among its staff was an old cadre in semiretirement (lizhi) from over thirty years of service in state commercial offices. He was engaged by the corporation because of his rich experience in business and his vast network of guanxi cultivated through the years in different sectors of industry, government, and commerce. Old acquaintances, subordinates, and trading partners could be called on to provide information on supply sources and to give the corporation special low prices. In return, the corporation had much to offer these people because of its privileged affiliation with a major hotel in Beijing. Whenever its business contacts needed to make business trips to Beijing, they could stay at the hotel free of charge or at reduced charge instead of hunting for hotel or dormitory rooms all over a city that was becoming more and more crowded with visitors. The hotel restaurant was often used to entertain business friends of the corporation. And since the corporation had guanxi contacts inside the Chinese airlines office, it could easily buy a "guanxi ticket" (*guanxi piao*) in only one day's time for its favored suppliers or clients leaving town.

The corporation sold its products to retail corporations or other middlemen at three different prices: the lowest was "factory price" (*chu chang jia*), then "wholesale price" (*pi fa jia*), and finally "retail" or "market price" (*shi chang jia*). It was legally free to discriminate in pricing, as long as it did not surpass the maximum market price for any given product set in advance by the state. The level at which the corporation pegged prices depended on the degree of guanxi intimacy and indebtedness to the buyer, as well as the buyer's potential for providing help to the corporation in the future.

The logic of price discrimination was explained to me by the manager of the corporation, a shrewd and very businesslike man in his late thirties, wearing a western-style business suit. He was the son of a high cadre and so enjoyed particular advantages in his work because of his wide guanxi network and social influence. "Business relations are those of mutual benefit, so we cannot act out of renqing all the time, even with good friends," he said. He generally tried to avoid doing business with friends. He did admit that there were two situations in which he would respond to renqing appeals. First, in choosing which customer to do business with, he might pick someone with a previous tie to him, such as a relative or friend, over a stranger. Second, if an old friend or classmate turned up and wanted to buy his products, he would give them a low price in recognition of their special relationship, but only for the first transaction. After that they would be treated like everyone else, as the corporation could not afford to behave on anything other than pure business principles for long. The overriding reason for giving customers lower prices, according to the manager, was that those customers could in turn provide something for the corporation. For example, to their guanxi in the Chinese airline office, they were willing to sell him a washing machine at wholesale price for his personal use. For the manager, this was good business sense. He believed that the future direction of society's development would be toward more money relations.

After several years of being a worker with a high absentee rate because he could not stand the discipline, Yuan Dahua finally found his true calling in life. Now that controls have loosened on commercial activity, he has managed to attach himself to the Shandong Provincial Native Products Corporation as a sales representative. He is responsible for finding buyers for Shandong's many native products such as canned foods, handicrafts, leather goods, and so on. His customers include both native Chinese dealers and Hong Kong businessmen. His income consists of a monthly basic wage and commissions on his sales, so he has become an aggressive salesperson, tracking down potential buyers and making sure they are satisfied so that they will come back to him. He observes the ritual of a banquet each time he reaches a large sales agreement. He makes a point of inviting the buyers to a dinner at the Sichuan Restaurant, a reputable restaurant in town where he knows some of the kitchen staff. They give him a special low price on the dinner and go to some trouble preparing an impressive spread, devoting more time to this preparation than they do for their non-guanxihu customers. In return he thanks the kitchen staff by giving them expensive cigarettes and taking them out to dinner too, at another restaurant where the prices are lower than what he spends for the original dinner and the cigarettes added together. By choosing this restaurant, he saves a lot of money on dinner expenses.

The change in social-exchange relations in China since the introduction of market forces and the reemergence of a strong money culture can be seen as a double movement. First, impersonal money has begun to replace some of the affectively charged relationships created by gifts and reciprocal favors. Second, at the same time, guanxi, gifts, favors, and status have acquired many features that make them money substitutes. In other words, change impinges on the art of guanxi from two directions. One, by a process of *displacement*, in which the direct payment of money reduces the practice of guanxixue in certain contexts, as in monetary compensation for labor and in bribery. Two, by a process of *commodification* of guanxi, in which the "exchange value" of guanxi, gifts, and favors overrides their "use-value," as when guanxi is employed with a view to expanding a person's or corporate group's means of buying and selling. The spread of the art of guanxi to a commodity economy has meant that guanxi begets money or the means for acquiring money. This relatively novel twist in guanxi exchange is a departure from the old *non*-monetary objectives for cultivating guanxi: self-protection, political advancement, and the acquisition of goods and services for direct consumption and use. In the meeting of the gift economy with the commodity economy, what has resulted is a crossfertilization of their principles of exchange. Furthermore, there is also an ongoing process of mutual colonization, as each economy tries to appropriate the other into its system of operation.

This is the schematic history of guanxixue in socialist China I pieced together from discussions with urban people. Throughout the 1950s and early 1960s, as China was experiencing a fundamental social, structural, and ideological transformation, the personalistic "nepotism" or kinship orientation of prerevolutionary social life all but disappeared. Then in the years 1966–69, the society underwent another major political reconstitution, only this time the methods and effects were much more drastic and, for many, traumatic and devastating. The political mobilization of the masses in the Cultural Revolution meant that state ethics penetrated into the very fabric of the social-cultural makeup, deeply affecting personal relationships. The ascendancy of "political relationships" left very little room for the sphere of private/personal relationships and sentiments. What resulted was a social body that had become so politicized that it could not be differentiated from the state. In the period between 1969 and 1972, signs of social resistance against total state saturation began to appear. What emerged were personalistic ethics in everyday life, often in the form of guanxixue or renqing ethics very much at odds with the dominant state system of universalistic ethics. Then in the 1980s, during the economic reform period, guanxixue took on new life and in many respects experienced a transformation as it intersected with a growing commodity economy with its attendant social mobility and consumer desires.

Still, in the face of continued state control and an incompletely rationalized market system in which social and material resources are still limited and differential access to them is still the norm, the form that a rebuilding of the social realm has taken is the revival of some prerevolutionary non-state relationships and ethics. What has emerged is a dense structure of individual connectedness as opposed to atomism, in which reciprocity is a form of social solidarity and social investment. The personalism of guanxi exchange created a social patterning in which people are juncture points embedded in webs of interdependent social relationships. This endless series of dyadic contracts as a mode of exchange is very different from market-dominated Western societies in which people are created as independent agents with formally equal access to goods and services, checked only by the size of their individual monetary income bases. In such societies, people find little need or encouragement to weave networks of mutually dependent exchange and reciprocity. Therefore, we can speculate that the postsocialist forms of capitalism developing in China today will assume a different form from the individual-based capitalism of the West.

PART II

THEORETICAL
FORMULATIONS

There is no event, no phenomenon, word or thought which does not have a multiple sense. . . . A thing is sometimes this, sometimes that, sometimes something more complicated—depending on the forces . . . which take possession of it. . . . The pluralist idea that a thing can be seen as "this and then that" is philosophy's greatest achievement. . . .

—Deleuze 1983:4

The history of a thing, in general, is the succession of forces which take possession of it and the co-existence of the forces which struggle for possession. The same object, the same phenomenon, changes sense depending on the force which appropriates it.

—Deleuze 1983:3

In Part 1 I showed the many ways the art of guanxi is understood and evaluated by its native practitioners and observers. The different "dialects" of guanxixue discourse reflect the various native interpretations of it in contemporary Chinese life. Guanxixue is variously understood as an unhealthy spread of privatism that if unchecked, could threaten the orderly institutions of the socialist system (official discourse); an example of official class privileges and official corruption; a way to beat the system through devious routes when official channels are closed or difficult; a facilitator for the return of market transactions and economy; and the revival of "human feeling" or renqing such as kinship and friendship ethics in everyday life. It would seem that guanxixue is at heart ambiguous and multidimensional, that different readings of it are possible, indeed, inevitable. These divergent views of a common phenomenon show that guanxixue can be appropriated by diverse interpretive-narrative grids.

The task of Part 2 is to explore an interpretation of guanxixue which has not been sufficiently articulated as a theoretical framework, the notion of guanxixue as *oppositional* to state power.[1] In Part 2 I introduce a new discursive "force" that can "take possession" of guanxi practices for another end, that of stitching together a post-state-socialist fabric of a *minjian*, a "people's realm," or a social realm separate from the state. This reinterpretation of guanxixue is intended as a performative act,[2] a process of counter-politics against the state.

In Part 2 I also take issue with a set of dichotomies, found in both China and the West, which are commonly assumed to be homologous: modernity is to tradition, as the West is to the East, as rational universalism is to personalism; as Enlightenment and liberation is to traditional oppression. It seems to me that all of these dichotomies, and the homologies between them, break down when we consider Chinese modernity. That the personalistic ethics of guanxi has resurfaced and prospered despite (or because of) the modernizing universalism of the state shows that personalism is not to be relegated to the past or to tradition, but also has an important present and future in modernity. Furthermore, state power in China today is both the product of the Western Enlightenment optimism in reason, social engineering (hence "scientific socialism"), and "modernization," as well as the eruption of an older, native rationality of the state.

In Chapter 6 I show that the categories "traditional" and "modern" cannot be easily grafted onto or conflated with the categories "East" and "West." Impersonal rule and political rationalization are not alien to Chinese tradition; they can be found in the ancient Legalist discourse that launched China's first centralized and bureaucratic state. Indeed, two Western sinologists have observed that although Chinese tradition did not develop a "science" of astronomy or physics, the Legalist tradition was "scientific" in politics, and was very close in spirit to modern Western nineteenth and twentieth-century social

---

[1] Andrew Walder has shown how Chinese workers are controlled by guanxi, which he defines as patron-client ties in which workers become dependent on their work-unit leaders for the needs of everyday life (1986). Although there is merit to this view, it portrays workers only in passive compliance before leaders. As the example of the worker forcing a gift on his factory manager in Chapter 3 illustrates, people are constantly manipulating principles of personalism and renqing, the very tools said to shackle workers, to do the opposite, to control their leaders and thwart the system.

[2] I thank Prasenjit Duara for pointing this out.

sciences in its utilitarian realism, its amoralism, and its behavioralism (Graham 1989:269; Schwartz 1985:348). Legalistic state power was hostile to personalistic kinship ethics; this tension persisted even after the imperial state appropriated Confucianism.

If modern state power has this native element in it, then calls by Chinese dissident intellectuals for "democracy" (*minzhu*) and "individual liberation" (*geren jiefang*) may not be sufficient, or simply may not work, since these concepts have no strong roots in China and may not address the particular structures and configurations of power in China. Therefore, we must also look for *native* mechanisms that subvert or counter state power. Furthermore, native mechanisms may perhaps also provide ways to avoid some of the problems encountered in Western modernity, such as the social disconnectedness and isolation of individual lives.

In the following chapters I also seek to go beyond another explanatory framework for guanxixue, which is found among both Chinese and Western scholars. This is the view that the art of guanxi serves to extend state power: officials feed off the people by demanding gifts in exchange for favors granted through their privileged positions. By giving gifts or banquets to officials above them, people affirm, express, and implement the hierarchy of state power. This may be so, but if it is, why does the state spend so much time in the official press denouncing such practices and reporting on how nepotistic and corrupt officials have been brought to justice? Certainly the reason is not simply to demonstrate the legitimacy of rule by officials, or else a system of elected short-term office would have been instituted. Rather, in its battle with official corruption, state discourse is pushing both the people and the officials to aspire to a higher loyalty.

A distinction needs to be made between "official power" and "state power." State power is a form of state rationality whose scope of operation and concern extends beyond the narrow class interests of official power. These two types of power formation do not represent two separate groups or institutions, but are two dimensions of power, often exercised by the same people. Officials may serve state power in carrying out its edicts, seeing to social control, and disciplining wrongdoers and even other officials. The same officials may also employ guanxi methods to promote their private gain, for they too are subjects of the state. The state controls its officials by using other officials to supervise, monitor, and discipline their colleagues, and by the especially ingenious method of unleashing the aroused masses to attack officials in political campaigns such as the Four Cleanups in 1963 (Madsen 1984:69–71, 88–90) and the Cultural Revolution.[3] Indeed, officials are just as subject to state surveillance, "rectification campaigns" (*zhengfeng yundong*), and indoctrination efforts as intellectuals. As Claude Lefort observed of totalitarian state power and its systematic eviction of officials: "The bureaucracy was . . . everything, and the bureaucrats nothing" (Lefort 1986:293).

It is my belief that state power genuinely objects to official involvement in corrupt guanxixue, not just because it makes the existing system of distribution and administration illegitimate in the eyes of the people but also because officials engaged in guanxixue are showing a loyalty to narrow, "privatistic," and "local" family, class, and regional interests, instead of loyalty to the state. From the state's point of view, official involvement in the personalism of guanxixue expresses a growing official power divergent from and threatening to state power; for although the art of guanxi may at times serve to extend official power, it always does so by weakening state power.

Each chapter in Part 2 takes guanxixue as a point of departure for delineating some of the contours of an elusive phenomenon, the logic and operations of "state power" in China. Unlike "official power," which can easily be accounted for by native notions of official privilege and corruption, as well as Marxist class analysis, "state power" has not been adequately thematized and examined as an independent force in Chinese cultural processes. Often concerns for official power have obscured the workings of state power, so that we need to develop new conceptual tools with which to grasp and describe it. By tuning into certain pitches of guanxi discourse, I seek to make more audible the humming and rumblings of the machinery of state power in the background. I wish to carve out a space in the social theory of China for something that has not been adequately developed or theoretically articulated: the tension, rather than the convergence, between a certain guanxi-cum-kinship polity and a certain recurring form of the state in China.

---

[3] Since Yan'an 1942–44, there have been at least nine other "cadre-rectification" campaigns: the Anti-Rightist campaign, 1957; the Anti-Rightist Tendency (*Fan you qing*) campaign, 1959; the Socialist Education campaign, 1962; the Four Clean-ups campaign, 1963; the most intense years of the Cultural Revolution, 1966–69; the Criticize Lin Biao and Confucius campaign, 1973; the Anti-Spiritual Pollution campaign, 1983–84; and the Party Rectification campaigns of 1985 and 1989–90. See Whyte 1974 for a discussion of political study and discipline among cadres and Party members.

CHAPTER FIVE

The Political Economy
of Gift Relations

["Governmentality"] has as its target population, as its principle form of knowledge political economy, and as its essential technical means apparatuses of security.

—Foucault 1979a:20

The state apparatus in socialist China has assumed for itself almost total responsibility for administering the social and economic domain. The welfare and control of the population, the organization of production, the distribution of the means of subsistence, and other activities have become primary concerns of organs of the state. The types of power relationships and their social and symbolic expressions, which have crystallized around the distribution and circulation of desirables in such a politicized economy, are the subject of this chapter. In this chapter I also examine how certain countertechniques of power deviate from the larger strategy of power exercised through the state-socialist political economy, forming pockets of intransigence from within.

The dissemination of state power in the political economy of state socialism in China conforms in many ways to what Michel Foucault has called bio-power (1980), a specifically modern mode of power characterized by the "[ever-] increasing organization of population and welfare for the sake of increased force and productivity" (Dreyfus and Rabinow 1983:7–8). The overall strategy of bio-power is carried out through techniques of discipline and techniques of normalization. "Disciplines" are those technologies of power which distribute bodies in space and promote or restrict their movements and actions, their development and reproduction. "Normalizing techniques" exert their power by the construction of a unilateral discourse of right and wrong, by measuring and regulating conduct according to its uniform and universalistic standards, and by defining fixed identities and persons on the basis of this particular discourse.

Foucault's thesis of a modern regime of power immanent in, constitutive of, and coextensive with society instead of exterior to it, as with an earlier monarchical mode of power (1980:92–95), is extremely compelling. Yet there are two areas in which the notion of bio-power could be further developed. First, when this novel notion of power is applied to the case of modern socialist China, much of its formulation is found to be lacking in institutional specificity. Most people would agree that the contours of power are different in a capitalist welfare-state economy and a state-socialist economy. Since Foucault was only looking at the genealogy of power in the modern capitalist West, the question of the specific historical relationship and linkages between bio-power and Chinese socialist political-economic structure and social institutions needs to be addressed.

Second, although Foucault was fully aware that there is no such thing as a perfect totalization of power and that "freedom" and recalcitrance are the conditions for the exercise of power (1983:221, 211), in his empirical works he did not elaborate on how power orders are riven with internal contradictions. Although the power techniques operating through the structures of a state redistributive apparatus have assumed dominance, they have not completely displaced other techniques of power, which continue to operate on the margins and in the interstices of state power as an "immense reserve" of alternative tactical possibilities (de Certeau 1984; de Certeau 1986:188). These other maneuvers of influence enjoy no formally recognized status, nor are they articulated by the dominant discourse. In given situations, the very different principles and forms of their operations may subtly challenge dominant power techniques and constitute an oppositional force.

Three distinct modes of exchange or domains of power techniques may be discerned in the contemporary political and cultural economy of China: (1) the state distributive economy, (2) the gift economy, and (3) a resurgent commodity economy. Each mode follows its own rules of operation and its own corpus of etiquette and good form in social relations, produces its own system of valuation and rates of exchange, and represents a unique style of the tactics and strategies of domination. Though representing distinct tactical styles, these domains of power techniques are not mutually exclusive in the sense that they comprise separate institutions or functions of the social structure; rather, they traverse institutions and are intertwined within them.

Furthermore, the practices of each mode of exchange can be seen as reactions to the practices of the other two modes, so that their boundaries are marked by conflict. In this chapter I am concerned mainly with the first two modes of exchange, and also with practices found in *urban* rather than rural Chinese society.

Note that I propose a tripartite scheme[1] for the cultural economy of power in Chinese socialist society rather than a dual-economy scheme, which opposes an "official" or "first economy" to a "shadow" or "second economy" (Grossman 1977, 1982; Galasi 1985); or a "formal sector" to an "informal sector" (Sampson 1985). There is a tendency in the writings on the second economy of Eastern European and former Soviet societies to conflate the dynamics of the gift economy and the commodity economy. Both involve practices and discourses oppositional to the power techniques operating through the state distributive mode of exchange, but in China (and perhaps in other former socialist societies too), their tactics of power follow distinctly different logics and genealogical trajectories. I will explore the differences between gift and commodity economies which are overlooked by the notion of second economy later in this chapter.

The Techniques of Power in the State Redistributive Economy

State socialism started out with the central aim of redistributing material wealth, services, and opportunities in an equitable, planned, and coordinated fashion, usually after the society had suffered through a war, impoverishment, or a period of corruption.[2] In this sense there was perhaps nothing cynical about the intentions of the revolutionaries or the strategists of state-socialist economies. What happened as these intentions and programs were translated into new social institutions and practices is a sobering illustration that even resistance and revolution are not outside power. Power has the uncanny ability to adopt new forms even while it is being resisted. In the process of constructing a unified and, in principle, egalitarian distribution system for the population, the state distributive economy also provided

---

[1] This tripartite scheme was inspired by the work of economic historian and anthropologist Karl Polanyi, who outlined three modes of economic integration for world-historical economies ranging from primitive to socialist and capitalist: reciprocity, redistribution, and market exchange (1957). For Polanyi, these modes are not evolutionary stages, but often coexist and interact within one social formation.

[2] For an official exposition of the aims and virtues of state-socialist economies, see Xue 1981.

an institutional framework that exerted new technologies of control over the population. Through the relationships between distributor and recipient, which ostensibly carry out merely distribution functions, the state distributive apparatus was transformed from within. The infiltration of new techniques of discipline and normalization in the centralized distributive apparatus means that it came to adopt *extraeconomic* functions not only in the political sphere but also in the social and cultural spheres.

The rationale for the state distributive economy is that the centralized state can best determine social needs and distribute necessities in an equitable fashion according to objective needs. But experience has shown that needs seldom present themselves "objectively"; rather, they are organized through a system of interpretation derived from the larger social and political discourse.[3] The values and elements of this discourse may recognize some needs but remain blind to others; prioritize and legitimate certain needs; and when needs are in excess of the means to fulfill them, construct criteria for assigning certain individuals and groups with special rights to the satisfaction of needs. It is precisely this interpretive space opened up by the state distributive economy that the new techniques of power have colonized and from which they exert power effects over the larger social body.

The point is not that the structure of a state distributive economy creates these power techniques and that a market economy does not, but that the distributive economy promotes certain types of power techniques not common in the market economy or employs them in a different manner.[4] A state distributive economy sets the conditions for

[3] In a survey of two Hungarian cities, Ivan Szelenyi showed that contrary to everyone's assumptions that socialist allocation of housing is for the most needy, it was the middle class (bureaucrats, intellectuals, professionals, clerical workers) rather than the working class who got the best state-subsidized housing. His explanation is that socialist urban inequities are not inherited from the capitalist past, but "arise logically from the socialist system of production and distribution" (1983:4). The inequities produced by administrative allocation are not due to mismanagement or official corruption but rather to the socialist logic that scarce services such as housing should be used to reward those who do the more important jobs for the country. See his *Urban Inequalities under State Socialism* (1983).

[4] The formal rationality of market economies tends to harbor techniques that extract the optimum efficiency and utility from bodies through the minute segmentation of time; through the exercise and training of bodies, the coordination and control of gestures and postures, to move in synchrony with machinery; and according to strict routines and schedules (Foucault 1979b:149–69). Another technique of power central to market economies is the incitement of consumer desire and commodity fetishism. Although these techniques have become universal features of the modern world, they do find fewer points of anchor in the substantive rationality of state distributive economy, which tends to be more interested in order and docility than in productive efficiency.

the coordination of techniques from diverse origins and histories and furthers their systematization. At the same time, many techniques are shared by different socioeconomic structures and discursive formations so that one can speak of the modern forms of power and knowledge.

How does distribution according to needs come to be carried out by resorting to microtechniques of power? Take, as a case in point, the following "List of Conditions for the Allocation of Housing," which was drawn up by the state-owned electric fan factory in Beijing which I studied for one month. This particular factory had just finished constructing a new apartment building for its own workers and staff and so drew up a list of logical criteria for awarding each apartment, with a point system to help determine who among the applicants were the most needy. The list, in its original order, follows:

1. Those with over twenty years service in this factory, and those who have made great contributions to the factory. (10 points)
2. Those old cadres who participated in the Revolution before the establishment of the country [The Peoples' Republic]. (10 points)
3. Intellectuals and scientific-technical personnel. (10 points)
4. Those who have obtained a "Certificate of Intention to Have Only One Child" (dusheng zinu zheng). (10 points)
5. Those who have been chosen municipal model workers. (10 points)
6. Both spouses working in this factory, and with no other source of housing. (10 points)
7. Those with three generations under one roof. (10 points)
8. Those with existing housing to exchange for this one. (10 points)
9. Those whose living space is less than five square meters per person. (20 points)
10. Those waiting for housing to consummate their legal marriage (male 28, female 25; who have already obtained their marriage licenses at least one year ago). (20 points)
11. Those with a spouse currently serving in the armed forces. (5 points)
12. Those applicants who are *male* workers or staff at this factory. (5 points)

It can be easily shown that in this list, the conception of "neediness" is intertwined with the normative categories of the "deserving." It would seem that only conditions 6 through 9 deal with material concerns for cramped living space, whereas embedded in all the rest are subtle techniques of normalization. Condition 1 leaves a lot of room for interpretation, as "great contributions to the factory" may refer to technical innovations that have improved factory production, but also may equally refer to consistent loyalty to the factory leadership or to political activism in recent social or political campaigns promulgated by the Party center. Conditions 2, 3, and 11 would reward on the basis of currently exalted "class-status" groups and not on the basis of actual living conditions of specific persons and families. The ostensible aim of number 3 is to redress past discriminations suffered by intellectuals, but it also continues the tradition of the imposition of a common and single will and set of values which created the current situation when workers were the exalted social category. This tradition exercises what can be called "temporal power effects," that is to say, the subsuming of situational needs to a power that determines universal needs according to its own agenda. The requirement of a "Certificate of Intention to Have Only One Child" in Condition 4 makes sure that only those who abide by state population policy can obtain government or enterprise housing. Condition 10 standardizes marriage throughout the land, demarcating a difference between male and female, imposing a norm that the male spouse is to be older than the female, encouraging young people to get married not before and not after a certain age. Thus power is also the regulation of the growth, reproduction, and sexual practices of the population. The fifth criterion ("model worker") favors not only industriousness, obedience, and political conformism but also those who do not have abnormal habits, family lives, or pursuits, for the latter type of people would not easily be awarded public recognition as model workers. Finally, the age-old gender effects of power where men are accorded diverse conditions for domination are again reinforced.

Normative techniques creep into a distribution according to needs at the state level as well. I can show this best with a quick survey of various power techniques operating throughout the state distributive economy in China, first in their disciplinary forms and then in their normative forms.

The investment of space with power follows from the regulation of population movements. The enclosure and partitioning of the population in the urban economy of power is achieved through three interrelated distribution systems: the distribution of "household registration" (hukou); the allocation of labor; and the rationing of basic foodstuffs. The system of household registration requires that every person be registered with local authorities at birth and apply to move permanently or temporarily to another location. It was started in 1959 in order to deal with the problems caused by the inability of cities to absorb massive influx of immigrants from rural areas.[5] This system enables the state to account for each citizen as a resource of the state and to fix the particular geographic, economic, social, and cultural site of each individual life. The effect is to impose a rigid order on the random movements of the population, to segregate the population into clearly defined urban and rural classes and cultures, and even at times to reconstitute families and kin networks, as when husbands and wives, parents and children, kin and neighbors are separated for countless years by household registration restrictions.

Before 1979, virtually all urban jobs were assigned through the state distributive system, and individual energies were channeled into a set of predetermined functional tasks and work sites. There was little room for variation and difference in the employment of energies, talents, and inclinations. Although recent urban reforms have allowed for individual enterprises, still the state allocation of labor remains the dominant form of employment.

The corollary of the labor allocation system is the "work-unit" (*gongzuo danwei*) system. Derived perhaps from military organization, the work-unit system assigns individuals to total institutions that oversee functions of production and reproduction, social welfare, indoctrination, and surveillance. Through a whole army of "well-meaning" personnel (Party sermonizers, Party moral-political activists and evaluators, labor union directors, Women's Federation representatives, Youth League leaders, and so forth)[6] who staff every work unit, the normative and political administration of the material and spiritual "welfare" of its members is achieved. The disciplinary power that assigns labor to work units and supervises the labor process there also makes possible the operation of normalizing techniques. For example, taking out a loan from labor union funds, the mediation of family disputes, and applying to join the Party, to marry, to give birth, or to divorce must be done through the work unit and are thus occasions for the exercise of normative power. The disciplinary and normative functions of the work unit are illustrated by a student who applied to my university for graduate study in the United States, but could send

[5] See a translation of the document "Regulations Governing Household Registration" issued by the National People's Congress, 9 January 1958 (Tien 1973:378–83). For a discussion of how the restrictions of the household registration system affect the social position of peasants, see Potter and Potter 1990, chap. 15.

[6] These positions can be seen as the Chinese counterparts to the normalizing and disciplinary roles of social workers, psychologists, doctors, and psychiatrists that Foucault discusses.

neither college transcript nor TOEFL examination scores. The reason was that after college graduation, she refused what she thought was a bad state job assignment and has been making a living on her own without attachment to any work unit. As a result, her former "unit," the university, refused to release her transcripts for five years, and she could not get permission to take the TOEFL because one must even be recommended by one's current work unit just to apply to take the test.

Disciplinary techniques are also found in the universal rationing of basic foodstuffs for urban residents.[7] Each individual and family becomes subject to an alien determination of needs, which sets down just how much people should consume based on their assigned social categories: office worker, student, athlete, manual worker, and so on. Rationing also aids in the control of populations because not only must one establish household residence in a new place in order to migrate there, one must also establish one's "grain-and-oil relationship" (liangyou guanxi), that is, get permission to receive one's basic food rations there. Throughout the 1980s, rationing steadily decreased, so that previously rationed foods such as sugar, cloth, soybean products, meat, and eggs were taken off the list. Rationing has been replaced by the market mechanism of higher prices.

In the systematic regulation of marriage, childbirth, and divorce lies another realm in which disciplinary techniques have proliferated. Not only is marriage before the age of twenty-two for males and twenty for females forbidden (in actual urban practice, permissible marriage age is three to four years later), but the need to get married, and to get married before the age of thirty, is also encouraged by virtue of this need being established as a norm and common expectation. Those who still remain single by a late age become the objects of the state's paternal concern and the discursive power of society's pity. Divorce is also mediated by the disciplines of the distributive economy. Permission to divorce is granted or withheld, first, on the basis of a thorough investigation into the nature of the couple's relationship (involving the collusion of work-unit leaders, neighbors, relatives, children, and so on), to determine that their bonds of affection are truly shattered (ganqing polie). Second, state permission to divorce is linked to whether divorce rates in the population are rising or falling, as indicated by state statistics, and is also affected by the

[7] See the document "Provisional Measures Governing Grain-Rationing in Cities and Towns," issued by the State Council in 1955 (Tien 1973:372–78, Appendix K).

state's concern with how much divorce the moral fiber of the society can tolerate.

Finally, childbirth and the fertility of the population have also fallen into the strategic relations of power. Population control in China cannot be thought of according to a simple "natural-growth and state-response" model in which state power is exterior to demographic growth and heroically responds to a situation created independently of it. The investment of population size and fertility with state power did not start with the One-Child Policy of 1979, but in the 1950s when the state promoted large families as a revolutionary duty to build up the population and strength of the new socialist order. The government banned sterilization and induced abortions and allocated grain, housing space, and living subsidies according to the number of persons in a family to encourage population growth (Liu and Song 1981:58). Another indication that the population size and fertility is not a "natural" process, but intricately tied in with the changing logic of the state is found in the fact that in the 1950s, 1960s, and early 1970s, arguments for a reduction in the already alarming population growth advanced by Ma Yinchu were branded a reactionary return to Malthusianism, which the state had labeled an apologist doctrine for capitalism in nineteenth-century Europe (Ma 1979; Liu and Song 1981:62).[8] In other words, the One-Child Policy of 1979 was *both* a response to threatening objective demographic conditions and the result of a changing logic of state power which produced a different set of disciplinary measures within an ongoing power complex of state and population.

Through the One-Child Policy the searching gaze of power has expanded its field of vision. Doctors, nurses, and representatives of planned birth committees, labor unions, and Women's Federations participate in the monitoring of women's bodies, their menstrual cycles, their sexual conduct, their use of contraception, and their relationships with husbands, parents, and in-laws. In the process, what is controlled is not merely the size of the population but also the body of the mother and the sexual, reproductive, and familial practices of the population. That the distributive economy also controls the access to "child nutrition supplements" (*yinger baojian buzhu*) and nursery

---

[8] In the 1950s through the early 1970s in China, it was thought that Malthus's grim thesis that population expands geometrically while food production grows only arithmetically was a convenient way of removing the blame for the impoverishment of the working classes from capitalist and state exploitation (Ma 1980:5).

care, as well as the mother's wages and bonuses, facilitates the spread of these techniques of control.

Besides the reign of the disciplines, the state distributive economy is also densely threaded with strategies of normalizing through classification, surveillance, and judgment. After the Revolution, the redistribution of wealth was effected by a vast social-classification grid imposed on the whole society. In urban society, people were assigned to "class status" (jieji chengfen) categories (Billeter 1985) on the basis of their economic status before the Revolution and of their birth, such as those of worker, peddler, and capitalist. They were also divided up into occupational categories in the new society, such as cadre, worker, peasant, soldier, and intellectual. Other classifications that carve up the population and have been used as a basis for segregating one portion from another are the division between Party members and "the masses"; the "Five Black Categories" (hei wulei) of landlords, rich peasants, counterrevolutionaries, bad elements, and rightists; and the "Five Red Categories" (hong wu lei) of workers, peasants, cadres, revolutionary martyrs, and revolutionary intellectuals.

Though originally inspired by the economic class analysis of Marx, these categories are in no way purely for the purposes of descriptive economics, but have come to play crucial political and normative roles. "Theoretically the status system was justified because it was seen as derived from Marxist class analysis, which was reputed to be scientific and objective. Actually, it originated from the determination to organize social relationships according to a rational and controllable order—a determination which no doubt must be interpreted both as the resurgence of a very ancient Chinese tradition and as a specifically contemporary phenomenon" (Billeter 1985:136). In the new discursive formation of power, the class-status categories embody different amounts of prestige, privilege, rights, virtues, and trust. To fall into one category is to be totally suffused with that particular class nature, to be assigned an identity stamped by the moral-political judgments levied on that class, and to be rewarded, avoided, or punished according to one's class. This normative technique of classification and identification has infiltrated and at times inundated the conduct of the distributive economy. In recent years class-status classification has fallen from the strategic dominance it enjoyed during the Cultural Revolution, but its subtle influences can still be detected at work.

There are also techniques that work vertically to break up the social body into a hierarchy of ranks and to establish chains of superior-subordinate relations. Techniques of hierarchization invest certain offices, ranks, positions, and occupations with power effects. They draw the lines of confrontation within the state distributive economy between the powers of distribution and the desire for access, between the state and the population, and between officials and the people. At the microlevel, vertical techniques are played out in the domination of the official over the applicant, of the clerks behind the counter over the customer, of the supplier over the buyer, and so forth. Office and rank in the distributive structure are transformed into loci of disciplinary and normalizing power.

Normalizing techniques can also be found in the routine public rituals for the expression of moral-political rectitude: political study sessions, criticism and self-criticism sessions, and struggle sessions. But these are crude forms of power which have often easily been subverted by countertechniques in which participants (interrogators and targets alike) play out games of posturing and charade. More effective perhaps are other techniques that promote rectitude, such as the interrelated techniques of individualization and surveillance. The system of individual dossiers (*dangan*), which follow each urban resident throughout his or her lifetime, exerts normalizing effects. Kept under lock and key in the work unit, dossiers record all awards and disciplinary actions (*chufen*) received by an individual and the evaluations and comments of peers and superiors. They serve to monitor the moral-political development of each individual. Dossiers stamp each person with the enduring records of an irreversible individual past and make the individual's life transparent for observation. The surveillance of individuals is accomplished not only by superiors but also by inciting coworkers, neighbors, and (especially during the Cultural Revolution) friends and family members to reveal their true natures. Thus mutual surveillance breaks down horizontal bonds to increase the individualization of the society, and the creation of individuals through dossiers, labor allocation, household registration, classification, and so on, expands the possibilities of surveillance.

The state distributive economy consists in more than the simple exchange of the means of subsistence for productive labor. Techniques of power operating in the exchange process ensure that the resulting dependence of the population is put to good use. The social body must pay for its subsistence by making itself available to be reshaped and put into order by a new mode of power. Yet the disciplinary and normalizing techniques of this mode of power in conjunction with a state distributive economy do not exhaust the total field of power relations. Like weeds that have managed to survive in the cracks of a building, countertechniques or oppositional practices have also multiplied and cross-fertilized to form a stubborn strain of resistance in the shelter of another mode of exchange, that of the Chinese gift economy.

Countertechniques in the Gift Economy

In Chapter 2 I outlined some typical contexts and goals in the deployment of guanxixue, from getting a movie ticket to changing residence. All of these use-contexts involve getting permission from and access through an official, a clerk, or some other representative of the all-pervasive state distributive economy. These are the fronts where the gift economy can be said to be challenging or whittling away at state power.

As noted in the preceding ethnographic chapters, there is both an official discourse and a popular discourse of guanxi, which feed on each other. Official discourse concentrates on how people use the art of guanxi to engage in official corruption detrimental to the good of the whole society, on how private and individual interests are furthered at the expense of playing havoc to a system of fair and equitable distribution. A corpus of practices often labeled "crooked winds" (*waifeng*) is well documented and excoriated in the official Chinese press: the use of public position for private gain, nepotism, patronage, factional favoritism, bribery, the exchange of special privileges (*tequan*) of office among officials, and so forth.

The popular discourse of guanxi also participates in denouncing the art of guanxi in this manner, but at the same time it also reinterprets the official denunciations of guanxi. Embodied in popular discourse are the contradiction of condemnation on the one hand and admiration and even approbation of the art of guanxi on the other. There is a pleasure derived from recounting tales of the exploits and small victories of guanxi in everyday life. Incited by examples of ingenious practices of guanxi, popular discourse plants the suggestion that if others are doing it, one should not be left out. And so popular discourse both encourages guanxixue and teaches the tactics of the gift economy. Perhaps more important, it superimposes onto official discourse a respect for and affirmation of the alternative relational ethics of the gift economy, the ethics of obligation, reciprocity, and mutual aid, and of the responsibilities of friendship and kinship.

By feeding off official discourse and twisting it for other ends, popular discourse illustrates how official corruption and popular practices of guanxi are related. Both are, in a sense, "produced" by the distributive economy, which relies on a bureaucracy of distributors to dispense livelihood and discipline. Some officials do take advantage of the system to promote their own class status positions, but on the underside of personal official power there dwells a repertory of the tactics of guanxi for the population. The gift economy not only challenges official power, it also subverts the dominant mode of economy. In other words, prefigured in the distributive economy are the seeds and possibilities of challenges to its power. The gift economy did not arise in a vacuum, nor is it a totally independent mode of exchange lying completely outside state distribution. Rather, it "poaches" on the territory of another mode of exchange, seeking the right occasions to strike and divert resources to its own method of circulation. In the process, it alters and weakens in a piecemeal fashion the structural principles and smooth operations of state power.

Here de Certeau's distinction between strategies and tactics is pertinent (1984:xix, 35–39). Strategies are manipulations of power relations that result from the isolation of a subject with a delimited *place* of its own. This subject exerts will and power from its own place or base of operations over the place of its objectified environment. Whether in the form of an army, a scientific institution, or a state, this subject engages in strategies to establish and maintain its territory independent of changing circumstances; it tries to conquer *time* by grasping space. Strategies want to locate and categorize each particular element in a proper place, to systematically organize, control, and predict all types of movement. In contrast, tactics enjoy no proper place or distinct and recognized discourse of their own, but are the "art of the weak" and must operate in the very place already marked out and claimed by strategies. They are furtive and "calculated"; they can only rely on *timely* occasions that have slipped by the organizing power of strategies. Caught up in discrete instances of struggle, tactics have neither an encompassing vision of the whole nor a unified program for its activities. It would seem that the gift economy, by operating on the underside of the space carved out by distributive power, represents very much the tactics rather than the strategies of power. The question then is, How can the tactics of the gift economy bring about oppositional effects on the dominant mode of power?

It was Marx who pointed out that commodities have a twofold nature, that of use-value and that of the "mysterious" and "transcen-

dent" character of exchange-value.[9] Use-value appears straightfor-
wardly as the value arising from the material utility of a product;
however, "the first step made by an object of utility towards acquiring exchange-value is when it forms a non-use-value for its owner,"
that is, when it gains for its owner another utility, a "utility for the
purposes of exchange" (Marx 1906:99–100). Exchange-value can
only be realized when commodities are exchanged, for it is through
relations of equivalence between commodities in circulation that exchange-value is produced in the form of money for their owners. Just
as commodities are composed of two different kinds of value, so it
must also be pointed out that gifts, in addition to their use-value, also
possess a *symbolic* value, which, like Marx's exchange-value, derives
from or can only be realized in the process of exchange or circulation.

   Anthropologists have long discerned the symbolic value of gifts:
"The point is that there is much more in the exchange itself than in
the things exchanged" (Lévi-Strauss 1969:59). Bronislaw Malinowski
rejected the utilitarian fallacy, which construed kula exchange as one
of necessities for material life. He saw it rather as an important organizational principle of Trobriand society, establishing rank, affirming
the bonds of kinship, and relationships in law (1961:166–67). Mauss
showed that the exaggerated generosity and wastefulness in Native
American potlatches in the Pacific Northwest were displays of wealth
and symbolic struggles for prestige and that gift-giving in general promotes social solidarity (1967). Marshall Sahlins stressed that gifts
promote peace and can be viewed as the original social contract
(1972:169). I would like to explore another effect of gift exchange, a
very salient one in the context of Chinese society, that although the
immediate goal of the art of guanxi is to acquire some material utility,
it exerts a subversive effect on the microtechniques of administrative
power.

   How does the gift economy produce this effect? We must look at
the minute mechanisms activated in each instance of guanxi transaction. Since the oppositional practices of the art of guanxi are embedded in culture and rich in symbolism, it seems appropriate to resort to
a cultural and symbolic analysis developed by anthropology to look

---

[9] Marx writes in *Capital*: "Commodities come into the world in the shape of use-values,
articles, or goods, such as iron, linen, corn, &c. This is their plain, homely, bodily form.
They are, however, commodities, only because they are something twofold, both objects of
utility, and, at the same time, depositories of value. They manifest themselves therefore as
commodities, or have the form of commodities, only in so far as they have two forms, a
physical or natural form, and a value form" (1906:54–55).

at the anatomies of cultures (those patterns of practices mediated by the construction of meaning) to elucidate these mechanisms of the gift economy.

In order to bring out the symbolic dimension of gifts, their symbolic qualities were likened to the material exchange-value Marx discovered hidden in commodities. When we delineate the mechanisms through which the gift economy operates furtively within the space of the state distributive economy, we need to recognize a fundamental distinction between the non-use-values of gifts and of commodities. The gift, unlike the commodity, is *inalienable* from its owner (Gregory 1982:18–19, 24). Since possession of a gift is contingent on repayment, a recipient does not have full rights of ownership over the gift. These rights are subject to the obligations owed by recipient to donor. There is no subject-object dichotomy in gift-exchange as in the owner-property relation in commodity transaction (Strathern 1983). The lack of a disjunction between person and thing in gift-exchange means that donor, gift, and recipient share a common symbolic substance, a linkage made possible through the medium of the gift. According to Mauss, gift-exchange creates spiritual bonds between "things which are to some extent parts of persons, and persons and groups that behave in some measure as if they were things" (1967:10–11). The gift is therefore never totally alienated from the donor, since he or she still has a hold on the gift in the form of a moral right to something in exchange for the gift. In contrast to gift-exchange, commodity-exchange establishes objective quantitative relationships between the objects exchanged, not personal qualitative relationships between the subjects exchanging the objects (Gregory 1982:41). Therefore, it is in this very space of personal relationship established by the gift that the art of guanxi unleashes its countertechniques of power.

The symbolic mechanisms that produce the oppositional effects of the gift economy can be viewed at two levels: the *personal* and the *systemic*. The personal level refers to the concrete instances of each guanxi transaction, in which microstruggles and acts of what Pierre Bourdieu has called symbolic violence take place (1977). The systemic level represents the cumulative power effects of all acts of guanxi exchange, which pose an abstract and general challenge to the dominant means of power. Proceeding with the anatomy of power at the personal level, I have isolated five movements or processes of tactical engagement found in each enactment of the art of guanxi. These are (1) transformation, (2) addition and layering, (3) moral subordination or status antagonism, (4) appropriation or possession, and (5) conversion.

These five mechanisms of symbolic violence in the gift economy hinge on a cultural construction of personhood which is in many ways different from the construction of the autonomous individual dominant in the West. That the individual is an "indivisible, 'elementary' man, both a biological being and a thinking subject [who] incarnates the whole of mankind [and] is the measure of all things" is a unique element of modern Western ideology with roots in Christianity and the Enlightenment, has been shown by scholars of comparative culture such as Louis Dumont (1970:9). In surveying the category of the person cross-culturally, Mauss also concludes, "Those who have made of the human person a complete entity, independent of all others save God, are rare" (1985:14).

Rather than creating discrete and unified ontological categories of persons each having the same equality of rights, the Chinese subscribe more to a *relational* construction of persons. That is to say, the autonomy and rights of persons and the sense of personal identity are based on differences in moral and social status and on the moral claims and judgments of others. Chinese personhood and personal identity are not given in the abstract as something intrinsic to and fixed in human nature, but are constantly being created, altered, and dismantled in particular social relationships. Furthermore, the boundaries of personhood are permeable and can easily be enlarged to encompass a scope beyond that of the biological individual. As a result, Chinese culture presents a frequent lack of clear-cut boundaries between self and other, as one Western-educated Chinese scholar has noted, "In Chinese culture, the 'dyadic' relationship where 'there is a me inside of you; and there is a you inside of me' is something that approximates a 'cultural law.' It can be played out with many possibilities" (Sun 1983:137). One of these possibilities is the art of guanxi, which has appropriated this cultural construction of persons as the basis of its operations and plays out its ramifications to the fullest.

It is interesting that in a Western context, the relational and intersubjective construction of persons describes a feminine gender while "separation" and "objectivity" are regarded as typically male (Chodorow 1974, 1978; Keller 1987). In defining persons, Western individualism adopts a male-oriented emphasis on setting boundaries between the self and the other. From a Western psychoanalytic feminist perspective, the Chinese relational construction of persons preserves more of the feminine and maternal principles of identity in its cultural formation of both women and men. Since the art of guanxi is very much relational, it would appear relatively "feminine" from those constructions which emphasize the separation and independence of the individual. The gender of the art of gunaxi is taken up again in the Conclusion.

The first movement to be examined in a guanxi transaction, "transformation," occurs during the preparation for a guanxi overture. Guanxi exchange cannot take place without first establishing a basis of "familiarity" in the relationship between two parties. At this stage, the logic of guanxi tactics is expressed in the attempt to transform the other into the familiar, to bridge the gap between the outside and the inside.

The insider/outsider dichotomy is an important feature of Chinese cultural ideology, perhaps because Chinese culture is rooted in a kinship-based sedentary agricultural society. When my uncle from a small and remote town in southern China visited me in Beijing, I took him to Beihai park and to lunch in a restaurant there. The restaurant service personnel were even ruder than usual. At the counter for buying beer, the woman eyed my uncle's somewhat shabby clothes and impatiently denied that they sold any beer. Only when I insisted and pointed to the cases of beer on which she was resting one foot, did she open a bottle for us, unabashed by the fact that her lie was so evident for all to see. My uncle's explanation for the treatment we received that day was that they knew we were "people from outside" (*waidiren*), that is, not Beijing natives, and that was how people treat outsiders. Some everyday expressions also manifest this dichotomy: "Do not take me for an outsider" ("Buyao jianwai") is employed when a host wants a guest to make herself at home, or when a person wants someone to dispense with formalities and treat him as an insider. The differential treatment of kin and non-kin, friend and stranger, fellow Chinese and foreigner is expressed in the saying "Distinguish between the inside and the outside" ("Neiwai you bie"). This cultural dichotomy can even be politicized, as when a citizen is accused of leaking information to a foreign country (*li tong waiguo*). Not only are outsiders not to be trusted, they are also under no obligation to help a person. Therefore, in the art of guanxi the pull of obligation must be introduced or strengthened by encompassing the outside within an expanding sphere of the inside.

The categories of inside and outside are also couched in food metaphors. A "familiar person," one with whom guanxi exchange can take place more easily, is also a "*cooked* person," whereas its opposite, the "stranger," is an "*uncooked* or *raw* person," according to the literal meanings of the words *shouren* and *shengren*. In addition, *shouren* can also be rendered literally a *"ripe* person," one who is "developed" or "mature" (*chengshou*), and *shengren* is also literally the *"unripe* person," connoting the sense of "newborn" (*xinsheng*). Bridging the gap between the inside and the outside in order to make guanxi exchange possible is accomplished by a transformation of the "uncooked" into the "cooked," in a sense preparing the other to make him/her palatable or ready for guanxi overtures. Likewise, the "unripe" must pass through the transformative process of time or length of personal contact to attain "ripeness," that is, maturity or familiarity.

In the art of guanxi, this transformation occurs in the process of appealing to shared identities between persons. Hence the emphasis on "shared" (*tong*) qualities and experiences that shape the identities of classmates (*tongxue*), or persons from the same county or province (*tongxiang*), colleagues (*tongshi*), as well as kinfolk, teachers and students, masters and apprentices, and so on. Familiarity, then, is born of the fusion of personal identities. And shared identities establish the basis for the obligation and compulsion to share one's wealth and to help with one's labor.

Where these relationships of familiarity are already well established and the parties involved are quite close, as in relationships of kinship and friendship, transformation can be dispensed with because identities are already fused. Tactics of transformation are found most often in situations in which two persons are not already bound within a common sphere of familiarity and therefore need to play up some objective link. Between strangers, transformation of identities is often achieved through a mutual acquaintance. "You worked in the same office as Ye? Oh, he and I were elementary school classmates. We haven't seen each other for years, but we used to play together." No matter how tenuous the social connection asserted, identities have been slightly realigned around a common link and the relationship now begins to assume a different light. The intermediary acts as a connector cable, so to speak, infusing a common current of identity into the two persons and draws them within a single circle of insideness. Mutual obligation may thus be activated because if one shares a basis of identity or familiarity, one should be prepared to share oneself with the other, to put oneself at his or her disposal, to do to the other what one would do to oneself, since the other has become an extension of oneself.

In the mechanism of "adding and layering" what occurs is more than the conceptual rearrangement of identities of persons, it is the symbolic breaking down of boundaries as a substance or gift from one person is attached to the person of the other, thus reducing the barrier of otherness between them. When one receives a gift, banquet, or favor, one shares not only an identity with the donor in terms of native place of origin, kinship, school, or workplace, but one also shares the donor's personal substance, since the gift embodies the donor's labor and wealth.

Heart is a central symbol for person or self in Chinese culture. Whereas in the Enlightenment West, the mind is the key to the self ("I think, therefore I am"), in the Chinese context, the heart and its feelings signify persons. Even such a modern Western invention as psychology, which examines the individual mind, is translated "the study of the principles of the heart" (*xinlixue*). When a gift is given, it is often accompanied by the phrase,

Zhe liwu shi wode yidian xinyi.

This gift is a small token of my regard.

The word for "regard," *xinyi*, means literally, "sentiments" or "spirit" of the heart. Since heart represents person, the gift is really a token of the person of the donor. Personal efforts and labor are also called "heart and blood" (*xinxue*); therefore, when these are given in the form of gifts, favors, or banquets, they signify a transfer or penetration of personal substance to another. And the term "heart and liver" (*xingan*) can designate either personal conscience or a beloved daughter or son, who are extensions of one's own substance. That is why, between close friends, family members, and kin, obligations need not be activated by giving gifts, nor are debts carefully accounted (*bu jijiao*), because there is already a sharing of hearts or a fusing of persons in these relationships.

How does gift-giving represent the adding on of personal substance? As noted above, gifts are not alienable from persons in exchange, there is no subject-object dichotomy in gift-exchange as in the owner-property relation in a commodity transaction (Strathern 1983). The lack of a disjunction between person and thing in gift-exchange means that the gift remains symbolically attached to and identified with the person of the donor, thus the gift becomes a medium for introducing the personal substance of its donor into the person of the recipient. Adding and layering, then, represent tactical incursions into the recipient's personal substance, from where he or she can be manipulated, which is what happens in the next stage of the art of guanxi.

The third movement, "status antagonism," is often played out in the struggle for "face" (*mianzi*) and moral superiority between donor and recipient. Face is not only a matter of prestige, but an emblem for personal identity, for the autonomy and integrity of personhood (Hu 1944). Intact face is a source of a sense of well-being, self-respect (*zizunxin*), and security. Face and identity are linked because they do not depend on conformity to abstract norms and ideals, but depend more on internalizing the approbation of others in the context of particular relationships. That is to say, the Chinese relational construction of personhood represented by the importance of face provides the mechanism for the art of guanxi to constrain the actions of a gift recipient. Threats to one's face constitute threats to one's identity, which is constructed relationally by internalizing the judgment of others in oneself. And reduced or fragmented face poses a disadvantage in a person's position and leverage in social interaction.

Chinese is rich in portraying the things that can happen to face. Besides "wanting face" (*yao mianzi*), "losing face" (*diou mianzi*), and "having face" (*you mianzi*), one can also "borrow face" (*jie mianzi*), "give face" (*gei mianzi*), "increase face" (*zengjia mianzi*), "contest face" (*zheng mianzi*), "save face" (*liou mianzi*), and compare face as in the expression "His face is greater than others" ("Tade mianzi bi bieren da"). The larger one's face, the more prestige and security one possesses and, therefore, the more self-determination one enjoys in social transactions. By losing or giving away part of one's substance in guanxi exchange, one paradoxically gains or increases one's face. Conversely, the size of one's face is inversely related to the amount and frequency one receives of another's substance in the art of guanxi.

This inverse relation between giving and gaining is illustrated by the example an informant named Wang gave me of what is meant by "giving him some face": "I don't really want to waste my money and buy something from an individual enterpriser friend named Lao Chen, but another friend says, 'Think a bit on Lao Chen's behalf, give him some face.' So I buy something from that Lao Chen." I asked Wang if that meant that he ended up short (*chi kui*) in the transaction. "Yes, that's exactly the point. Lao Chen gains face while I end up short [*chi kui*]." The moral of the story is that Wang's material loss results in Lao Chen's symbolic gain, which in Wang's mind, overrides Lao Chen's material benefits from the sale. Wang does not gain face himself unless Lao Chen knows that Wang really did not want to buy his merchandise.

By a similar logic, one sacrifices the material wealth and labor that goes into transferring a part of oneself in the form of a gift, banquet, or favor, but what one gains is an important moral (and at the same time, material) advantage over the recipient of one's generosity. The effect of adding one's substance to the other is that one can in turn take the other's face and add it to one's own. In other words, the donor becomes the moral and symbolic superior of the recipient and can thus subject the latter to his or her will. The creation of this asymmetrical microrelationship is a crucial step in the mechanisms of the gift economy. It obtains regardless of the status positions of the two participants in the larger society, but this microantagonism of status within the art of guanxi takes on special significance when the recipient has a higher status in society than the donor. This is perhaps why the higher the social status of the guest, the greater the generosity that is unleashed to subdue him or her, and why it is usually the case that those who give are lower in social status and influence than those who receive. Through this tactical movement of moral subordination in the art of guanxi, donors are able to effect a symbolic reversal of the larger social hierarchy, a reversal with material consequences.

The fourth stage is centered in the recipient of the gift. For the recipient, accepting another's substance is to be "appropriated" or "possessed" by the other in oneself. Having lost face to the donor, the recipient becomes subject to the internalized will of the other; and having been morally subordinated, he or she is now beholden to and dependent on the person of the donor. Since her face has been taken away and part of her person is occupied by another's substance, her person is reduced in stature. This is experienced as a softening of her will, as indicated by this saying:

Chi ren zui ruan; Na ren shou duan.

Eating from others, one's mouth becomes soft.
Taking from others, one's hand becomes short.

The saying has been explained to me in the following way: After one has eaten of other's food, one's mouth finds it difficult to "harden" and purse up to refuse the other's request for help or to say bad things about the other. When one takes a gift from someone, the hand grows short, and so cannot reach out to push that person away when he or she needs help. Nor can the shortened hand easily reach out to hit or make trouble for the other. Mouths that have eaten and hands that have taken become "easy to persuade" (*hao shuo hua*) and likely to "speak well" (*shuo hao hua*) of their hosts to others, especially their superiors. Thus for face, mouth, and hand, accepting a gift is not so much a gain as a loss or reduction of stature and control. It follows that indebtedness is couched in terms of a state of loss, a loss of wholeness of person and independence. To restore one's face, identity, and self-respect, the debt must be repaid, either to restore the balance of relationships or to create a new asymmetry by giving back more than was first given.

Finally, a fifth step in the anatomy of the operations of the gift economy is that of the "conversion" of one kind of value into another and then into a third. Conversion of values takes place when the recipient repays the debt he or she owes in order to compensate for the loss sustained in the acceptance of the gift. Repayment may take either the form of a *material object* such as giving a gift in order to acquire medicines or train tickets, for example, or the form of *personal labor* such as making furniture, or more important, helping one's donor to "accomplish a task" (*banshi*), such as using one's position to locate and persuade the right official to grant a request or writing a note to a subordinate in the office to give the donor's son a job in the desired department. Personal wealth and labor may also be combined to give a banquet as a gesture of thanks for help rendered. Here it must be pointed out at length that the gift economy is so called because the structure and logic of its operations are distinct from those of state distributive economy and the fledgling commodity economy. A purely economistic approach derived from a capitalist milieu cannot adequately explicate the workings of the gift economy, nor can it distinguish between guanxi or gift transactions and such things as bribe, barter, and private market exchange.

In the step of conversion the distinctiveness of the gift economy is revealed.[10] The conversion of values in the gift economy follows a

[10] Pierre Bourdieu challenges both the narrow economistic approach, which sees only the cash nexus and individual economic interest (in the restricted sense) in noncapitalist exchange, as well as "naively idyllic representations of 'pre-capitalist' societies," which deny they give play to any economic calculation. Rather, in understanding exchange in noncapitalist societies, Bourdieu proposes to recognize economic calculation in the pursuit of material and symbolic goods, at the same time that no distinction is made between economic and symbolic capital, a distinction that is alien to these economies. "The only way in which such [an approach] can apprehend the undifferentiatedness of economic and symbolic capital is in the form of their perfect interconvertibility." That is to say, noncapitalist economies

more complex structure than either barter or simple commodity-exchange. Barter is a mere direct and immediate exchange of use-values: product A for product B. Commodity-exchange involves an additional step of conversion to money as an objective medium of exchange. Take Marx's example in *Capital* of the weaver who must sell the linen he weaves in order to purchase a family Bible for use (Marx 1906:116–28). First, the universal value of socially necessary labor time (exchange-value) is translated from its commodity form to its monetary form during sale. Thus the linen's use-value is converted into exchange-value. Then the monetary form is in turn converted into another commodity form during purchase. In other words, the exchange-value of the linen is reconverted into the use-value of the Bible through a crucial detour into labor's money form. The common and universal value underlying all of the items involved, the weaver's labor, the linen, money, the Bible, and the labor of making the Bible is that of exchange-value. Commodity-exchange represents the circulation of different forms of this value until the chain of circulation is broken by consumption adopting the use-value of an item. In this scheme the relative status of persons and the quality of social relationships are rendered secondary concerns by the leveling process generated by money-price equivalences.

In guanxi exchange, however, the range of basic items circulated is much wider, and they cannot be measured by a single objective value. Their equivalences are not systematized or universalized, but remain context- and person-specific. The forms of value which can be converted and circulated are the following:

Gift capital. This category of exchange items can include gifts proper (such as cigarettes and alcoholic drinks [*yanjiu*], cakes and fruit, watches, TVs); banquets or more modest dinners; and the whole variety of favors, especially bureaucratic permissions and privileges. Gift capital is composed of two subcategories: *material capital* or wealth and money that come from state or collective wages, and in some cases, from private earnings in the petty market economy which is spent on the gift, and *body capital*, the labor energy and time expended in buying or making a gift or banquet or in performing a favor.

---

entail the pursuit of both economic (material) and symbolic interest, where symbolic interest is not merely "gratuitous," but essential because of the importance of the conversion of one kind of capital into another (1977:176–78).

Symbolic capital. Symbolic capital accrues to a donor when a social investment or the penetration of personal substance yields such benefits as the loss or reduction of face or an unbalanced state of indebtedness, gratitude, or obligation on the part of the guanxi target.

Office capital. The capital of office refers to the social capital provided by occupying positions and ranks that give special access to desirable products and opportunities unavailable otherwise. Office capital is especially high for household registration officials, municipal housing bureau officials, work-unit personnel-department heads, hospital leaders, and the like. This capital can also refer to the broader sense of an office that is outside the formal government organs but directly controls some desirable, such as those "offices" of shop clerk, driver, nurse, or pharmacist.

Political capital. In the native system of categories, political capital [*zhengzhi ziben*] is the asset a person enjoys from being (1) a Party member, (2) born with a good (i.e., low-class) family background, or (3) a powerful official. These assets provide not only some material privileges but also political security (especially in the event of a political campaign) and further upward mobility. I have chosen to install office capital as a separate category to emphasize the difference between political and social capital. Since the Cultural Revolution the "conversion power" of political capital has diminished somewhat.

Whereas commodities must usually be converted into money in order to realize a desired use-value, the art of guanxi aims at building up symbolic capital, which can be converted into usable gift capital. In the distributive economy, often it is office capital or sometimes political capital, not money, that controls access to desirables. The symbolic capital generated by the art of guanxi is the crucial bridge to office and/or political capital and the ultimate conversion of material and body capital to the desired end. Gifts invested with wealth and labor are converted into the symbolic capital of face, gratitude, indebtedness, or obligation. Symbolic capital can then be translated into office and political capital when, say, an official in charge of dispensing desirables grants the request of the donor and waives considerations of the donor's bad class background or other political fault.

At this point, the reasons that the Chinese gift economy cannot be confused with bribery, barter, black market, or commodity economies and thrown together with them into a catchall "second economy" become evident. The second economies in state-socialist societies have been defined in many ways by scholars of Eastern Europe: as consisting in activities for private gain or which are considered illegal (Grossman 1977); as being outside state plans (O'Hearn 1980); or as subordinate but complementary counterparts to the first economies, distinguished from them by budgetary constraints that decree survival on the basis of profitability (Galasi 1985). The assertion that the second economy serves as "a partial substitute for the missing market mechanism" which avoids the "rigidity, delays, inefficiency, disequilibria, and inconsistencies" (Grossman 1982:101) of the command economy is better applied to the Chinese commodity economy than to what I call the gift economy. Yet Steven Sampson would subsume what appears to be the gift economy under the rubric of the second economy. For him, the activities that compose the second economy can be placed in three categories: (1) the "parallel economy"—legal activities outside of planned economy, such as private farm plots; (2) the "underground economy"—illegal activities such as theft of state property, black marketeering, graft, and bribery; and (3) the "hidden economy"—undocumented activities such as family labor, the exchange of goods and favors between kin, friends, and neighbors, and gift-giving (Sampson 1983). Perhaps the confusion of the gift economy with the profit-oriented second economy arises from concentrating only on the purely economic categories and functional outcomes of exchange. An examination of the microdynamics of power in gift relations argues for a conception of the gift economy as a sphere of practices which operate very differently from those of the second economy.

First, unlike the commodity economy, the art of guanxi does not entail a disjunction between subject and object, or between the "law of persons" and the "law of things" (Gluckman 1965). In other words, the exchange of gifts is inextricably tied in with the identities of the transactors, their relative statuses (defined both at the level of gift exchange and at the level of larger social categories), and the nature of the mutual obligations that inform their relationship. The exchange of things is governed not only by the material values of the things or their supply and demand, but also by the quality of the personal relationship between transactors. As Christopher Healey has noted of two types of exchange relations among the Maring of New Guinea, "Trade is overtly concerned with relations between material objects mediated by social relations; prestations with relations between people mediated by material goods" (1984:45). Since gifts are parts of persons, donors do not separate from them completely; and recipients never own them totally, since recipients are still bound by obligations to the donor. In the gift economy, there is no distinction between the transaction of material utilities and the discharging of obligations in social relationships such as those of friendship, kinship, and superior and subordinate.

By contrast, bribery, barter, black market, and legal market economy transactions are not as embedded in ongoing social relationships but tend to be restricted to that dictated by the purely economic relationship at hand. Hence such transactions can take place between any strangers and are generally discrete rather than continuous. Whereas in gift-giving, the return of a favor is structurally uncertain, in commodity transactions, payment assures the rendering of service. This argument, that the gift economy and the second economy are qualitatively different, is supported by Joseph Berliner's distinction between *blat* and bribery in the former Soviet Union. In *blat* there is a "personal basis for expecting a proposal to be listened to," whereas bribery is conceived of as only a relationship linked by material interest and characterized by direct and immediate payment (1957:191). In the Chinese cultural discourse, on the one hand, there is often a fine line between the art of guanxi and bribery (*xinghui*). Yet on the other hand, the two are still conceptually distinguished by such things as cultural judgments of the level of instrumentalism; the form and art of gift-giving (gifts or money, ordinary gifts or expensive gifts, temporal lengths of familiarity and repayment, and so on); and whether the effects are considered ethical or unethical (whether it is using office for self-gain or an ordinary person seeking solutions to legitimate problems).

The Chinese gift economy cannot be confused with the commodity features of the second economy for a second reason. Traditional Chinese society also had a developed petty-commodity economy, which included both barter and money transactions. Although with socialism the society saw a temporary eclipse of this commodity tradition, the art of guanxi is still embedded in a set of discourse and practices that self-consciously defines itself *against* the impersonal elements of money transactions and direct buying and selling in this tradition. The decorum and rules of etiquette of the art of guanxi stress the importance of the length and quality of personal relationships, of dealing with those who are "inside," and the inappropriateness of immediate repayment and precise accounting of gift and return equivalences. This is reminiscent of an account of village life in the 1920s where the local villagers would feel obliged to walk outside the village to a market in order to engage in trade and bargaining with their very neighbors. They did not trade on each other's doorstep, but in the market, because there they could shed their ties of obligation and etiquette and adopt the status of strangers, which is more appropriate to impersonal trading and haggling (Fei 1983:80–81).[11] For the gift economy, the style and manner in which exchange is carried out is not merely gratuitous, but constitutive of a mode of exchange based on very different principles of operation than commodity economy. As J. Kenedi puts it, "An outside observer would only see the choreography: friendly conversation, polished manners, courteous behaviour. In fact, these are not mere formalities, but the essence" (1981:79).

A third distinguishing feature of the art of guanxi which sets it apart from the other forms of exchange is the centrality of symbolic interest or capital in the conversion of values. In the gift economy, a relationship is not simply a transparent medium for the exchange of commodities, but also a medium for the exchange of a component as crucial as the thing given: symbolic capital in the form of face, moral advantage, social debt, obligation, and reciprocity. Guanxi exchange makes possible the production of symbolic capital either as a means or as an end in itself, as in the desire for political and social security. Possession of symbolic capital compensates for the lack of material, office, or political capital, and is often more effective and easily convertible than money when engaging a state distributive economy.

All this concern to distinguish the Chinese gift economy from what has been written about the second economy is not to deny its economic and instrumental aspects, but to argue that it cannot easily be encapsulated by definitions of economic exchange or gift-giving derived from a Western market context. In the West, a capitalist market society, "gift-exchange—in which persons and things, interest and disinterest are merged—has been fractured, leaving gifts *opposed* to exchange, persons *opposed* to things and interest to disinterest. The ideology of a disinterested gift emerges in parallel with an ideology of a purely interested exchange" (Parry 1986:458). In other words, a society in which the market and the pursuit of individual economic interests are dominant easily results in *either* a certain romanticization of gift-giving as "pure" and disinterested, a refuge from the inexo-

---

[11] Malinowski also noted that Trobriand Islanders made a clear distinction between the gift economy of the kula exchange which precluded any ungraceful haggling, and the practice of barter (*gimwali*), in which the value equivalence of two objects is thoroughly bargained about and computed (1961:95–96).

rable motivations of the market, *or* the dismissal of gift-giving's form and principles of decorum as merely obfuscatory rationalizations for underlying market transactions. So in perceiving instrumentalism in the gift economy in modern societies, the tendency is often to equate it with what is readily understandable in economic and market terms, and to construct mutually exclusive categories of pure gift and economically interested gift. I would like to argue that in the context of a state distributive economy, market relations are embedded in the gift instead of the reverse, and the art of guanxi embodies the features of the primitive nonmarket gift explicated by Mauss: a combination of both interest and disinterest, both voluntary and constrained. Yet whereas the primitive gift can be seen as a form of social contract in which there is no state to assume the role, the Chinese art of guanxi takes on added significance in the context of the particular forms of power that have crystallized around the state distributive economy in socialist society.

Propositions

Writing on the ruses of popular culture which furtively play within the space of the capitalist and consumerist production of power (such as TV programs), de Certeau has explored how elements of popular culture can *reappropriate* these motifs of domination (1984). Users and consumers of the products of a capitalist culture-industry can escape domination by putting such products to creative uses and subjecting them to meanings not originally intended, in the same way that people who rent an apartment can reappropriate an alien space and make it their home (1984:xxi). In a similar manner, the art of guanxi *redistributes* what the state economy has already distributed, according to people's own interpretation of needs and the advantages of horizontal social relationships.

That which distributes has a tendency to ask for compliance in return. For all its discourse of fair and equitable distribution and guaranteed security, the distributive economy is also a one-sided system of state generosity which creates a one-sided dependency on the part of the population it administers. Through the techniques of bio-power the state avails itself of the opportunities provided by its particular conditions of exchange to normalize and discipline the social body. Such categories of exchange as individuals, class, needs, shortages, rank and prestige, and morality are not objectively given in the world, but are actively constituted by a certain mode of power. The gift economy *reconstructs* these categories in ways that deflect and wreak some havoc on the operations of bio-power.

One way the gift economy reconstructs the categories of bio-power is its substitution of a discourse of relational ethics for the dominant discourse of universalist ethics which pervades the state distributive mode of exchange. The gift economy stresses a contextual and expandable circle of social relationships and commitments rather than fixed class-status categories or loyalties to abstract and universal notions of the state, the country, the Party, and a particular political-economic system. The social relationships and obligations of the gift economy are immediate and revisable, contingent on personal circumstances and specific power situations. Relational ethics foregrounds relative insider/outsider concerns over normative concerns and moral-political criteria for exchange and distribution. This is anathema to the discourse of universalistic ethics, in which the units of loyalties are fixed, and therefore not subject to reconstruction, and are to be uniformly applied, regardless of contingent situations and particular relationships.

At the systemic level, the gift economy carves out a sphere of oppositional tactics against techniques of normalization and discipline. This is shown in the fact that the art of guanxi is practiced not only in conditions of economic scarcity, but can be detected everywhere state power tries to extend and systematize its control over the population. The sites of struggle between two approaches to distribution are found in the contested realms of population movement, biological reproduction, health and welfare of the population, marriage and divorce, labor assignments, promotion in office and access to political authority, definition of social needs in both consumption and production, and supply and marketing relationships between units of production such as factories, classification of the population into class identities, among others.

The gift economy harbors another sort of oppositional tactic at the systemic level. Its bonds of obligation and indebtedness effect a subversion of disciplinary techniques of individualization, as well as the spatializing power of the distribution, enclosure, and partitioning of the population. Guanxi can be used to elude the constitution of individuals and individual needs by state power. This is accomplished when the relational ethics of guanxi are introduced into the administration of the household registration system, the rationing system, the labor allocation system, the work-unit (*danwei*) system, the social welfare system, and the dossier surveillance system. Guanxi practice in these areas also helps corrode the edifice of spatializing power which would control population movements and the conditions of that population's reproduction and growth. Furthermore, the situational time scheme of the art of guanxi (long-term symbolic investment, payment on need) also provides a challenge to the workings of a temporal power that subjects needs to its own timing.

Status antagonism, another mechanism in the art of guanxi, can in given situations dismantle the construction of official and universal hierarchy and rank. In anthropology, it has been shown that efforts are often made to keep "inalienable possessions" out of gift circulation, because retention of these precious objects (such as scepters, crowns, feather cloaks, and Kwakiutl coppers) establishes the difference between their owners and others, and this difference is transformed into rank, authority, and political hierarchy (Wiener 1992: 40). This means that initiating gift-exchange with these owners is also a way to force them to become exchange partners and "to snare what is not part of that exchange" (1992:42). That is to say, gift-exchange can serve as an attempt at leveling hierarchy by indebting those with rank and pressuring them to give up some of their goods or authority.

Similary, in contemporary China, it is often people of lower status and rank who feel obliged to give gifts to officials and clerks who have the "inalienable possession"[12] of the office, rank, or work position that gives them access to goods and opportunities. Gift-giving creates a microcosmic world in which hierarchical relations are to a certain extent reversed. Donors become the moral superiors of recipients, who now owe favors to their donors. Symbolic capital compensates for the lack of material, office, or political capital. Thus face and the morality of reciprocity, obligation, and indebtedness become in a sense the ammunition of the weak. This mobilization of the forces of gift morality effects a subtle displacement of the abstract principles of bureaucratic hierarchy and defuses their potency by diversifying the state economy's principle of classification and distribution by rank.

A young woman worker explained the proverb "A county official cannot compare with an official in charge" ("Xian4guan1 buru xian4 guan3") in this way:

Take for example, the president of Beijing University: he is a famous and powerful person. But even he cannot get his son a job in a certain

---

[12] Gift-giving can seldom totally alienate these officials from their office or rank. Only state power, with its disciplinary and surveillance techniques, can affect official power.

factory without a "familiar person" there. The person in charge of personnel at this factory won't feel compelled to do it. He would first give a job to the son of a friend or to someone who has done him a favor, or to whoever his superiors want him to let in. The president of Beida poses no threat to this personnel director.

The personnel director does not fear the university president because the president's authority is limited to the jurisdiction of Beijing University and so cannot harm him, whereas his immediate superiors in the factory or the corporation or bureau above the factory can. The president has general high status (*xian4guan1*), but he is not "the person in charge" (*xian4guan3*). The power of the president's office is not boundless and omnipotent throughout society, but must also be exercised through guanxi channels. That is to say, the spread of guanxixue has meant that office must now be situated in a network of personal relations, reciprocity, and loyalty in order to realize its power and authority. Although the Beida president's office is objectively of greater rank and status than that of the personnel director, within the social order created by the art of guanxi, their relative statuses are reversed. The president must beg the personnel director for a favor, which once granted, renders him a debtor and the moral inferior of the personnel director. As a result of the workings of the art of guanxi, the universalistic legitimation and power of high office or political position are not always effective, for often the particular and personal relations of local authority and local guanxi networks block their extension. By constraining the exercise of power to the principles of the gift economy, non-officeholders are able to gain a certain leverage against official power.

By pointing out the subversive effects of guanxi practices, I do not mean to cast them in the light of a heroic and organized stance of defiant uncompromising resistance. Indeed, many cases of guanxi practice are actually instances in which the techniques of bio-power and governmentality have appropriated the tactics of the gift economy to bolster their own strength. Where gift-giving is obligatory and merely serves to confirm official hierarchy, where it takes the form of tribute rather than social investment, where the gift economy leaves the basic structures of the distributive economy intact by seeking permission to acquire or do something through the established specialized offices, or where the gift economy accepts the need to convert symbolic capital into the right office capital, then it cannot be termed a form of active resistance. It is an oppositional economy "in-itself" rather than "for-itself." That is why I have preferred the word "sub-version" over "resistance." This choice avoids a totalizing representation of the art of guanxi, but suggests the rich arsenal at its disposal for some control over the conditions of the dominant form of power embedded in the state distributive mode of exchange. The challenge to the principle of state distribution by the tactics and ethics of the gift thus pose as obstructions and limits to the extension of modern bio-power in China.

CHAPTER SIX

"Using the Past to Negate the Present": Ritual Ethics and State Rationality in Ancient China

I would like to write the history of [the] prison. . . . Why? Simply because I am interested in the past? No, if one means by that writing a history of the past in terms of the present. Yes, if one means writing the history of the present.

—Foucault 1979b

I would like to rewrite the history of the art of guanxi in contemporary China.[1] To do this I must answer the following questions: What past corpus of ethics and practices did guanxixue draw on, revitalize, and reconfigure as adaptations to its present context of a state-organized order? If it is true that during the 1950s, guanxi ethics retreated in the face of new state loyalties, then what was the shape of a past Chinese order without, or before, a state? How does the present of guanxixue replicate or differ from a past when guanxi-like ethics (and not the state) were the central social principles? What are the ancestral forms of guanxixue gifts and etiquette, the power of obligation and reciprocity, and kinship/friendship ethics? Understanding former incarnations of guanxixue will throw light on its present reappearance.

This genealogy of guanxi does not, however, trace it to its immediate past in republican and late imperial China, but to an ancient past of the transition from a kinship order to a centralized state order, when a conflict between two discourses, *Rujia* (later called Confu-

---

[1] A French version of this chapter has been published in the journal *Annales* (Yang 1991). I am greatly indebted to David Keightley, Ken Dewoskin, Ron Egan, Prasenjit Duara, Tani Barlow, and Don Munro for their valuable comments and reference suggestions for my interpretation of ancient Chinese philosophy and history. Needless to say, I am solely responsible for any mistakes.

cian) and *Fajia* (or Legalist), first took place. Why write the ancient but not the modern history of guanxi? Because a genealogy looks for thematic and structural similitudes that bring to light certain aspects of the present, instead of predictable linear developments of cause and effects (Foucault 1984). That this ancient period has something significant to say about the present was brought home to me in a comment by a professor of ancient Chinese political philosophy in Beijing. Perhaps in all of Chinese history, he said, there were only two times when Legalism was explicitly and publicly espoused (as opposed to secretly practiced) by the rulers: in the fourth and third centuries B.C.E. and after 1949 C.E. I do not deny that there is a past outside the present; I merely seek to unearth and salvage from the past for the present that portion which is the present-in-the-past.

It is generally agreed that the recording, writing, and interpretation of history is a venerable tradition in Chinese civilization. What is perhaps less often recognized is that in China, the evaluations of past and present by historians writing history have been an intrinsic part of state functioning, and of opposition to the state. I would like here to explore a recent manifestation of the relationship between history and the state in China by taking as my point of departure the discourse concerning the past contained in the "Criticize Lin Biao, Criticize Confucius" campaign of the 1970s. Furthermore, by writing an alternative history of the same period in ancient China, I would also like to appeal to and illustrate an oppositional tradition in Chinese history-writing, which is not the history of "the victors" (Benjamin 1969a:256), but a history that refuses to further the project of the state.[2] Both sorts of history are "histories of the present" in that they are interpretations of the past from the standpoint of what is meaningful for the present; however, they issue from two very different positions in the present.

"Criticize Lin Biao, Criticize Confucius"

In 1973, shortly after his designated successor Lin Biao had betrayed him and then died mysteriously, Mao Zedong officially launched the "Criticize Lin Biao, Criticize Confucius" campaign (*Pilin pikong*), which lasted until his own death in 1976. The campaign looked back into ancient Chinese history to seek meaning for

---

[2] For two recent critiques of the Qin unification of China (*da yi tong*) as despotic centralized control of both material resources and thought, see Lei 1988 and Chen 1988.

the present, and in the process, it departed radically from the past two millenia of Chinese historiography in its interpretation of the crucial issues of that period (Li 1975; Li 1977; Kandel 1978). In the voluminous publications of this campaign, the struggle between the philosophical schools of Legalism and Confucianism was taken to be the defining issue of the Warring States period, the short-lived Qin dynasty, and the Western Han dynasty.[3]

The significance of this campaign cannot be reduced to a matter of internal court intrigues and struggles of policy factions within the central Party, as suggested by both Chinese and Western commentators (Moody 1974; Shi et al. 1977). Certainly the campaign was orchestrated as an attack on the disgraced Lin Biao, who had dared to criticize Mao for being like the ruthless and despotic First Emperor of Qin (Qinshihuang). There also seems to be no question that the campaign attacked Confucian restorationism as a way of taking aim at certain Party leaders such as Zhou Enlai, whose name linked him with the duke of Zhou (Zhou Gong), much admired by Confucius and his disciples. Analyzing the campaign in terms of internal Party struggles does not enable us to deal with the important questions of what substantive components in Legalism made it particularly suitable as the rallying ground for renewing the 1949 Revolution in the 1970s and why it was Confucianism that was identified as so threatening to the socialist order.

By adopting a longer historical and cultural perspective, and by closely analyzing the substantive content of its discourse, the *Pilin pikong* campaign can be shown to have a much deeper significance. I suggest that the campaign was an articulation of the self-understanding and aspirations of modern Chinese state power through a narrative interpretation of the progressive development of Chinese history. As such, the campaign represents a "history" written from the standpoint of the "present" of modern Chinese statism.

---

[3] The traditional chronology of ancient Chinese historical periods referred to in this chapter are as follows:

Xia dynasty	2205–1766 B.C.E	
Shang	1766–1122 B.C.E	
Zhou	1122–770 B.C.E	Western Zhou
	722–481 B.C.E	Spring and Autumn ⎫ Eastern
	403–221 B.C.E	Warring States ⎭ Zhou
Qin	221–206 B.C.E	
Han	206 B.C.E–8 C.E	Western Han
	8 C.E–220 C.E	Eastern Han

Three main themes can be extracted from the campaign's treatment of this ancient period. First, there was a class analysis of the "two-line struggle" between Confucianism, which represented the corrupt class ideology of the declining "slave-owning aristocracy," and Legalism, which stood for the progressive interests of the new "feudal landowning class" (Yang 1972). A second theme concerns history: Legalism and the Qin dynasty represented the great historical breakthrough that catapulted China from the "slave society" of the Xia, Shang, and Western Zhou dynasties to the more advanced "feudal society" of a unified imperial order under the Qin and later dynasties. Thus Chinese history was made to conform with the tenets of Marxist-Leninist evolutionism.[4] It was argued that in fulfilling the inevitable course of history, the Qin dynasty (and by implication, contemporary socialist society as well) needed to stamp out the forces of Confucian restorationism and reaction. The ancient expression "Emphasize the present while slighting the past" (*Houjin bogu*) was revived and used to attack the ancient notion of "using the past to negate the present" (*yigu feijin*) (Hong 1972), attributed to the Confucians who wanted to preserve the "ritual government" (*li zhi*) of "slave society" (Shi 1973: 34–35; Yang 1973).[5]

Third, the establishment of China's first centralized state and empire through military unification of the six Warring States was hailed as an event whose brutality was entirely justified by the greatness of the accomplishment. The premier Legalist social engineer Shang Yang (Liang 1974) and the emperor Qinshihuang were applauded for their leadership in the reforms and state policies they instituted. These included the expropriation of the "fiefs" of the old aristocracy and the forced transfer of aristocratic households to the capital; the institution of "private property," which established the new classes of landlords and peasants; the establishment of thirty-six administrative and geographical units called commandaries, with counties underneath

[4] See Lee 1991, in which Lee traces the socialist discourse of "modernity" and linear time to the introduction of nineteenth-century Western evolutionism to China. He argues that unlike what developed in the West, the Chinese version of the discourse of modernity was unrelieved by a skeptical counterdiscourse of "aesthetic modernism."

[5] At a central Party meeting in 1958, Mao Zedong had already said, "Qinshihuang advocated that those who 'use the past to negate the present will have their lineage lines cut off.' Qinshihuang is an expert at emphasizing the present and slighting the past. . . . [The intellectuals] accuse me of being a Qinshihuang. They are wrong. We have surpassed Qinshihuang a hundred times. They accuse us of being Qinshihuang, of being despotic. We have always acknowledged this. It's a pity that [their descriptions] don't go far enough, so that often we have had to supplement them ourselves" (Mao 1969:195).

them; a bureaucracy of officials representing the centralized state to administer these units; a unified system of penal laws; the emphasis on the occupations of agriculture and military service to strengthen the empire and the abolition of secondary occupations such as those of merchants and scholars; and finally, the standardization of writing, weights and measures, money, and cart-axle widths (Yang 1973:39–54).

Such admiration for the Legalists' radical launching of a new order reveals the strong affinity the campaign participants felt between their own revolutions (1949 and 1966) and the ancient Legalist project and rejection of its past.[6] The campaign discourse made it evident that the new socialist order was to model itself on that other major breakthrough in Chinese history, except that the present socialist project was more historically advanced since it was now overthrowing both the "feudal" order that was the Legalist legacy and the later capitalist order as well. Their identification with the Legalists shows that their vision of socialist society was not that found among Western Marxists, of a coalition of cooperatives giving free expression to the individual, but a society ordered and provided for by a powerful state.

What especially fueled the campaign was the hatred for the recalcitrant "Confucianists," both in that ancient period as well as in socialist society. Ancient Confucianism was represented as the ideology of the slave-owning class and its scholars as parasitic apologists seeking to restore the old order and perpetuate the subservience of the people by preaching on ritual status distinctions, virtue, filial piety, brotherhood, and loyalty. By analogy, what was implied was that in socialist society, modern Confucian dangers still lurked in the form of the reactionary classes and their apologists, the intellectuals. Mao himself at a Party meeting in 1958 had made a revealing statement: "What does Qinshihuang amount to? He buried only 460 scholars alive; we have buried 46,000 scholars alive. Haven't we killed counterrevolutionary intellectuals?" (Mao 1969:195).

It can be readily seen that the themes of the campaign—the discourses of class struggle, of historical progressive time, and of the necessity and virtues of a strong state order—are closely related and mutually reinforcing. First, from the vantage point of class struggle, in order to displace the slave-owning aristocracy, the new landowning

[6] There is of course, a deep irony to be found in this affinity between the *Pilin pikong* campaign and ancient Legalism. Legalist concerns for universal laws and legal procedures, their formulation, public promulgation, and strict observance and implementation have not been the hallmarks of the modern socialist order.

214 Theoretical Formulations

class needed to negate the past and dare to institute a new present, while relying on the help of a strong state. Second, in terms of the logic of historical necessity, the class struggle and the buildup of centralized state power were the fulfillment of the inevitable progressive movement of the universal and fixed stages of history. These two ways of linking up the three themes of the campaign are both well developed within the discourse of the campaign, since they accord with the dominant themes of Marxist-Leninist theory.

Yet one can also detect in the campaign a third overriding logic, which subsumes the other two themes to itself. This third point of departure is the logic and interests of state power, which are served by the other two themes. That is to say, state power relies on fomenting class struggle because it weakens the structures of society. State power also relies on a notion of the superiority of the present over the past to support its radical restructuring of society and to project itself as the necessary fulfillment of history: "If it does not represent the inevitable developmental scheme of history, then how could the commandary-county system have lasted nearly 2,000 years and not be changed?" (Shi 1973:40). That ancient Legalism rather than Marxism was what was elevated in the *Pilin pikong* campaign suggests that this third theme is the controlling subtext in the campaign discourse.

This pivotal state logic of the campaign is further revealed through a bold reassessment of Confucius in an article written by the scholar Li Zehou just a few years after the end of the *Pilin pikong* campaign (1980, 1985). First published in 1980, this article implicitly challenged the assertions of the campaign in every way. Li's article examines the discourse of the philosophical school known as *Rujia* or "School of the Weak"[7] of the Spring and Autumn period. It draws an important distinction between this early school and later Confucian schools and doctrines that the Han and later dynasties had integrated into state orthodoxy.

According to Li, Confucius lived in a time when the social order of the Zhou dynasty was breaking down, and in order to stem the growing tide of warring states, Confucius sought to restore the "rituals of Zhou" (*Zhouli*). Instead of decrying Confucian restorationism, Li Zehou argues that the rituals of Zhou were "the set of decrees, regu-

---

[7] In order to distinguish between the early Confucian philosophy of the Spring and Autumn period from the Han and later versions of state Confucianism, I will hereafter refer to the former as "Rujia" and to the latter as "Confucianism."

lations, institutions, customs, and ceremonials" the Zhou inherited
from much more archaic times, from the "late clan-ordered society"
of the Xia dynasty, whose ritual order provided the system of "patriarchal social control for primitive society" (1980:78). Analyzing the
notion of ritual (li), which plays such an important role in the classical texts such as Analects (Lun Yu), the Book of Rites (Li Ji), The
Rituals of Zhou (Zhou Li), and the Yi Li, he concludes that ritual
began with primitive shamanistic ritual for the paying of respect and
worship of deities, which later developed into the worship of human
ancestors, and was expanded into a system of customary law guiding
everyday life in primitive kin-ordered society (1980:78–79). For the
early Rujia, returning to rituals meant the revival of a social order
whose mode of power consisted of the extension of the ritual practices and ethics of kinship to all aspects of life, especially the political.

By pushing Zhou dynasty Rujia thought back so far into archaic
primitive society, Li Zehou emphasizes certain redeeming elements
that had been overlooked by most interpretations of Confucius over
the subsequent course of Chinese history, elements also significantly
absent in the Pilin pikong campaign discourse. He discovers that en-
veloped within the early Rujia's folds of aristocratic hierarchical
Shang and Zhou dynasty ethics are the still vibrant remnants of
"primitive democracy" and "primitive humanism" from the very archaic Xia dynasty (1980:86). Although by Zhou times the ritual system had become a monopoly of the aristocracy, the preservation of
the Xia communal clan structure in the economic foundation of Zhou
society meant that the Zhou ritual order still harbored the "democratic and popular nature of primitive society" (1980:78). These elements are found in the Rujia emphasis on the moral leadership and
accountability of the ruler, which is based on the clan-leader model of
primitive society and in the applications of the principle of kinship
ethics and ritual form not just to the familial system but also to the
political system. In this way, the early Rujia sought to "oppose the
separation of politics and punishment from [the realm] of ritual and
virtue" (1980:83).

For Li Zehou, the establishment of the Qin-Han empire may have
been a great historical advance, but the remnants of primitive democratic and humanistic spirit and the "small clan-based city-state de-
mocracies of the Spring and Autumn period were abandoned and
swallowed up" by the development of the autocratic centralized state.
"History has always developed in this tragic manner, through contra-

puntal variations: civilization develops at the price of ethics" (1985:1). Li Zehou's exegesis of the early Rujia represents one of the first public expressions of doubt after the *Pilin pikong* campaign about the achievements of the Qin, its strengthening of the state, and the unilateral progressive construction of history. The archaic primitive elements of the Rujia he brings to light represent one emerging strain of oppositional discourse in China after the Cultural Revolution.

In this contrast between Li Zehou's positive reevaluation of Confucius and the *Pilin pikong* campaign, the third and pivotal theme of the campaign becomes more apparent as the controlling narrative subsuming the other two themes to itself. By championing Legalism and castigating Confucianism and by asserting the superiority of the present over the past, the campaign was calling for the eclipse of archaic kin- and ritual-ordered society and affirming its replacement by a new, efficient state machinery. In this logic, the replacement of an aristocratic order of clan and lineage leaders by a new landlord and peasant class constructs a convenient population base for state taxation and control, while destroying the regional autonomy of kinship units. The rejection of the past implicates time in the strategies of a new and unprecedented form of state power which cannot appeal to the past.

A Reinterpretation of the Past

According to traditional Chinese historical sources, Confucius (ca. 550–479 B.C.E.) was born in the state of Lu in the Spring and Autumn period, an era that saw the beginnings of the collapse of an older sociopolitical order of hierarchical clan and lineage groupings and hereditary social strata. The emergence at this time of contending militaristic states, which no longer recognized the suzerainty of the royal Zhou clan, led directly to a period of turmoil later labeled appropriately, the Warring States period, and culminated in the unification of all China under a new centralized empire by the state of Qin, the most militaristic and powerful of the states. As a witness to the beginnings of these changes and social disorder, Confucius traveled from state to state as an itinerant philosopher preaching a way of life and a set of ethics to stem the tide of social disintegration. Several generations of his disciples helped record and transmit his teachings to posterity. Reference will be made here only to these early pre-Qin

Rujia and not to the different Confucian traditions and commentaries of later imperial times.[8]

Although the institution of written penal law codes can already be found toward the end of the sixth century B.C.E., the articulation of government by law and punishment did not become a coherent body of philosophy until later, with the emergence of Legalism in the Warring States. The Legalists themselves represented a very different response to that process of social disintegration and general state militarism which, although much more severe later on, had already begun in Confucius's lifetime. The implementation of Legalist doctrines and reforms were important, if not central, to the strengthening and ultimate victory of the state of Qin, which established the first unified imperial state system in China in 221 B.C.E.[9] Although the Qin dynasty lasted only fifteen years, it laid the foundations for the centralized state system that operated in later dynasties all the way into the twentieth century. The two main Legalists referred to here are Shang Yang (390?–338 B.C.E.) and Han Feizi (280?–233? B.C.E.).

Government by Kinship and Government by the State

In the Rujia text *Analects* there is a passage in which Confucius is informed of the uprightness of a man who dutifully reported his father to the authorities for having stolen a sheep. Confucius replied, "Among us, in our part of the country, those who are upright are different from this. The father conceals the misconduct of the son, and the son conceals the misconduct of the father" (*Analects* 13.18; Legge 1961:270). A similar parable about another man who reported his father for stealing sheep is also found in the *Han Feizi*, a Legalist text, only in this version the man is executed by the authorities for being "loyal to the ruler but undutiful to his father." The Legalist response to the execution of this man, and Confucius's praise of the

[8] Of course, it may be an impossible task to separate pre-Qin Rujia discourse from Han Confucianism, since many of the extant Confucian classics were written, compiled, or reinterpreted during the Western Han dynasty when Ruism experienced a court-sanctioned revival. See the appendix in Hsu 1965, Creel 1970, and Legge 1961:1–44 on the authenticity and dating of ancient texts. The point I wish to make is that we must assume a distinction between early Rujia and its various later interpretations in imperial times, because it is highly likely that once it became part of imperial state orthodoxy and had attained the status of cultural hegemony Rujia changed character.

[9] See Dean and Massumi 1992 for an excellent and irreverent comparison between the Legalist state logic of ancient China and the late twentieth-century U.S. militarist state. This work is written in the spirit of Deleuze and Guattari (1983, 1987).

man who deserted the battlefield in order to take care of an old father, is to ask, "How can a state attain order and strength" when it upholds incompatible principles of filial piety and loyalty to the ruler (*Han Feizi* 1982:670–71)? Although the examples here point to a line of disagreement between Confucian and Legalist discourses threaded throughout the texts of the two schools, their differences cannot be reduced to a mere matter of conflicting loyalties to one's father or to one's ruler. It will be more fruitful to examine the differences between them at the level of the general principles of government.

The early Rujia did not necessarily see the heavy stress they placed on kinship relations as being in opposition to loyalty to the state and the ruler, which they also upheld. Rather, they sought to improve government by realigning its principles of operation according to the correct roles, virtues, and mutual obligations of kinship relations, which include such elements as status distinction, affection, and obligation. Even the position of the dynastic ruler was to be embedded in kinship relations, to assume a paternal role with regard to the people, and that of a filial Son of Heaven (*tianzi*) who sacrifices to his ancestors and to Heaven. Indeed, in Rujia discourse, the "state" was modeled on the family, and represented an extension of kinship principles, so that "[The rulers'] persons being cultivated, their families were regulated. Their families being regulated, their states were rightly governed. Their states being rightly governed, the whole kingdom was made tranquil and happy" (*The Great Learning* "Cha Yi," 5, Legge 1961:359). Thus the Rujia tendency to favor the father rather than the ruler is not due to any championing of the family in opposition to the state, but is in keeping with the principles of kinship distance where one has a duty first to the closer kin.

The Rujia stress on interpersonal ethics, as seen in the virtues of filial piety (*xiao*), brotherhood (*di*), humaneness (*ren*), righteousness (*yi*), sincerity (*xin*), mutuality (*shu*), and reciprocity (*bao*), were to be applied not only within the family or clan, but also in government: "When those who are in high stations perform well all their duties to their relations, the people are aroused to virtue. When old friends are not neglected by them, the people are preserved from meanness" (*Analects* 8.2; Legge 1961:208). Thus family, social life, and government were not distinct institutional spheres in Rujia discourse; rather, all three operated according to a single logic of the extension of kinship ethics.

To be sure, the Rujia vision of a kinship polity was a very male-gendered one, as the stress on father-son relationships and brotherhood make clear. Women usually did not figure as full-fledged persons, as in a passage in the *Analects* in which Confucius declares that since the ten able ministers of King Wu of the Zhou dynasty included a woman, the king actually had no more than nine able ministers (*Analects* 8.20; Legge 1961:214). There is some irony in the deep patriarchal attitudes of the Rujia, given that they looked to the Western Zhou past for inspiration, a past in which, according to historical records and bronze inscriptions, women had a considerable political role (Creel 1970:129–31).

Given the Rujia approach to government based on kinship ethics and kinship forms of power, it is appropriate that Confucius always looked back to the ancient past of the Three Dynasties (the Xia, Shang, and Western Zhou) for inspiration.[10] Although all the features for the emergence of the state (urbanization, ceremonial and military centralization, systematic social stratification) can be found in these dynasties, the "state" in these periods was quite different from what started to develop in Eastern Zhou and imperial times. The "states" in the Three Dynasties period resembled what anthropologists call tribal federations and political kinship and ritual orders of agnatic clan and segmentary lineage systems (Chang 1983; Chang 1986:364; Hsu and Linduff 1988:147–85; Cooper 1982; Li 1962; Lewis 1990: 8–9, 28–36; He 1992; Savage 1985). The royal house of each dynasty was actually a clan that had managed to dominate other, coexisting clans. Members of each clan traced descent to a common mythological paternal ancestor, practiced exogamy, and shared a common emblem (totem), which signified their common character. Within each clan, there was a system of stratified segmentary lineages and branch sublineages, comprising a genealogical system of differentiated degrees of political status in the social order. Thus it would seem that what crystallized into a stratified order of hereditary aristocracy in this period was the extension of a system of kinship-ranking derived from pre-state social systems.

It is also probable that during the Shang dynasty kinship and lineage groups were the basic units of organization for the military, the state, and agricultural labor (Schwartz 1985:26–27; Hsu and Linduff

---

[10] Rujia discourse cannot be regarded as simply a wholesale invocation of the Three Dynasties kinship ethics. Rather, the Rujia were selectively appropriating those elements of the past which suited their present, while introducing innovations of their own. These include disseminating the kinship ethics of the ancient aristocracy to the common classes in their own era and the notion of "humaneness" (*ren*), according to which kinship and friendship are virtues applicable to any fellow human.

1988:164). The hierarchical society of Zhou was also an integration of familial relations with "state" relations, in that the clan and lineage nobles of the subordinate yet autonomous segment states came from the same clan as the ruler (Hsu 1965:3) and, therefore, the ruler was only first among equals with his aristocratic kin (Hsiao 1979:323). The familial concept of the state meant that "the ruler reigned but did not rule" and the "sovereignty of rulers was not at all absolute," because respect to nobles and rulers was accorded to them personally as heads of families or clans, and not as institutionalized offices (Hsu 1965:78–79). Therefore, the "state" of the Three Dynasties was not a purely political institution, but "resembled an enlarged household" in which the nominal king shared power with his brothers and close relatives, who were the nobles: "The Son of Heaven has his dukes; princes of states have their high ministers; ministers have [the heads of] their collateral families; great officers have the members of the secondary branches of their families; inferior officers have their friends; and the common people, mechanics, merchants, police runners, shepherds and grooms, all have their relatives and acquaintances to aid and assist them" (*Zuo Zhuan*; Legge 1872:466). Although there is relatively little information left to us about the social structure of the common people and the nature of their relationship with the nobles, this passage suggests that they too were integrated into the "state" order through kinship principles. These principles assigned them lowly kinship ranking and status, but they also may have prevented a clear line of demarcation from being drawn between rulers and subjects.

All this started to change in the Warring States period. As strong states tried to annex weaker states, the kinship ties that had held the sociopolitical order together began to disintegrate. Seeking to protect itself in times of war, the new state formation came to treat the people's labor and wealth as material resources to be manipulated through systematized measures of reward and punishment made possible through the introduction of written law.

In the school of Legalism, which arose during this period, the bifurcation of the Rujia ideal of a continuous kinship-state order is especially evident. The overriding concern of the Legalists was loyalty to the monarch and the state, which came to be seen as forming a single entity, whereas all other ethics of interpersonal relationship were interpreted as threats to the well-being of the state. This is evident in the repeated invocation of the opposition between "private" and "public" as in this Legalist passage on etymology:

In olden times, when [Cang Jie] invented the system of writing, he assigned the element "self-centered" [zihuan] to the character "private" [si]; and combined the elements, "opposite to" [bei] and "private," to form the character "public" [gong]. The contradiction between "public and "private" was thus from the beginning well understood by [Cang Jie]. Today, to regard them both as serving an identical interest is a calamity born of neglecting to investigate. (Han Feizi 1982:671; Liao 1959:286)[11]

Legalist discourse also sought to challenge the relational ethics of kinship and friendship:

To perform private favors [xing si] for old friends, is called not neglecting [friendship]. To distribute alms with public funds [gong cai] is called being benevolent. To make light of [government] rewards and instead stress the [cultivation] of the self[12] is called being a "superior person." To strain the law to shield one's relatives, is called having [good] conduct. To desert one's official post for cultivating personal friendships is called having a knightly sense of justice [you xia]. To keep aloof from the world and ignore one's superiors is called being high-minded. To be disputatious and disobey orders is called showing unswerving spirit. To pass out favors and gain a mass following is called winning the people. (Han Feizi 1982:631–32; Liao 1959:248)*

For all these private virtues, the Legalists substituted a public ethic, only in their discourse, "public" no longer meant simply the opposite of private, in the sense of a larger community, but came to be subsumed under the category of the ruler and the state. Thus by relegating all the ethics of interpersonal relationships of Rujia discourse into the category of the private, the Legalists set kinship up in opposition to the state.

In Rujia discourse, the "state" (guo) was only a part of the hierarchical kinship order; in Legalist discourse the strengthening of the

---

[11] Translation is modified. Hereafter, I will use the asterisk (*) to indicate that I have modified an original translation. If no translator is cited, the translation is my own and follows modern Chinese commentaries and annotations.

[12] The translation of this paragraph follows closely the version rendered by Hsiao Kung-chuan (1979:387). For the third passage, Qing lu zhong shen weizhi junzi, Liao translates "Who makes light of bounties but thinks much of himself, is called a superior man." It is obvious that rendering zhong shen as "thinks much of himself" cannot capture the Confucian concept of "superior man." The Confucians believed in self-cultivation through the practice of ritual, which involves movements of the body according to proper ritual form. In this way body and self (shen) were transformed. I discuss the Confucian meaning of the word shen at greater length later in this chapter.

state becomes the raison d'être of all social life. The Legalists believed the state was served by only two occupations: agriculture and warfare, and that these alone would make the state an efficient fighting machine and give it internal stability and order. However much the people wished to avoid these occupations, they must be persuaded to follow them by rank and reward or force and punishment. All other occupations, such as those of scholar, sophist, knight-errant, merchant, and artisan, were secondary, parasitical, or dangerous to the state (*Shang Jun Shu* 1988: chap. 3; *Han Feizi* 1982, "Wu Du").[13]

Inspired by Shang Yang, certain measures implemented by the state of Qin during and after its ascendancy, hastened the total decline of the old kinship-based form of government. First, the Qin broke up large family systems by decreeing that henceforth any family with two or more males living under one roof would have to pay double taxes (Duyvendak 1928:15, 18). Second, the Qin in 221 B.C.E. dealt a blow to the hierarchical system of hereditary aristocracy by moving about 120,000 noble families away from their ancestral lands to the capital in Xianyang under the watchful eye of the centralized state (Bodde 1967:178). Third, hereditary titles of nobility were replaced with a state-instituted system of eighteen degrees of rank based on one's military accomplishments and informing on the wrongdoing of others (Duyvendak 1928:61–63). The decline of the aristocracy reduced social stratification by reducing the mass of the population to a level inferior to the monarch and his state in every way. Finally, clan and lineage lands were converted into thirty-six commanderies (*jun*) and their respective subdivisions, the counties (*xian*), throughout the realm. These local units were brought under central state administration, and each was supervised by officials sent from the capital (Creel 1964). Far from inaugurating a "feudal" era according to the Marxist stages of history, the Qin dynasty launched a new imperial bureaucratic state order.

Ritual Power and the Power of the Law

Rujia discourse placed an inordinate emphasis on the significance and practice of ritual (*li*) and advocated a return to the rituals and

---

[13] It is perhaps no accident that the *Pilin pikong* campaign looked to ancient Legalism for inspiration. Both the 1949 Revolution and especially the Cultural Revolution elevated peasants and soldiers as revolutionary classes and made other classes the targets of socialist struggle. Furthermore, kinship principles, lineage structures, and "privatism" have also been attacked by official revolutionary discourse.

music of Zhou. Yet however much they looked back to the rituals of the past, the way that the early Rujia talked about ritual marked a significant departure from previous times. It is evident that rituals were a constitutive component of ancient Chinese life. The archaeological record, resplendent with Shang and Zhou dynasty bronze ritual vessels of various shapes and patterns, shows the highly ritualistic nature of these clan-based state societies and the importance of access to ritual for political authority (Chang 1983:40–41, 95; Chang 1980). Yet in pre-Rujia texts, the word for ritual was seldom used, and when it was, it usually referred merely to a specific rite or body of codes of conduct (Eno 1990:23, 212). The early Rujia were probably the first to thematize ritual as a general category of practices, to point out self-consciously its psychological impact on the person and its ethical and political effects on the social order.

The Chinese character for ritual, *li* 禮 , has a very interesting etymology. The oldest Chinese dictionary, the *Shuowen Jiezi* written by Xu Shen of the Han dynasty, defines *li* as "a step or act, that whereby we serve spiritual beings and attain happiness" (1959: *juan* 1; Legge, *The Li Ki* 1885:9–10). The radical *shi* 示 on the left originally referred to the suspended heavenly bodies (sun, moon, stars) that provided omens for humans and over time came to be associated with the affairs of spiritual beings, so that it is found in such characters as those for spirits 神 (*shen*), sacrifices 祭 (*ji*), and ancestor or origin 祖 (*zu*) (ibid.). The element on the right of the character is the phonetic *li* 豊 , but it also has a semantic content of its own. It signifies "vessels used in performing [sacrificial] rites" and the lower half of this symbol refers to "vessels for food and meat in ancient times" (1959: *juan* 5). So from very early times, the notion of ritual was associated with the the cosmos and nature and with the sacrifice of food offerings to spiritual beings and ancestors in special vessels (see also He 1992:102), which by the Shang and Zhou dynasties had become the highly elaborate bronze ritual vessels prominent in the archaeological record until the early Han dynasty.

In Rujia discourse the notion of ritual attains a pivotal metaphoric status. "Ritual" comes to denote a whole range of philosophical as well as practical ethico-political tenets of life. The following quotation from the *Li Ji*, a Rujia-influenced text of the Han dynasty, with very archaic elements predating Confucius, gives an idea of the wide-ranging meanings of the Rujia notion of ritual. After some passages stating that ritual originates with the unity of the cosmos before it was divided and conforms to Heaven's constant principles of operation, the text goes on to say, "[This cosmic principle to which ritual conforms] resides in the human world and can be called nurturance [the basis of human life]. Its realization is based on making offerings and laboring, and the [rituals] of declining and yielding, drinking ceremonies, feasting ceremonies, capping rites, marriage ceremonies, funeral rites, sacrificial rites, archery contests, chariot-driving, court audience ceremonies, and friendly missions [to other states]" (*Li Ji* 1987: 382).* First, ritual signified the *cosmological order* or principle of operation that was embedded in nature. The practice of rituals according to the forms laid down in the past had the effect of enabling a person or the whole of social life itself to tap into or partake of this original cosmic order and unity. Second, ritual referred to *concrete and formal rites and ceremonies* performed by a community, such as various forms of sacrifice, capping (initiation for boys), marriage, funeral rites of passage, and other occasions for social gathering which adhered to sets of prescribed behavioral procedures and forms, and were hailed by the Rujia for promoting communal harmony and love (*Li Ji* 1987:808). Third, through the extension of the rules of formal ceremonial performances to everyday life, ritual can also mean *propriety, custom, habits, and etiquette* in the conduct of social relationships. Such a meaning is suggested by the words "declining and yielding" (*ci rang*) above, postures of respect and politeness featured in banquet scenes, in which the guest initially declines the host's hospitality and both try to yield precedence of entering, seating, and eating to the other (*Li Ji* 1987:17, 28–31, 570).

Finally, the ancient usage of the word *li* also included the notion of "gift," in either the sense of a present given, an offering made, or a favor or hospitality rendered, as well as the ritual of a formal banquet (Morohashi 1955–60, 8:501).[14] Among scholars and aristocrats, it was the etiquette that courtesy visits must always be accompanied by greeting gifts (Xu 1990:1–6). Ancient gifts often took the form of meat, wine, jade, or silk, which were also a kind of currency. Much etiquette was also prescribed to accompany the act of giving; there were rules concerning the kinds of gifts appropriate to each rank of people in each season of the year, how to hold and present each kind of gift, what deprecatory things to say about the gift being presented, how to receive a gift depending on the donor and recipients' relative

---

[14] For a useful catalogue of the myriad ways to write the words "gift" and "to bestow," see Xu 1990:10–22.

social positions, and so forth (*Li Ji* 1987:568–70). In the *Book of Rites*, banquets and feasts were also guided by many ritual prescriptions.

In an encyclopedic examination of the history of Chinese gift-giving customs, Xu Ping notes that the polymorphic meanings of the word *li* in ancient Chinese "is definitely not a linguistic coincidence" (1990:9). Ritual in ancient China prescribed an ideal social order through different ritual acts, and these set the guidelines for the conduct of interpersonal and intergroup relations.

That the ritual form achieves its social ordering effects through "performance" and the positioning of the body was recognized by the Rujia, who "performed" their philosophy through music and dance and archery as part of their regimens of self-cultivation (Eno 1990). Many scholars have pointed out the absence of mind/body dualism in ancient Chinese notions of the "person" and "ritual" as integrated psychosomatic processes (Ames 1984; Tu 1983; Fingarette 1972; Zito 1994).

This early Rujia understanding of ritual coincides remarkably with the approach taken by Roy Rappaport in analyzing the "obvious aspects of ritual" (1979a). A symbolic, structuralist, or functional analysis of ritual does not take into account the special character of ritual in comparison to myth, poetry, and art, whereas an examination of the "surface" forms of ritual shows that "certain meanings and effects are intrinsic to the ritual form" (1979a:174). For Rappaport, the performer of ritual "is not merely transmitting messages encoded in the liturgy, he is also participating in—becoming part of—the order to which his own body and breath give life" (1979a:192).

The notion that ritual creates social order through bodily performance is illustrated in this marvelously suggestive passage about a country feasting ceremony held once every three years in early Zhou times:

> The host honors the guest, therefore he seats the [principal] guest in the northwest and the accompanying guests in the southwest in order to assist the guest. The guest, whose demeanor toward [the host] is one of righteousness, sits in the northwest, [that he may imbibe of the force of righteousness]. The host, whose demeanor toward [the guests] is one of benevolence, virtue, and generosity, sits in the southeast, [that he may imbibe of the force of benevolence]. The host's attendant is seated in the northeast, in order to assist the host. [In this way,] as the forces of benevolence and righteousness come together, and guest and host each have their proper assignments, and the stands and dishes are presented

in the proper numbers, then it is called [attaining] the sacred. Having
established [a state of] sanctity, and also treating [the occasion] with
reverence, it is called propriety [li]. When ritual [li] embodies [ti] the
distinction between elder and younger, it is called virtue [de]. Virtue is
that which is obtained [de] through the body [shen]. That is why it is
said: "The ancients who studied the arts of the Way sought thereby to
moralize [de] the body." This, therefore, is the reason why the sages
paid attention to the [practice of ritual]. (Li Ji 1987:974–75)*

My translation of the last three sentences differs markedly from that
of Legge, who renders the third to the last sentence "Virtue is that
which is the characteristic of the person" (Legge 1885, vol. 28:438).
His translation of the word shen as "person" instead of "body," I
believe, is not in keeping with passages earlier in the chapter describing the mutual bowing and yielding of precedence three times at the
first meeting of host and guest. Nor does it adhere to the spirit of the
rest of the passage above about the physical positioning of guests and
host according to the directions of vital forces, and of the previous
sentence about ritual "embodying" the distinction between elder and
younger. Finally, the passage makes two word plays. There is a pun
on the words "virtue" and "obtain," both pronounced de: virtue is
"obtained"; and the way to obtain "virtue" is to somaticize it, or to
"moralize" the body through ritual action. There is also an affinity
drawn between the characters for "ritual" and "embody" (li 禮 and
ti 體), since both characters have the same phonetic element, which
means "ritual vessel." The implication that can be drawn from the
linkage between the two characters is that the body is a ritual vessel
for holding the virtues obtained through ritual practice.

   This importance of ritual and music for Rujia lies not only in what
can be called the regimens of "self-ritualization" followed by Rujia
disciples in their study groups, such as those of ritual performance,
music and dance, archery and charioteering, and the interpretation
and discussion of ancient texts on ritual, history, and ethics (Eno
1990:55–60). More pertinent for this history of the present is how
the Rujia recognition of the performative effects of ritual led also to
a discourse on what may be called the "reritualization of politics"
or the will to recreate the social order and to conduct government
through ritual.

   Zi Zhang asked about government. The Master said, "Zi, did I not
   speak to you on that subject before?" The person of learning who understands ritual and music has only to take and apply them [in order to

practice government], and that is all." (*Li Ji* 1987:813; Legge 1885; vol. 28:276)*

Confucius said, "Lead the people with governmental measures and regulate them by law and punishment, and they will avoid wrongdoing but
have no sense of honor and shame. Lead them with virtue and regulate
them by the rules of propriety [*li*] and they will have a sense of shame,
and, moreover, set themselves right." (*Analects* 2.3; Chan 1963:22)

What the Rujia proposed was to use the various forms of ritual as a
system of "dikes" (*fang*) to shore up and channel human actions. The
repeated performance of rituals serves to instill in the people customs
and habits of daily life which are in accord with propriety (*Li Ji* 1987:
823–24; Li 1931:15). For instance, at the periodic rituals of sacrifice
to the ancestors, the way that kin are physically arranged in order of
precedence distinguishing between elder and younger, between male
and female, and between more closely related and more distant kin,
inculcates the principles of social ordering in the people and ritually
assigns them roles and statuses (*Li Ji* 1987:782–86). The solemnity of
the performances and the music inscribes in the participants (and simultaneously expresses) reverence and mourning for the deceased.
The sharing of the sacrificial meats creates a sense of solidarity among
all the living and deceased kin. The ritual of "declining and yielding"
in greeting, visiting, and feasting serves to inculcate mutual consideration while damping tendencies for competition and self-gain. Ritual is
all the more powerful as it relies not just on words, but on the involvement of the body.

There is much in the textual records to suggest that the Rujia discourse on ritual government did not arise in a vacuum, but was an
elaboration on knowledge of the actual state of affairs in the Three
Dynasties before Confucius's time. The ancient usage of the word *li*
also included that of "the *system of governance* of a state" (Morohashi 1955–60, vol. 8:501; *Zhongwen Da Cidian* 1967, vol. 24:95).
A passage in the *Zuo Zhuan* describes how a Duke Zhuang wanted to
go to another state to witness its sacrificial rite for the Spirits of the
Land: "The ritual is conducted for the rectification of the people
[*zhengmin*].¹⁵ Hence there will be meetings of the princes to inculcate
the [differential] duties of the high and low, and for determining each
of their contributions of wealth. There will be court visiting rites to
rectify the different ranks of nobility, and to arrange the order of the

¹⁵ The verb *zheng* also has the sense of "putting into order."

young and old" (*Zuo Zhuan* 10.2a; Legge 1872:105). It would seem
that ritual in this society—like the display, symbolism, and drama of
the nineteenth-century Balinese theater state described by Clifford
Geertz (1980)—was not a mere extrinsic embellishment or legitimation of the proper workings of government, but an intrinsic component of government and an end in itself. This literal notion of government by ritual was lost or overshadowed very early in China by
Legalistic notions of the workings of the state in terms of law, force,
statecraft (*shu*), and administration, and in the West in the sixteenth
century by a "command-and-obedience conception of political life,"
which reduced the state to matters of "regnancy, regime, dominion,
mastery—statecraft" (Geertz 1980:121–22).

Since the Ruists lived amid the gathering storms of warfare and
statism in the Eastern Zhou, for them, government through ritual and
music must have presented an alternative to emerging new forms of
government later favored by the Legalists, such as administrative bureaucracy, increasing military might, written law, and the meting out
of punishments. For the Ruists, political and social order were to be
brought about through ritual, and ritual was at the same time the
conduct of politics: the two terms were regarded not as separate institutions, but as two aspects of one and the same thing. The order
within ritual would serve as a vehicle to reproduce order in society.
Furthermore, since the order found within ritual ultimately derived
from the cosmic order and from the rhythms of nature, it meant that
the principles of government were inextricably linked to the cosmic
forces. This hearkening back to what was taken as an older mode of
power can be seen as a way to resist the frightening new power order
in which politics was beginning to cast off the encumbrances of ritual
and kinship.

Let us examine how power exerted through ritual is different from
what was to prove victorious during the Warring States period: a
pure form of political rationality and an intensified state power. In
ritual, power is *intrinsic* to the performance of ritual. According to
Rappaport, there are two kinds of messages transmitted in ritual acts:
(1) indexical messages, which transmit the current individual psychic
and emotional states or roles of individual performers, and (2) canonical messages, which because they are concerned with enduring aspects of nature, society, and the cosmos, do not issue from participants but are already encoded in the prescribed sequential acts and
utterrances of the ritual (1979a:179). Rujia discourse touched on

both these aspects of ritual,[16] but it is with the latter that the present work will be concerned.

Canonical messages embedded in the arrangement of objects, bodies, and utterances in ritual are directives and elements of power carried from the past, and as they are reproduced, they exercise power on performers and witnesses. In the very act of performing a ritual, performers accept the directives encoded in the ritual, whether or not they believe them, because through their bodily enactments and utterances, they become fused with, and a part of, the messages they are transmitting and receiving. It is their performance, not their thought, which conforms with the prescribed ritual code and realizes and carries through the particular type of order and power implicit in the ritual (1979a:192–94).

When ritual is employed as the primary means of establishing social order, it has certain implications for how power relations are arranged. The way that ritual exerts power from within itself is quite distinct from power imposed externally through decrees and commands backed by force or control over resources, as when power becomes crystallized in the machinery of a full-fledged state. When power is applied from without, through fixed laws and decrees, it means that the political function has attained an existence separate from the process of the reproduction of social order through ritual. When power acquires an autonomous base, the acceptance of the subordinated is not elicited through the very medium of the coded directives transmitted, but predicated on something external to the directives which can impose acceptance. *Therefore the implication of the Rujia discourse on government based on ritual is a society in which power is contained in the reproduction and conduct of social relations and not objectified and externalized in a universal state opposed to society.*

Instead of ritual government, the Legalists called for a system of objective laws (*fa*) and punishments drawn up by the monarch and made public for all to see. Just as a carpenter's various measuring tools are more accurate and objective than his unaided eyesight, so also the law provides an objective standard of judgment that does not discriminate between those of high and low intelligence or between

[16] See *Xunzi Jinzhu*, Book 19, "On Ritual," for an eloquent assessment of how ritual transmits "indexical messages" to participants, bringing out deep emotions and appreciation for beauty (*Xunzi* 1975; Dubs 1928).

ministers and commoners (*Han Feizi* 1982:50). This objectivity is the best way to control the wrongdoing of both the high and the low and to unify and standardize the behavioral norms of the people (ibid.). Thus law was understood not as a safeguard of the people's rights and privileges but as a way of strengthening the positions of the monarch and the state and insulating them from the threats posed by those of high rank or intelligence (ibid.).

The legal system required a new bureaucracy to supervise and execute the laws. Two complete sets of laws and mandates were to be kept in the capital, one in the palace of the Son of Heaven, one locked up in the Forbidden Archives, safe from tampering. These would serve as the absolute standards for the land. Three high-level law officials were to be designated by the Son of Heaven to officiate from the capital, and one of whom would be assigned to the palace, each of the other two to other centrally located state offices. One law officer and various law-enforcement officials would also be assigned to each commandary and prefecture throughout the empire, replicating the pattern of the capital. These officials were expected not only to apply the law but also to inform the people about the laws and to answer their questions, so that they would be deterred from violating the law themselves and at the same time would be able to prevent any wrongdoing on the part of officials (*Shang Jun Shu* 1988:194–96).

Besides a bureaucratic system, what also was to uphold the laws and to serve as its very strategy was a system of rewards and punishment (*shang xing*).

> What I mean by the unifying of rewards is that profits and emoluments, office and rank should be determined exclusively by military merit, and that there should not be different reasons for distributing them. For thus the intelligent and the stupid, the noble and the humble, the brave and the timorous, the virtuous and the worthless will all apply to the full whatever knowledge they may have in their breasts, exert to the uttermost whatever strength they may have in their limbs, and will be at the service of their ruler even to death, and the outstanding heroes, the virtuous and the good, of the whole empire will follow him, like flowing water, with the result that the army will have no equal, and commands will be carried out throughout the whole empire. (*Shang Jun Shu* 1988: 132–35; Duyvendak 1928:275)

An example of reward for military merit in the law of Shang Yang was the stipulation that whoever cuts off one enemy head is given one degree in rank and those who desire to become officials will receive an office worth the price of 50 piculs or exemption from taxes (Duy-vendak 1928:61, 297). Punishments fitting the crime were also writ-ten into the laws. No distinctions in punishment would be made on the basis of rank, kinship, or past good behavior. Shang Yang favored harsh punishments over light and also advocated that penalties be extended to three sets of kin related to the guilty (*Shang Jun Shu* 1988: 135– 37).[17]

The formulation and implementation of the law was intricately tied up with surveillance and mutual denunciation measures, both within the court bureaucracy and among the population. In Legalist dis-course, the ruler becomes fully elevated above all in the realm, and the figure of what Gilles Deleuze and Felix Guattari called the "para-noid despot" (1987:193) emerges. Strategies of secrecy and surveil-lance come to be explicitly formulated for the monarch and the state (Hsiao 1979:322–27). A remarkable passage of advice to the sover-eign suggests that the genealogy of the modern panopticon in China must be sought in the second historical disjunction between a hier-archical kinship order and the imperial state.

See but never be seen. Hear but never be heard. Know but never be known. If you hear any word uttered, do not change it nor move it, but compare it with the deed and see if word and deed coincide with each other. Place every official with a censor. Do not let them speak to each other. Then everything will be exerted to the utmost. Cover tracks and conceal sources. Then the ministers cannot trace origins. Leave your wisdom and cease your ability. Then your subordinates cannot guess at your limitations. (*Han Feizi* 1982:37; Liao 1959:32–33)

There were also precautions taken against the people.

When the people are weak, the state is strong. When the people are strong, the state is weak. Therefore, a state that understands the Way of governing, engages itself in weakening the people [*ruo min*]. When the people are simple, then the state's borders are secure. When the people are profligate [in living], then the state is weak. When the people are weak, then they follow the established rules, when they are profligate,

[17] The word used for the three grades or groupings of relatives of the guilty is *san zu*. According to the commentator Huo Linxu, it is not clear whether the three kin groupings refers to: (1) three lineages, those of the father, the mother, and the wife; or to (2) three generations, those of father, son, grandson; or to (3) three sets of relations within the extended family, parents, brothers, wife; or to (4) three generations of male siblings, the brothers of the father, the self, and the son (*Shang Jun Shu* 1988:136).

then they follow their own desires. When the people are weak, then they are useful [to the state]. (*Shang Jun Shu* 1988:160)*

In addition to limiting the desires of the people and making them simple, another measure to weaken the people was the *lianzuo* system, or the system of collective responsibility for mutual surveillance. Thus in the history written in the Former Han dynasty, it states: "[Shang Yang] ordered the people to be organized into groups of fives and tens mutually to control one another and to share one another's punishments [*lianzuo*].[18] Whoever did not denounce a culprit would be cut in two; whoever denounced a culprit would receive the same reward as he who decapitated an enemy; whoever concealed a culprit would receive the same punishment as he who surrendered to an enemy" (Si-Ma 1972, *juan* 68:2230; Duyvendak 1928:14). *Lianzuo* was a system of social control instituted by Shang Yang in which not only the person who had committed a crime but also the other members of the person's unit of five families would be punished (Yates 1987:222). The logic of *lianzuo* and that of extending punishment to three kin groups (*san zu*) continue to inform some state practices in China today.

From the Segmentary State to the Bureaucratic State

Rappaport has suggested that the sustaining of social order through ritual power predates power based on resource control and the application of external force (1979a:197). If this premise is accepted, I would argue that the major discontinuity in this regime of ritual power was the eruption of the state out of primitive egalitarian and ahistorical society, so well dealt with by Pierre Clastres for South America (1987).[19] The Three Dynasties period can be taken as the result of the first thrust of the "state" in China. By Confucius's time, this "state" in the sense of a system of hierarchical ranks and classes and the concentration of the means of production, consumption, rit-

[18] The word for "control" is *mu si*, literally "to shepherd" each other, in the sense of to supervise and to surveil.

[19] With Nietzschean spirit, Clastres explains how some South American Indians have managed to avoid developing a state, or in other words, crystallization of "the Many into the One": by maintaining the centrifugal forces of plural descent and residence communities, by detaching political power from the relations of exchange so that the chief does not enjoy surplus extraction or accumulation, through laughter at shaman and chief, through inscribing tribal law into the memories and bodies of each member instead of entrusting it to an external authority; and by making the office of chief a position of responsibility without power.

ual, and warfare in the towns of clan and lineage nobles and in the capital of the royal clan was already about one and a half millenia old (Chang 1980). Yet, as the Rujia discerned, and as we can make out today, ritual continued to play a central role in this sociopolitical order, and not just as legitimation to prop up a military regime.

It would seem, then, that the "state" of the Three Dynasties period was of an order quite different from that which developed during the Warring States period and under the Qin, which was articulated in Legalist discourse. For instance, the principles of hierarchy in the former were an extension of, not a departure from, the lines of division by age, sex, and kinship of primitive non-state societies. Furthermore, textual and archaeological sources suggest that there was unevenness in the scope of the "state" in the Three Dynasties, so that the disjunction should be understood not as one of a total shift in a "stage" of history, but as a period in which elements of a more dispersed and less stratified segmentary clan society coexisted with hierarchical and centripetal elements of the kinship state.[20] This accords with Deleuze and Guattari's claim that the first appearance of the state represents an "overcoding" or a reassemblage of elements of a primitive past into a new unity, rather than a leap into a progressive linear evolutionary stage (1987:427–32).

Recent writings on ancient China informed by anthropology and archaeology (Chang 1983; Keightley 1982, 1983; Savage 1985; Lewis 1990; Cooper 1982; Fried 1983; Li 1962) have all departed from an older Western scholarship (summarized in Bodde 1956) that took Western feudalism as an implicit model for the Three Dynasties social order.[21] The problem with the "feudal" model is that it places inordinate stress on the quasi-legal lord-vassal contractual relationship, enfeofment, and gradations of nobility and does not fully recognize the central importance of the principles of kinship, ancestor worship and, ritual to the ancient Chinese social order. Therefore, many of the

[20] For example, the frequent presence of neolithic Longshanoid sites over the whole area "ruled" by the Shang shows that that "state" was "at various stages of development" (Keightley 1983:547). Furthermore, historian Li Yanong finds that the three books of Zhou ritual preserve many primitive clan society elements of the Zhou people dating back to when they were still a tribal people and had not yet overrun the Shang and learned their "slave system" (Li 1962:217–18).

[21] Even though Hsu Cho-yin and Linduff in their recent book continue to describe the Western Zhou as a "feudal society" and to interpret *ceming* documents as written investiture contracts between lord and vassal, they also acknowledge that Zhou society departed from the more rigid and explicit formulations of rights and obligations found in European feudalism in that the Zhou relied on personal kinship ties and ritual to cement relations between the court and its segmental units (1988:177–85).

kinds of non-Western societies with rudimentary states studied by anthropology through fieldwork might give better insight into the development of a pristine state in ancient China than medieval Europe, which had already known a full-fledged imperial Roman state system, itself a secondary state.[22]

The concept of the "segmentary state," first developed by an anthropologist looking at precolonial African states, may provide a better working model than that of "feudalism" for trying to understand the Three Dynasties period (Southall 1956, 1988). For Africa, Aidan Southall posits three types of social formations: stateless societies, segmentary states, and unitary (or centralized bureaucratic) states (1965:126). The segmentary state implies a centralizing force in the form of a royal clan gathering a number of local segmentary lineages, clans, and even tribes into a larger comprehensive entity in which the segments maintain their independence. No administrative organs can be found that integrate the various parts of society into a centralized unitary structure. A central office of the king and his court exists, but in the absence of coercive power it mainly serves a ritual function representing and inculcating the unity of the people and the land. Kinship, as genealogical relatedness or as fictive interpretation, remains the primary idiom of social organization and stratification. The centralizing force that brings the segments together relies as much or more on ritual dominance and gift relations as on military and political-administrative dominance: "The spheres of ritual suzerainty and political sovereignty do not coincide. The former extends widely towards a flexible, changing periphery. The latter is confined to the central, core domain" (Southall 1988:52). As revealed in oracle-bone and bronze inscriptions and in archaeological sites, the Shang state was "a thin network of pathways and encampments . . . laid over a hinterland that rarely saw or felt the king's presence and authority" (Keightley 1983:548). Therefore, the tenuous hold of this kind of state over its various segments leads one to look to other principles of centralization and subordination, such as the dependence of the segments on the royal sacrifices to ensure rain, good harvests, and good relations with spirits, ancestors, and Heaven.

Besides ritual centralization, the Three Dynasties also relied on a network of gift relations to cement the segmentary polity. A passage in the *Book of Historical Documents* (*Shu Jing*), a book Confucius is known to have studied, has this to say:

[22] See Fried 1983 for a discussion of pristine and secondary states.

The intelligent kings have paid careful attention to their virtue [de], and the wild tribes on every side have willingly acknowledged subjection to them. The nearer and the more remote have all made offerings of the productions of their countries—clothes, food, and vessels for use. The kings have then displayed the things thus produced by their virtue, and [distributed them to the princes] of the States of different surnames, [to encourage] them not to neglect their duties. The precious things and gems they have distributed among their uncles in charge of States, thereby increasing their attachment [to the throne]. The recipients have [thus] not despised the things, but have seen in them the power of virtue. (*Shu Jing*, "Books of Zhou"; Legge 1865:346–48)

The passage shows that, besides kinship relations, gift and tribute relations were an important means by which the Western Zhou "state" was held together. The various clan-states as well as other tribes within the Zhou orbit were threaded together with gift relations established between the leaders of these various social segments and the court. It would seem that total prestation, which Mauss discovered in primitive societies (1967), in which gift relations between groups reverberated with legal, moral, economic, political, and religious force all at once, continued to operate in the segmentary state.

The classical literary texts are not the only sources that indicate the extreme importance of gift relations in the ancient segmentary polity. David Keightley has observed that Zhou bronze ritual vessel inscriptions "scattered all over North and Central China serve as records of a vast network of donor-recipient relations" which established political obligations (1981:17). A great many of these bronze vessels were cast and inscribed on the occasion of their owners receiving a charge from the king to oversee a local area or people or to assume an office at the court. The inscriptions carefully itemize the gifts given by the king which accompanied the charge and often record the gift ceremony, banquet, or ritual outing that surrounded the event (Creel 1970: 125–26, 391–95, 403–5). Gifts were also made by nobles to lower-ranking kin or subordinates, and gifts sometimes also moved upward from nobles to the king during ceremonial court visits. One of the longest inscriptions is found on the famous bronze vessel the Mao Gong Ding, where it is recorded that on "conferring on" (*ming*) Duke Mao (a relative) the charge of an office of the court, the king "bestowed on" (*xi*) him the following gifts: one jar of millet wine, a set of ritual implements, a red robe, a jade ring and tablet, a carriage with bronze fittings, a bow and quiver, four horses, and a red flag with two bells to be used for annual rituals. The duke "responded" (*dui*) by praising the king's "generosity" (*xiu*) and casting the tripod for his sons and grandchildren to treasure (Way 1983).

The importance of the principle of gift reciprocity in government can also be illustrated in the notion of "virtue" or "power" (*de*). The Shang and Western Zhou texts and bronze vessel inscriptions are full of references to the importance of cultivating *de* in the person of the king because *de* gives the king access to Heaven and the Mandate to rule and because it is a power more effective than force for attracting and winning the people (Savage 1985:186). *De* could be obtained by the king in many ways: by bestowing benefits and kindness to the nobles and the people; by sacrificing to the spirit and natural world, by sacrificing to the royal ancestors, and by cultivating his moral character and observing the proper rituals of state. The first two ways can be shown to rely upon the logic of gift-giving. Since *de* (virtue) is semantically and phonetically connected with *de* (to get or to obtain), one way to understand the term is in this sense: A gains credit (*de*) for giving B something, and is due something in return from B. In other words, "power" (*de*) is "obtained" (*de*) by the king through giving, which is also an act of virtue because "the felt force of the compulsion [to repay], in the receiver of the favor, is psychologically transferred to the giver, and perceived as a psychic power in the giver to elicit response, [and] this power is his *de*" (Nivison 1978:53).[23]

The discursive emphasis the Ruists of the Eastern Zhou placed on the ritualized conduct of reciprocity in social relationships can be seen as an elaboration of the gift element in Three Dynasties culture. What the Ruists did was to extend and generalize this principle of reciprocity from its older aristocratic and political context to the context of everyday life in their own times. In this frequently quoted passage of the *Book of Rites*, the notion of reciprocity is tied into the observance of the correct principles of ritual, so that ritual and gift obligations are linked in interpersonal ethics: "In the highest antiquity they prized (simply conferring) good; in the time next to this, giving and repaying [*bao*] was the thing attended to. And what the rules of propriety [*li*] value is that reciprocity. If I give a gift and nothing comes in return, that is contrary to propriety; if the thing comes to me, and I give nothing in return, that also is contrary to propriety" (*Li Ji* "Qu Li," 1987:7; Legge 1885:65). In Rujia ethics, giving, receiving, and repaying are not valued so much for the interested outcome of the ex-

---

[23] Another interpretation the ancient usage of *de* sees it as a personal quality derived from emulating and conforming to moral norms and sages (Munro 1969:99–112).

change, as for the ritual form to which such acts adhere and for their exemplification of the ritual rules of social conduct. Embedded in ethics and the objective cosmic principles of ritual, reciprocity in Rujia discourse is a ritual performance, or an extension of ritual to everyday actions which maintains the linkages between human actions and cosmic forces.

It is interesting to contrast the Legalist attitude to gift-giving with that of the Rujia. In the *Han Feizi*, there is a story about King Zhao of the state of Qin who fell ill. "The hundred surnames [his subjects] in every hamlet bought an ox and every family prayed for the king's earliest recovery" (1982:476; Liao 1959:124). When this was reported to the king, instead of being pleased, he was angry and ordered every village to pay a fine of two suits of armor. Said he, "When the people love me, I will have to alter the law and bend my will to comply with their requests. In this manner the law will not stand. If the law does not stand, it leads to chaos and ruin" (ibid.). In other words, the king did not wish to be obligated to the people, and he refused to assume the subordinated position of a receiver of their gifts and goodwill.

The Eastern Zhou witnessed the gradual breakdown of the segmentary state order as kinship, ritual performance, and gift relations no longer proved adequate to hold the segments to the center. The old order of kinship and ritual gave way to new organizational principles of general militarization and bureaucratization as each of the segments developed into contending states. By the time of the Warring States, gift relations no longer enjoyed the prominent role they had in the Three Dynasties polity. Indeed, it is interesting that in the archaeological record, the number of bronze ritual vessels declines in the Eastern Zhou and traces of them taper off in the Qin-Han period. Thereafter, the state was no longer constituted by ritual performance or kinship and gift relations, but relied on a well-developed administrative machinery of taxation, bureaucracy, and laws to ensure centralized control. As local segments lost their former autonomy in the new imperial state order, the center no longer depended on gift obligations to bind them.

In the Legalist vision of the perfectly ordered state, the people were made dependent on the state through a process in which the state, more systematically than ever before, gathered up all the means for distribution. Thus in the *Shang Jun Shu*, the sovereign is advised that a strong and effective state must rely on "statistics" (*shu*), a word that has the dual meaning of "counting and measuring" (*suan, liang*) and "method of control" (*shu*), with which it shares the same pronunciation (1988:59–65). What was to be counted and measured by the state was the strength of its army, the extent and wealth of its land, the size and distribution of the population, and the number of mountains, forests, highways, dikes, and pastures. Should there be an imbalance in the proportion of cultivated to arable land, of the population to arable land, or of farmers to soldiers, and so forth, then the state must take measures to correct the imbalance. These measures could range from granting free land and houses and exemption from taxes for three generations to encouraging immigration when necessary to barring people from taking up other occupations or changing residence (1988:16–17, 65–71, 119–29).

Another means whereby the state was to take control of resources away from the clan and lineage nobles and administer them rationally was in instituting new population registration, classification, and taxation systems. Thus in 375 B.C.E. population registers were introduced in the state of Qin in order to submit the male adult population (from 17 to 60 years old) to taxes, corvee labor duties, and military service (Yates 1987). There were several types of registers, based mainly on occupation: military, household, royal clan, official, market (for merchants), criminal, bondservants or slaves, and perhaps scribes. This system of registration by occupation interacted with a complicated system of ranking in ways that are still unclear to us today. The ranking system was based in part on military merit and on heredity, so that within the stratified categories of royal clan, aristocracy, commoners, convicts, and slaves, there were differential degrees of rank open to upgrading and demotion based on merit and wrongdoing. Thus the second historical eruption of the state in China destroyed the old kinship hierarchy based primarily on heredity, but only to replace it with a state classification system no less hierarchical.

It is in the discourse of the Legalists that the second great historical eruption of the state can be seen in China, this time resulting in a pure form of a unitary and fully centralized state completely released from the principles of kinship, ritual, and gift power. This second thrust of the state inaugurates the bureaucratic state with its "modern" mechanisms of direct territorial administration, legal and penal system, systematic taxation, surveillance, and rigid classification of the population.

The Past in the Present

It is a commonplace that the early Ruists looked to the past for their models of the good social order (Creel 1970:103): "The Master said, 'I am not one who was born in the possession of knowledge; I am one who is fond of antiquity, and earnest in seeking it [knowledge] there'" (*Analects* 7.19; Legge 1961:201). The Ruists hearkened back to the semilegendary rulers Yao, Shun, and Yu of a largely prehistoric period. They also admired the Western Zhou dynasty, especially the reigns of the first two Zhou kings Wen and Wu, and the duke of Zhou:

[Confucius] handed down the doctrines of Yao and Shun as if they had been his ancestors, and elegantly displayed the regulations of Wen and Wu, taking them as his model. Above, he harmonized with the temporal order of Heaven, and below, he conformed [with the order of] the waters and the land. (*Doctrine of the Mean* 30.1; Legge 1961:427)*

Yan Yuan asked how the government of a country should be administered. The Master said, "Follow the calendar of the Xia. Ride in the state carriage of Yin. Wear the ceremonial cap of Zhou. Let the music be the Shao [music of Shun] with its dancers." (*Analects* 15.10; Legge 1961:297–98)*

The Rujia position on the recuperation of the past was not to advocate a wholesale reversion to the past, but to promote certain rituals and institutions of the past. For example, it is interesting that Rujia discourse never advocated emulating the founder or adopting the government rituals of the Shang dynasty, only some of its minor customs of private life (Hsiao 1979:96). Furthermore, Confucius thought that the customs of Qi, a "hegemonic state" that had imposed its authority by force and where the ways of the Shang were deeply entrenched, was not up to the level of the rituals of the state of Lu, where Zhou ritual and customs were strong (95). Not only were the Ruists interested in reviving those aspects of the past that were more conducive to Rujia definitions of humaneness (*ren*), they also attempted to extract certain principles from the vanishing old order and extend their applicability outside the court and nobility to everyday life for different classes of people.

The past that appealed to the Rujia the most were rituals and personal ethics that were simple and sincere and served to blunt the coercive thrust of the state. "Confucius said, 'The people of former times, in their rituals and music, were wild people [*yeren*], while the people of later times, in their rituals and music, are cultivated men [*junzi*]. If I were to adopt [ritual] practices, I would follow the people of former times'" (*Analects* 10.1; Legge 1961:237).* In this passage Confucius recognizes one connotation of "wild people" (*yeren*) as crude, coarse, and vulgar, in contrast to the refined and learned gentleman (*junzi*). Yet the effect of his explicit preference for the "wild" rituals and music of former times is to affirm the other connotations of *ye* current in his time. These other ancient associations of the word *ye* deserve to be explored.

Many usages of this word in Zhou texts suggest the meaning of something that is "outside of the state."[24] For example, *yeren* could refer to the common people, in the sense of "people without ranks of nobility or emoluments of office." The term "in the wilds" (*zaiye*) meant someone who was not recognized by the center or who was out of office. It was used in contrast to "in office" (*zaiwei*) or "in court" (*zaichao*) (*Shu Jing*, "The Books of Yu"; Legge 1865:64–65). *Yeren* could also mean people who lived far away from the city, in the fields and open spaces, or in the frontier wastelands not yet brought under full control by the state. Such people were *ye* because they displayed the qualities of simplicity and crudeness, in the sense of unadorned. In the *Rituals of Zhou*, *ye* is also defined as the area between 200 and 300 *li* (a unit of distance) outside the royal city. Indeed, textual evidence suggests that in both predynastic and Western Zhou times, there existed an ideal template for the classification of spaces radiating outward from the "imperial domain" to the domains of the cities of various clan nobles and princes and, further, to the remoter regions of the wild tribes such as the *Man* and the *Yi*, and banished criminals (*Shu Jing*, "The Tribute of Yu"; Legge 1865:142–49). Therefore, in affirming the simpler rituals of the past, and describing them as "wild," Confucius was also implying that he preferred rituals that came from places away from the imperial center or beyond the reaches of the state.

Indeed, there are many passages that suggest that Confucius frowned on assuming an official state post or adopting statist methods. Rather, he advocated what can be called deinstitutionalized or non-statist politics as methods of governing. "Someone addressed Confucius, saying, 'Sir, why are you not engaged in the government?' The Master said, 'What does the *Shu* [*Book of Historical Documents*] say of filial piety?—"You are filial and show friendship to your brethren. These qualities are displayed in government." This then also constitutes the exercise of government. Why must this be taken as government: that one must be engaged in the government?'" (*Analects* 2.21; Legge

---

[24] Morohashi 1955–60, vol. 11:431. Legge's translation of *yeren* in this passage is "rustics."

1961:152–53).* By selectively quoting from the *Shu*, which records the personages, utterances, and events of the Three Dynasties period, Confucius can be seen as rhetorically invoking certain elements of ancient segmentary state politics to resist the growing tides of statist modes of power in his day.

By the time of the Warring States, the old segmentary state order had all but disappeared, except in the old books and preachings of philosophers. The Legalists, in promoting a strong state system they knew to have no precedents in history, deployed a different construction of time. Theirs was a temporal order in which the past was no longer relevant, and the precarious new political institutions of the present had to be constantly defended with resolve and imposed with strength.

> Generally speaking, men hesitate to change ancient traditions because they are diffident about affecting the peace of the people. Indeed, not to change ancient traditions is to inherit the traces of disorder; to accord with the mind of the people is to tolerate villainous deeds. If the people are stupid and ignorant of disorder and the superior is weak-willed and unable to reform traditions and institutions, it is a failure in the process of government. The sovereign, who understands with clarity the way to rule the state, must proceed to put it into strict practice, so that even though it violates the wishes of the people, he must establish his method of rule. (*Han Feizi* 1982:165; Liao 1959:154)*

Even after the state of Qin's victory and the establishment of the empire in 221 B.C.E., these radically new practices and instititutions were felt to be poised precariously in history, always threatened by the examples of tradition. When the new imperial state order was challenged by the Rujia for not following tradition, the emperor Qin Shihuangdi, at his minister Li Si's suggestion, issued the decree for the notorious Burning of the Books. Here is the famous record of Li Si's suggestion in the *Shi Ji* (*Historical Records*):

> Your servant suggests that all books in the bureau of history, save the records of Qin, be burned; that all persons in the empire . . . daring to store the *Shi* [*Book of Songs*], the *Shu* [*Book of Historical Documents*], and the discussions of the various philosophers, should go to the administrative and military governors so that these books may be indiscriminately burned. Those who dare to discuss the *Shi* and the *Shu* among themselves should be (executed and their bodies) exposed on the marketplace. Those who *use the past to negate the present* [*yigu feijin*]

should be put to death and their lineages terminated. (Si-Ma 1972, vol. 1:255; Bodde 1967:82–83; my emphasis)*

Only the books contained in the imperial archives and practical books on medicine, divination, and agriculture circulating among the people were exempt. The *Shi* and the *Shu* were especially objectionable because these were constantly invoked by the Ruists to hearken back to a golden age of sage-kings who ruled by virtue and ritual instead of by force and law (Bodde 1967:164).

The policy later dubbed as "burning the books and burying Ruist scholars alive" *(fenshu kengru)* did not last for very long. With the ascendancy of the Han dynasty in 206 B.C.E., a great effort to recover the ancient books was mounted with official patronage in the first two centuries of the new dynasty. Calls were sent out over the empire to collect any books in private possession that had escaped burning, and transcriptions were made of the classics from the oral recitations of old scholars who had committed the texts to memory. It is in the compilation and editing of the old books during this period that many alterations of the ancient texts were probably made to conform to the standpoint of a new imperial state order. Passages were reinterpreted, interpolated, and falsified (Legge 1961:3–11; Bodde 1967:164–66). Thus the Rujia texts are an amalgam of layers of different times and interpretations and contradictory passages: the segmentary state order, elements of which Confucius sought to revive, coexisted with the imperial state order, which found its way into the texts and which later commentaries tended to emphasize.

The character of the Rujia itself changed as it gained ascendancy in the Han court as state orthodox discourse.[25] No longer was it an oppositional discourse outside the state; now it served the state and legitimated its rule by softening its impact on the people. The Han and later imperial dynasties preserved all the imperial state structures established by the Qin and inspired by Legalist discourse (such as the commandary-county system, the penal and surveillance system, and the bureaucracy),[26] but replaced Legalist discourse with the moralism

[25] Modern scholars have observed that in Han Confucianism there was more stress on rigid status distinctions and stratification than in the pre-Qin era (Hsu 1970–71; Wasserstrom 1989) and that beginning with the transitional text of *Xunzi*, Warring States and Han notions of "ritual" *(li)* incorporated a Legalist-informed perspective (Li 1985:110–12, 115–16; Fehl 1971:151, 181–83). These observations support the argument made here that the emergence of Legalism and the new imperial state order altered the substantive teachings of the Rujia and also brought it more in line with the needs of the state.

[26] For an analysis of debates on the role of the state in the Western Han dynasty, which succeeded the Qin, see Loewe 1985.

of Confucianism as its orthodoxy. Once the imperial state system was established, pre-Qin Rujia oppositional discourse became state Confucianism, which was predicated on and served as a cover for Legalism.

Rujia "employed the past to negate the present" (*yigu feijin*); Legalism "emphasized the present and denigrated the past" (*houjin bogu*); but except for occasional reformist attempts, state Confucianism under the empire used the past to strengthen the present of imperial power. According to early Rujia, the larger field of power, which invested the leader with the virtue and Mandate to rule and the social realm with order and regulation, was constructed as something dependent on ritual. Ritual practice, which involved the people, carved out and reproduced social order while bestowing sanctity on it. Under state Confucianism, the relationship between social institutions and ritual was reversed; ritual and the sanctity it produced became instruments of the state. Although the Han and later imperial orders revived the political role of ritual, once a systematic state administration appeared, ritual could never recover the importance it had had in the polity of the Three Dynasties. When the state relied mainly on its coercive institutions and resource extraction procedures, ritual power was neutralized, disconnected from the role envisioned for it by the early Rujia as the space in and through which the social order could be worked out involving the participants themselves.[27]

From the first traces of the imposition of the state onto primitive societies, through each successive historical upsurge or renewal of the state, older and more archaic elements were absorbed and integrated. The state "overcoded" its logic of centralized organization onto the segmentary kinship units of local communities so that they formed concentric circles revolving around the same central trunk of the state, all resonating with each other. The state, which Deleuze and Guattari call an "arborescent" structure because of its branches stemming from a singular, rooted, fixed, and rigid central trunk, becomes the "axis of rotation" for formerly independent kinship units (1987: 208–13). It has been able to absorb older elements, such as ancestor worship, gift and kinship relations, clan and lineage organization, and reorient them to fit its own purposes of infiltrating into local communities.

At the same time, these remnants of another social order can also pose as centrifugal forces countering the centripetal project of the

---

[27] This argument on pre- and postimperial Confucianism parallels Rappaport's contrast between ritual as generative of social order and ritual as hypocritical lies (1979b:240).

state. This alternative history of the present recognizes the now rarely conceded point that an appeal to the past is not always conservative or reactionary, but can be oppositional. If it is true that the early despotic state achieved a gathering of primitive kinship filiations into the direct filiation of the state machine (Deleuze and Guattari 1983: 198), then it must also be true that within each new state order, the primitive past will always reappear and form oppositions to the present.

CHAPTER SEVEN

The Cult of Mao, Guanxi Subjects,
and the Return of the Individual

Most of the time, the [modern] State is envisioned as a kind of political power which ignores individuals, looking only at the interests of
the totality or, I should say, of a class or a group among the citizens. . . . That's quite true. But I'd like to underline the fact that the
State's power (and that's one of the reasons for its strength) is both
an individualizing and a totalizing form of power. Never, I think, in
the history of human societies—even in the old Chinese society—has
there been such a tricky combination in the same political structures
of individualization techniques, and of totalization procedures.

—Foucault 1983:213

In Chapter 5 I discussed the various ways the centralized bureaucratic state orders, classifies, and disciplines the population in the
course of carrying out its distribution prerogatives. Yet two questions
may be posed at this point concerning how it is that state redistributive power can tolerate such segmentation and individualization of
subjects. First, would not the totalizing unity of state and society be
threatened if the individualization, classification, and segmentation of
the population were allowed to go unchecked? Second, what happens
when the very state apparatus that administers the population itself
comes under attack, as was the case during the Cultural Revolution,
when the state simultaneously strengthened itself and promoted its
own destruction? Both these questions can be dealt with by looking at
the modern phenomenon of the "cult of Mao," a unique type of state
power, which is both complementary to and in tension with state
redistributive power.

In this chapter I wish to show how "subjectivity," or the construction of personhood and self in guanxixue, counteracts not only redistributive power but also state-centering power or the subjectivity produced in the cult of Mao. In addition, I touch on a reemerging

245

subjectivity, the free and universal individual, which stands apart from the state-redistributive, the Maoist, and the guanxi subjects.[1]

In exploring the cultural and historical construction of the person in the Mao cult, the anthropology of personhood[2] does not provide a satisfactory theoretical tool. This is because it still tends to assume, first, the coherence and stability of the category of person (however defined) *within* a single cultural formation; second, the uniform nature of the construction process therein; and third, the homogeneity and constancy of the culture itself. The anthropology of personhood has seldom been concerned with charting the inner borders that mark a fragmented self, often divided against itself. Furthermore, except for life-cycle developmental changes, the stability of the category of person has been stressed over transformations of the self, especially changes resulting from the linkages between the self, or its segments, and historically shifting discourses. Given the rapidity of historical transformations from the nineteenth through the twentieth centuries in China, what is needed is a way to delineate the multiple, coexisting, and conflictual constructions of the subject often found in one and the same person, and the alternating and commingling layers of modernity and tradition. Since modern discourses shift and are transformed with history, and the subject is an entity intricately connected to discourses, the subject embodies history.

The word "subject," it seems to me, dissociates itself from the notion of a coherent, stable person or self by its importance in the language of psychoanalysis, where "the Freudian subject is above all a partitioned subject, incapable of exhaustive self-knowledge.[3] Its parts do not exist harmoniously: they speak different languages and operate on the basis of conflicting imperatives" (Silverman 1983:132). The

---

[1] A version of this chapter was presented in the Anthropology Departments at the University of California at San Diego (November 1989) and the University of Chicago (February 1990), and at the American Ethnological Society meetings in Atlanta in April 1990. A version was also presented in Chinese at the Center for Psychosocial Studies, Chicago, February 1990. I very much appreciate the many useful comments.

[2] This literature is enormous; see, for example, Geertz 1973b and 1984, Dumont 1970, Mauss 1985, and M. Rosaldo 1984. An exception to the assumption of a culture-specific monological subject can be found in Kondo 1991.

[3] The argument may arise that Freudian analysis, which assumes the universality of psychic processes, is incompatible with the relativism of poststructuralist theory. My own position is that Freud discovered some psychic processes common to the species, but that each culture or historical period translates and combines these psychic processes differently. Therefore, I believe that psychoanalysis can be employed fruitfully in conjunction with poststructuralist frameworks. Efforts to historicize psychoanalysis and the psychological disorders it studies in the modern Western condition include Foucault 1980, Deleuze and Guattari 1983, and Sass 1987.

usage of the word "subject," then, is intended to serve as a way of introducing fluidity, divisiveness, and antagonism to the processes of both self and culture.

The word "subject" also corrects for the problem of giving too much credit to the self as the seat of consciousness, intention, and self-knowledge. The subject "speaks [for itself while] simultaneously being spoken" by discourse (Silverman 1983:128). Anthropology's portrayal of culture as the unconscious and automatic transmission and socialization of thought and action just does not seem adequate to account for what has actually been involved in "making a revolution." The revolutionary experience in China has included the deliberate and systematic state mobilization of the masses to actively transform themselves, their thoughts, motivations, values, and modes of social interaction.

Michel Foucault has pointed out the twofold meaning in the term "subject": "There are two meanings of the word *subject*: subject to someone else by control and dependence, and tied to his own identity by a conscience or self-knowledge. Both meanings suggest a form of power which subjugates and makes subject to" (1983:212). Subject-formation then, is a process of domination as well as self-subordination.

To thematize the state is to give a more concrete representation of the dominant structure of power in China today. Louis Althusser explicitly links subjectivity with the state by showing that there is more to the state than the repressive machinery of the army and police. Another dimension of the state is what he calls "ideological state apparatuses" such as the institutions of education, religion, family, media, literature, art, and sports (1971). State power also works positively by defining and classifying subjects who are at once free and subjected. They submit themselves freely to the state, thus participating in their own subjection. Therefore, they are also active agents who do not always need the repressive state apparatus but can "work by themselves" to further state power (Althusser 1971:168–69).

A Sweep of Red: State Subjects and the Cult of Mao

Historian Takashi Fujitani has shown that modern Japanese emperor-worship, with its national holidays and state rituals, was a product of late nineteenth- and early twentieth-century efforts to promote nationalism and the drive to modernize (1993; 1994). This "invention of tradition" (Hobsbawm 1983) was a new religion with no precursors in a past that had no concept of loyalty to a unified entity of Japan. Similarly, the Mao cult no longer relied solely on awesome monarchical displays or the linking of people to binary and ever-expanding superior-subordinate kinship relationships of correspondence (father/son, emperor/subject, husband/wife, and so on) (Hamilton 1984; Yang 1988:416). Mao, the new leader, no longer assumed the old dynastic emperor's ritualized "pivotal" or "centering" role of mediating the boundaries between Heaven and Earth, upper and lower realms, inside and outside, ancestors and descendants (Hevia 1990; Zito 1987, 1993).[4] Nor did he bring "Heaven's symmetry to earth's confusion" (Geertz 1977:159) by aligning the order created in ritual to the order of the cosmos, as the Qing dynasty emperors did through imperial state rituals.

What separates Maoism from the reigns of dynastic emperors is the process of modern state-building (Duara 1987, 1988a), and more than half a century of the conversion of "the motley . . . peoples in the Chinese empire, which used to be 'All under Heaven'" (Sun 1992:245), into "the masses" of a national state. The cult activated mechanisms that cut through the old layers of hierarchy which intervened between the emperor and the people. In Maoism, each individual was brought to an equal distance from the leader or state center, and state surveillance was directly embedded in the interiority of each subject. This conversion process benefited from the fear and hatred of Western and Japanese imperialism. At the same time, it also had the help of Western metanarratives of linear historical progression (Christian, Social Darwinist, Marxist) and perhaps of imported modern psychology, especially the racial and crowd psychology of Gustav Le Bon (Sun 1992).

The present analysis follows in the Foucaultian spirit of detecting a historical rupture between the old Chinese imperial system and the mid-twentieth-century phenomenon of the cult of Chairman Mao. In other words, I propose that the cult of Mao was not so much a continuation of a traditional Chinese penchant for emperor-worship as a novel product of a Chinese modernity that had to deal with the profound loss of the traditional order.[5] Maoism is better understood in light of various other leader cults and fascist movements in the twen-

---

[4] Zito (1987) uses the notion of "centering" differently from how I use it when describing a key mechanism of the modern cult of Mao.

[5] This does not mean that traditional elements cannot be found in the Mao cult, but that new and traditional elements come together to form a new social force and technique of power to deal with a novel situation.

tieth century, an era that Benjamin has described as the shift from religious or ritual life to the dominance of the political (1969b:224).

Throughout the first three decades after Liberation, the figure of Mao acted as an icon of the Revolution and the new Chinese nation. The love and yearning for Mao reached a climax in 1968–1971 during the Cultural Revolution, when the cult of Mao pervaded the everyday symbolic and ritual life of the people across the nation.[6] In the 1980s in Beijing I found many people who were ready to reminisce, sometimes sheepishly, sometimes bitterly, about what my friend Hu Peng called a "long nightmare [from which] the Chinese people have at last awakened." What follows are selected oral accounts of Mao worship I collected in the field, as well as material I gathered from primary and secondary sources on the Cultural Revolution.[7]

During those years, many people across the country pinned Mao buttons on their shirts, next to their hearts. Buttons were aluminum or plastic, sometimes ceramic, and they were usually round. Portraits of Chairman Mao on these buttons came in various guises, as a young man striding resolutely forward in his student days, as a Yan'an revolutionary in a soldier's cap, or as a round, beaming, middle-aged leader of the Party surrounded by wheat stalks or the famous mangoes.[8] On the backs of the badges, characters such as "loyalty" (zhong), or slogans such as "Long live Chairman Mao for ten thousand years without limit!" were printed, often along with the name of the work unit that had manufactured or distributed the button. The more fervent-minded wore several buttons, and some were known even to pin them directly onto their skins to show the seriousness of

---

[6] The worship of Mao can be found both before and after this period. I will only address the most extreme form of Maoism. Any analysis of the minor reemergence of the Mao cult in the years after the 1989 Tiananmen tragedy must take into account the loss of faith and the new ironic twists of the 1980s.

[7] By the 1980s, most of the people interviewed about the Cultural Revolution tended to speak in generalities about the period because in their memories the times and places of important events had become blurred, even confused. I thank Michael Schoenhals for pointing this out.

[8] The story of Mao's mangoes has many versions, each one considered the real and authoritative account by the person telling it. The story has it that in the 1960s some overseas Chinese from Southeast Asia (an African head-of-state in another version) paid a visit to Chairman Mao, bringing along some mangoes as a present. Mao wanted to share the mangoes with the people, so he sent them as a present to Qinghua University's Workers' Propaganda Team (or some poor peasants) who received them with awe and reverence. Those who ate the mangoes were criticized, but those who did not were praised. Another version circulating in Beijing in the early 1980s took this story a step further. These workers (or peasants) could not imagine eating such sacred objects directly from the Chairman himself. They kept the mangoes on a table in the center of their homes as if they were a sacrificial offering. When the fruit rotted, they had wax replicas made, and worshipped them instead.

their commitment. There were also those who had the Chinese characters for "Loyalty to Chairman Mao" and "Toward the Party" tattooed directly onto their bodies.

Mao's physiognomy and bodily stature were taken as proof of and justification for his exalted status. His tall and robust build marked him as a leader, even "emperor-like," it was said, and his obesity in a land of thin people and his long earlobes were seen as marks that his was a destiny of greatness and good fortune (*you fu*). Many believed that Mao would actually live to be 135. His presence was felt everywhere, from portraits painted on walls and hung in homes to statues in public squares, so that it seemed that he was omnipresent and omniscient. Thus, in Mao's mechanically reproduced portraits can be seen the lingering "aura" and "cult value" of preindustrial art finding a last refuge in the human countenance of a modern mass movement (Benjamin 1969b:226). In the Mao cult can be found the "aestheticization of politics" that Benjamin ascribed to fascism (Falasca-Zamponi 1992).

Elder Sister Su, a factory accountant, recalled to me the wedding presents she and her husband received in 1970. "Back then weddings were very simple. We both distributed some candy to our coworkers in our units. All our relatives and friends gave us the same things. We got seven or eight busts of Chairman Mao and I don't remember how many volumes of *Collected Works of Chairman Mao* we got. . . . You know, back then, you didn't dare throw these things away, so you just had to wait until your friends got married and you passed these things on to them." In their two-room home, I could see the large wooden trunk, a wedding present provided by the groom's family, emblazoned with the calligraphy of Lin Biao praising Mao.

Around 1968, a daily series of rituals evolved called "asking for instructions in the morning and making a report at night" (*zao qingshi, wan huibao*). Each morning in every home, family members would wake up and go to the portrait of Chairman Mao. They would each bow three times and tell the Chairman what efforts they would make for the Revolution that day. Then each night before they went to bed, they would again bow to the Chairman and report on their accomplishments or failures for the day and their resolutions for the next day.[9]

The "loyalty dance" (*zhongzi wu*) was another way to show one's dedication to Chairman Mao. For a period of about two years, all

---

[9] These and other oral accounts of the rituals of Mao worship can be found in *Collection of Laughing Materials from the Cultural Revolution* (Cheng 1988). These practices, which seem so comical to many Chinese in the 1980s and 1990s, were in most cases sincere and deadly serious in their time.

work units were given orders from administrative levels above to hold collective loyalty dance sessions periodically. To the strains of such popular tunes as "The Red Sun within Our Hearts" and "Ten Thousand Years! Ten Thousand Times Ten Thousand Years!" people would assume various heroic poses of head held high and chest thrust forward and go through dance steps such as raising the hands as if holding *Quotations of Chairman Mao* and kicking out the feet as if making rebellion (Yu 1988:1–2).

The height of the Mao Cult is remembered as a period when many people were swept away by their fervent love for Mao, when many became so "fanatical" (*kuangre*) that they totally "lost their reason" (*shiqu lixing*). In both oral and written accounts, a major motif emerges regarding the ecstatic experience of seeing Chairman Mao in person in Tiananmen Square in Beijing. In a collection of personal testimonials of loyalty to Mao, a middle-aged Party secretary of a Beijing shoe factory writes about a scene he witnessed in 1970:

We stood on the Gate of Heavenly Peace, waiting for the most fortunate moment of our lives. At precisely ten o'clock, to the imposing music of "The East Is Red," our great leader Chairman Mao mounted up onto the Gate with vigorous strides. Immediately, the crowd on the Gate and in the square seethed with excitement. The cries of "Long live Chairman Mao" resounded to the skies and merged into one massive cry. I stood in the midst of the crowd on my tiptoes, gazing at the Red Sun. Glowing with health and radiating vitality, Chairman Mao's face shone with a red light. With a slight smile, he waved to us. A powerful flow of warmth suddenly flooded my whole body. My heart pounded violently and hot tears burst forth from my eyes. The great savior star that we had been longing for day and night stood today before us. How could it not move me ten thousand degrees? Oh, you sparkling tears, do not block my vision, but let me get my fill of this most fortunate scene! Gazing at the kind and loving face of Chairman Mao, I just could not stay calm. (Zhang et al. 1977:36–37)

Youth were especially vulnerable to revolutionary fervor and longing for the Chairman. It was every Red Guard youth's dream to travel to Beijing and catch a glimpse of him during one of his several tours through crowds of hundreds of thousands of people in Tiananmen Square. In 1966, many made the journey from around the country on crowded trains that were free to Red Guard youth. Liang Heng (Liang and Shapiro 1983) was one such youth from Changsha who got close to the Chairman one day. The frenzied scene he describes attests to the intense impact that Mao had on people's deepest emotions. That day, after Mao had briefly passed through the crowd and shaken hands with a few lucky people, everyone around them reached out to touch those who had touched the Chairman. A sudden centrifugal ripple-flowing effect occurred, as these people were in turn eagerly touched by a larger circle of people, who in turn transmitted Mao's "mana" or totemic force (Durkheim 1961:223), so to speak, to even more distant areas of the crowd, and all were suffused with joy (Liang and Shapiro 1983:123).

The compelling force of Mao was not limited to his images, his deeds, or his commanding personal presence. It also magnetized the people through language, specifically Mao's utterances and writings, which were collected in lengthy volumes and condensed in the widely distributed small book with a red plastic cover called *Quotations of Chairman Mao* (*Mao Zhuxi Yulu*). The People's Liberation Army Political Department printed almost a billion copies of it between 1964 and 1967 (Meisner 1982:165). The *Quotations* were the objects of intense daily study, and whole passages were learned by heart.

There were two types of Mao's utterances revered during this period: "the Highest Directives" contained excerpts of Mao's speeches and writings from the 1930s to the 1960s, and "the Newest Directives" were Mao's pronouncements during the Cultural Revolution. Chen Zhongwang, a school teacher who was only a thirteen-year-old girl in Wuhan in 1966, recalls that the Newest Directives of the Chairman were often promulgated at night. Each new directive was usually announced over the speakers of the public-broadcast system of work units and neighborhood committees, sometimes in the middle of the night when everyone was sleeping. Residents would awake to the sound of gongs outside on the streets and would pour out of their homes, heading for their work units or nearest congregating area. There, they would listen to the words of the Newest Directive from Mao and parade around in the night to celebrate the latest bestowal of wisdom from above.

Modernity and the Mao Cult

The groundwork for the Maoist subject was laid in China's modernization and Westernization in the first half of the twentieth century. As Lydia Liu and Tani Barlow point out, modernist discourse derived from the May Fourth Movement sought to "liberate" individuals from traditional family, kinship, lineage, and local community bonds, but the effect was to facilitate their insertion into a new apparatus of power: the modern nation-state (Liu 1993a; Barlow 1989,

1991a).[10] Similarly, in an insightful and poignant analysis of Lu Xun's *Madman's Diary*, Wu Xiaoming traces how the desire of May Fourth intellectuals for a society of autonomous individuals produced a "paranoia" of tradition and a "melancholia" for the loss of objects of emotional identification (Wu 1992). Once unmoored from the social relationships of a Confucian culture, the new and barely formed individuals sought refuge and security, and this led them paradoxically to embrace and merge with a new revolutionary collective subject, a subject that was to swallow up the very individual they once desired.

It is important to note that the Mao Cult developed *after* most elements of traditional beliefs and practices had been swept away, first by May Fourth iconoclasm, then by the modernizing Guomindang Party (Duara 1991), and finally by the Communists in massive socioeconomic structural transformations, thought reform, and mass-mobilization campaigns. Antitraditionalism was tied in with the growth of the modern state, and it reached its zenith during the Cultural Revolution when old books and old art objects were burned and temples and historical monuments were pillaged. The worship of Mao must therefore be seen as a novel and modern phenomenon, and not as any kind of return to some ancient Chinese emperor-worship.

Two mechanisms of inner propulsion of subjects can be discerned in the construction of Maoist subjects: (1) the centering of subjectivities on a common fixed object of emotional identification; and (2) the division of internal subjectivities so that one part of the subject monitors and disciplines the other. One mechanism tries to integrate individuals to the larger collective and center their social and emotional bonds onto a single pivotal point of the nation-state. The other promotes the interiority of individuals by making them examine their inner selves for transgressions. They reinforce each other in achieving a common end: the merging of all subjects into a giant and awesome totality, the image of the state as the embodiment of the unified "People-as-One" (Lefort 1986:297).

The Centering of Subjectivities

What drove so many people to act as one uniform mass and so elevate the person and words of one human being? The following

[10] May Fourth 1919 was the day when intellectuals, students, and other city dwellers demonstrated in Beijing against the Versailles Treaty. This event helped launch an urban movement by students and writers against traditional Chinese culture and a campaign to adopt "progressive" Western ideas (democracy, science, and freedom of the individual). For a detailed examination of the May Fourth Movement, see Chow 1960.

excerpts from interviews with people who were urban youth during the Cultural Revolution reveal at least six emotions that shaped the Maoist subject: (1) gratitude; (2) denigration of the self; (3) hero worship; (4) love of the country or nationalism; (5) fear; and (6) hatred of cadres, teachers, class enemies, and the imperialist West.

For Lin Hui, a Shanghai youth at that time, his fierce love for Mao was a mixture of gratitude and deep respect. He was grateful to Mao for saving China from the imperialists and for creating the New China. It was Mao and the Communist party who had driven out the "foreigners" (Europeans and Americans), the Japanese, and the Guomindang forces. "Mao really wanted to do something for the people." He also admired Mao's boldness of vision and flair—Mao could fight a war, mobilize the people, and write beautiful poetry and calligraphy.[11]

Peng Guanghua, now an economist, who was eighteen years old in Beijing when the Cultural Revolution broke out, gave me this analysis of his own inner feelings (*neixin*) for Mao at that time. First and most important was his desire to "struggle with the private or selfish" (*dou si*) in himself. Mao had instructed people to overcome selfishness and merge with the collective. Peng developed tremendous feelings of guilt (*fuzuigan*) over his selfishness. He struggled with himself so that he could give more of himself to the nation and to the Revolution: "This kind of thing was a religious experience. Worshipping Mao Zedong was a replacement for religion."

A second aspect of Peng's love for Mao was the worship of revolutionary heroes (*geming yingxiong*). Mao was of that generation of revolutionaries who had risked their lives and sacrificed themselves for an ideal. As youths, Peng and his friends read countless moving stories of revolutionary heroes and martyrs. He had great admiration for Mao because in his eyes Mao represented the epitome of heroes. Third, for Peng there was also the element of nationalism (*minzu zhuyi*). Love for Mao represented for him love for country. After China was humiliated by the West, Mao provided a rallying force for unifying and rebuilding the country and gave it hope for future greatness. Finally, mixed in with these other sentiments was also the element of fear. In the back of his mind, there was also a fear that if he

---

[11] Speaking in the 1980s, Lin also added that his feelings for Mao had undergone a "thorough reevaluation" and that he no longer felt the same way. Mao did build the New China, but he also destroyed it in the Great Leap Forward and the Cultural Revolution. Yet he also believed that the mass of people still did not question Mao.

did not go along with worshiping Mao like everyone else, he might be accused of being a counterrevolutionary.

Fear was a component as well as a byproduct of the incredible awesomeness and sacredness of Chairman Mao. Chen Zhongwang remembers two incidents in Wuhan which she believes are hard to imagine in the 1980s. A worker was helping to put up stage props for a show in an auditorium. He was cradling in his two arms a bundle of plaster busts of Mao when he tripped on the stairs and fell, smashing the Mao busts into pieces. No matter how unintentional, this sacrilege was so serious that the worker was taken away and either locked up or executed. I, the anthropologist, wanted to clarify exactly to whom his act was so grave, so I asked Chen whether Public Security had taken him away and the people were too afraid to defend him, or whether everyone in the community had condemned him. She replied without hesitation, "Not only did everyone condemn him, but the worker most likely condemned himself. He probably felt very guilty and believed that he should be punished. It was like that back then."

The other incident involved a professor at Wuhan University, which was located in the neighborhood she lived in. He had been branded a rightist in the Anti-Rightist Movement of 1957–58, and now he was eager to redeem himself, so he made a very grave confession at one of the many "criticism, self-criticism" meetings that were held in the late 1960s. He confessed that one day he had a counterrevolutionary "flash of thought" (*shan nian*) that he wanted to get out in the open so as to cleanse and reform himself. He had inexplicably imagined himself killing Chairman Mao, and then thought of the various consequences of this act. Chen explained that the professor most likely revealed this horrible thought in order to show that he was sincerely trying to reform himself and that he was not hiding anything from the Party, but of course it had exactly the opposite effect. He was beaten and put into prison.

"Flash of thought" was a term popular during the Cultural Revolution to refer to those ideas and images that erupted unexpectedly from the brain and had to be controlled so that one would not deviate from the revolutionary path. Thus, a monological, unitary, and centered subjectivity had to assert its dominance over the disruptive multiplicity that constantly broke through.

Looking back on those days, Chen marveled and shuddered at the thoroughness and intensity of the emotional forces ruling the masses in their idolization of Mao:

In the whole world, who could achieve such a feat of getting everyone to think and act exactly alike, totally as one? The whole country was one vast sweep of red [*yi pian hong*]. If anyone said or did anything against the tide, that person would be attacked at once by the masses. Mao became a god [*shen*]—nobody dared oppose him. It was like a giant flood. . . . Don't even consider opposing it or going against the waves. You couldn't even stay still, not to mention go against the current. No matter how hard you clung [to the banks], you'd also be swept away like everyone else.

Finally, there was the deep-seated hatred of officials, indeed of anyone occupying a seat of authority. Wang and Lei, a middle-school teacher and a factory supply agent in a southern provincial town, are both grandsons of a landlord and have met with difficulties in life because of this family background. They also felt deep sentiments for Mao because he told them to "make rebellion" (*zaofan*) against bad officials. At the time, they were grateful to Mao for realizing that the new society had spawned a lot of people who, once they attained office, used their power to serve themselves and oppress the people. Following Mao's exhortation to continue the Revolution, they readily joined Red Guard factions that terrorized local officials in power.

Shen, another Shanghai youth, also supported Mao's call to attack the "bourgeois power holders within the Party" or the "capitalist roaders," which in his mind included all of officialdom. To my question why officials were thought of as capitalist, he replied, "At the time, I thought that they treated their office like private property for their own selfish gains. For seventeen years after 1949, the people were oppressed by greedy and despotic cadres. The cadres made the people examine themselves and confess their faults, but they were the ones who should have accounted for themselves to the people. So the attack on 'bad officials' was supported by the people. There were, of course, good officials and they were protected by the people." Shen went on to say that Mao kept himself well above the Party and the bureaucracy, so that the people thought of him as a "good person" (*haoren*), unsullied by the evil bureaucracy.

Hatred also extended to other categories: intellectuals and teachers, counterrevolutionaries, former capitalists and landlords, the imperialist capitalist West, and the "backward" and "feudal" traditional Chinese culture. These hatreds gave rise to an astounding level of violence during the Cultural Revolution. Luo Ying, a forty-year-old screenplay writer, will never forget the gruesome scene he witnessed when many of his junior high school classmates dragged their teacher into a field and beat her to death, her head swollen into a giant balloon of blood and anguish. Wen Wei remembers how at the age of nine in 1966, in a hospital in which he was staying, one horrible night was filled with the screams and shrieks of a person being slowly whipped to death by two girls with leather belts. Hatred for traditional culture and the West was expressed by the destruction of historical monuments, old temples, old and foreign books, ancestral halls and graveyards, and Western-style clothing, and by the persecution of people with overseas connections.

Identification, Idealization, and Filial Piety

The elements of hero worship, gratitude, and nationalism work in concert to unify and propel subjects from within. Chairman Mao was the model that eclipsed all other revolutionary heroes in that he was the single model imitated by the heroes themselves. The Revolutionary Committee of Beijing Normal University declared in 1967: "When we learn from the glorious example of [revolutionary] heroes, the most, most fundamental principle is to learn from their . . . boundless heartfelt love for our great leader Chairman Mao, their boundless faith in him, their boundless worship of him, and their boundless loyalty to him" (*Hongweibin Ziliao* 1975:579). How did hero worship serve as part of the Mao cult's centering mechanism?

In psychoanalytic terms, "identification" is the expression of an emotional tie for another person by molding one's subjectivity according to an exalted model, in other words, by taking the object as an "ego-ideal."[12] This process achieves a substitution for the desire to possess a love object by subjectively assuming the characteristics of that object instead (Freud 1951:60–65), translating a desire to *have* into a desire to *be*. Thus the libidinal constitution of groups can be summarized as follows: individuals in a group all substitute one and the same love object, that of the beloved and feared leader or leading idea. Since they all share the same internalized love object, group

---

[12] In Freud's later works, the term "identification" is applied to the processes that all persons go through in the normal development of their character through a series of bondings with different objects in their lives; however, here I am using the term in a pathological sense, the main sense Freud focuses on in *Group Psychology*, in which he explains how subjects come to submit themselves to a leader, and the sense he later assigned to the term "idealisation," which is a substitution for the lost narcissism of childhood (Laplanche and Pontalis 1973:144–45, 202–8; Freud 1951, 1989). I thank Elliot Jurist for pointing this out.

members not only identify with the object, but also with themselves (1951:80), thus producing a degree of mass uniformity.

Identification can at times assume a pathological character, which Freud called "idealisation." The object is inflated into an unattainable ideal, so that it comes to dominate the subject who becomes more humble and self-sacrificing, and in extreme cases may be in danger of being overpowered and consumed by the object (1951:74–75).

Just as Freud's essay inspired Theodor Adorno (1982) and Wilhelm Reich (1970) to analyze the libidinal construction of sexually repressed subjects in German fascism, a similar process of modern subject-formation around the love object of Chairman Mao can be detected in China. The pervasiveness of Mao on the physical and cultural landscape and the tears of excitation, loyalty, and longing for the Chairman recounted in the reports above attest to a certain libidinal quality in the formation of individual, group, and national subjects. Despite the social divisiveness, "class struggles," and fighting between political factions, all social segments shared a common point of anchor in their intense loyalty and admiration for Chairman Mao.

Not only was Mao a role model as the quintessential revolutionary hero, he was also regarded as a parental figure. Lei Feng was a People's Liberation Army hero whose diary was first published and promoted in 1963. During the Cultural Revolution, Lei Feng enjoyed a minor cult status as one of the most faithful of Chairman Mao's followers. In his diary he composed a poem called *My Feelings*:

> Ah, Chairman Mao is like a father,
> Chairman Mao's Thought is like the sun.
> Father constantly takes care of me.
> The sun nurtures my growth into maturity.
>
> (Lei 1968:7)

So deep was the love for Mao as a parental figure that one's own parents came under a pall of suspicion as not measuring up to Mao's standards.

Toward the words of your father and mother, and those of an old superior [in office], you must examine them in accordance with Mao Zedong Thought and ask a "why?" If what they say is not in accordance with Mao Zedong Thought, then you must criticize them and definitely not do as they say. If they go counter to Mao Zedong Thought, then you must rebel against them, regardless of whether they are your father or mother, no matter how high an official they are. (*Hongweibin Ziliao* 1975:255)

This exhortation by a Red Guard organization at Qinghua University in 1967 suggests that the larger-than-life persona of Mao and its projected image of moral and political perfection increasingly came to displace the authority of subjects' own parents. Millions of pubescent and adolescent youth substituted Mao for their parents as an object of idealization and loyalty with an intensity and ardor their parents probably never enjoyed.

If hero-worship illustrates the psychological mechanism of identification, how does it relate to feelings of gratitude? Toward both revolutionary heroes and parents, there was not only admiration and identification, but also the sentiment of gratitude for all that they had done. The traditional virtue of filial piety (*xiao*) was based on gratitude toward parents for having brought oneself into the world and for having raised one up into an adult. In the Mao cult, this gratitude was transferred to a new authority figure: "By a strange coincidence, I saw Chairman Mao last night in my dreams. Like a kind father, he stroked my head, and with a gentle smile, said to me, 'Study well, always be loyal to the Party, be loyal to the People!' I was so happy I could not say anything, but could only shed hot tears of gratitude" (Lei 1968:8). During the Cultural Revolution, Mao was referred to as the "Great Savior Star" (*Da Jiuxin*) of the people for having saved the country from feudalism, imperialism, and capitalism: "In the old society, I had my fill of suffering and hardships. Under the unceasing nurturance and education of my kindly mother, the Chinese Communist Party, I have quickly matured into a People's Liberation Army soldier and a glorious Communist Party member. [Therefore], I must constantly prepare to sacrifice all my individual interests, even my very life, for the greatest interest of the Party and the class" (Lei 1968:33). That this ultimate gift of life from mother (the Party) and father (Mao) must be reciprocated, appeals to the same logic that decrees that parents must be repaid with filiality for bringing one into this world. Thus the discourse of Mao was able to appropriate a traditional value, filial piety, and adapt it to a modern project of state power.

Introjection

The discourse of Mao worship is full of descriptions of the corporeal experience of loving Mao. After Lei Feng's encounter with the

Chairman in his dream, he experienced a physical sensation in his body: "In the morning when I woke up, it was as if I had really seen Chairman Mao. Energy suffused my whole body, and I felt as if this load of energy could never be used up" (Lei 1968:8). Here is a depiction of internal bodily processes triggered by the absorption of something external, a psychosocial mechanism Freud called "introjection."

The heart is a central metaphor in Maoist discourse. The following three passages representing the title and first few sentences of an article in a Red Guard publication bear analysis.

1. Presenting our Red Hearts to Chairman Mao.
2. The Red Sun shines into our hearts and hot blood wells up like a wave. Our hands carrying the valuable book, we look toward Beijing, [while] our hearts long for our great leader Chairman Mao.
3. June 19th was the day when the most red, most red of red suns in our hearts, Chairman Mao, came to see the revolutionary play performed by our troupe. (*Hongweibin Ziliao* 1975:35)

In the second passage, all hearts are oriented to a single love-object. Although the Red Sun does affect the subjects' bodies by stirring up their blood, it still shines from outside the subjects. In the third passage, the reddest sun or Mao is described as being located *within* the hearts of the subjects' bodies. From this location, the redness of the sun can better transform hearts, or in other words, hearts directly absorb an attribute of the sun (redness) therefore becoming like suns themselves. Once Mao had been introjected as an intrinsic part of the internal composition of subjects, then those subjects could be said to "offer their hearts," or give themselves totally to Mao, to become part of him and what he represented.

The notions of centering, heart, and submission are all encapsulated in the Chinese word for "loyalty" (*zhong*) 忠 , which is written with the characters for "center" and for "heart." During the Cultural Revolution, *zhong* appeared everywhere: on the backs of Mao buttons, painted in red ink or etched on walls, rooftops, and on machinery. Loyalty to the leader was expressed by the centering of each person's heart around the pivotal Chairman Mao.

In introjection, the subject transposes an object and its inherent qualities from "outside" to "inside" itself, and this object is "put in the place of" a psychical segment of the subject (Laplanche and Pontalis 1973:206–7, 229). Those who pinned Mao buttons or tattooed Mao images directly onto their skins can be seen as attempting to insert Mao into their bodies, to become one with Mao. Whereas in identification, subjects are only centripetally oriented to the central love object, in introjection, the love object is diffused centrifugally into all subjects, causing a welter of perturbations throughout their psychic-bodily processes.

Incorporation and Melancholia

In her diary, Yang Weihong, a fifteen-year-old girl in Liuzhou, Guangxi Province,[13] referred to Mao Zedong Thought as something ingested like food which nourishes the spirit and gives strength to the body: "The staple foods of my spirit everyday are the majestic thoughts of Chairman Mao. Each time I open up the *Works of Chairman Mao*, a red sun emerges in the midst of my heart and a warmth spreads over my whole body. Each time I gaze upon the portrait of our Great Leader Chairman Mao, it's as if all up and down my body I've gained an inexhaustible strength" (Yang 1970: June 5).

An entry by Yang Weihong's teacher in her diary also employs corporal metaphors: "Our bodies' every vein is filled with the thoughts of our Great Chairman Mao, and every single one of our accomplishments are all flashing with the magnificent brilliance of Chairman Mao's thought. . . . When a belief protects Chairman Mao, then the wild winds and vicious waves cannot budge it. When a red heart follows Chairman Mao, then the body and its bones and marrow will not falter" (Yang 1970: January 20). One of Lei Feng's diary entries also describes the presence of the Party within himself: "It can be said that every single cell in my whole body is suffused with the blood of the Party" (Lei 1968:18). Introjection becomes "incorporation" when Mao's personal and symbolic qualities (such as, Mao Zedong Thought or revolutionary heroism) are said to be ingested by the subject as food, or transfused into the bloodstream. Food or blood for the body invigorates even as it constitutes and alters the intrinsic substance of the subject.

At this point in our analysis, the distinction between two mourning strategies, "introjection" and "incorporation," becomes relevant. According to Nicholas Abraham and Maria Torok (1980),[14] the mourn-

---

[13] I thank Michael Schoenhals for bringing this diary to my attention, and lending me the original handwritten copy from the Far Eastern Library of Stockholm University.

[14] I thank my colleague Larry Rickels for bringing this work to my attention. See the useful introduction to his book on psychoanalytic approaches to death and mourning (1988).

ing for a lost or deceased love object takes two different forms: (1) introjection—a benign healing *process* involving two oral enactments of coming to terms with (or "swallowing") the loss, such as eating (funerary banquets, and so on) and talking about the loss, and (2) incorporation—an aberrant form of mourning which works through *fantasies* of the body absorbing the lost object rather than literal enactments.[15] The second type of mourning is really an inability or refusal to mourn because admitting the loss poses a tremendous threat to the stability of the psychic system. When a loss is sustained, but only fantasies of incorporation are offered as a substitute for proper enactments of mourning, then the "grief that cannot be expressed builds a *secret vault* within the subject" (Abraham and Torok 1980:8). When this vault is threatened, "the phantom of the crypt may come to haunt the keeper of the graveyard, making strange and incomprehensible signs to him, forcing him to perform unwonted acts, arousing unexpected feelings in him" (ibid.).

In making use of this psychoanalytic distinction to think about the cult of Mao, we need to switch our focus from an individual's psyche to a collective psyche at the level of a whole social and historical formation. The Mao of the Cultural Revolution can be understood as the phantom who emerged from a secret crypt buried deep within the cultural psyche of modern China.

The Mao cult was the product of a culture that had failed to introject, through mourning rituals and verbal acts, the loss of a traditional order in which roles, social relationships, and rank were clearly laid out in a hierarchy that was ritually anchored and centered in the pivotal person of the emperor.[16] The inability to mourn this object of emotional identification derives from the modern Chinese cultural ambivalence toward tradition. Compared to the modern military, technological, and democratic power and allure of the West, Chinese tradition seemed hopelessly backward and corrupt, it deserved an early death; however, emotional attachment to tradition was difficult to break; it had offered security and stability, as opposed to the destabilizing forces of modernity. Tradition was what linked the living in a continuous line with the past world of the ancestors, a world that had a highly developed culture of mourning.[17]

[15] Freud called pathological mourning "melancholia" (1973).

[16] For an example of the cultural nostalgia for a bygone era of ritual wholeness, see the case of the peasant who declared himself emperor (Anagnost 1985).

[17] For examples of the rich traditions of Chinese rituals of mourning and death cults, see Ahern 1973, Hsu 1967, Watson and Rawski 1988, and Wolf 1974.

Abraham and Torok further posit that for the subject to build a secret crypt, the lost object must have played the role of "ego-ideal" for the subject, a role that for some reason the subject finds too shameful to admit (1980:9). In modern China, the discourse of modernity instills a cultural shame at being attached to a tradition that is now regarded as bankrupt and "backward." Perhaps it is not a coincidence that the Cultural Revolution was a period that saw the extreme of *both* Mao worship *and* angry assaults on religious temples and monks, the burning of old books, the defacing of historical monuments, and the desecration of the graves of historical "class enemies." The more the people tried to disentangle themselves from the hated tradition, the more they buried the loss deep within themselves, and the more they made room for the return of the repressed in the distorted figure of Mao, a new love object who promised to set the world in order. The Mao cult represented a desperate attempt to incorporate this unmourned ghost into the social body, to fill in the empty void left behind by the thorough uprooting of traditional culture. Thus, the Cultural Revolution, in its attacks on tradition, can be seen as May Fourth iconoclasm carried to its extreme.[18] When the crypt is threatened, as it was during the Cultural Revolution, "the ego will fuse with the enclosed object, becoming one with it" (Abraham and Torok 1980:14). That is why Maoist subjects went to any lengths to defend the object, because any injury to their ego-ideal threatened their very survival and the survival of the whole group.

> The seas may dry up, stones may get mashed, but the red hearts of us hundreds of millions of people's militia will remain forever loyal to you without cease. Whoever opposes you is digging out our hearts, wanting to end our lives. In order to defend you, we are willing with all our hearts to ascend mountains of knives, descend into the sea of fire; fling down our heads and skulls, and splatter our hot blood. (Luo 1966:16)

So identified is the subject with the object buried inside it that virtually the only way for it to recover from this obsession is for the object and ego-ideal to die a physical death, so that the subject can finally go through proper mourning for the lost object (Abraham and Torok 1980:15–16). This is at the same time a way to reconcile the subject with the loss of the unspeakable object that Mao represented.

In the West, modernization was gradually introduced over several

---

[18] By an interesting coincidence, Wu Xiaoming also argues that the Cultural Revolution was not the antithesis of May Fourth enlightenment and individualism, but its exaggerated outcome (1992:189).

centuries, and there was no blanket rejection of tradition. Germany is the exception in the West that proves the rule, for its late modernization led to the phenomenon of a mass worship of the leader. China's encounter with modernity and its loss of tradition were also sudden and traumatic, compounded by the fact that it was also part of the modernizing state's agenda to obliterate traditional mechanisms of coping with traumatic change, loss, and mourning.[19]

A Unified Body and a Single Head

So far the themes of hero worship and gratitude have been dealt with, but how does nationalism,[20] the love of one's country, fit into Mao worship? Lei Feng writes, "We must read Chairman Mao's books, obey Chairman Mao's words, be loyal to the Party, loyal to the people, loyal to Chairman Mao" (1968:26). In this passage, a logic of sequential identification and association is at work here so that Mao stands for a whole series of equivalent and related notions larger and more enduring than himself. Shen Ling, a student studying in the United States, drew this sequence: "the individual and the self ⇒ the collective [*jiti*] ⇒ the people [*renmin*] ⇒ the Chinese race and culture [*minzu*] ⇒ the nation [*guojia*] ⇒ the Party [*dang*] ⇒ Mao Zedong Thought ⇒ Chairman Mao ⇒ the individual and the self." The individual must be subsumed to the collective; love for the collective means love for the people and the masses; love for the people means upholding the Chinese race and culture, which is tantamount to loving the nation; loving the nation is equal to loving the Party; loving the Party is adopting Mao Zedong Thought; adopting Mao Zedong Thought is loving Mao; loving Mao is the duty and feeling of each individual. So the logic comes full circle to link the individual directly to Mao through a relationship of worship.

In such a logic, the person of Mao is located at the endpoint of a series of equivalent notions and acts as a unifying metaphor for them. Since Mao incarnated the unified body of the "People-as-One" (Lefort 1986), and since this unified body was sustained and protected by a Party-state organization, then the people's longing for Mao and their introjection or incorporation of his at once paternal and authoritarian persona into their psyche wedded each of them both to the

[19] See Whyte 1988 for a discussion of how traditional rituals of dealing with death have been replaced in the post-1949 period with restrained and simplified services.
[20] For extended discussions of modern Chinese nationalism, see Gladney 1991, Liu 1993b, and Duara 1992a.

image of the perfect unified and totalizing state and to each other. Thus, the state is embedded inside subjects with a thoroughness perhaps never attained by the attenuated system of identification found in the old emperor system.

This process of centering subjects from within represents a new departure from past imperial state subjectivization techniques in the extreme attention paid to individual subjects. The old imperial and Confucianized mode of power secured social order and state loyalty through a series of graduated levels and increasingly inclusive units of moral commitment, from the individual to family to kin group to community to province to empire (Yang 1988:416). For most of the people, loyalty to the emperor in his court in the capital was only attained as a culmination of loyalties to various intervening figures of identification and authority: father and mother, lineage elder, local official, and so on. After the Revolution, these cumbersome old methods, which cluttered the path of the relationship between the individual and the top leader, were abandoned in the rush to destroy "feudalism." Aided by the mass media, Mao-centered subjectivity drew a direct and unmediated line between each individual psyche and the state center.

The May Fourth discourse of individual liberation, equality, and antitraditionalism had the unintended consequence of creating free-floating atomized individuals who were easily inserted into the workings of the nation-state, the only entity to benefit from the processes of modernity. What the May Fourth movement provided the seeds for, and the Communist Revolution carried out, was a "flattening" or "leveling" of the social order, in which the old system of basing identity and status on distinctions of rank, class, age, and kinship distance was dismantled. At the same time, a "homogenizing" process took place, in which differences (of religion, ethnicity, intelligence and education, and gender) were reduced and almost erased. Out of these dual processes emerged "the masses," individuals who formed the body of a new society, and who were brought to an equal distance from the head. This is what Claude Lefort means when he proposes that modern totalitarianism is a reaction to the indeterminateness and divisiveness of democracy and egalitarianism (1986:303–4). When a hierarchical order that keeps people in place is leveled, then a homogenizing force steps in to create a new unity of the People-as-One. Old social divisions give way to new oppositions, that between "the masses" and the outside world (the imperialist West), "the masses" and internal class enemies. And perhaps no modern culture has seen a social body as tightly unified, uniform, and state-saturated as that of the Mao cult of the Cultural Revolution.

The Division of Internal Subjectivities

Although the emotions of fear and guilt were not as publicly articulated as love and loyalty in Mao worship, they were also key ingredients in this discourse, as indicated by the frequency with which subjects during this period publicly confessed their faults and subjected themselves to severe self-criticism in the new state rituals. Contrary to essentialist or Orientalist notions of China as a "shame culture," guilt can be detected here as a more dominant technique of power than shame. Persons feeling shame tend to conceal or rationalize their wrongdoings, whereas persons feeling guilt are propelled into self-disclosure as a way of seeking redemption and expiation (Wu 1979: 33). A psychoanalytic approach again helps to bring to light the interconnections between fear and guilt, the categories of public and private, and their implication in the making of the Maoist divided subject.

The fear that people experienced, especially during the Cultural Revolution, of incurring the masses' anger and being attacked as counterrevolutionaries stems from both the external social world as well as the internal subjective world. The condemnatory voices echoed by the masses out in the society were internalized as the voice of the state residing within the subject.

Dividing the subject was a mechanism explicitly employed by the campaign of "Struggling against the Private and Selfish and Criticizing the Revisionist" (*dousi pixiou*), which got underway in 1967. The idea was to "start up an intense clash and struggle in the brain between collectivism and communism [against] individualism" by "incessantly dissecting [*jiepou*] the self, incessantly undergoing self-criticism (*ziwo piping*], so that one's own worldview would experience a fundamental reconstruction [*gaizao*]" (*Dousi pixiou* 1967:44–45). Besides individualism, the category of the "private" or the "self" (*si*) also stood for such faults as anarchism (as opposed to discipline [*jilü*] and obedience), factionalism, the private property of slavery and feudalism, and "capitalist-roader revisionism" within the Party. Through constant self-monitoring and self-criticism, all these aspects of the selfish and the private would be weeded out and eliminated from state subjects.

As part of the *dousi pixiou* campaign, diary writing of a special political nature was instituted and encouraged among urban youth across the country. These diaries were called "*dousi pixiou* diaries" or "red diaries" (*hongse riji*). They were semi-public texts in that they were started either at the prompting of a teacher or by the student herself, and they were written in private, but with a view to being read by teachers, parents, and fellow students. Ironically, although the goal of political diary writing was to obliterate the self, it relied on a very private and individual effort at strengthening the voice of the state within.

The red-diary movement followed closely on another related campaign, the "Learn from Lei Feng" campaign of 1962, which featured the selfless young People's Liberation Army soldier Lei Feng as a model hero.[21] After his death, Lei Feng's diary was edited and widely disseminated, and became the model par excellence, for the diary writing of both the Lei Feng and *dousi pixiou* campaigns. Although the confessional mode is not prominent in Lei Feng's diary, in which the main motifs are gratitude to the Party and resolutions to be selfless, it became a distinctive feature of how red diaries were written during the *dousi pixiou* campaign.

Of course, these political diaries were not the only form of confessional after 1949. The ingredients of diary writing—self-examination, self-criticism, and confession—have appeared separately or combined in other forms as well. For example, in small-group rituals called "living a democratic life" (*guo minzhu shenghuo*) or "political study" sessions (*zhengzhi xuexi*), participants engaged in what is called "criticism and self-criticism." Each person took turns criticizing themselves or someone else in the group (Whyte 1974). Social gatherings known as "struggle meetings" (*pidou hui*) were usually much more public and larger-scale affairs, in which the accused, with head bowed, was brought before a crowd and loudly denounced by the assembled masses. Finally, a form of writing called "examination" (*jiancha*) served as a written confession and resolution to improve, which a person accused of wrongdoing was asked to write.

Nor were these diaries the first instance of such internal dividing techniques. In 1939 in Yan'an, when the Communist Party was still an oppositional force fighting for survival, Liu Shaoqi called on Party members to submit themselves to "self-cultivation" (*ziwo xiuyang*) (1981). Although he did employ the word "self-criticism" and called

---

[21] Lei Feng was again made a model of emulation for people in a minor campaign in 1983–84 and in 1989 after the Tiananmen Massacre.

for inner Party struggles to eliminate deviation from the correct line, the general thrust of Liu's ideas on cultivation had not yet attained the extremes of self-abnegation and remorseful confession of the 1960s and early 1970s.[22]

Teachers in elementary, middle, and high schools assigned diary writing to their students as part of their homework, to be read and corrected by the teacher. In addition, students who "placed higher demands on themselves" would also voluntarily undertake to write political diaries in order to improve their "political consciousness" (zhengzhi juewu). Chen Zhongwang was an elementary school teacher at the time, and she remembers asking students to write these diaries. She regarded them as opportunities to improve their composition skills, although some other teachers treated them as a way of improving their students' political characters. In high school just a year before she became a teacher, she herself would stay up late at night writing her own diary with a flashlight after the lights were turned out. Typical themes and formats included "self-examination" (ziwo jiancha), in which one reviewed one's thoughts and deeds of the day and criticized oneself for wrongdoing; copying down a quotation of Mao or Lin Biao (sometimes Marx, Engels, Lenin, or Stalin), and writing down the "insights gained" (xinde tihui) from it and how it could be applied to one's concrete life; making resolutions to improve oneself; and criticism or exposure of the political shortcomings of family, friends, and workmates.[23]

During the Cultural Revolution, red diaries came to supplant traditional diaries, which were not explicitly political or revolutionary in spirit. Everyone stopped writing traditional diaries because of the dangers such "privatistic" acts harbored. If they fell into the wrong hands, their contents would expose their authors' political backwardness. In those days, one never knew when one's home might be broken into and searched by roving bands of Red Guards or hoodlums masquerading as Red Guards. The writing of red diaries declined in the early 1970s, but the practice continued on in schools until at least

---

[22] Liu's long speech and essay "On the Cultivation of a Communist Party Member" is sprinkled with quotations from Confucius, Mencius, and others from the Classics, appealing to a long tradition of self-cultivation and self-improvement. The evidence suggests, however, that in this Confucian tradition, the elements of guilt, self-reproach, and confession did not emerge until the late fifteenth century during the Ming dynasty with Wang Yangming's brand of Neo-Confucianism (Wu 1979:22).

[23] Chen also remembers that sometimes other teachers would give out such diary assignments to students as "enumerate your father's mistakes."

the late 1970s, when traditional diary writing seems to have witnessed a gradual and cautious revival.

In the diary of Yang Weihong, the confessional and self-reproach mode is marked, in keeping with the *dousi pixiou* campaign at the time.

> Today, . . . I participated in "organizational life."[24] . . . Were there still any "selfish heart and distracting thoughts" [*sixin zanian*] in me? There were. There were also thoughts of avoiding hardships and fear of getting tired. Originally, after participating in "organizational life," I intended to go to the tunnels just to take a look and then go back home to rest. However, when I arrived there, classmates informed me that they were going to work [at the tunnels] all night. I thought that it might be kind of "fun" to labor at night, and so prepared to stay and work. However, as soon as this thought surfaced, another set of "selfish heart and distracting thoughts" also appeared. Would working at night affect the next day's performance, would it be too much for my body to take? This conflict between two kinds of thoughts started a struggle [inside me]. Torn in this direction and that, I came to realize that both these thoughts were wrong. One kind of thought was to have "fun," while the other represents the word "selfishness" [*si*]. Whichever way you look at it, both thoughts are in the service of "selfishness"—having fun is only to serve oneself. . . . I came to understand that digging a tunnel is not for "fun," but for going into battle. If we participate in a battle with a view to having "fun," then we will not win this battle. (Yang 1970: January 15)

This passage shows some inner thought processes and the struggle between different parts of herself: that which wants to have fun, that which wants to protect her health, and that which represents the internalized voice of the state counseling responsibility, seriousness, and self-sacrifice. In the end, the superego of the state overrides all others with its absolute authoritativeness and its call to subsume petty private concerns to a transcendental cause.

Sometimes the internalized judge can cause the other part of the subject, the accused, intense anguish and a sense of worthlessness, as in this passage:

---

[24] "Organizational life" (*zuzhi shenghuo*) refers to any activities of a political nature organized and conducted collectively by a group, in this case, her local youth league. Activities include "criticism, self-criticism" sessions, political study sessions, and "struggle sessions" in which a target of the Revolution is put on display to face the verbal condemnation of the assembled people.

What contributions have I made toward the Party and the people? For shame! I feel so totally ashamed [*can kui*]! This is because during vacation, I have changed. And I have not changed for the better, but for the worse. I feel unworthy of our great leader Chairman Mao, and unworthy of the nurture bestowed on me by the Party and the people. My shame is hard to put into words. During vacation, I did not conduct political study sessions properly. When "lively thoughts" [*huo sixiang*] rose among my classmates, I did not help them. Most important of all, I have relaxed the vigilance on my thoughts. I have not studied the works of Chairman Mao, and have not written even one piece of "insights from study" [*xuexi xinde*]. I have become lax about my "thought reconstruction" [*sixiang gaizao*]. This is really dangerous! (Yang 1970: February 17)

"Lively thoughts" are bad or wrong thoughts that erupt suddenly in the brain and are not under control. It is the goal of thought reform and the duty of a friend to bring these negative thoughts under control through criticism, self-criticism, and persuasion.

In his examination of patients suffering from delusions of being watched, Freud discovered that a "critical agency" splits off from the rest of the subject, so that "one part of the ego sets itself over against the other, judges it critically, and, as it were, takes it as its object" (1973:247). Whereas the subject harbors sentiments of love and feelings of inferiority toward the "ego-ideal," this "superego" is an internalized object of dread and a source of guilt feelings for the subject. It is a power that works through "watching, discovering and criticizing" from within the subject (Freud 1951:118). Thus, in Mao worship, both the love/loyalty cluster of emotions and a fear of punishment born of the dividing of the subject into the harsh and watchful judge and the guilt-ridden defendant centered the subject to an ego-ideal. This is not to say that the partitioning process was initiated by Mao worship, but that this historical process exaggerated and appropriated a preexisting division within the subject.

When the subject is bombarded by criticism from within and without, while at the same time linked inextricably to the state center by a process of introjecting a key symbol of the state, then she has incorporated the will of the state in herself and is ready to give up herself to merge with the its subjectivity. In a passage that refers to Lei Feng, who had declared himself a common "screw" of the Revolution, Yang Weihong substantiates this thesis.

As a Youth League member, I should make myself into a common screw [*luosiding*] of the Revolution. Wherever I am placed, I should want to be there, assuming the function of a screw. When the Party assigns me to a work station, I will go there and exuberantly continue the Revolution. When the Party assigns me to a study station, in dealing with myself, I shall follow the dictum "study without becoming weary," and toward others, I shall follow the dictum "humiliate them without rest," in order to complete the task of study which the Party and the people have entrusted to me. From the day that I entered the Party, I delivered my whole body [yishen] to the disposal of the Party. If the Party wants me to be an "old yellow cow" of the Revolution, then I will exuberantly serve the people. To sum it up in one sentence, "the needs of the Party are also my own aspirations." (Yang 1970: April 10)

How does the willingness of Yang Weihong to serve wherever the state redistributive apparatus assigns her reconcile with the hatred of the bureaucracy, the sixth element of Mao worship? How is it that on the one hand, the incorporation of Mao absorbs the subject into the will of the state, yet on the other hand, Maoist subjects were also fired up to attack the very agents and institutions of the state with a vehemence seldom seen? These questions point to a major paradox of the Mao cult, the at once statist and anarchist character of the Cultural Revolution, and the complementary yet antagonistic relationship between state apparatus and Maoist subjectivities.

Molar Construction, Molecular Deconstructive Flows

In order to understand the mechanism of this paradox, I propose to treat these two divergent aspects of the Cultural Revolution as part of a larger, social-structural process. Here we need to think of two distinct levels of the construction of state subjects. The deeper level is the creation of libidinal and emotional Maoist subjects through such processes as identification, introjection, and incorporation, processes that affect the intrinsic substance of subjects from the inside. The second level is the formation of state subjects through the external attachment of labels, dossiers, classification categories, and bureaucratic controls on the life of each subject. These two levels usually complement each other, but during the Cultural Revolution, they came to be opposed.

In *Group Psychology and the Analysis of Ego*, Freud draws a parallel distinction between two types of group formation: the short-lived unorganized crowd and the more stable associations and social institutions held together by external organizational constraints such as, for example, the Catholic Church or an army (1951:25–31). Unorganized groups are characterized by excessive emotion, the absence of personal interest, inhibited intellectual and critical faculties, the lack of independence of its members, the strength of collective will, and the respect for heroes (1951:14–17, 33, 81–82, 91). It can be said that in China during the Cultural Revolution the orderly and stable institutions of the bureaucratic apparatus, which had been established in the 1950s collapsed into the unorganized masses of the cult of Mao. This new Maoist order of minimal social structure came to bind subjects in an intensely libidinized way to a central image of unity, Mao the supreme leader of the People. For the moment, the first level of subject-formation was enough to create loyal state subjects, and even enough to sustain their attacks against the state apparatus of the second level.

This distinction also fits well with the explanatory model developed by Deleuze and Guattari, in which social phenomena have both a "molecular" and a "molar" level of articulation, both of which give form and substance to one and the same object (1987:213). The molar level of integration refers to the structure of an organism, its segments and divisions. This level of structure is "distinguished from the properties or motions of its molecules or atoms" (Webster's 1973: 734), which compose the organism, but which interact with one another in a fluid and less structured way. Class segmentarity and bureaucratic divisions in a society are examples of more rigid molar and macro-structures, while molecular motion describes the more unpredictable movements of unorganized crowds and the modern phenomenon of "masses." "Classes are indeed fashioned from masses; they crystallize them. And masses are constantly flowing or leaking from classes" (Deleuze and Guattari 1987:213). Mass movements in modern history such as fascism can be represented as a molecularization process that shook the rigid molar state apparatus from within until it collapsed. "The segmentation and centralization of [Stalinist totalitarianism] was more classical and less fluid. What makes fascism dangerous is its molecular or micro-political power, for it is a mass movement: a cancerous body rather than a totalitarian organism" (Deleuze and Guattari 1987:215). What fascist leaders have at their disposal which is more powerful than (indeed, threatening to) state administration, is the micro-organization of the molecular flows of crowds, gangs, factions, and the huge masses.

In the Cultural Revolution, the emotions of anger and hatred were unleashed by the masses against the bureaucracy and the enemies of the people. Local gangs, Red Guard factions, mobs and crowds, families and neighborhoods were mobilized to tear asunder the authority and molar organization of the state. These molecular processes were of such a fluid character that state power itself lost its rigid Stalinist structure and, attaining an uncontrollable life of its own, easily penetrated to almost every social segment and molecular subject. In this way, the politicized and mobilized masses came to embody and express state power themselves, and no longer needed the external structure and directives of the molar state apparatus.

Countless examples of destruction in the Cultural Revolution show a state-society continuum bent on pushing itself to the very brink of existence. Red Guards and other factions fought each other from building to building and in the streets. Reminders of the backward past and "feudal" tradition were smashed and desecrated by zealous youth. The whole formal power structure erected after the Revolution was attacked as students stood up against teachers, workers against managers, office workers against superiors, and the common people against intellectuals and cadres. Nor were the common people themselves spared, as witch-hunts for enemies of the people were often indiscriminate in the search for targets. There was an urge to erase, to level, and to replace knowledge and thought with the monological common denominator of Mao Zedong Thought, as evidenced by the pressure to be "red versus expert," the sending down of students and intellectuals to the countryside, and the burning of nonrevolutionary books.

The repeated refrain of such verbs as "beat down" (dadao), "pulverize" (fensui), "exterminate" (xiaomie), "criticize," and "struggle" filling the air gave added impetus to the general demolition of the molar state structure, tradition, and culture itself and created what Deleuze and Guattari call a suicidal state. "In fascism, the State is far less totalitarian than it is *suicidal*. There is in fascism a realized nihilism . . . [it is] pure destruction and abolition" (1987:230).

Yet what stamps the Maoist molecular subjectivity with a distinct state character, no matter how destructive, oppositional, or anarchic, is the presence of the common anchoring point shared by all molecular segments or subjects: the body of Mao as the incarnation of a unified society-state. Mao was carried inside each subject as an ego-ideal and stood as the icon of every factional social segment. He served as the central pivot around which swirled the fluid molecular energy forces of the mobilized masses. Unlike other contemporary social movements, such as 1968 Paris, and the 1960s and 1970s in the

United States, the molecularized and energized flow of the Cultural Revolution was never able to extricate itself from the very fabric of the state. It was able to harness the tremendous social energies that wanted to tear down the molar apparatus and its officials, but its very means and ends were a strengthening of another mode of state subject formation, the Mao-centered subject.

The Death of Chairman Mao

Throughout the 1970s the Mao-centered subject was in decline, although subjects remained for the most part attached to what Mao symbolized. Gao Liqun, an artist, remembers that after Mao's death in 1976,[25] he was called to participate in building Mao's mausoleum and that he considered the assignment a great privilege. He remembers looking down while perched high up on a wall overlooking the central hall where the body would be laid out and thinking that every brick he laid in place was his contribution to a glorious project of honoring a great leader.

Yet he also remembers a strange and inexplicable incident that occurred at about the same time. He and a few friends in their dormitory one night got onto the subject of what Mao's daily routine was like. From there they realized that Mao must have had to go to the toilet. "Yes," said a friend, "Chairman Mao had to go to the toilet just like everyone else. He even has sexual organs just like we do." This statement stunned everyone for a second, and there was a hushed silence. Then for some reason, the realization that Mao had indeed had sexual organs started a round of nervous chuckles, which burst uncontrollably into raucous and stomach-pinching laughter, and everyone rolled around helplessly on their dorm beds. Gao had "never laughed so hard or so painfully" in his life.

Indeed, the death of the Great Helmsman spawned a good crop of Mao jokes. One joke I recorded in Beijing in the mid-1980s concerns a man from the provinces who had journeyed to Beijing to visit the Mao mausoleum. When he approached the guard and asked to see the Chairman, the guard replied, "Go away. Don't you know that Chairman Mao is dead? And besides, the mausoleum is not open to the public."

The man left, but on the next day, he returned to the mausoleum, and again he requested to see Chairman Mao. Again the guard re-

[25] See Wakeman 1988b for an interesting comparison between the funeral ceremony for Mao Zedong and that for Jiang Jieshi in Taiwan.

plied, "Go away. Don't you know that Chairman Mao is dead? And besides, the mausoleum is not open to the public."

The man left, but on the next day, he returned once more. This time the guard recognized him and demanded, "Why do you keep coming back? Why do I have to keep telling you that Chairman Mao is dead?"

"Because I like hearing you say it," the man replied.

In another joke, Zhou Enlai was walking outside Mao's bedroom one day when he saw one of Mao's bodyguards peering into the window eagerly. He asked the bodyguard what he was looking at, to which the startled guard nervously replied that he hadn't seen anything. Zhou also peered in, and of course Mao was inside romping with another one of his female nurses. Said Zhou to the guard, "Do not tell anyone what you saw. After all, Chairman Mao is human too" (*Mao zhuxi yeshi ren*).

As Freud pointed out, jokes, like dreams, reveal the hidden world of the unconscious (1960). These jokes provide a convenient medium for expressing the otherwise forbidden thought (or desire?) that Mao could die and his project could end. Each of these jokes drives home the fact that Mao is not a god, but a man, as mortal as anyone else, with human physiological functions and sexual appetites just like anyone else.[26] The psychology of laughter here depends on the juxtaposition of two images: the one, a great leader surrounded by a fear-inspiring aura of power, dignity, and sacred historical mission; the other, an ordinary man going to the toilet or having sex. The incongruity of these two images and the shock of seeing the potency of the first reduced to a ridiculous parody in the second are what triggers laughter. The second image is a transgression of the proper way to see Mao, and laughter is a cover for, and a willful release from, the fear and nervousness brought on by this transgression. Through laughter, the charisma and awesome state totemic force of Mao are stripped away so that he becomes an ordinary person with weaknesses of the body and a finite life.

If Mao is a mere mortal, then his death is real, and he can be properly mourned and laid to rest in a state funerary ritual. Then the culture would not have to go through a fantasy of incorporating him in order to deal with a profound sense of loss so long denied. His ghost, or the

[26] Ma Fengchun, a student studying in the United States, remembers that after Mao's death he happened to see a statue of Mao. He looked up at the massive form and thought, "Can he really die? If he can die, then the world is mortal, and it can change." He felt a great sense of relief.

ghost of the unmourned past, would then cease to haunt the present, and the secret crypt could finally be dismantled. However, the story of the Mao cult is not yet finished. Mao's body still lies unburied and on display in a glass coffin in his mausoleum in Tiananmen Square. In the early 1990s, Mao images reappeared, hanging from rearview mirrors of taxis in many Chinese cities. It would seem that the culture has yet to resolve the loss of a traditional order. The void inside still needs to be filled.

The Return of the Individual Subject

With the decline of Maoist subjects, what took place was a re-strengthening of the redistributive state apparatus,[27] even as economic reforms in the 1980s introduced new market forces, which began to curb some spheres of its operations. It is in this space of contestation between a state redistributive economy and a new commodity economy that two different subjectivities, oppositional to both Maoist and redistributive power, have reemerged in urban culture: the universal free and individual subject and the guanxixue subject.

After its last appearance in the May Fourth era of the 1920s and 1930s, the individualist subject returned to urban China in the 1980s. Its operational discourse is made up of two distinct yet often inter-linked themes, one of which can be called "individuality" (*ziwo zhuyi*) and the other "humanism" (*rendao zhuyi*). The most avid participants in and practitioners of this discourse are to be found among the urban youth and students of different classes and among the urban intellectuals and artists.

Although this individualist subjectivity can be traced directly to the May Fourth movement and to the importation of Western intellectual and cultural discourses, it would be a mistake to reduce it to the process of Westernization (Liu 1993a). Two other forces need to be considered. First, there is a long native tradition, both Confucian and non-Confucian, of the category of the self and the will to individuality, as reflected in the fourth-century B.C.E. poetry of Qu Yuan, the radical individualism of the philosopher Yang Zhu, the Confucian emphasis on moral autonomy, and the Neo-Confucian notion of the

---

[27] This, I believe, is the point made in Vivienne Shue's book *The Reach of the State* (1988), although she does not make the distinction between the two kinds of the state which I do here and thus runs the danger of seeming to promote nostalgia for the Maoist state.

mind as the seat of consciousness, knowledge, and moral judgment (Elvin 1985; Lin 1974–75; Tu 1968). Second, in the 1980s commercialization of culture, forms of economic and cultural individualism reemerged from China's traditional petty-commodity economy which are not reducible to European or American discourses of liberalism, laissez-faire, or rugged individualism.

At least four elements of the humanistic construction of the subject can be detected: individual autonomy and uniqueness; individual thought and expression; individual dignity and rights; and "human" (*ren*) as an abstract universal category of being. These elements are found singly or in interesting combinations. They are repeatedly condemned by official discourse as "bourgeois liberalism." When a young worker told me that the social system he lived in was good at "taking each person and grinding [him or her] down, grinding down all the sharp and irregular points . . . it's like making smooth round balls out of squares," he was expressing a yearning for individual uniqueness. The points or edges of the square signify the individuality of subjects, and these are ground down in a systematic way to transform subjects into uniform and indistinguishable balls so that the machinery of the state may operate smoothly.

The above sentiment has much in common with the assertion by the well-known young poet Gu Cheng that what makes the new poetry of China new is the emergence of the voice of the "self" (*ziwo*).

> Our past literature, art and poetry always advocated a kind of "I" [*wo*] that was self-negating. It was an "I" that wanted to abolish the self, to destroy the self. For example: it was an "I" that, in the face of this or that, was a speck of sand, a piece of stone used to pave a road, a gear wheel, a screw. In sum, it was not a person [*ren*], not a person who can reflect on things, who can have doubts, or who has feelings and desires. Put simply, it was a machine person, and a machine "I." . . . The new "self" is born right out of this rubble [of the destruction of the old "I"]. It smashes the molding shell that alienated it, and in the face of a wind devoid of the fragrance of flowers, it extends out its body. It believes in its own scars, believes in its own brain and sensory nerves, believes that it should be its own master as it walks back and forth. (Gu 1985:29)[28]

The critique of the Lei Feng type of state subjectivization, as indicated by the reference to the screw and the machine, is subtle yet unmistakable. Similar sentiments are expressed by Li Zehou, a highly regarded

---

[28] I thank Tu Guo-ch'ing for bringing Gu Cheng's work to my attention. In 1993, Gu Cheng shocked the international Chinese intellectual community by brutally killing his wife out of jealousy, and then taking his own life.

philosopher of Kant and classical Chinese thought: "Today, more than at any other time in modern history, it is all the more imperative to emphasize the rights and desires of the individual entity [*geti*], to emphasize the freedom, independence, and equality of individual personalities, to enhance the self-initiative and creativity of the individual, so that it will no longer be a kind of obedient instrument or passive screw, and the mighty force of tradition may be dissolved" (Li 1987:289). In these statements, tradition is opposed to the new liberating force of individuality, reflecting a prevalent theme and structure of this humanistic discourse.

When I asked how people are showing their individuality and expressing themselves, two answers were invariably given. First, clothing and hair styles are becoming more differentiated and individuated. Emerging from the uniformity of the Maoist masses of blue and olive-green unisex clothing and hair, could be seen a growing concern to express difference, individual, gender, age, and regional differences, through clothing and hair.[29] Second, young people are increasingly pursuing "free love" (*ziyou lianai*); they want to meet their prospective mates on their own, instead of having everything arranged by their elders. There is also a general perception that sexual relations have increased dramatically, especially pre- and extramarital ones. Indeed, the "sexual liberation" (*xing jiefang*) of the reform period deserves a whole discussion by itself.

A 1989 newspaper story featured a combination of elements different from the above examples, one that included the principle of individual dignity and value. That year, some college students in Beijing took to climbing onto rooftops, baring themselves to the waist (I take it these were men), and crying out defiantly into the wind, "I am me! I am me!" ("wo jiu shi wo!") (*SJRB* 20 September 1989:3). Asked for his interpretation of this practice, a student whom I knew in Beijing and who now studies in the United States answered that before he left China in 1987, he also had an intense desire to do something like this. "It's a way of saying, 'I'm not your servant, I'm not your slave, I'm not a screw in some revolutionary machine!'" he declared with emotion. "I'm a human being, and like every other human being, I have rights [*quanli*], and a basic individual value [*geren jiazhi*]. China has always cast people as sons or subjects or fathers, but never as individuals."

The intellectual feminist discourse of the reform period also par-

---

[29] The issue of whether curling one's hair should be allowed was publicly debated (*ZGQNB* 28 November 1979).

takes of this humanistic discourse of individual liberation. It self-consciously opposes both the imperial Confucian construction of women as subjects defined only by their relations with men (mother, sister, wife), as well as the Communist statist discourse of *funu* (woman), which cast women as a state-defined category of masculinized women "liberated" by the state (Barlow 1994).[30] In a discussion of the high suicide rate among young peasant women, Zhang Yini attributes the cause to the conflict in their lives between traditional patriarchal practices and the fact that "their self-valuation [*ziwo jiazhi*] was changing, and their self-consciousness was awakening [*ziwo yishi zai juexing*]" (Zhang 1989). The issue of divorce is often addressed in feminist terms of women developing a new "female consciousness," which enables them to initiate or go through with a divorce from an unhappy or abusive marriage, instead of being dependent on their husbands and defining themselves by their ability to maintain a hollow marriage (Ning 1988, 1989). In an interview, film director Zhang Yimou described his film *The Story of Qiu Ju* as being "about a woman who comes to recognize her own self-worth [*ziwo jiazhi*], a woman who realizes that she herself controls her own fate" (Yang 1993).

An intriguing discussion of women and sexuality was couched in terms of the evolution of "women's right to control her own sexual activity" (*nuxing xing quanli*) (Pan 1987). Women in agrarian societies are said to have lost their sexual rights when men controlled material production and came to buy women's bodies for their exclusive use and control. What modern society must do is recapture the "full female human dignity" [*nuxing wanzhen de renge*] that women once had in primitive society.

Yet another combination of elements in individual humanist discourse is found in a conversational exchange that took place when I was studying a factory in Beijing. A young male worker said to an older male worker, "I don't want to risk my life working so hard for the Motherland [*wei zuguo war ming de gan*], that is slave mentality [*nuli yishi*]." The older worker chastised him, "This type of thinking is wrong. You must love the Motherland because you are a Chinese person [*ni shi zhongguoren*]." The younger worker replied without any trace of shame or guilt, "But I am also a human being [*ren*] first of all. As a human being, I would like to visit and even live in other countries too. Why should I be bound here just because I happened to

[30] See also Barlow 1989 and 1991.

be born here?" In this exchange, the notions of individual dignity and value, individual autonomy, and human being as a category transcending nationality, ethnicity, and class are combined into a political statement, made political because it is diametrically opposed to the constructions of official discourse.

In intellectual discourse, this last element of universal humanism takes on a familiar, but also very different and problematical cast. Chinese intellectual discourse, especially the Marxist humanist variety, systematizes and rationalizes these elements and translates what was always a situational opposition (as in the last example) into a coherent theory characterized by universalism and a heroic optimism concerning human progress. The protagonist in the novel *Humanity, Oh Humanity* writes a book called *Marxism and Humanism*, in which he fervently declares:

> We must respect human beings, respect individual human personality, nourish and strengthen human dignity. I believe that in our society today, human self-respect is not too strong, but actually too weak. Several thousand years of the feudal system have gradually trained us to become a certain kind of person: unused to thinking about the worth of a human being, unable to form independent opinions about life, uninclined toward developing independent personal character. It would almost seem that the value of a person's existence does not reside in the degree to which [that person] can introduce into society a unique [self],[31] but rather in the degree to which that person can meld or subordinate [that self] to something else, that is to dissolve individual character in the general character of the group. *How monotonous life would be, however, if human beings had no individual character! And how slow-paced would be the progress of society! Fortunately there are always a few people in history . . . who are the first . . . to lead forth a vast army, and to push history forward.* (Dai 1985:277–78; Duke 1985:171–72)

The problem, as I see it, with this kind of humanist discourse is that it shares with the very statist revolutionary discourse it seeks to oppose, the metanarrative of progressive liberational history that elevates humanity, individual hero/martyrs, in order to submerge them in the end into the great project of History with a capital H.

In Wang Ruoshui's formulations of a philosophy of Marxist humanism (1983, 1984, 1988), he upholds the rights of individuals, of women, and of workers and other oppressed groups in the face of

---

[31] Here I depart from Duke's translation of this passage in order to bring out the sense that what a person should bring to society is his/her uniqueness (*dute de*). I also correct for Duke's masculinist translation.

property owners or the oppressive state bureaucracy. Yet he does so by positing a transcendental category of "human essence" (*ren de benzhi*) that is prior to and independent of social relations. Indeed, for Wang, social relations, whether Confucian or socialist, distort essence by constraining its development. This original human essence is self-conscious action and freedom. Human nature is no mere passive element shaped by history and social relations, but an active agent striving to move history toward the realization of human essence. Wang then employs this ahistorical and universal essence as a fixed objective standard for being human and pits it against concrete and historical existence, with a view to measuring existing social systems according to how they fulfill and give full play to human essence. Those social systems like his own which suppress human essence produce persons alienated from their original essence. The task then, is to awaken self-consciousness of essence and push history forward.

One can sympathize with this positing of a pristine subject in order to judge the social relations that constrain it, but this theoretical framework also produces some troubling features. To declare the transcendence and universalism of human essence is to deny that each definition of human nature is historically and socially constituted and to close oneself off from the constant reinterpretation of ongoing history. Positing a universal human essence always means that it must be defined, which means that the way is opened up for a new and more authoritative normalization of subjects. At the same time, the universal human subject posed by humanism is a rational, naturally moral, unified, and internally coherent subject. There is no sense of conflict, division, or amalgamation between the more socialized and individualized coexisting segments, between tradition and modernity, between desire and the death instinct, or between good and evil. Finally, to define human essence as individual freedom and to pit it against social relations is to adopt a position that is exactly opposed to that of the state, and thus to remain caught up in a rigid and polarized state discourse of total freedom versus total subjugation. To adopt a position that is the exact opposite of the state's is to fulfill its need for a nemesis against which and through which it can expand its power, instead of sliding past statist discourse and subverting the state's project.

Guanxi Subjectivity of Addition and Subtraction

An alternative opposition to the two state subject-formations can be found in the art of guanxi. As mentioned earlier in the book, guanxi practices and their discourse, building on a cultural tradition of the ethics of obligation and reciprocity in human relations, surfaced around the middle of the Cultural Revolution, a few years before the reemergence of the discourse of individuality and humanism in the 1980s. These two different forms of subject-formation, then, have been in operation in urban centers more or less contemporaneously, coinciding with the gradual decline of the Mao-centered subject and the reascendancy of the state-apparatus subject. Yet compared to the pervasiveness of guanxi practices and discourse, the construction of the free and individual subject seems still relatively weak and limited.

There are at least three ways in which guanxi subject-formation differs from the other three types.

Metonymic rather than Metaphoric

In guanxixue, the gift, the object given and received, does not exhaust in its representation, either the person of the donor, of which it is a part, nor the recipient, of which it becomes a part. The art of guanxi constructs relational subjects by detaching a part of the donor's personal substance in the form of the gift and attaching it to the recipient. What is added to the person of the recipient is only a part of the donor's substance, and what is lost by the recipient in the act of accepting a gift is only a part of his or her "face," which is added to the face of the donor as a gain of symbolic capital. Since gifts are only parts of subjects to be added or subtracted from other subjects, guanxi transactions construct relatively autonomous subjects. Although guanxi subjects are constrained by obligation and indebtedness to others, their intrinsic identities are not exhausted or exchanged with the other, unlike the introjection or incorporation of Mao into his subjects. That is to say, guanxi subjects are formed by a process of addition and subtraction, gain and loss, which augments or reduces their "face," but does not fundamentally transform the intrinsic identity and internal makeup of the subjects involved.

Thus, guanxi subjectivity undercuts Mao-centered subjectivity by producing subject/object relations based on *metonymic* addition rather than *metaphoric* identification or substitution. In semiotic theory, a metonymic relationship is one characterized by contiguity, difference, and disproportion in which an object is only an attribute, an adjunct, or a part of the subject it represents or interacts with. A metaphor on the other hand, sets up a relationship of similarity, identification, and substitution between subject and object (Jakobson 1956:76–82; Silverman 1983:109–21; Strathern 1983, 1987).[32] Metaphoric subjectivity is one of libidinal identification in which the subject must totally reconstitute its internal makeup around the introjected object such as the person of Mao.[33]

Guanxi's metonymic subject-formation also differs from the metaphoric linkages made by the redistributive state apparatus between state subjects and their roles and identities as formulated and classified by the state. These elementary components of the state (individual dossiers, class and family statuses, written confessions, ration booklets, work-unit positions, bureaucratic ranks, and household registrations) stand in a metaphoric relationship to subjects. That is, they are not constructed as extrinsic aspects of a subject, but as representations of the total instrinsic natures of subjects in the sense that a subject's dossier *is* that subject's personal history and moral-political character.

Fluidity and Instability

A second way that the art of guanxi constructs an alternative subjectivity is found in its constant creation of fluid and unstable subjects. There is a permanent instability built into the guanxi construction of subjects. Gift and debt relations continuously deconstruct and reconstruct the subject through the circulation of symbolic and material capital. For example, between two guanxi partners, reciprocity ensures that what is taken away will be given back, so that the temporary loss experienced by a person will be compensated for in a return gesture that, for a moment, will restore wholeness. Furthermore, with each new guanxi transaction, parts of different persons are added to the recipient, and parts of the donor find their way to link up with new recipients, creating ever-expandable and contractable subjects, made up of the parts of several persons in a guanxi network. This versatility is in contrast to the two state subjectivities, which are of a

[32] Marilyn Strathern employed these two tropes to look at different constructions of gendered persons in New Guinea. She found a difference, first, in how the identities of men and women in Hagen society were attached to clans and, second, in how Hagen as opposed to Wiru women were attached to natal and affinal clans. She used the terms "metaphoric" and "metonymic" in her original draft (1983), but switched to "literal" and "figurative" later (1987).

[33] Of course, Mao is also a metonymn of the country, the Party, and the State. The point made here, however, is that the relationship individual subjects have with the Mao metonym is a metaphorical one.

fixed and abiding nature, one metaphorically fixated on the person of the leader, the other on the self constructed by the state organization.

The guanxi subject does not incorporate a single object such as the person of Mao, but many gifts (many parts) from different sources or donors. At the same time, no single gift object is given to or incorporated in every single subject in the population. Furthermore, there is no prolonged libidinal identification with any particular guanxi donor because built into the structure of guanxi exchange is the right and the obligation to repay. Repayment means that the temporary addition of the other in oneself has ended, and that the balance of prestige has been adjusted and symbolic status ranking has been overturned, so that now the other is augmented by oneself. What is low can become high and vice versa. This contrasts with both the Maoist and the redistributive constructions in which the subject is forever caught in a relationship of unpayable debt to Mao and dependence on the state apparatus and its officials. The fluidity and unstable character of guanxi subjects also stands in contrast to the free and independent subject created by the discourse of individuality and humanism. The individual autonomous subject emphasizes complete differentiation from others, but its very discreteness and its efforts to close up the boundaries of the self to the penetration of outside objects means that it will remain fixed to an image of itself, with transformation coming only from within itself.

The Circulation and Interconnectedness of Subjects

Third, by effecting a series of metonymic linkages between persons through the medium of the gift and the debt, guanxi constructs subjects that are mutually dependent and constituted by more than one person, so to speak. The circulation of personal substance means that particular linkages are constantly shifting as new favors are performed for different persons and new debts incurred from others. The result of the gift economy practiced on a massive scale in society is the forging of an interlinking of subjects into a series of open-ended networks that cut across state divisions of class, rank, region, and so forth. Such a construction of horizontal, intersubjective linkages can only serve to diminish the isolating and individualizing tendencies of the state-apparatus subjectivity found in such institutional practices as mutual surveillance and criticism. It also counters the spread of Mao-centered practices, which dissolve all subjects into the unified body of the supreme subject.

Although the guanxi construction of subjects depends on establishing metonymic relationships of difference and disproportion between subject and object, how it organizes power and produces power effects has something in common with processes of Maoist subjectivization. Both these techniques produce a molecular micro-organization of power, as opposed to a rigid molar arrangement of social segmentation and classification. Maoist subjectivization can mobilize sweeping waves of destructive social and molecular forces that endanger the neat order laid out by molar state organization, but the gift economy's construction of interlinked subjects also subverts molar organization in a piecemeal but cumulative fashion. By forging links of indebtedness and mutual dependence among subjects carved out by bureaucratically defined segments and categories, guanxixue introduces stresses and strains into the foundation of molar organization. Should these stresses build up, they may also begin another kind of molecular dismantling process.

The increasing pervasiveness of guanxi practices throughout the 1980s can be seen as a mounting pressure toward a social molecularization that would reduce or dissolve the carefully constructed state edifices of segmentation, individualization, classification, and rigid organization and return to a more basic level, to the very fabric of society, the warp and woof of interpersonal relations. The art of guanxi represents a movement away from vertically integrated individuals, classes, and box-like work-units, whose organizational principles all resonate and are concentric with one another around a pivotal state center. To this guanxixue substitutes a fluid social assemblage of open-ended and shifting chains and networks of relationships. By creating the interwovenness of subjects, guanxi exchange begins to weave the basic fabric of an incipient new order that is not suffused with the state, even while it must operate within its structure.

Guanxixue introduces heterogeneous organizational principles into state molar organization. These personalistic relationships and networks are "system-foreign" elements that have emerged out of the state redistributive apparatus. It is possible to think of them as the beginnings of a Chinese "second society" (Hankiss 1988), an interconnected and relatively autonomous social domain operating both within and without the state.

In positing a "second society" that does not operate according to state principles, we must also consider the role that the free and individual subject might have in its formation. Although they both stand in opposition to the two state subjectivities (individuality explicitly so and the art of guanxi implicitly so), their relationship is nevertheless an uneasy one. The discourse of individuality and humanism does not distinguish between the relational subject of guanxi and the subjugated and libidinal subject of the state. It finds both subject-formations oppressive to the individual and condemns them both as stubborn holdovers of a stifling feudal tradition. On the one hand, the free and independent subject perceives relational ties of obligation and reciprocity to be just as constraining as the state on the full realization of individual will and expression.[34] On the other hand, guanxi discourse finds the subject who wishes to be liberated from ties of obligation and reciprocity ethically dubious. What we have here are two different approaches to the forging of a second society. The individual subject and the guanxi subject are competing, as well as, complementary constructions of this emerging second society.

For the time being, at least, it would seem that guanxi subjectivity will predominate in the construction of a second society for the following reasons. Individuality is constructed so that the terms freedom [ziyou] and discipline [jilü], individual [geren] and collective (jiti) or state or nation [guojia], are understood as polar opposites. Ironically, this opposition is contained in *both* statist and individualistic constructions. The will to individuality risks falling into the social atomism created by state individualization techniques such as mutual surveillance and dossier-keeping. At the same time, the still incompletely formed individual subject must confront the megalithic state head-on as a visible threat to a force that overpowers it. Guanxi subjectivity, however, does not oppose the state directly, but forges a multiplicity of links through and across state segments. Where the state creates atomized individuals through mutual surveillance, guanxi joins these individuals together in relationships of exchange. Where the state binds persons together into collective state segments, guanxi subjects form networks that cut across such divisions. Thus guanxixue poses a more effective challenge to state power than a collection of individuals, for guanxixue subverts state power but individualism must confront it.

[34] Liu Zaifu, personal communication, Chicago, 1990.

CHAPTER EIGHT

Rhizomatic Networks and the
Fabric of an Emerging Minjian in China

We're tired of trees. We should stop believing in trees, roots, and
radicles. They've made us suffer too much.
                              —Deleuze and Guattari 1987:15

In contrast to centered (even poly-centered) systems with hierarchical
modes of communication and preestablished paths, the rhizome is an
acentered, nonhierarchical, nonsignifying system without a [com-
manding] General and without an organizing memory or central au-
tomaton, defined solely by a circulation of [flows].
                              —Deleuze and Guattari 1987:21

In the modern history of the West, the discursive and social formations of what was called "civil society" have emerged twice: first in
Western Europe in the eighteenth century, and more recently in Eastern Europe and the former Soviet Union beginning in the 1970s. Both
formations of civil society are defined in terms of a social realm
breaking free from the despotic state, whether the monarchical absolutism of the eighteenth century or the totalizing bureaucratic apparatus of state socialism in the late twentieth century (Taylor 1990).
Both movements wished to recover a society's original self-governing
forces before they were politicized by the state. They were conceived
as the resuscitation of a society's own non-state structure of integration. This process is necessary for the development of an independent
society in which the state does not control all social activities.

Taking this modern Western social dynamic of state and society
and applying it to an understanding of China is fraught with the dangers of imposing one interpretive framework on a different social and
historical context (Wakeman 1993). That is why I adopt the native
category of *minjian* which has emerged in 1980s language usage in

China.[1] The sphere of minjian refers to a realm of people-to-people relationships which is non-governmental or separate from formal bureaucratic channels. However, I still assert that discussions of civil society and the state are relevant to what is happening in China today, even though the Chinese minjian may have very different contours than its equivalent in the West. As I pointed out in the introduction, part of the global experience of modernity is the unleashing of the secular political domain and its displacement of the religious domain (Benjamin 1969b). In global modernity, the rise of the nation-state has been one of the most impressive and awesome developments. The experience of twentieth-century China has more than conformed to this rule. Therefore, the search for an autonomous realm of social activity that can counterbalance state power is also extremely important in a Chinese modern context which has seen the introduction of nationalism, fascism, Marxist-Leninism, and so on.

To claim that the discussion of civil society and the state is relevant to China and to theorize the conditions and forms of the emergence of the minjian are not just academic exercises in description and comparison (in this case, of China with Eastern and Western Europe and North America). Nor is it an evaluation of whether or not a Western-style civil society has appeared in late imperial or modern China. This is not just a descriptive empirical task but a performative act in which to search for its traces is at the same time to invoke the non-state sphere and make it a conscious project in a society still very coextensive with state. At present the legal system is not enforced to protect society; there are virtually no legal, public, or institutionalized structures or associations that are not part of or subordinated to the state bureaucracy; public assembly and discussion, even in small groups, is difficult unless it is condoned by the state; and between social groups, there are very few public or formal horizontal linkage across geographic and institutional boundaries independent of the state.

Elemer Hankiss, analyzing Hungary in the 1970s and 1980s, identified a "second society" (1988) which operates "in-itself" according to non-state principles, but whose discourse and practices do not consciously form a separate and independent civil society "for-itself." Whereas the "first" or official society exhibits (1) vertical organization, (2) downward flow of power, (3) state ownership, (4) centralization, (5) politicization of culture, (6) official ideology, (7) visibility, and (8) official legitimacy, the "second society" is characterized by their absence, and even some opposition to them (1988:36). These

---

[1] I thank Lydia Liu for discussing this notion of minjian with me.

parallel societies do not represent two groups of people, but "two dimensions of social existence" that people skillfully negotiate, switching as necessary from one to the other.

The art of guanxi can be seen as a dominant theme of the Chinese minjian. Like the Hungarian second society, the Chinese minjian operates in a transitional space between the state and a fully developed self-organizing social formation. By closely examining guanxixue, one can detect "some incipient forms" or contours of a new minjian order that will become strong enough to deter the state.

Many civil-society discussions deal with the formal and legal institutions of democracy (such as, voting, constitutional law, and multiple political parties) (Wang 1991). This discussion will deal with the minjian at the level of the basic social fabric from which social organizations are created. The term "social fabric" refers to the warp and the woof of social relationships which intertwine and weave out the very substance of a given social order. Since the present inquiry into the fabric of Chinese society is situated in an ongoing and unpredictable history, there are great risks in making any pronouncement about the future of this unfolding; however, these risks must be taken if one is to speculate at all about China's changing social order.

Just as Hankiss delineated some conflicting "organizational principles" at work in the Hungarian state-socialist system and identified "a process of emerging and self-asserting 'system-foreign elements,' of 'alien bodies,' of 'seeds of [a] non-state-socialist steering mechanism'" (1988:15), in this book I have also set about exploring guanxixue as a "system-foreign element" in the state power of China. The question now before us is, What is the relationship of guanxixue to an as-yet-to-emerge Chinese social body whose formation does not depend on or replicate the state?

A case could be made that since many guanxi tactics are employed by corrupt officialdom to advance their private family and class interests through nepotism and oligarchic networks, guanxi does not belong to the second society but actually works to strenthen the first society. Nevertheless, these official practices can be shown to have four of the eight features of the first society listed earlier: vertical organization, downward flow of power, state ownership, and centralization. Therefore, guanxi relations among officials are best understood as a subset of the first society, forming an area that "borders on, and is partly intertwined with, the second society" (Hankiss 1988:36).

In the history of the West, civil society as the social realm autonomous from the state has been conceptualized in two distinct ways: in terms of individual rights, citizenship, and civil liberties on the one hand, and in terms of intermediate associations and groups on the other. Given these two elements of civil society in the European experience, can the Chinese art of guanxi, which privileges neither the individual nor the group or association, play a role in the emergence of an independent minjian in China? And will the art of guanxi contribute to shaping a Chinese minjian along Chinese, not Western, lines?

The Enlightenment notions of individual rights and citizenship are an important component of Western European civil-society discourse. For thinkers such as Thomas Paine in the late eighteenth century, despotic states violated the "natural rights" of originally "free" individuals. His solution was a juridical one: unlawful governments must be made to give way to a system of popular sovereignty and government by law (Keane 1988b:44–48). The various contract theories popular at the time all supposed that in the state of nature, before the founding of society, there were already fully formed individuals with their rights, freedom, and equality intact. It was thought that for self-preservation these individuals entered into a social contract that formed the basis for civil society. Even for someone like Rousseau, who elaborated on the theory of the general will, the task was "to find a form of association which may defend and protect . . . the person and property of every associate, and by means of which each, coalescing with all, may nevertheless obey only himself, and remain as free as before" (1967:17–18). Thus civil society at this time was for the protection of its members who were conceived of as male, propertied, and, above all, autonomous individuals engaging in exchanges of mutual interest in the market and associating to fend off the depredations of the state.

Corresponding to the emergence of the private realms of market exchange and the conjugal family, there was at this time in Europe an increasing consciousness of individual rights and an expansion of the realm of individual subjectivity. According to Jürgen Habermas, the historical birth of the bourgeois public sphere of debate on public issues in eighteenth-century Europe was preceded by a literary "public sphere in apolitical form," which provided the "training ground for critical public reflection" (1989:29). Through personal letters, diaries, and epistolary novels, there was performed "a process of self-clarification of private people focusing on the genuine experiences of their novel privateness" (ibid.). The kind of individual self- and social reflection engendered through these reading and writing practices served as a basis for critical debate and participation in the public sphere and for the construction of a more or less self-regulating civil society (49). Thus an emerging European civil society independent of the state was made possible by the formation of a critical public sphere of debate and discussion of public issues, which in turn was derived from the evolution of autonomous individual subjectivity.

The other focus of civil-society discourse in Western Europe in this period was the role of intermediate or "civil" associations in engineering a self-governing civil society independent of state administration. De Tocqueville was especially attentive to these "societies" within a civil society as a way to counterbalance the increasing government administration of the minutest details of social life (Keane 1988b:55–62). Such forms of civil association as "scientific and literary circles, schools, publishers, inns, manufacturing enterprises, religious organizations, municipal associations and independent households" were seen by de Tocqueville as examples of participatory democracy and self-government which resisted state despotism (Keane 1988b:61). In the United States and Western Europe today, despite increasing encroachments by market forces on the one side, and the welfare and military state on the other, nonprofit voluntary organizations continue to serve as a viable base for democratic forces in the society (Wuthnow 1991).

From the late 1970s to the present, the discourse of civil society has experienced a revival in a new historical and political context. The social movements against socialist state despotism in Eastern Europe and the former Soviet Union are understood by many of the participants as a resuscitation of civil society (Kligman 1990; Hankiss 1988). These movements seem to focus more on independent associations and institutions and less on individual rights and subjectivity. In Poland the Catholic Church and Solidarity trade union were two such organizations challenging the state from the outside and promising a "new self-managing society." Solidarity was not a mere labor union, for under its umbrella arose a "plurality of interests" and independent associations (Arato 1981; Wojcicki 1981). Civil society in Poland is seen as a coalition of the interests and organizations of industrial workers, private farmers, humanistic intellectuals, and students (Pelczynski 1988:370). When rights are discussed, the emphasis is placed on values of abstract universalism, so that basic human rights rather than individual rights are stressed in Eastern Europe.

If we turn to contemporary China, we see that the question is whether the European notion of civil society can be applied to a context where historically, unlike Europe, there have been no religious institutions (like the Church) or political institutions (like city-states) independent of centralized state control. Towns and cities in imperial China were presided over by officials sent from the capital to govern the local population according to imperial directives. The imperial state also sought to monitor and restrict religious institutions and activities throughout the empire by requiring that new temples and monasteries (Buddhist, Daoist, deity cults), as well as the ordination of priests, be registered and approved by the state.[2] Indeed, even the supernatural bureaucracy of gods and deities did not transcend the temporal human bureaucracy, but was often subjected to its system of rewards and punishment. Human officials and the emperor could grant honorific titles to gods who were at subordinate levels to them. They could also order the thrashing of gods who had failed to protect the people from a natural disaster (Yang 1961:182).

Nor can we find a strong tradition of the articulation of individual rights in China. To be sure, as Chapter 7 indicates, especially in urban areas today, there is a growing sensibility of individuality and the independent self, often intertwined with a discourse of universalistic humanism. In many ways, this represents a revival and further elaboration on an interrupted May Fourth urban discourse of modernism earlier this century; however, the general situation described by Liang Shuming in the 1940s, when an overwhelming "99 percent" of the Chinese people would treat the notion of "individualism" (*geren zhuyi*) as a term for selfishness and self-gain (1949:50), still leaves a deep imprint on popular habits and attitudes today.

The other element of civil society which has played an important role in both Western and Eastern European contexts, intermediate and voluntary associations, self-governing groups, and sites for public discussion, has more counterparts in late imperial Chinese social institutions. These include gentry management and local self-government (Rankin 1986); guilds (Burgess 1928; Strand 1989; Rowe 1984, 1990); neighborhood and religious organizations (Skinner 1977b;[3] Crissman 1967); clans and lineages (Watson 1982); and teahouses and native-place associations (Skinner 1977a; Rowe 1990; Goodman 1990). There is, however, much historical evidence to suggest that in late imperial and republican China, there was a great deal more state monitoring, restricting, and coopting of these organizations than in early modern Europe (Wakeman 1993; Hsiao 1967; Yang 1961).

The Communist Revolution swept away all of these traditional

---

[2] Yet, as C. K. Yang points out, in the early Qing dynasty, imperial records show that 84 percent of all listed temples and convents were built without government permission (1961:188). Just as today, the will of the state for total control is sometimes stronger than its ability to carry it out.

[3] See in the Skinner 1977b the articles by Donald DeGlopper, G. W. Skinner, Kristofer Schipper, Hugh Baker, and Perter Golas.

semiautonomous associations and put in place a Stalinist "mono-organizational" society in which all social organizations were linked to an arm of the state bureaucracy and had to be subordinated to a higher administrative level or "leader" (Rigby 1977; Yang 1989b). There occurred a sharp historical rupture when this native tradition of forming corporate groups according to a diverse array of organizational principles (kinship, native-place, occupation, neighborhood, religion, and so on) was radically excised from the social body. In urban China it seems questionable whether the revival or reinvention of lineages, temples, and monasteries today will have a large role to play in the development of a postsocialist independent social realm. They may very well play a role in rural areas, along with Christian churches.

In 1990 and 1991 I made two short excursions to China, visiting places in Shandong, Hubei, Zhejiang, and Shaanxi Provinces, as well as Beijing, in search of local voluntary associations, or signs of a self-organizing realm outside the state. Those people to whom I explained the theoretical framework of my social investigation, generally shook their heads and told me that the Party would never allow truly independent organizations, no matter how nonpolitical these were. The Communist Party rose to power, they said, through its organizational skills, so it is especially attentive to and easily threatened by new organizations.

Although the Chinese constitution guarantees citizens "the right to form associations" (*jie she quan*), the actual situation is much more complicated. In order not to be branded an "illegal clique" (*feifa jituan*), an organization must be properly registered with the authorities. This is a very difficult process, which involves a great deal of red tape and a lengthy processing period. Most people I spoke with did not know which office to go to for registration, nor what the exact procedures entailed. Even if an organization is legally established, people assured me, the state will still try to integrate it into an existing arm of its bureaucracy.

In a town in Zhejiang Province, a woman told me of how she and other amateur folklorists had founded a local folklore studies society in 1989, which was spontaneously initiated (*zifa*) and totally self-funded. Nevertheless, they had to agree to be under the jurisdiction of two wings of the state bureaucracy overseeing cultural affairs and activities: the local social science federation, composed of scholars, and the local cultural federation (*wenlian*), which has branches organizing the writers, artists, musicians, photographers, and calligraphers in the town. This is called "dual leadership" (*shuangchong lingdao*).

Both of these superior levels of administration are in turn under the authority of the propaganda department of the town's Party committee. Indeed at the central level in Beijing, the Party even has a Masses Affairs Department (*qunzhong gongzuobu*) devoted to coordinating just such "organizations of the masses." The experience of this folklore society is typical because it is the Party's policy not to allow any social group formation to go unsupervised by a responsible branch of the state organization. In this way, voluntary associations formed by the people themselves generally end up as new extensions of the mono-organizational apparatus.

Given the difficulties of independent group formation in the present Chinese political context, the inability of the legal system to protect individuals and associations and the relative weakness of a discourse of "rights" and of "individualism" in the culture, the prognosis of civil society according to the European model does not look good in China. Perhaps we must focus on informal group and individual units for the seeds of an autonomous social realm in China.

Despite the overwhelming importance assigned to independent associations in the formation of civil society in Eastern Europe, other aspects of their recent experience can provide us with a clue to the shape that civil society may assume in China. Hankiss describes the Communist takeover of Hungary in 1948 as a process whereby "Hungarian society was systematically disintegrated and atomized. . . . [However], fragments of some of the [traditional] networks survived in a state of semilatency and semilegitimacy and, in the mid-1960's, the slow regeneration of the 'life world' of social networks began" (1988:28). A similar account of Poland in the late 1970s may also be relevant to our thinking about minjian in China:

> Informal, familial, and small-scale *private networks of social relations* . . . can provide self-defense even in the absence of formal movements. This largely spontaneous, defensive response makes possible a higher, more organized level of social plurality. Circles of family and friends protect the private sphere from an administered public one. They permit the defense of a given society, its customs, mentalities, its national and local identities. The reconstruction of society is possible because *the foundations are there.* (Arato 1981:29; my emphasis)

According to Kazimierz Wojcicki, the independent unions and every other form of autonomous organization represent "the re-establishment of more complex structures where there had been elementary forms" (1981:103). If "private networks of social relations" are the "elementary forms" laying down a "foundation" for civil society in Poland and Hungary, how much more of a role would guanxi and renqing networks play in the emergence of a Chinese minjian, where the ethics of kinship, friendship, and reciprocity have, since ancient times, enjoyed a canonical status in both Confucian and peasant traditions?

I propose that in China, an area to watch for in the development of the minjian, is the art of guanxi, a dynamic element of the second society. It assumes a network form similar to those "elementary forms" described in Poland and Hungary; however, the Chinese guanxi network version will be so much more culturally elaborated that it will overshadow what in the history of Europe have been the two forms of a full-fledged civil society: the individual and the association or group. Projecting from guanxixue, the faint features of a Chinese minjian order can be described in terms of two "in-between" statuses: between the individual and society, and between the individual and the formal group or association.

In-between the Individual and Society

In his book *The Essential Meanings of Chinese Culture*, published in 1949, the Confucian philosopher Liang Shuming argued that from the Middle Ages to modern times, the West has been swinging back and forth between two extremes: the collective group and the individual (1949:49). This dynamic can be found in such struggles as those of "liberalism" and "individualism" against "collectivism," "socialism," and "totalitarianism." In the West the individual and the society are invariably set up in opposition to each other. Liang thought of British and American societies as "individual-based" (*geren benwei*) societies, and the Soviet Union as an example of "society-based" (*shehui benwei*) society (1949:86). China, he wrote, is neither of these, but a "relationship-based" (*guanxi benwei*) social order.

Although we may not wish to subscribe to such essentialist characterizations, it is significant that in the midst of warfare, geographical and social dislocation, and the twentieth-century breakdown of the traditional Chinese social order, Liang should see "relationships" as the feature most characteristic of Chinese culture. Liang writes:

> Our closest and dearest feelings go toward those who are naturally related to us through bone and flesh, and then extends out to all those we associate with. Depending on the relative depth and length of the association, there develops a corresponding amount of affect [*qingfen*].

From affect arises right conduct or obligation [*yi*]. . . . Relationships of ethics [*lunli guanxi*] are also relationships of mutual favors, that is to say, there is a relationship of mutual obligation. The logic of ethical-relational principles [*lunli*] is found in the components of feeling and obligation. (Liang 1949:86)

A "relationship-based" social formation, then, is constituted by relational ethics, which start with particular and concrete dyadic relations of family and kin and radiate outward to all types of interpersonal relationships. In this quotation, the art of guanxi in urban China today can be seen as a further extension of kinship ethics, as well as a derivative product of Confucian relational ethics.[4]

It is appropriate that the character for *ren* 仁 , the Confucian virtue of "humanity" or "humaneness" is written with a "human" radical and the sign for "two," "designating the primordial form of human-relatedness" (Tu 1972:188). In such a system, what is considered human or humane is never thought of in the singular, with qualities issuing from within itself, but is understood as the outcome of a process involving at least two persons in a relationship. Thus the focus in the ethics of a "relationship-based" system is neither the intrinsic rights of originally autonomous individuals nor the good of the larger social whole, both of which represent universalistic ethics. Rather, such a social structure features a relational ethics that occupies the space "between" self and society.

Chinese anthropologist Fei Xiaotong made a similar contrast in 1949 when he categorized modern Western social structure as an "organizational mode of association" (*tuanti geju*) and the Chinese system as a "differential mode of association" (*chaxu geju*) (Fei 1983: 31; Fei 1992:62). In the Western system, relations between individuals are based on a common linkage to a shared collectivity, which serves as an overarching unity, such as the way citizens are linked to "the nation." In the traditional Chinese system, relations with the whole society are secondary, and there are few ethics governing the relationship between the individual and the collectivity. Instead of relying on an overarching and all-inclusive collectivity, relations expand from multiple centers or persons to the scope necessary for different occasions. In Chinese culture, family and kinship ties form an ever-expandable horizon of relationships, and they provide a metaphor or idiom for other social relations.

---

[4] In the countryside, kinship values have been more dominant and there is a finer line between kinship and guanxi than in the cities (Madsen 1984:50–51).

What Liang and Fei did not see was that what they called the "Western" social pattern was taking hold in the China of their time and, after 1949, came to curtail and displace the traditional pattern altogether. Collectivism was part of the rise of the nation-state in modern China. It is possible to speculate that at the height of the Cultural Revolution, when the eclipse of the social realm by politics and by the state was the most totalizing, there occurred a reaction-formation in the social body. It took the form of private and person-alistic relationships of mutual aid and obligation which implicitly challenged the universalistic ethics of self-sacrifice, national identity, and state loyalty internalized in each citizen. The emergence of a sec-ond society in China in the aftermath of this long period of "state saturation" can be seen in the uncovering and reinventing of what Liang called the "relationship-based" core of Chinese culture.

The art of guanxi operates in the space between the individual and society and can be described as both individual-centered and individ-ual-decentered. Individuals situate themselves at the center of each network. They exercise discretion concerning whom to include in their networks, which gifts to give, how to present them, and of whom to ask a favor. Yet gift-giving and the notion of "face" are very other-dependent, in the sense that the kinds of persons they construct are never complete in and of themselves. Rather, guanxi persons are constituted by the sum of exchange relations in which they are em-bedded. They are large or small depending on the relative proportions of gifts and favors given out or taken in. Their "face" is in inverse relation to the degree of their indebtedness to others. Through the art of guanxi, a person or group can gain a certain *political* autonomy from state regulations, policies, cadres, and bureaucracy, but at the expense of making themselves more *socially* dependent on the gener-osity and help of their network.

Individual decenteredness in the art of guanxi constructs persons who are not sufficient unto themselves, but are completed or constitu-ted by their relations with, and gifts to and from, others. It is interest-ing that this observation can be found in both Liang Shuming's Con-fucian discourse, as well as in anthropological descriptions of gift economies in Melanesia. The opposition between self or individual and society, so important in Western constructs of civil society, is simply not germane to these social systems. Marilyn Strathern has pointed out that in the West, "relations are, so to speak, after the fact of the individual's personhood and not intrinsic to it" (1990:10). In Melanesia, persons are not distinct from nor prior to relationships, but are the products or by-products of a changing constellation of relationships that intersect through them. "Melanesian persons . . . contain a generalized sociality within. Indeed, persons are frequently constructed as the plural and composite site of the relationships that produced them" (Strathern 1988:13).

In both Melanesian and Chinese gift economies, the totalizing notion of "society" as an abstract force to which the individual must be subsumed or subordinated is inappropriate and even irrelevant. If the persons in these economies are not self-sufficient and autonomous individuals in the first place, then how can it be said that they must be made to lose their rights and serve the demands of society? Rather, in the art of guanxi, persons are subject to the control of concrete and particular other persons in a network through relations of indebtedness, not to the universal and abstract principles and sanctions associated with the notion of "society" or "the state."

In the very year that Liang and Fei published their studies, the private and relational ethics of kinship and friendship underwent dramatic contraction. Ezra Vogel has noted the ascendance of an impersonal and politicized "comradeship" over friendship in the 1950s (1965). In the countryside, systematic efforts were made to destroy renqing and traditional kinship bonds among the peasants (Madsen 1984:181–87). The still nascent discourse of individuality was also rooted out. This process represented the logical end of the modern development of Chinese nationalism, which had started at the turn of the century. Therefore, the very inception of the notion and the ethics of a collectivist entity such as "society" in China was tied up with the establishment of the modern state.

The basic social unit in the West has been taken to be the individual, or the group construed as a collection of individuals. Social movements in the West continue to take the form of the expansion of basic civil rights to an ever-wider portion of the population: women's suffrage and the Equal Rights Amendment, ethnic minority rights, gay and lesbian rights, and even children's and animal rights. Two exceptions to individual rights movements are the environmentalist and antinuclear movements, which subscribe to holistic visions of the earth and nature and to a vision of humanity which transcends national boundaries.

Given a cultural point of departure quite different from that of the West, Chinese minjian will probably not find individual rights and citizenship the most fertile ground for its emergence or reemergence. Where the history of civil society in the West was propelled primarily by a discourse of rights, specifically, individual rights, the formation of a social realm outside the state in China, will most likely be fueled by a discourse of relatedness and obligations.[5] In China, the cultural emphasis has not been on the abstract universal person, but on the person as defined in terms of relationships and roles.

No doubt the distinctive cultural histories of Europe and China have something to do with this difference in the basic patterns of their social fabric. As Max Weber (1958) has pointed out, Protestantism, which dispenses with intermediate hierarchies of clergy and saints, has been a main driving force in the modern West. It has emphasized the direct relationship between the individual and the transcendent realm beyond the monarch. In China, the dominant ethics have derived not from the religious realm, but from kinship relations. The recent resurgence of the art of guanxi is the latest extension of kinship ethics.

Although, as shown in Chapter 7, the discourse of individuality has been gaining ground in urban areas during the reform period, it cannot compare with the depth of the discourse of renqing and guanxi obligations in the cultural unconscious. Nor will an equally abstract notion of "Chinese society" or the "Chinese nation" be adequate to nourish a social realm independent of the state, since these have already been too thoroughly colonized and appropriated by the state. Indeed, neither the roots of individuality nor collectivity are very historically elaborated or deep; they can be traced to the very soil that has sustained the modern expansion of the state as a reaction to the forces of imperialism and modernity. In contrast, in Chapter 6, the genealogy of guanxixue was traced to ancient forms of ritual and kinship government before the eruption of the centralized and bureaucratic state. At a time when revolutionary idealism, the main vehicle for collectivism and societism, seems to have lost its captivating power, and when weariness of universalistic ethics has set in, there will be a retreat to relational ethics. Therefore, I posit here that the art of guanxi, which occupies a space between the "individual" and "society," will provide a basis and form for a Chinese minjian emerg-

[5] The distinction drawn here between Chinese and Western civil societies cannot be labeled a reductive dualism because it does not form any symmetrical oppositions. Guanxixue is not the exact opposite of Western individualism; collectivism is. Nor is it a version of Indian holism described by Louis Dumont (1970). Nor does the Chinese context lack a discourse of individuality and universal humanism, or a universalistic collectivism, as I point out in Chapter 7. What is suggested here is the genealogy of Chinese relational ethics in the kinship order, and its roles in countering the collectivist state order.

ing out of state socialism. And since the discourse of obligations is as yet not conscious of itself as oppositional to the state, a step has been taken here to harness it to the development of an autonomous social realm.

In-between the Individual and Groups or Associations

If a Chinese minjian order is unlikely to take either the "individual" or "society" as its dominant form and basic unit, what about "intermediate associations and groups," that other form so important to the history of civil society in Europe and North America? As noted above, late imperial and even republican China were full of local and voluntary associations whose organizations were conceived as outside the state, although not always independent of it.

According to Liang Shuming, traditional Chinese culture did not have the distinct group associations that have existed in the West since the Middle Ages when Christian organizations undermined kinship organizations such as family and clan. He did, however, see the continuity of ancient Zhou Confucian principles down to his own time, a set of organizational principles which formed a Chinese "relationship-based" system. In this social order, group formation is muted because social units and group boundaries are infinitely flexible and expandable and blur into the larger social fabric (1949:53, 59, 73). For Liang, a "relationship-based" system such as China did not have true bounded groups, but adhered to a principle of construction based on the outward extension of kinship ethics.

Rather than a collectivity of individuals, as found in a bundle of rice straws, Fei Xiaotong describes Chinese sociality as the concentric circles of ripples widening outward from a stone thrown into the water. In the Chinese "differential mode of association" (chaxu geju), according to Fei, each person is at the center of his or her social or kinship network of ever-expandable relationships of familiarity (1983: 24,31). Each ring represents a differentially graduated sphere of obligation, the more distant the ring, the weaker the ties. The Chinese concept and practice of "family" (jia) is elusive in that this social entity is seldom a fixed and well-defined one, but in practical usage, it is subject to a rule of situational elasticity in its boundaries. For both Fei and Liang then, the most important principle of Chinese social patterning is the reckoning of kinship and relational distance. They looked not to the individual or the group as the basis of Chinese sociality, but to that space between, to personal networks adhering to the principle of kinship extension.

Fei and Liang studied Chinese culture in the 1930s and 1940s, a time of great social turmoil, dislocation, and warfare. It is perhaps significant that in the midst of the Cultural Revolution, also a period of severe social stress, atomization, and the breakdown of state order, what emerged was a growing importance of cementing relationships and relying on networks. In Deleuze and Guattari's terms, when the molar organizational system is disintegrating, it is easier to see through to the molecular level, where social integration and social dynamics take on added significance because the social order now rests on the very fabric of their relationships.

After the Revolution, any independent groups that did exist were either disbanded or gathered into the folds of state administration. As of this writing, it is still very difficult to form voluntary associations in China, although many such new organizations bloomed very briefly in the spring before the great storm of 1989 in Beijing. In such a hostile environment, the art of guanxi can assume the role that formal groups and associations play in Western civil societies. There is abundant evidence that guanxi networks often function in such a capacity.

On a visit to Beijing in 1990, I had a fruitful discussion with Zhou Wenhou, a reporter who writes on economic affairs for a newspaper. I asked him whether in recent years he had noticed any spontaneously formed groups or organizations that "revealed an independent life-force (shengmingli) in the society." He thought for a moment, then replied that most organizations invariably get integrated into the government organs; however, he offered, he could think of a great many "informal organizations" (fei zhenshi zuzhi). For example, in the acquisition of coal for a factory, there is a "guanxi network" composed of people who are the producers, the sellers, the transporters, and the buyers.

> It's all guanxi. But they form a sort of group which no one else knows about. It is the same with acquiring things for your own home. Getting a telephone installed, or finding propane gas for cooking, all these rely on guanxi networks. The members [of these networks] do not publicly announce [bu xuanbu] that they have formed a group. They have no charter [xianzhang], and they pay no membership fees [bu jiao huifei], nevertheless, these networks are very important.

Then Zhou proceeded to recount how he himself recently participated in the formation of something he described as "half-guanxiwang,

half-organization." After June Fourth 1989, a "leave-the-country fe-
ver" (*chuguore*) broke out all over Beijing. He himself went to the
Australian embassy to try to obtain a visa for himself and his son.
While standing in line, he made the acquaintance of several like-
minded persons, and they exchanged telephone numbers. Soon they
were calling each other up and swapping information about Australian cities, working conditions, schools, and universities. The network
grew larger until someone thought to formalize things a little by getting a few people together to form the "Students-in-Australia Information Service School" (*fuao liuxue zixun fuwu xuexiao*). Occupying
a small rented office, this "school" gave out free information on how
to get to Australia and the living conditions there. For a fee, it offered
a service of helping people with the complicated process of negotiating bureaucracies and paperwork (*banshouxu*) involved in going
abroad. It advertised its services in a local newspaper. Since private
schools are legal now in China, they were able to register with the
Bureau of Education of the Beijing Municipal Government.

Inspired by our discussion of recent social changes in China, Zhou
thought of one more sign of society's reviving "lifeforce." These days,
he noted, the making of TV dramas has become a regular industry.
The making of any given drama involves many people of diverse
backgrounds from a range of different work units. For example, a
drama production team may include an organizer who is an editor of
a newspaper, a novelist from the Writers' Association, a camera crew
from one TV station and a producer from another, and a film director
from a film studio somewhere in the country. They are all put together through various kinds of guanxi they have with the organizer
or each other. With finance money from one or more industrial enterprises who wish to feature their companies and their products on
TV commercials during the show, a production group is formed.
Through guanxi, their show gets air time on TV, and thereafter they
divide up the money and the group dissolves.

This process can be described as a collection of friends and acquaintances which form a guanxi network, which for the purposes of
producing a TV drama solidifies for a time into a coalition or loosely
defined work group and which on completion of the project then dissolves. Such a social phenomenon fits what network analysis in anthropology has called a quasi-group: "A coalition of persons, re-
cruited according to structurally diverse principles by one or more
existing members, between some of whom there is a degree of pat-
terned interaction and organisation. It is not a permanent social entity

nor can it become one unless it undergoes further structural transformation. . . . It has a structural form which is given by the regular and often purposive interaction that takes place" (Boissevain 1968:550; Mayer 1966).

There is a difference between the egocentric guanxi networks I described in the Introduction and Chapter 3 and the purposive quasi-groups introduced here. A simple network may be egocentric, but its purposive goals and actions are understood and coordinated only by ego. Relationships within the network tend to be single-stranded or low in density. That is to say, persons in the network know only one or a few of the others, so that there is very little interaction among the members of the network. In quasi-groups, however, all of the members understand and share in the common goal, they communicate it to each other, and they see themselves as working in concert to further certain ends. Furthermore, in quasi-groups, the egocentric nature of guanxi networks develops into a leadership function. This centralized nucleus of a leader or leadership group can approximate an office or even assume a title. Such is the case with a new social phenomenon in the cities, loosely translated here as "going underground" (*zouxue*).

In early 1991, in the dressing room behind the stage of an auditorium one night in the city of Hangzhou, I queried a young woman pop singer about this new phenomenon. Her work unit was a state-run "song and dance company," but she also performed secretly on the side for extra income and amusement. Her idol is the African-American singer Whitney Houston. According to her, "going underground" involves a "cave head" (*xuetou*) bringing together entertainers (singers, TV and movie stars, "cross-talk" comedians, musicians, and so on) from different work units to put on special performances for the public. These activities are carried out almost entirely outside the state structure in that they are organized by anyone who has a large guanxi network among entertainers, and the participants split the money made from the concerts among themselves. A "cave head" usually holds a regular state job, but he uses his spare time or steals away from work to engage in this "second career" (*di er zhiye*), which provides him with an income much higher than his official wage. In his capacity as a "cave head," he goes to municipal governments and large enterprises across the country to propose that performances be held in their city or factory and to rent auditoriums. He also assembles a cast of performers through his guanxi network, trying to include one or two famous stars for audience drawing power.

She knows a "cave head" in Beijing who occasionally calls her up long distance to ask her perform at one of these privately organized events. Performers like her slip away from their work units for a few days when her company is not busy with shows, and their work-unit leaders generally do not know about it. In order to buy an airplane ticket, she needs to have a letter of introduction (*jieshao xin*) from her work unit. She did not elaborate on how she wrangled such letters, but implied that she had "familiar persons" here and there. The more she performs, she said, the more she enlarges her guanxi network, and the more she gets called on to perform all over the country.

The "going underground" phenomenon began in China around 1986 and reached a peak just before the events of June Fourth 1989. Thereafter such performances subsided because of a general political tightening on activities not organized by the state. In mid-1990, however, there was renewed life in these privately organized public events. According to a middle-aged university professor in Beijing, the terms *zouxue* and *xuetou* are a revival of prerevolutionary usages, which since the Revolution had disappeared from the vocabulary.

Although the leadership function of these performance quasi-groups is important, they cannot be considered full-fledged groups or organizations because of their relative impermanence. As Tian Meng, a middle-aged artist said, "Guanxi networks are like casting a fishnet into the sea; when the fish have been caught, the people [holding the net] disperse. When the net is recast, not all the same people are in the new network."[6] His friend, Old Pan, added that guanxi networks cannot be fixed with permanent members and titles because they have to be secret in order to operate. That is what guanxi networks are good for. The flexibility, relative anonymity, and weak integration that characterizes guanxi networks are what enable them to withstand incursions made by the state. The quasi-group can continue to function even though occasionally a few members get caught. Given the current political conditions in China, quasi-groups are better off not becoming crystallized and institutionalized into full-fledged and visible formal associations and corporate groups.

At this writing, it is not clear whether the minjian realm in China can only assume the form of guanxi networks and quasi-groups. Most likely, this form is only a transitional phase, so that once the state can guarantee the legitimacy of formal associations, through a working legal system that actually protects the right to group formation, quasi-

[6] This is an allusion to Zhuangzi's Daoist insight.

groups can be transformed into open associations that contribute to the welfare of a community or the larger public.

Rhizomatic Kinship and Guanxi Polity: From 'Guanxi Networks' to a 'Minjian'

In Chapter 6, I traced the contemporary art of guanxi to an ancient genealogy when a segmentary state based on kinship principles was overtaken and "overcoded" by the first centralized bureaucratic state in China. Guanxixue has been an offshoot of both kinship ethics and a Confucian discourse that gives systematic expression to kinship values. This link between guanxixue and kinship can be made only if we take kinship in its broadest sense, which Meyer Fortes defined as a system of social classification and fiduciary morality in which can be found "the mutual dependence of person on person in a network of dyadic reciprocities" (1969a:107; Fortes 1969b). Urban guanxixue preserves out of traditional kinship only certain aspects. It dispenses with the other elements associated with kinship: genealogical tracings, descent and inheritance, marriage and affinal ties. The notions of connectedness, familiarity, obligation, reciprocity, mutual assistance, generosity, and indebtedness are the kinship principles retained in the art of guanxi.

Several anthropologists have pointed out that there are two dimensions of kinship. In the patrilineal kinship order of the Tallensi in Africa, there is a difference between agnatic bonds and other kin relations that link members of different agnatic groups. Agnatic bonds form the foundation of corporate social units of lineage and clan, whereas the other types of kinship establish connections between persons of one kinship unit with another and enable them to maintain bonds of amity and mutual assistance, regardless of the political relationship between their two (agnatic) clans (Fortes 1949:281, 286, 341–42). The latter kind of shifting and fluid horizontal personal ties allow persons to cross alien clan territory safely. They are usually matrilateral, uterine, or sororal ties because the crucial links in these relationships are women as mothers, sisters, or father's sisters. Before the imposition of a colonial state, the Tallensi social order was constructed in terms of multiple centers of patrilineal clan corporate groupings, each latently hostile to nearby rival clans. This system of multiple centripetal forces was relieved by the centrifugal force of matrilateral kinship connections that provided flexibility and variability to an otherwise rigid system.

A similar opposition of kinship principles is noted by Deleuze and Guattari in their distinction between filiation (usually patrilineal), which ensures the vertical continuity of structure through time, and alliance, which sees to the lateral connections between structures through affinal ties and is maintained by a continuing chain of debt relationships. "Filiation is administrative and hierarchical, but alliance is political and economic, and expresses power insofar as it is not fused with hierarchy and cannot be deduced from it, and the economy insofar as it is not identical with administration" (1983:146). Alliance exercises power in a way different from, and even in opposition to, hierarchical filiation. The economics of debt through which alliance operates is a process of negotiated and shifting asymmetries between social entities, rather than an orderly administrative imposition.

The difference between "official kinship" and "practical kinship" has also been pointed out by Pierre Bourdieu:

> As soon as we ask explicitly about the *functions* of kin relationships, or more bluntly, about the usefulness of kinsmen, a question which kinship theorists prefer to to treat as resolved, we cannot fail to notice that those uses of kinship which may be called genealogical are reserved for official situations in which they serve the function of ordering the social world and of legitimating that order. In this respect they differ from the other kinds of practical use made of kin relationships, which are a particular case of the utilization of *connections*. (1977:34)

Whereas official kinship instills order, classification, and fixed identity in human relationships, the practical kinship of connections is situational, shifting, and flexible. In each of these distinctions in the way kinship operates, it is the latter aspect that the art of guanxi in urban China has retained. Urban guanxixue adopts only a portion of Confucianism—it dispenses with the vertical filiational ties of filial piety, ruler and minister, and unequal spousal gender relations. It retains occasional elder and younger relations, such as those between teacher and student or leader and subordinate, but most important, it develops the realm of friendship.

Here I venture a speculation: in the history of Chinese patrilineal kinship, with each eruption and renewal of state organizational power, there has been a progressive but intermittent state appropriation of the first function in each of the above distinctions of kinship.

The imperial state had over the centuries been able to restrict and make use of the kinship order by "overcoding" its own organizational principles and administrative apparatus onto the agnatic, centripetal, hierarchical, filiative, and corporative dimensions of patrilineal kinship. This can be seen in the skillful way that the imperial state made local lineage and clan leaders into degree-bearing gentry and scholar-officials who served the state.

Unlike the poly-centered system of lineages, clans, and clan-states, the despotic, centralized state in China desired to gather the population into a unity, a single hierarchy revolving around a pivotal center. This unity forms what Deleuze and Guattari call an "arborescent" structure, a mono-organizational bureaucracy with a central trunk from which branches extend in different directions, the better to attach all manner of organizations to them. Arborescent structures are also deeply "rooted," that is to say, concerned with both origins as well as hidden foundations of power; hence the importance of history writing to every dynastic order, and underground surveillance to the modern state.

The furthest development of arborescent structure was in the mid-twentieth century when the revolutionary state "e-radicated" or "up-rooted" all lineage, religious, and other corporate organizations, and planted new arbors—a rural system of state-run communes, brigades, and production teams and an urban system of state-administered work units and neighborhood committees. Both are territorial systems of control which attempt to fix the population in specific places and arrange it into classification units by political category and assigned work and residential sites. This mono-organizational grid on what had been a system of multidimensional principles of organization erased the traces of independent social groupings outside state administration.

The question of "kinship polity" is especially relevant to pre-state social formations or those with only rudimentary state organizations where kinship is not relegated just to the familial-domestic domain. In a kinship polity, the lines between the familial and domestic relationships and the political relationships are blurred. There is no structural differentiation between the domain of interpersonal relationships based on familial ties and the political-economic domain (Fortes 1969a:101, 118). In the absence or weakness of a state organizational apparatus, kinship in primitive societies provides the idiom for the conduct of political, economic, religious, ritual, and sexual practices. The social order in stateless societies is held together by kinship morality and the balance of countervailing kinship principles (Gluckman 1965b; Van Velsen 1964). It can be said that if the notion of a "kinship polity" is important in understanding primitive societies without a state structure, then the notion of a "guanxi polity" is relevant to an examination of a potential minjian realm disengaging itself from a socialist state.

Although the state has successfully appropriated and overcoded the hierarchical, vertical, filiative, and corporative dimensions of Chinese kinship (as seen in state Confucianism), it would seem that the lateral and practical dimension of kinship as the fluid interpersonal transactions of centrifugal dispersal have continued to elude it. The modern art of guanxi can be identified as a new "socialist" version of the second dimension of kinship. Practical kinship, or the art of guanxi, has a "rhizome" form, an uncentered and meandering growth that quickly makes itself a nuisance in the centripetal "arborescent" structures of the state (Deleuze and Guattari 1987:3–25). Rhizomatic guanxi "are non-hierarchical, horizontal multiplicities which cannot be subsumed within a unified structure, whose components form random, unregulated networks in which any element may be connected with any other element" (Bogue 1989:107). Like rhizomatic tubers, guanxi networks can be broken at any spot, but they can start to grow again, taking up where they were interrupted, forming new networks for each occasion.

Guanxi practices constitute an alternative and even subversive realm of operations, weaving webs of personal relationships which crisscross and overlie one another. A successful person negotiates his or her way through a maze of bureaucratic obstacles by having familiar persons in different work units, occupations, cities, and so forth. Whenever there are problems of access, one goes to one's network. Each person in a network can also tap into their own networks to help their friend. Thus guanxi are rhizomatic or vinelike growths extending across state arborescent organizations and offices to form their own linkages.

In this book we have seen how the art of guanxi works to constitute a polity of its own by extending into and "poaching" on the public domains monopolized by the state. This guanxi polity poses as an alternative system of relational ethics and social integration subverting and displacing state structures. Thus the power of official channels, state rules, and state regulations are neutralized. They are made to bend and change with the circumstances and with each particular constellation of persons involved. In the art of guanxi, personal and private ends are attained ironically through a process and an ethics that breaks up any unitary construction of the individual by stressing obligation, indebtedness, and interpersonal loyalty. Therefore, through the art of guanxi, it is possible to recuperate from the state's monopoly the category of "public" and return it to the realm of the social.

In contrast to the arborescent cult of Mao in which "being" and "identity" were fixed in the self so that its intrinsic substance revolved around a pivotal state icon, rhizomatic guanxi work through a "conjunctive" process of addition, "and . . . and . . . and . . ." (Deleuze and Guattari 1987:25), creating an outwardly expanding network of lateral relationships. Yet the art of guanxi also resembles the Mao cult in that both achieve an incremental molecular deconstruction of molar state organization. But the Mao cult relied on roving bands of fired-up youth and destructive crowds to dismantle the state, whereas guanxixue quietly corrodes the state edifice through deflecting its ethics and diverting state distribution. Unlike the Mao cult, however, guanxixue does so without a subjectivity that hooks up each individual to a state center.

The art of guanxi does not base itself at fixed sites of operation, but grows dispersed and unregulated, at different sites of state construction. Kjeld Brodsgaard is right when he points out that in Gramsci's understanding, civil society is not necessarily in a relationship of externality to the state (1991). For Gramsci, the state can also "encompass" civil society. Therefore, in China, perhaps we should not expect an autonomous social realm to arise only outside the state in the form of independent and oppositional group associations. It can also be found in the fluid flows of relationships and networks operating both within and without the state according to different ethics and principles. Fluidity, the situational expansion and contraction of networks, the purposive establishment of relations in different sectors and levels of bureaucracy according to need, allow a second society to avoid assuming a tangible form or an identifiable fixed site of operations. Thus it is able to elude the state.

An objection could be made that since the art of guanxi has a strong instrumental component and works to strengthen the private realm, it cannot be linked to any construction of a social order that is for the public good.[7] There is instrumentalism in contemporary

---

[7] Indeed, there are signs that the gift economy may affect the development not only of society but also of capitalism in China. Depending on the extent of state involvement, a newly emergent form of Chinese capitalism could be different from the individualism of early Western capitalism, as well as the "political economy" or state-corporate type of capitalism found in Japan, and to a lesser extent, in the West today. Gary Hamilton has

guanxixue, to a higher degree perhaps than in the older renqing discourse, and certainly more than in the idealized relations envisioned by Liang Shuming and other Confucians. This is due perhaps to the extra social loads that guanxixue has to bear, such as market relations, the impoverishment of the people, and political power plays. For a long time, market relations, which were forbidden by the state, did not operate in a sphere of their own, so they had to hitch a ride on something else, such as guanxi. The lack of resources and wealth on the part of the people also made it necessary for them to use whatever they had access to: their jobs, their friends, and so on, to strengthen their material and social positions.

This does not mean that once people become more prosperous, and the market becomes legitimate, the art of guanxi will disappear. So long as the state redistributive apparatus predominates, there will be a need for guanxi to obtain through political channels what is not available through the market. What keeps the art of guanxi apart from market or commodity relations though, is the fact that ironically its instrumentalism can only work through nonmarket guanxi ethics and nonobjectified human relations. Similarly, so long as the state dominates, the art of guanxi will challenge it with relational ethics. In the process of guanxi exchange, the social realm's internal linkages are strengthened, and the threads of a society whose basic fabric has been severely torn for nearly two centuries can be gradually rewoven. However, in urban areas this process will not be simply going back to the order before the social disintegration process of modern China, but will be the construction of a new order, based not so much on kinship and family, but on friendship.

The charge that guanxixue, being private, cannot contribute to civil society, which is public, can be answered in the following ways. First, China's minjian order will emerge in a very different context than that of the West in the eighteenth century. In Western Europe and the United States, civil society assumed a public form because it emerged along with, and in order to counterbalance, capitalism and its often socially destructive forces of privatism. China today is in a postsocialist phase, which means that the minjian is emerging in the aftermath of extreme state penetration of the social order and state appropria-

---

found that overseas Chinese capitalism (Taiwan, Hong Kong, Singapore, Southeast Asia) often assumes a transnational family and guanxi-network form (1992). The small size and flexible form of these enterprises enable them to insert themselves into small and shifting niches of the global market. This sort of guanxi-network capitalism may also develop in mainland China, but most likely in conjunction with large state monopolies.

tion of the public sphere. In this respect, China has more in common with Eastern Europe and the former Soviet Union, where private networks protected pockets of society from a state that wanted to make everything public and all of culture political. It is likely then that an independent social realm in China will appear first in expanding circles of private relations and networks, whose oppositional stance is often expressed by a politics of antipolitics, and then crystallize into more public groups and associations.

Second, despite official discourse that brands the art of guanxi as belonging to the category of "private and selfish" (*si*) activities harmful to the benefit of the "public" (*gong*), the art of guanxi actually operates in both private and public realms. Guanxi is practiced for private individual and familial ends but relies very much on public means: generosity, mutual assistance, indebtedness and obligation, strings and networks of acquaintances, friends and intermediaries.

In the art of guanxi, a second society has appeared in which "every person in the whole society will become locked into one another and their relationships will ramify and spread outward, so that out of a [social] formlessness will emerge a sort of organization" (Liang 1949: 87). In this way, guanxixue serves as the basis for the reweaving of the social fabric of an emerging minjian. It is a fabric based on a "web of kinship" pattern in which personal networks of guanxi do not yet form clear contours or group boundaries, but "stretch out indefinitely, and result in a kaleidoscopic fluidity of social relations" (Fortes 1969:108). The effect is to promote public and social life by connecting and bringing together disparate people into networks that crisscross state-imposed institutions to form a second society according to a multiplicity of organizational principles. Thus the first steps have been taken toward a social order that can activate and organize itself.

Back to the Source

Let me close, not by repeating what has already been said, but by recounting two final guanxi, or rather, renqing stories, whose very freshness and distinctiveness from stories told earlier will paradoxically throw more light on the book as a whole. They should properly be called renqing stories because this time they are collected from the countryside in southeastern China in 1993. In this rural peasant culture, I found renqing to be preponderant in discursive practice over the more instrumental guanxi. As mentioned in Chapter 2, one urban Chinese told me that rural life is the "issuing source" (*fayuandi*) of the art of guanxi. As the stories show, the rural gift economy in contemporary China differs in many ways from the urban one I have described in this book. However, the rural form reveals more vividly its genealogical connections with the ancient gift-ritual economy roughly sketched out in Chapter 6. The rural gift economy perhaps also illustrates better the role of gift exchanges in the formation or strengthening of the minjian sphere in relation to the state, as well as the role of gender in this structural relationship. Of course, it should be kept in mind that rural customs differ greatly in the huge cultural range of China, and that what I found in this prosperous part of rural China is not found everywhere.

The Female Supple Force of Exchange

The first story is about the reemergence of all kinds of gift-giving practices in rural Wenzhou, Zhejiang Province. Throughout the 1980s and early 1990s, this area has seen the revival or renewal of gift-giving in traditional festival or ritual contexts. The festivals include the Spring Festival or Lunar New Year's; the Qing Ming Festival, when families go to sweep the graves of their ancestors; the Duan Wu Festival, celebrating the ancient dissident scholar Qu Yuan; the Xi Qiao Hui Festival, when the Cowherd star in the sky meets his beloved Weaving Woman star; the Mid-Autumn Moon Festival; and the Winter Solstice. Besides the gift-giving among kin and friends during these festivals, there is another category of gift-giving which is called "giving renqing" (*song renqing*), and which takes place in the ritual contexts of weddings, funerals, birth celebrations, house construction banquets, and the rowing of dragon boats during the Spring Duan Wu Festival. The difference between the festival gift-giving and "giving renqing" is that the former is obligatory, while the latter is voluntary, occurs on no fixed dates, involves no fixed amounts or types of gifts to be given, but is based on personal or family income and inclination.

For much of the twentieth century, both kinds of gift-giving were curtailed because of poverty and state restrictions. Traditionally, gifts were delivered in a pair of painted wooden, multilevel round boxes called "ritual or gift containers" (*lisheng*), which were attached to a shoulder pole and carried to the homes of kin and friends. In some homes, these boxes were very old, having been passed down through the generations as family heirlooms. During the Cultural Revolution, in the campaign to "Smash the Four Olds" (*po sijiu*), each family was told that these things were "feudal" and must be destroyed. Since there were too many of them for the committee appointed to destroy them, each family was required to destroy its own boxes. Two middle-aged male peasants told me that the practive of "giving renqing" was greatly curtailed but never fully stopped during the Cultural Revolution; it continued secretly (*toutou momode*) on a small scale. People would still give relatives money and gifts on ritual occasions but did not dare do it openly until the early 1970s. I asked why gift-giving was not allowed. The men replied that all they know is that people above said it was "feudal superstition" and a "wasteful practice." Today there are virtually no old "ritual containers" left; instead, gifts are now delivered in large bamboo baskets attached to shoulder poles.

The focus now will turn to just one example of the second category of gift-giving, the giving of renqing for the "rowing of dragon boats" (*hua longzhou*). A village I shall call Bridge Village decided in 1993 to organize a dragon boat-rowing for the Duan Wu Festival. The last time they had done so was in 1984. In 1993, however, they decided to go along with the old custom of accepting renqing in the form of money to finance the outfitting of the boats and rowers.[1] An old peasant told me that this custom is an old one that existed long before Liberation, but just a few years ago, in the late 1980s, "accepting renqing started to blow up a wind" (*shou renqing feng qilai*).

What is interesting is the way that dragon boat gift-giving is structured along gender lines, whereas in urban China, gender is not such a salient category in guanxi transactions. In this strictly patrilineal, patrilocal, and still largely patriarchal rural culture, only women, those who have married *out* from Bridge Village to surrounding villages, give renqing gifts of money to support the boats of their natal village. Similarly, the women who married *into* Bridge Village and now are residents here send money back to their own natal villages if they are rowing this year. When I asked why only women gave renqing on this occasion, I never received what to me was a clear answer, only that it is a way for the women to show their ganqing to their natal homes (*niangjia*). One woman peasant said she did not mind giving, for she was giving to her own "family" (*jia*). Here she was playing on the double meaning of the Chinese term *jia* as both "family" and "hometown." A woman cadre informed me that all of the women, whether of the younger generation who recently married out, or the older generation who have been out for many years, would give, because not to give would be a terrible loss of face for their parents. On the day of the boat-rowing, each married-out woman prepared a small table of food along a waterway of her adopted village with which to greet the boat-rowers of her natal village as they made a friendly tour of the neighboring area.

In return, Bridge Village prepared vinyl briefcases as gifts to present to those women who gave 100–200 yuan. Those who gave more got something better. The village expected to receive a total of 300,000 yuan this year from the married-out women, more than the 100,000 yuan needed to sponsor the boat-rowing. The extra money was to be spent on building a park and an Old People's Pavilion and activity center in the village.

Another kind of gift-giving was associated with boat-rowing in Bridge Village. Gifts were also given to the rowers of the dragon boats from their direct (*zhixi*) relatives who lived in other villages. Such kin can include daughters (but not sons), maternal and paternal uncles (*jiujiu* and *shushu*), siblings, paternal or maternal grand-

---

[1] It should be noted that Bridge Village in particular does not have a history of accepting renqing gifts and money for dragon boats, because it was always a wealthy village that did not need money. However, in surrounding villages, the custom of accepting renqing for dragon boats was in practice before Liberation for as long as the old people can remember.

parents, and parents. Of the three dragon boats, one was rowed by a team of peasant women, the other two by men. Since this is a prosperous area of rural China, gifts can be expensive—a color TV or even, amazingly, a motorcycle, which costs 45,000 yuan including the license. The rower recipient must then return part of the value of the gift to the donor in cash. Rich families might return 70–80 percent of the worth of the gift, while poor families might return only 30 percent. This custom is also very old, but it is only in the early 1990s that these gifts have become so inflated.

The direct kin first solicits from the rower the kinds of things he or she would like to have, and through the give and take of discussion, the giver gets an idea of how much the recipient can afford and whether other kin are also giving to the same person. Otherwise, the recipient might be faced with too many expensive gifts and find it impossible to give back the customary return money. "That would be disastrous!" (*Na hai de liao!*) declared a peasant woman in such a comical way that I could not resist a hearty laugh.

Finally, the Duan Wu Festival is also an occasion for a third kind of gift-giving, from the parents in Bridge Village to their married daughter in her first year of marriage, whether the daughter now lives there or in another village, and regardless of whether the village is rowing dragon boats. These gifts are household items such as bamboo bed mats (*xizi*), mosquito netting, or clothing.

In all three kinds of gift-giving associated with dragon boat-rowing or the Duan Wu Festival, women play an important role in maintaining and expanding inter-village and inter-lineage relations. Several ethnographies have pointed out such a role for women in diverse cultures. Among the Tonga of Africa, a married woman moving into her husband's village becomes the conduit for maintaining linkages among three sets of kin: her matrilateral and patrilateral kin, and the kin of her husband's village (Van Velsen 1964:53–55). Malay peasant women are also crucial in maintaining social ties across families and communities in their exchange of cooked foods, childcare, and festival preparations (Ong 1987:96). Ellen Judd has shown that in rural North China, women after marriage maintain close links with their natal families (*niangjia*) and home villages (1989). In the Wenzhou dragon boat case, peasant women were either the givers, the receivers, or the transmitters, the persons through whom the gift passed. Here women were not the gift objects themselves; therefore analyses that explain female subordination by seeing women as passive objects and victims in male bride exchange (Rubin 1975) must also take into account other contexts of gift-giving besides marriage.

What this example bears out is the strong female component in that aspect of rural Wenzhou kinship which Deleuze and Guattari call "alliance" as opposed to "vertical, hierarchical filiation" (1983), and Bourdieu describes as "practical" rather than "official kinship" (1977). This female dimension of gift-giving coincides with Fortes's finding among the Tallensi that the random inter-agnatic and "individual bonds of amity" among people of different lineages and clans were often "matrilateral," passing through a mother or sister, and that those bonds that tied people to fixed corporate agnatic kinship groups were male (1949).

In this example at least, it seems that the supple and fluid force that leads to the mobile circulation of social relationships across groups and boundaries is often a female one, while the rigid force that fixes individuals into kin groups based on a tracing of roots, and that maintains corporate group solidarity and security, is the male principle of agnation or descent in rural China. If we consider the imposition of state administrative divisions onto existing rural kinship group formations, we can also say that the state structure preserves the male principle of group formation, even though the old kinship groups themselves often did not survive the state. Thus, compared with either traditional kinship structures such as lineages, or new state socialist structures like work units or production teams, the flexible lines extending social relationships and networks outward and across fixed social groups or divisions can be described as more compatible with a female gender construction.

It seems to me that this gender analysis of the gift economy in rural Wenzhou can be carried over to a consideration of the urban art of guanxi, even though in urban areas gender does not seem to be a salient category in guanxi transactions. As mentioned in Chapter 2, we can get a better sense of gender in urban guanxi if we look not so much at the gender of persons engaged in the art of guanxi, but at the gender of the art of guanxi itself. The gender of guanxixue can be described as female because it promotes relational subjects, each of which is not whole unless completed by others in exchange. American feminist psychoanalytic theory describes this interrelatedness as typical of the construction of female subjects (Chodorow 1974, 1978), whereas the construction of men features separation and independence from other subjects.

Psychoanalytic object-relations theory has also tried to retrieve an alternative system of morality to the dominant morality in the West, of abstracted universalistic rights and rules. This other morality—which speaks "in a different voice," one that stresses responsibilities that arise in "a network of connection, a web of relationships that is sustained by a process of communication" (Gilligan 1982:32)—has been submerged in Western culture because it belongs to the female domain. Modern Western science illustrates, par excellence, the radical methodological separation between the scientific knower and the object of knowledge, making it a powerful male force for the domination and control of nature (Keller 1987). In comparing the modern West with modern China, we can say that, whereas in the West, relational ethics are assigned to women and are muted in public discourse, in China there is a strong public (but not state) discourse of relational ethics, to which both men and women subscribe.

Although the stronger presence of relational ethics in China perhaps infuses Chinese culture with a larger "feminine" component than in the West, it would be a big mistake to say that China is essentially female while the West is essentially male. For if we look at different ethical discourses *within* China, it seems that there are still discourses of *both* gender persuasions. For example, the practice of guanxixue in China gives rise to a proliferation of "feminine" relational ethics, which run counter to an abstract, therefore male, state universalistic ethics of loyalty to the nation and the Party. The relational ethics of the art of guanxi and renqing exert a supple, female traversing and transgressive force in a male-defined rigid statist formation which requires fixed and centered subjects. However, when compared with renqing, guanxi becomes male to renqing's more female qualities.

Such constructions as the Mao cult subject, which has infused a central icon of the state into its subjectivity, and the subject that is defined and restricted by state classifications and divisions, are both undermined by this alternative guanxi subject whose boundaries are open to new combinations and flows in the circulation of gifts and relationships. In this way, the lateral, as opposed to vertical, integration of the social realm, and its flexibility and openness to change, are strengthened at the expense of state-boundedness.

Ritual as a Self-organizing Vehicle of the Minjian

The second story is about a rural cadre in southeastern China I will call Zhao,[2] who found himself painfully caught between state and society after his father's death. Zhao's elderly father had been the

[2] It is not possible to say who told me the story without revealing the identity of the protagonist of the story as well.

Zhao lineage head because he was the oldest living member in both age and generation. Zhao himself never told anyone that his father had died, but his elder brother, "who is usually a very honest and obedient (*laoshi*) peasant," organized an elaborate funeral ritual for their father. Traditional ritual activity is discouraged by the socialist state, and anyone organizing large-scale rituals usually runs into trouble. One thousand people showed up for the funeral, and at the funerary banquet "there were several tens of tables." Altogether the Zhaos fed over five hundred people. Many of the guests gave unsolicited gifts and money, and all in all, the Zhaos collected 7,000 yuan. These people wanted to show their respect for the deceased and their approval of Zhao as one of their cadre leaders, while his brother wanted to show his loyalty to their father. Unfortunately, as so often happens in China, Zhao had some time ago offended another cadre, so the funeral provided this person with the opportunity to "inform" (*gao*) higher authority levels that Zhao was engaging in "corrupt and feudal" activities.

Zhao was arrested and subjected to internal Party discipline. He was accused of using his official position (*liyong zhiquan*) to accept bribes. The authorities detained him in a room for four days, then put him under surveillance and questioned him for several months. All kinds of state organizations got involved: the Party organization, Public Security, the county and city governments, the People's Court, judges, and so forth. They all sent special teams to study his past activities, and they questioned the local people about his behavior. Zhao was personally traumatized by this turn of events. His case became known far and wide. Everyone thought that he would be demoted for sure, perhaps even stripped of Party membership and cadre status; no one expected that he would emerge with a higher rank, which was in fact how his case ended.

What happened was that the local people all supported him. Several village Old People's Associations (*laoren xiehui*), a new type of public organization, made special trips to the city to plead his case with the city government. Local school teachers also got together, telling as many higher-level officials as they could find that he was a good cadre, that he had done a good job for the community and had built up the local middle school. The local community said that an injustice (*yuanwang*) had been done to him. So what the official investigations uncovered was that he had a lot of respect and prestige (*weiwang*) among the people.

Said one local man who knew the case very well because he was personally involved,

> Actually, the higher levels don't understand the situation at the lower level. They don't know that this is renqing, that renqing is given and returned. In the six years that he was our leader, he gave out lots of gifts and money out of his own pocket to people's weddings, funerals, and births; he gave money to people in need, and when he made visits to the sick. All this amounted to a total of 4,000 yuan. Now at his father's funeral, they were just repaying. The higher levels don't understand that if he just quietly put his father in a coffin and buried him without doing a social ritual [*bubai xishi*], then everyone will think that this cadre has no respect among the people. They will think that the people don't have any human feelings for him [*gen ta meiyou renqing*].

This local interpretation of the event was confirmed by a woman who said to me that she and most people she knew approved of the way that Zhao could "speak the language of renqing" (*jiang renqing*).

In this story can be found many of the arguments set forth in this book. From the people's point of view, the funeral was not a "backward" or "feudal" institution, nor was Zhao using his position to extort money and gifts from them, but it provided an important social occasion for repaying debts owed or initiating a new round of debt relationship with Zhao and his family. The local people sought to transform their relationship with Cadre Zhao from an impersonal, administrative, ruler-to-governed top-down relationship into a personal renqing relationship of giving and repaying. It is noteworthy that, counter to the official policy of de-emphasizing and sometimes banning rituals, the local people attach much social significance to funerary rituals and feasts. The ritual provides a staging ground for the practice of renqing with an official,[3] so that there is a clear association between ritual or feast and renqing, and between ritual, renqing, and good government.

Zhao himself is a cadre whose attitude toward his job is tinged with a heavy renqing perspective and who allows himself to enter into debt relationships with the people. That is why when he got in trouble with his superiors, so many people organized themselves to support him. In this action the people were not just defending Zhao's personal integrity, but also a certain approach to government and the

---

[3] Helen Siu makes a similar point when she writes that contemporary rural rituals are not merely a revival of tradition but are transactions of new and ongoing social and political relationships (1990).

importance of ritual in their social life. In rural Wenzhou, minjian forces have begun to organize themselves and even to prevail against the state, and these forces include the discourse and practice of renqing and ritual.

Renqing over Guanxi

The contrast between the rural renqing gift economy and the urban art of guanxi suggested above brings us to a consideration of the difference between renqing and guanxi. Most of this book has dealt with the urban art of guanxi, which has been described as a particular instrumentalized and politicized form of a more traditional body of renqing principles and rural gift economy. As mentioned in Chapter 1, women tended to be more critical of the ethos of guanxixue than the men I interviewed, because of its aggressive tactics and instrumental aims. In Chapter 2, one woman noted that Chinese women have more renqing qualities than Chinese men, in that women are more attentive to the obligations, debts, warmth, and reciprocities involved in interpersonal relationships. Therefore, we can also detect a gender distinction between a more "feminine" art of renqing and a more "masculine" art of guanxi.

The art of guanxi seems more masculine because, unlike traditional rural-derived renqing, it has emerged in a historical postrevolutionary context where people have had to deal with a modern state perhaps more powerful and socially pervasive than any in the long history of China. As this book has argued, the art of guanxi arose as a way to defuse and subvert the elaborate regulations and restrictions that the state redistributive economy has imposed on everyday life. It is in this engagement with the state that the art of guanxi becomes more instrumental, hardened, cynical, and politicized than renqing, adopting some of the masculinist features of the state. In addition, the guanxi gift economy has also served in many ways as a substitute for market relations, which were severely curtailed by the redistributive and planned economy of state socialism. It is in this process that the art of guanxi has also become instrumentalized and commodified to a great extent into means-ends relationships. Traditional renqing ethics existed in a context where market relations were also present, and took care of a great deal of the distribution of goods and services. Therefore, in seeing the art of guanxi as an important way in which the fabric of the Chinese minjian will be rewoven, we must also call for its "de-masculinization."

However, when compared to the abstract universal ethics of state discourse and nationalism, which can be described as masculinist, *both* renqing and guanxi are more "feminine" in that both pay attention to the relational values and kinship distance of interpersonal relations. Whereas the state creates subjects of equal distance to the state center and subjects equally suffused and penetrated by the state, both renqing and guanxi set up differential combinations of relational subjects which can only be interpenetrated by first converting social distance into social familiarity and a sense of kinship. The art of guanxi can build up an alternative social realm by spreading its relational kinship ethics, which have been discursively relegated to a domestic, and therefore powerless, sphere by the state and the encroaching market. Thus, the ethics of ancient primitive and segmentary state formations will wreak their revenge on later social institutions such as the state and capitalism. Both state and market have evolved beyond kinship forms, but they have never fully supplanted them, and certainly have far from extinguished them.

Glossary

ai mianzi 爱面子	to love face; to value one's social standing
bai jiazi 摆架子	to put on airs
bangpai 帮派	a faction
banshi 办事	to get something done, especially bureaucratic paperwork
banzhang 班长	home-room teacher
bao 报	to repay; reciprocity
baojia 保甲	decimal system of household registration and mutual surveillance in late imperial and republican China
bu dong renqing 不懂人情	not understanding human feeling; not socialized in proper moral conduct
bu duiwai kaifang 不对外开放	not open to foreigners; off-limits to outsiders
bu gou gemenr 不够哥们儿	lacking in the ethic of brotherhood
bu jiang renqing 不讲人情	to treat someone on an impersonal basis (literally, not speaking the language of human feeling)
bu jijiao 不计较	not keeping strict accounts of giving and receiving
bu rendao 不人道	inhumane
bu shuo xinlihua 不说心里话	not speaking from the heart; not being honest
buyao jianwai 不要见外.	"Do not take me for an outsider."
bu zheng zhi feng 不正之风	crooked wind; a trend in which people's behaviors are not proper or upright
caigouyuan 采购员	supply agent (of a factory or enterprise)
chaojia 抄家	to raid people's homes (especially during the Cultural Revolution)
chaxu geju 差序格局	differential mode of association

323

chengbao 承包	to subcontract
chengshou 成熟	mature; ripe
chi kui 吃亏	to lose out; to be taken advantage of
chu chang jia 出厂价	factory price
chufen 处分	disciplinary action
chuguore 出国热	"leave the country fever"
cirang 辞让	to decline and yield (a Confucian etiquette)
congming 聪明	smart
dadao 打倒	to beat down
daguanqiang 打官腔	to speak in obfuscatory bureaucratic language
daiye qingnian 待业青年	youth-awaiting-employment
dajie 大姐	elder sister (often a fictive kinship term of address)
Da Jiuxin 大救星	the Great Savior Star (a title for Mao Zedong during the Cultural Revolution)
danchun 单纯	simple; naive; uncomplicated
dang 党	the Party
dangan 档案	dossier; personnel file
da xiao baogao 打小报告	to make a report; to inform on someone to the leadership
da yitong 大一统	unification and centralization (of the empire)
de 德	virtue; power; to moralize
de 得	to obtain
dezui 得罪	to offend
di 弟	brotherhood (a Confucian term)
di er zhiye 第二职业	second job; second career
difang jinggong 地方进贡	regional localities paying tribute [to the court; to the central government]
diou mianzi 丢面子	to lose face
diqu 地区	regional-district; a rural administrative unit below the provincial level
di tiaozi 递条子	to pass a slip of paper; usually refers to a superior covertly instructing a subordinate to help or hire a personal friend
dou 斗	to struggle; to attack a person of bad class background or a person who is accused of wrongdoing
dou si pixiou 斗私批修	"Struggle against the private and selfish and criticize revisionism" (during Cultural Revolution)
dui 对	to respond (in its classical Chinese sense)
duikangxing 对抗性	oppositional character
erdaofan 二道贩	middle-man in business
fa 法	laws; regulations (especially in Legalist thought and practice)

Fajia 法家	Legalism; School of Law
fangbian 方便	convenient; to facilitate
fangguanju 房管局	Bureau of Housing
fankang 反抗	to resist; resistance
fanmian wutuobang 反面乌托邦	dystopia
fa yuandi 发源地	issuing source or origin
feifa jituan 非法集团	illegal clique
fei zhengshi zuzhi 非正式组织	informal organization
fengjian 封建	feudal
fengjian canyu 封建残馀	feudal remnants
fenshu kenru 焚书坑儒	"burning the Books and burying the Confucian scholars alive" (refers to an act carried out by the Legalist state of Qin)
fensui 粉碎	to pulverize
funu 妇女	woman (term associated with official discourse; as opposed to *nuxing*)
fuwu taidu 服务态度	service attitude
fuwuyuan 服务员	service personnel; waiter or waitress; store clerk
fuza 复杂	complicated; complex
gaizao 改造	to reconstruct (one's thoughts and values)
ganbu 干部	cadre; leader
ganqing 感情	emotional feelings
ganqing polie 感情破裂	breakup of emotional feelings (usually refers to marriage breakup)
gao 告	to inform on
gaohao guanxi 搞好关系	to cultivate good relationships
gaoji ganbu 高级干部	high-level cadre or official
gemenr yiqi 哥们儿义气	ethic of brotherhood
geming yingxiong 革命英雄	revolutionary heroes or martyrs
geren benwei 个人本位	individual-based [society]
geren jiazhi 个人价值	the value of the individual
geren jiefang 个人解放	liberation of the individual
geren zhuyi 个人主义	individualism; selfishness
getihu 个体户	individual entrepreneur or small businessman or woman
gong 公	public
gongren 工人	worker (blue-collar)
gongshi 公事	official business
gongshi gongban 公事公办	"public matters should be conducted in accordance with public procedures"; to follow the letter of the law; not to bend to personalistic appeals

gongsi 公司	corporation; company
gongxiao gongsi 供销公司	supply and marketing corporations
gongxiaoke 供销科	supply and marketing department of a factory or enterprise
gongzuo danwei 工作单位	work unit
guakao 挂靠	to hide a private enterprise behind the facade of a collective or state enterprise (literally, "to hang and lean on")
guan 关	to connect; to make a linkage; a pass or gate; an obstacle
guan 官	official
guanhua 官话	language of officialdom
guanliao zhuyi 官僚主义	bureaucratism; red tape
guanxi 关系	relationship; personal connections
guanxi benwei 关系本位	relationship-based [society]
guanxihu 关系户	guanxi households; people whom one is obligated to help
guanxiwang 关系网	guanxi network
guanxixue 关系学	the art of guanxi; guanxiology; the study of guanxi
guo 国	a state
guojia 国家	nation-state; country (in modern Chinese)
guo minzhu shenghuo 过民主生活	"to live a democratic life" (to participate in political study and self-criticism sections)
haoren 好人	a good person; a virtuous person
hao shuo hua 好说话	to be receptive and open to persuasion
hefa 合法	in accordance with rules and regulations; legal
hei wulei 黑五类	"five black categories" (landlord, rich peasant, bad element, counter revolutionary, rightist)
heli 合理	in accordance with reason or popular opinion
heqing 合情	in accordance with human feelings
hong bao 红包	a present of money; a bribe (literally, a "red package")
hongse riji 红色日记	"red diary" (written as political self-reflection and confession during Cultural Revolution)
hong wulei 红五类	"five red categories" (workers, peasants, cadres, revolutionary martyrs, revolutionary intellectuals)
houjin bogu. 厚今薄古.	"Emphasize the present while slighting the past" (ancient Chinese expression)
hua 滑	slippery; sly and cunning
hua longzhou 划龙舟	to row a "dragon boat" (for the Duan Wu festival)
huaqiao 华侨	overseas Chinese; especially those who have not

changed their citizenship or who live in Southeast Asia

huaqing jiexian 划清界线 — to draw a line of separation; to separate oneself from someone [often family members] with political faults or a bad class background

huayi 华裔 — overseas Chinese; especially those who have become citizens of their host countries, which are usually in the West

huizhang 会长 — the head of a [usually] non-state group or association

hukou 户口 — household registration; a registration that assigns a person to live in a fixed area

huo sixiang 活思想 — "lively thoughts" (notion of uncontrolled thoughts which must be disciplined)

huo yuan 货源 — supply source

huxiang liyi 互相利益 — mutual benefit or interest

ji 祭 — to sacrifice

jia 家 — family, hometown

jia jiti 假集体 — false collective enterprise

jiancha 检查 — a verbal or written confession or self-examination

jiang renqing 讲人情 — to speak the language of renqing

jianli guanxi 建立关系 — to establish a relationship

jiaohuan 交换 — to exchange

jieji chenfen 阶级成分 — class status

jiemenr yiqi 姐们儿义气 — ethic of sisterhood

jie mianzi 借面子 — to borrow face

jieshao xin 介绍信 — letter of introduction

jie she quan 结社权 — the right to form associations

jilü 纪律 — discipline

jimi 机密 — strictly secret

jinbu 进步 — progressive

jingji guanli chengbaozhi 经济管理承包制 — the subcontracting form of economic management

jingqian guanxi 金钱关系 — money relationship

jiti 集体 — collective; an enterprise owned by a collective

jiurou pengyou 酒肉朋友 — "wine-and-meat friend"; ordinary friend

jiu sixiang 旧思想 — old thinking; tradition-bound thinking

ju 局 — a government bureau; an administrative unit in municipal government

jun 郡 — commandery; prefecture; an administrative unit in the Spring and Autumn period and under the Qin dynasty

junzi 君子 — a cultivated person; a gentleman (a Confucian term)

kuangre 狂热 fanatical

la guanxi 拉关系 "to pull guanxi"; to call on personal connections for help

laodongke 劳动科 labor department; a personnel office in charge of manual workers

laoshi 老实 honest; ingenuous; naive; obedient

laoxiong 老兄 elder brother (often a fictive kinship form of address)

lao youtiao 老油条 old oily deep-fried pastry; a cunning person

li 禮, 礼 ritual; etiquette; propriety; proper form

lian 脸 face (public recognition of the ego's moral integrity)

liangyou guanxi 粮油关系 "grain-and-oil relationship" (refers to food rationing)

lianpi hou 脸皮厚 to be thick-skinned

lianzuo 连坐 system of collective responsibility in which a criminal's kin, friends, or neighbors will also be punished (especially in Legalist practice)

Li Ji 禮記 *The Book of Rites*, one of the five classical texts of the Confucian canon

lingdao 领导 leader; especially of a work unit

lingshigong 临时工 temporary worker

liou mianzi 留面子 to save face

li sheng 礼盛 gift container

li tong waiguo 里通外国 to leak information to a foreign country

liwu 禮物, 礼物 ritual object; a gift (in modern Chinese)

liyi 利益 profit; gain; interest

liyong zhiquan 利用职权 to make use of one's official position

li zhi 礼治 ritual government

lunli 伦理 human relationships and ethics

lunli daode 伦理道德 morality and ethics of human relationships

lunli guanxi 伦理关系 relationship of ethics

luohou 落后 backward

luosiding 螺丝钉 a screw

luzi 路子 roads; paths; channels; personal routes to get something done

mai mai 买卖 "buying and selling"; to do business

meiyou mianzi 没有面子 lacking in face; shameless; not having requisite social position

meiyou renqing 没有人情 lacking in human feeling

mianzi 面子 face (publicly recognized prestige and social advantage)

minjian 民间 "people's realm"; a sphere of people-to-people relationships which is non-state and separate from its bureaucratic organizations

ming 命	to confer on (especially in the classical Chinese sense)
minzhu 民主	democracy (literally, "people as the masters")
minzu zhuyi 民族主义	nationalism
neibu 内部	internal classification; off-limits to unauthorized persons
neiwai you bie 内外有别	to distinguish between insiders and outsiders
niangjia 娘家	a woman's natal family
nuli yishi 奴隶意识	slave mentality
nuxing 女性	woman (term associated with liberal discourse valuing the individual; as opposed to *funu*)
pai ma pi 拍马屁	"to pet the horse's ass"; to flatter and be obsequious
pidou hui 批斗会	struggle meeting (during which persons accused of wrongdoing are verbally and physically abused by the crowd)
pi fa jia 批发价	wholesale price
Pilin pikong 批林批孔	"Criticize Lin Biao, Criticize Confucius" campaign, 1973–76
piping yü ziwo piping 批评与自我批评	criticism of others and self-criticism (of political faults)
puo sijiu 破四旧	"smash the four olds" (destroy traditional ways)
qian renqing zhai 欠人情债	to owe a debt of human feeling
qing 情	affect; feeling; emotions
qingfen 情份	degree of affective feeling
qingke songli 请客送礼	to play host and give gifts
Qinshihuangdi 秦始皇帝	First Emperor of Qin
qiyejia 企业家	entrepreneur
qu 区	district; an administrative unit of municipal government
quanli 权利	rights; power
qunzhong 群众	the masses [note: the word *qun* has the character "sheep" in it]
qunzhong gongzuobu 群众工作部	Masses Affairs Department [of the Chinese Communist Party] (an office in charge of associations formed "among the masses")
ren 仁	humaneness; humanism (a Confucian virtue)
rendao zhuyi 人道主义	humanism; humaneness (modern term)
rende benzhi 人的本质	human essence
renge 人格	individuality; personality; character
renmin 人民	the people
renqing 人情	human feelings; human sentiments; personal tie of affect and obligation
renqing shili 人情势力	the power of human feelings
renqingwang 人情网	network of human feelings

renqingwei 人情味	flavor of human feelings
renqing zouyang 人情走样	distorted human feelings; corrupt form of renqing
Rujia 儒家	Confucianist school of philosophy (here used to refer to its pre-Qin version); "School of the Weak"
ruo min 弱民	to weaken the people (especially in Legalist thought)
sha 傻	foolish
shang xing 赏刑	rewards and punishments
shan nian 闪念	"flash of thought" (uncontrolled thoughts that must be disciplined and made revolutionary)
shehui benwei 社会本位	society-based [society]
shehui fengqi 社会风气	social climate
shehui yulun 社会舆论	social opinion; public opinion
shen 身	person; body; self
shen 神	spirits; deities; gods
sheng 省	province; an administrative unit
shengren 生人	stranger
shi 市	city; town; municipal government
shi chang jia 市场价	market price; retail price
shifu 师傅	master (term of address for factory workers in general or for a teacher of a skill who is senior in age
shihui 实惠	substantial; practical
shiji 实际	realistic; pragmatic
shili 失礼	to fail to observe proper etiquette and morality in a relationship
shili yan 势利眼	an eye for power; ability to gauge another person's social position
shiyong jiazhi 使用价值	use-value
shou hui 受贿	to accept a bribe
shouren 熟人	familiar person; person who can be counted on to help
shu 恕	mutuality (a Confucian virtue)
shu 术	statecraft; method of control and political power (a Legalist term)
shu 数	to count; numbers, statistics
shuangchong lingdao 双重领导	dual leadership
shufang li de hua 书房里的花	flower in the study
shuo hao hua 说好话	to say nice things
shuo jiahua 说假话	to utter falsehoods; to be insincere; to be deceptive
shuo renqinghua 说人情话	"to speak the language of human feelings"; to appeal to a sense of personal obligation and feeling

si 私	private; personal; selfish
siren guanxi 私人关系	personal or private relationship
siren quanzi 私人圈子	private circles (of friends)
sixiang gaizao 思想改造	thought reform; reconstruction of thought
sixin zanian 私心杂念	"selfish heart and distracting thoughts" (uncontrolled thoughts that must be made revolutionary)
songli feng 送礼风	"gift-giving wind"
song renqing 送人情	to give renqing or human feelings
songshang men 送上门	to give a present at a person's home
tequan 特权	special privileges; especially of officials
ti 體, 体	body; to embody
tianzi 天子	emperor; "Son of Heaven"
tiemian wusi 铁面无私	"steel the face and counter the private"; to steel oneself against personal requests
tongshi 同事	colleague; coworker
tongxiang 同乡	person of the same native place
tongxianghui 同乡会	native-place association
tongxue 同学	classmate; schoolmate
tuanti geju 团体格局	organizational mode of association
tuo renqing 托人情	to call on human feelings to get something done
waidiren 外地人	a person from out of town; a non-native
waifeng 歪风	"crooked wind"; deviant behavior
wang 网	a net; network
wei renminbi fuwu 为人民币服务	"Serve the people's currency" (a play on the expression "Serve the people" *wei renmin fuwu* 为人民服务)
wenlian 文联	Cultural Federation (a state organization for artists, writers, calligraphers, photographers, poets, etc. in cities
wu tuo bang 乌托邦	utopia
wuzhi liyi 物质利益	material benefit
xi 锡	to bestow (in its classical Chinese sense)
xian 县	county; an administrative unit first developed in Spring and Autumn period and Qin dynasty
xiang 乡	township; a rural administrative unit which used to be called a commune
xiang qian kan 向钱看	"Look toward money" (a play on the expression "Look toward the future" *xiang qian kan* 向前看)
xian4guan1 县官	a county official
xian4guan3 现管	to be directly in charge
xianzhang 宪章	group charter
xiao 孝	filial piety
xiaomie 消灭	to exterminate

xiao ren 小人	inferior person
xin 信	sincerity (a Confucian virtue)
xinde tihui 心得体会	insights gained and experienced
xinghui 行贿	to bribe
xing jiefan 性解放	sexual liberation
xingyong 信用	trust
xinyi 心意	"token of the heart"; expression of personal feeling
xitong 系统	a system; a vertical bureaucratic division with multiple hierarchical levels (e.g. textile industry system)
xiu 休	to be generous; generosity (in its classical Chinese sense)
xuetou 穴头	"cave head" (head organizer for a cultural performance put together through non-state channels)
xuetu 学徒	apprentice
xuexi xinde 学习心得	insights from study
xueyuan guanxi 血源关系	blood relationship; kinship
yamen 衙门	office of the county magistrate in late imperial times
yanjiu 研究	to study [homonym of "cigarettes and wine"]
yaomianzi 要面子	to want face
yeren 野人	wild people; rural folk; the common people without rank or office (here referring to its classical Chinese usage)
yewuyuan 业务员	sales agent
yi 義, 义	righteousness; obligation; duty (a Confucian virtue)
yiban pengyou 一般朋友	ordinary friend
yigu feijin. 以古非今.	"use the past to negate the present" (expression found in the *Historical Records*, an ancient book of history written by Si-ma Qian in the Han dynasty).
yi pian hong 一片红	"a sweep of red"; a revolutionary social climate
yiqi 义气	ethic of righteous brotherhood; close bonds of friendship
you 油	greasy, oily; devious, sly, cunning, guileful
you fu 有福	to have good fortune
you li jiu xiang. 有利就想.	"If there's profit to be gained, then I want it" (a play on the word "ideals" *lixiang* 理想).
you mudi 有目的	to have an ulterior motive
youqian jiutu 有钱就图	"If there is money in it, then go for it" (a play on the word "future" *qiantu* 前途).

you xia 游侠	knight-errant
yuanze 原则	correct principles of behavior; rules of proper (especially political) conduct
zaofan 造反	to make rebellion
zengjia mianzi 增加面子	to increase face
zhanyou 战友	comrade-in-arms
zhaogu 照顾	to take care to of; to look after
zhengfeng yundong 整风运动	rectification campaign (cleansing of cadre class ranks)
zheng mianzi 争面子	to contest face; to struggle for face
zhengmin 整民	to rectify the people; to put the people into order
zhengzhi guanxi 政治关系	political relationship
zhengzhi jiaohuan 政治交换	political exchange
zhengzhi juewu 政治觉悟	political consciousness
zhengzhi waiqu 政治歪曲	political distortion [of a relationship]
zhengzhiziben 政治资本	political capital
zhishi fenzi 知识份子	intellectual
zhixin pengyou 知心朋友	intimate friend
zhong 忠	loyalty (to the ruler; leader; or the country)
zhongjianren 中间人	an intermediary
zhongyang 中央	the center; central government in Beijing
zhongzi wu 忠字舞	loyalty dance (during Cultural Revolution)
zichan jieji geren zhuyi 资产阶级个人主义	bourgeois individualism
zifa 自发	to arise or develop spontaneously
ziwo 自我	the self (modern term)
ziwo jiazhi 自我价值	the value of the self; to be self-valuing
ziwo xiuyang 自我修养	self-cultivation
ziwo zhuyi 自我主义	individualism; principles of individuality
ziyou lianai 自由恋爱	"free love"
ziyou shichang 自由市场	free market; usually refers to private vegetable and meat markets
zizunxin 自尊心	self-respect
zongfa zhidu 宗法制度	clan system
zou houmen 走后门	to go through the back door; to use personal connections to get something done
zouxue 走穴	"to go underground" (to put on a cultural performance through non-state channels)
zu 祖	origin; ancestor
zuzhi 组织	organization; the institutional authority of work-unit leaders
zuzhike 组织科	organization department; a personnel office in charge of cadres in a work unit or in a party organization

Chinese and Japanese
Bibliography

Beijing Ribao (*BJRB*) 《北京日报》
>   Beijing Daily (Newspaper.)

Bo Yang 柏杨
>   1985   *Chou lou de zhongguoren* 《丑陋的中国人》 (The ugly Chinese.) Taibei: Lin Bai Chubanshe.

Chen Jinzhong 陈锦忠
>   1988   *Da yi tong zhengju de dianjizhe—Qin diguo de jianli yu tongzhi* 《大一统政局的奠基者——秦帝国的建立与统治》 (The foundation of the unified polity—The establishment and rule of the Qin empire). *Lishi* 《历史》 (History), no. 5 (June).

Cheng Shi, ed. 橙实
>   1988   *Wenge Xiaoliao Ji* 《文革笑料集》 (Collection of laughing materials from the Cultural Revolution). Chengdu: Xinan Caijing Daxue Chubanshe.

Dai Houying 戴厚英
>   1985   *Ren a, ren!* 《人啊, 人!》 (Humanity, oh humanity!). Hong Kong: Xianggang chuban gongsi. (1980.)

Ding Xuelian 丁学良
>   1983   *Qieshi gaige: suqing fengjian zhuyi canyu yingxiang* 《切实改革: 肃清封建主义残余影响》 (Earnestly reform: Clean up the influence of the remnants of feudalism). *Xinhua Wenzhai* (New China Digest), October.

"Dousi pixiou" shi wuchan jieji wenhua da geming de gengben fangzheng 《「斗私批修」是无产阶级文化大革命的根本方针》
>   1967   "Struggling against the private and selfish and criticizing revisionism" is the great proletarian Cultural Revolution's fundamental direction. Beijing: Renmin Chubanshe.

Fei Xiaotong 费孝通
>   1983   *Xiangtu Zhongguo* 《乡土中国》 (Folk China). Mimeograph copy

by Beijing University Sociology Department Study Group. Originally published in China by Guan Cha Society. (1949.)

Fengci yu youmuo (FCYYM) 《 讽刺与幽默 》
Satire and Humor. Beijing. (Weekly cartoon periodical.)

Gongren ribao (GRRB) 《 工人日报 》
Worker's Daily. Beijing. (Newspaper.)

Gu Cheng 顾城
1985   *Qing ting women de shengying* 《 请听我们的声音 》 (Please listen to our voices). In *Qingnian shiren tan shi* 《 青年诗人谈诗 》 (Young poets discussing poetry), ed. Lao Mu. Beijing: Beijing daxue wusi wenxue she.

Han Feizi xiaozhu 《 韩非子校注 》
1982   The annotated *Han Feizi*. *Han Feizi* xiaozhuzu 《 韩非子 》校注组 (Annotating Group for the *Han Feizi*). Nanjing: Jiangsu Renmin chubanshe.

He Bingdi (Ho Ping-ti) 何炳棣
1992   *Yuan Li* 《 原礼 》 (The origin of rites). *Ershiyi Shiji* 《 二十一世纪 》 (Twenty-first century), no. 11 (June).

Hong Shidi 洪世涤
1972   *Qinshihuang* 《 秦始皇 》 (Qinshihuang). Shanghai: Shanghai renmin chubanshe.

Hongweibing Ziliao 《 红卫兵资料 》
1975   Red Guard Publications. Reprinted by the Center for Chinese Research Materials, Association of Research Libraries, vols. 1–20.

Hu Ping 胡平
1990   *Zai lixiang yu xianshi zhijian: du Muo Yingfeng "Taoyuan Meng"* 《 在理想与现实之间: 读莫应丰「桃源梦」》 (Between idealism and reality: On reading Muo Yingfeng's "The Dream of the Land of Peach Blossoms"). In *Zai lixiang yu xianshi zhijian* 《 在理想与现实之间 》 (Between idealism and reality), 1–29. Hong Kong: Tian Yuan Shu Shi.

Jin Yaoji 金耀基 [King, Ambrose]
1982   *Lun renqing* 《 论人情 》 (On renqing). *Ming Bao* 《 明报 》 17, no. 8: 69–76.

Jiushi Niandai (JSND) 《 九十年代 》
The Nineties. Hong Kong. (News magazine.)

Lei Feng 雷锋
1968   *Lei Feng Riji* 《 雷锋日记 》 (Diary of Lei Feng). Edited by the Memorial to Lei Feng, Chairman Mao's Good Soldier. (1963.)

Lei Jiaji 雷家骥
1988   *Luelun Zhongguo fenhe de kejiu* 《 略论中国分合的窠臼 》 (A brief discussion of the pattern of division and unification in Chinese history). *Lishi* 《 历史 》 (History), no. 5 (June).

Li Anzhai 李安宅
1931   *"Yili" yü "Liji" zhi shehuixue de yanjiu* 《「仪礼」与「礼记」之社会学的研究 》 (The sociological study of the *Yili* and the *Li Ji*). Shanghai: Shangwu Yinshuguan.

Li Ji Jinzhu Jinyi 《礼记今注今译》
    1987   *The Book of Ritual, with Contemporary Annotation and Translation.* Translated by Wang Mengou 王梦鸥注译 Taibei: Taiwan Shangwu yinshuguan.

Li Yanong 李亚农
    1962   *Zhouzu de shizuzhi yu tobazu de qian fengjianzhi* 《周族的氏族制与拓跋族的前封建制》 (The clan system of the Zhou people and the prefeudal system of the Toba people). In *Xinran zhai shi lunji* 《欣然斋史论集》. Shanghai: Renmin chubanshe.

Li Zehou 李泽厚
    1980   *Kongzi zai pinglun* 《孔子再评论》 (A reevaluation of Confucius). *Zhongguo shehui kexue* 《中国社会科学》 (Chinese Social Science), no. 2: 77–96.
    1985   *Zhongguo gudai sixiangshi lun* 《中国古代思想史论》 (On the history of ancient Chinese thought). Beijing: Renmin Chubanshe.
    1987   *Qimeng yu jiuwang de shuangchong bianzou—wusi huixiang zhiyi* 《启蒙与救亡的双重变奏——五四回想之一》 (Enlightenment and salvation's contrapuntal variations: Reminiscences of the May Fourth movement). In *Zou wo ziji de lu* 《走我自己的路》 (Walking down my own path). Taibei: Gufeng Chubanshe.

Li Zongwu 李宗吾
    1990   *Houheixue* 《厚黑学》 (Thick and black learning). Beijing: Qiushi Chubanshe. (1934.)

Liang Shuming 梁漱溟
    1949   *Zhongguo wenhua yaoyi* 《中国文化要义》 (Essential meanings of Chinese culture). Chengdu: Lu Ming Shudian.

Liang Xiao 梁效
    1974   *Lun Shang Yang* 《论商鞅》 (On Shang Yang). *Hongqi* 《红旗》 (Red Flag), no. 6: 22–29.

Liu Shaoqi 刘少奇
    1981   *Lun gongchandang yuan de xiuyang* 《论共产党员的修养》 (On the cultivation of a Communist Party member). In *Liu Shaoqi xuanji* 《刘少奇选集》 (Selected works of Liu Shaoqi), vol. 1. Beijing: Renmin chubanshe.

Luo Changxiu 罗昌秀
    1966   *Mao zhuxi, nin shi women xinzhong de hongtaiyang* 《毛主席,您是我们心中的红太阳》 ("Chairman Mao, you are the Red Sun within our hearts"). *Hongqi* 《红旗》 (Red Flag), no. 13.

Ma Yinchu 马寅初
    1979   *Xin renkoulun* 《新人口论》 (A new essay on the principle of population). Beijing: Renmin chubanshe.

Mao Zedong 毛泽东
    1969   *Zai bada erci huiyi shang de jianghua* 《在八大二次会议上的讲话》 (Minutes of the meeting of the second plenum of the Eighth Central Committee). In *Mao Zedong sixiang wansui!* 《毛泽东思想万岁》 (Long live Mao Zedong thought!). Taipei: Institute of International Studies reprint.

Morohashi Tetsuji 诸桥辙次
 1955–60   *Dai kan-wa jiten* 《大汉和辞典》. Tokyo: Taishukan Shoten.
Ning Dong 宁东
 1988   *Yige liangci lihun de nuren* 《一个两次离婚的女人》. (A twice-divorced woman). *Shehui* 《社会》(Society), no. 1.
 1989   *Meiyou juexing de nüxing* 《没有觉醒的女性》(A woman who has not awakened). *Shehui* 《社会》(Society), no. 1.
Pan Suiming 潘绥铭
 1987   *Nüxing xing quanli de lishi mingyun* 《女性性权利的历史命运》(The historical fate of women's sexual rights). *Zhongguo Funu* 《中国妇女》(Chinese Women), no. 12.
Ping 'sirenbang' de piru pingfa 《评「四人邦」的批儒评法》
 1977   Evaluating the "Gang of Four's" criticism of Confucianism and appraisal of Legalism. Guangzhou: Guangdong renmin chubanshe.
Qiao Jian (Chiao Chien) 乔健
 1982   *Guanxichuyi* 《关系刍议》(My humble views on guanxi). In *Shehui ji xingwei kexue yanjiu de zhongguohua* 《社会既行为科学研究的中国化》(The Sinicization of Social and Behavioral Science Research), ed. Yang Guoshu and Wen Congyi 杨国枢, 文崇一. Taibei: Institute of Ethnology, Academia Sinica.
 1988   *Zhongguo wenhua zhong de jice wenti chutan* 《中国文化中的计策问题初谈》(A preliminary examination of the problem of strategies in Chinese culture). In *Zhongguoren de xinli* 《中国人的心理》(The psychology of the Chinese people), ed. Yang Guoshu 杨国枢. Taipei: Guiguan Tushu Gongsi.
Quan Weitian 全慰天
 1949   *Lun "jia tianxia"* 《论「家天下」》(On "families under Heaven") In *Huang Quan yu Shen Quan* 《皇权与绅权》(The power of emperor and gentry), ed. Wu Han 吴晗 and Fei Xiaotong 费孝通 et al. Hong Kong: Xuefeng Chubanshe. (Originally published in China by Guan Cha Society.)
Renmin Ribao (RMRB) 《人民日报》
    People's Daily. Beijing. (Newspaper.)
Shang Jun Shu 《商君书》
 1988   The book of Lord Shang. Edited by Huo Lingxu 贺凌虚编. Taibei: Taiwan Shangwu Yinshuguan.
Shi Gao et al.
 1977   *Ping 'sirenbang' de piru pingfa* 《评四人邦的批儒评法》(Assessing the 'Gang of Four's' Criticism of Confucianism and Appraisal of Legalism). Guangdong: Renmin Chubanshe.
Shijie Ribao (SJRB) 《世界日报》
    World Daily. Los Angeles. (Newspaper.)
Shi Jing 《诗经》
 1980   The book of songs. Edited by Gao Heng 高享编. Shanghai: Guji chubanshe.

Shi Lun 石仑
1973   *Lun zunru fanfa* 《论尊儒反法》 (On respecting Confucianism and opposing legalism). *Hongqi* 《红旗》 (Red Flag), no. 10: 33–43.

Shu Xincheng et al., eds. 舒新城等编
1947   *Ci Hai* 《辞海》 (Sea of words). Hong Kong: Zhonghua Shuju.

Si-Ma Qian 司马迁
1972   *Shi Ji* 《史记》 (Historical records [of the Han Dynasty]), vols. 1–10, *juan* 1–30. Beijing: Zhonghua Shuju.

Sun Longji 孙隆基
1983   *Zhongguo Wenhua de "Shenceng Jiegou"* 《中国文化的深层结构》. (The "deep structure" of Chinese culture). Hong Kong: Taishan Publishing.

Wang Ruoshui 王若水
1983   *Wei rendao zhuyi bianhu* 《为人道主义辨护》 (In defense of humanism). *Wenhui Bao* 《文汇报》, 17 January: 3.
1984   *Tantan yihua wenti* 《谈谈异化问题》 (Discussion of the problem of alienation). *Zhongguo zhi chun* 《中国之春》, (China Spring), no. 9 (January).
1988   *Lun ren de benzhi he shehui guanxi* 《论人的本质和社会关系》 (On human essence and social relations). *Ming bao yuekan* 《明报月刊》, no. 12.

Wang Shaoguang 王绍光
1991   *Guanyu 'shimin shehui' de jidian sikao* 《关于「市民社会」的几点思考》 (Thoughts on "civil society"). *Ershiyi shiji* 《二十一世纪》 (Twenty-first Century), no. 8: 102–14.

Wei Shouxian 魏守先
1981   *Zenyang yifen wei er kan "guanxixue"* 《怎样一分为二看「关系学」》 (How to look at "guanxixue" with a dual attitude). *Gongren ribao* 《工人日报》 (Worker's Daily), 29 January: 3.

Wei Yaping 魏亚平
1981   *Dui "guanxixue" buneng yifen wei er* 《对「关系学」不能一分为二》 (We cannot have a dual attitude toward "guanxixue"). *Gongren ribao* 《工人日报》 (Worker's Daily), 29 January: 3.

Wen Congyi 文崇一
1982   *Bao-en yu fuchou: jiaohuan xingwei de fenxi* 《报恩与复仇: 交换行为的分析》 (Repaying kindness and revenge: An analysis of exchange behavior). In *Shehui ji xingwei kexue yanjiu de zhongguohua* 《社会既行为科学研究的中国化》 (The sinicization of social and behavioral science research), ed. Yang Guoshu and Wen Congyi 杨国枢, 文崇一. Taibei: Institute of Ethnology, Academia Sinica.

Wenhui Bao (WHB) 《文汇报》
Cultural Reports. Shanghai. (Newspaper.)

Wu Xiaoming 伍晓明 (Shang Duo 尚多)
1992   *Wangxiang, zilian, youyu yu xianshen: ershi shiji zhongguoren ziwo de dansheng yu siwang* 《妄想, 自恋, 忧虑与献身: 二十世纪中国人自我的诞生与死亡》(Paranoia, narcissism, melancholia, and

self-sacrifice: The birth and death of the Chinese self in the twentieth century). *Jintian* 《今天》 (Today), no. 4: 171–90.

Xu Ping 许平
  1990   *Kuizeng Lisu* 《馈赠礼俗》 (The rituals and customs of gift-giving). Beijing: Zhongguo Huaqiao chuban gongsi.

Xu Shen 许慎
  1959   *Shuowen Jiezi* 《说文解字》 (Explanation of words and characters [in the Former Han dynasty]). Facsimile reprint of Song dynasty edition. Taibei: Si Ku Shanben Congshu.

Xunzi Jinzhu jinyi 《荀子今注今泽》
  1975   Translated and annotated by Xiong Gongzhe 熊公哲. Taibei: Shangwu yinshuguan.

Yang Rongguo 杨荣国
  1972   *Chunqiu zhanguo shiqi sixiang lingyu nei liang tiao luxian de douzheng* 《春秋战国时期思想领域内两条路线的斗争》 (The struggle between two lines in the ideological sphere during the Spring and Autumn and Warring States periods). *Hongqi* 《红旗》 (Red Flag), no. 12 (December): 45–54.
  1973   *Kongzi—wangudi weihu nulizhi de sixiangjia* 《孔子——顽固地维护奴隶制的思想家》 (Confucius—a thinker who obstinately upheld the slave system). *Renmin Ribao* 《人民日报》 (People's Daily) 7 August: 2.

Yang Weihong 杨卫红
  1970   *Yang Weihong Riji* 《杨卫红日记》 (Diary of Yang Weihong, 1969–70). Manuscript, Stockholm University library, Sweden.

Yu Yingjie 余英杰
  1987   *Shilun guanxiwang* 《试论关系网》 (An exploration of the guanxi network). *Renmin daxue shubao ziliao zhongxin* 《人民大学书报资料中心》 (People's University Books and Periodicals Resource Center), January, C–4: 103–7. Originally published in *Shehuixue* 《社会学》 (Sociology).

Yuan Zhongren 原中人
  1981   *Tan "guanxixue" de shehui gengyuan* 《谈「关系学」的社会根源》 (A discussion of the social roots of "Guanxixue"). *Gongren Ribao* 《工人日报》 (Worker's Daily), 29 January: 3.

Zhang Yini 张恰妮
  1989   *Zisha, yige bei jihui de shehui wenti* 《自杀, 一个被忌讳的社会问题》 (Suicide, a tabooed social problem). *Shehui* 《社会》 (Society), no. 3.

Zhang Zhemin, et al. 张哲民 (与其他)
  1981   *Weida lingxiu Maozhuxi, caimao zhigong yongyuan huainian nin* 《伟大领袖毛主席，财贸职工永远怀念您》 (Our great leader Chairman Mao, the workers and staff of the finance department will always think of you). Beijing: Zhongguo Caizheng Jingji Chubanshe.

Zhao Ziyang 赵紫阳
  1981   *Dangdai de jingji xingshi he jinhou jingji jianshe de fangzhen.*

《当代的经济形势和今后经济建设的方向》(The present economic situation and the direction of future economic construction). In the *Government Report at the Fifth Conference of the People's Congress.* Beijing: Renmin Chubanshe.

Zheng Yefu 郑也夫
1984   *Shilun guanxixue*《试论关系学》(An exploration of guanxixue). *Shehuixue yu shehui diaocha*《社会学与社会调查》(Sociology and Social Investigation), no. 2–3. (For a partial English translation, see *The Chinese*, ed. Martin K. Whyte et al. Ann Arbor: University of Michigan, Center for Chinese Studies.)

Zhong Shi 钟实
1982   *Yiyuan buzhen zhi feng de qingkuan diaocha*《医院不正之风的情况调查》(Investigation of deviant winds in hospitals). *Shehui*《社会》(Society), no. 3..

Zhongguo Funu Ribao (ZGFNRB)《中国妇女报》
Chinese Women's Daily. Beijing. (Newspaper.)

Zhongguo gongchandang zhongyang junshi weiyuanhui《中国共产党中央军事委员会》(Chinese Communist Party Cental Military Commission)
1968   *Xiangjiang Liehuo*《湘江烈火》(Raging fire on the Xiang river). Decision of the Chinese Communist Party Central Military Commission Expanded Meeting Concerning the Strengthening of Soldiers' Political Thought.

Zhongguo Qingnian Bao (ZGQNB)《中国青年报》
China Youth Daily. Beijing. (Newspaper.)

Zhongguo shehui kexueyuan yuyan yanjiusuo cidian bianjishi《中国社会科学院语言研究所辞典编辑室》(Chinese Academy of Social Science, Institute of Language, Dictionary Editing Office).
1982   *Xiandai hanyu cidian*《现代汉语辞典》(Modern Chinese dictionary). Beijing: Shangwu Chubanshe.

Zhongwen Da Cidian《中文大辞典》
1967   *Encyclopedic dictionary of the Chinese language.* Taibei: Zhongguo Wenhua Yanjiusuo.

Zuo Zhuan《左传》
1814   *Commentary on the Spring and Autumn annals.* In *Shisan Jing Zhushu*《十三经注疏》(The annotated Thirteen Classics). Nanchang.

English Bibliography

Abraham, Nicolas, and Maria Torok

    1980   "Introjection—Incorporation: Mourning or Melancholia." In *Psychoanalysis in France*, ed. Serge Lebovici and Daniel Widlocher, 3–17. New York: International Universities Press.

Adorno, Theodor W.

    1982   "Freudian Theory and the Pattern of Fascist Propaganda." In *The Essential Frankfurt School Reader*, ed. Andrew Arato and Eike Gebhardt, 118–37. New York: Continuum.

Ahern, Emily

    1973   *The Cult of the Dead in a Chinese Village*. Stanford: Stanford University Press.

    1981   *Chinese Ritual and Politics*. Cambridge: Cambridge University Press.

Althusser, Louis

    1971   "Ideology and Ideological State Apparatuses." In *Lenin and Philosophy: Notes Towards an Investigation*, trans. Ben Brewster, 123–73. London: New Left Books.

Ames, Roger T.

    1984   "The Meaning of Body in Classical Chinese Thought." *International Philosophical Quarterly* 24, no. 1: 39–53.

Anagnost, Ann

    1985   "The Beginning and End of an Emperor: A Counter-Representation of the State." *Modern China* 11, no. 2: 147–76.

    1992   "Constructions of Civility in the Age of Flexible Accumulation." Paper presented at the meeting of the American Anthropological Association, San Francisco.

Appadurai, Arjun

    1990   "Disjuncture and Difference in the Global Cultural Economy." *Public Culture* 2, no. 2: 1–24.

Arato, Andrew

    1981   "Civil Society against the State: Poland 1980–81." *Telos*, no. 47.

Baker, Hugh
   1979   *Chinese Family and Kinship*. New York: Columbia University Press.
Bakhtin, Mikhail
   1981   "Discourse in the Novel." In *The Dialogic Imagination*, ed. Michael
          Holquist. Austin: University of Texas Press. (1953.)
Barlow, Tani E.
   1989   "Introduction." In *I Myself Am a Woman: Selected Writings of Ding
          Ling*, ed. Tani Barlow and Gary Bjorge. Boston: Beacon Press.
   1991   "Theorizing Woman: *Funu, Guojia, Jiating.*" *Genders* 10 (Spring):
          132–60.
   1994   "Politics and Protocols of *Funu*: Re-Making the National Woman." In
          Body, Subject, and Power in China, ed. Angela Zito and Tani Barlow.
          Chicago: University of Chicago Press.
Befu, Harumi
   1967   "Gift-Giving and Social Reciprocity in Japan." *France-Asie/Asia* 21, no.
          188.
Benjamin, Walter
   1969a "Theses on the Philosophy of History." In *Illuminations*, trans. Harry
          Zohn. New York: Schocken Books.
   1969b "The Work of Art in the Age of Mechanical Reproduction." In *Illu-
          minations*, trans. Harry Zohn. New York: Schocken Books.
Berliner, Joseph S.
   1957   *Factory and Manager in the U.S.S.R.* Cambridge: Harvard University
          Press.
Berman, Marshall
   1982   *All That Is Solid Melts into Air: The Experience of Modernity*. New
          York: Penguin.
Bernstein, Thomas
   1977   *Up to the Mountains and Down to the Villages: The Transfer of Youth
          from Urban to Rural China*. New Haven: Yale University Press.
Billeter, Jean-François
   1985   "The System of 'Class Status,'" In *The Scope of State Power in China*,
          ed. Stuart R. Schram. London: School of Oriental and African Studies.
Bodde, Derk
   1956   "Feudalism in China." In *Feudalism in History*, ed. R. Coulborn. Ham-
          den, Conn.: Archon Press.
   1967   *China's First Unifier: A Study of the Ch'in Dynasty as Seen in the Life
          of Li Ssu*. Hong Kong: Hong Kong University Press.
   1981   "Basic Concepts of Chinese Law." In *Essays on Chinese Civilization*.
          Princeton: Princeton University Press.
Bogue, Ronald
   1989   *Deleuze and Guattari*. New York: Routledge.
Boissevain, Jeremy
   1968   "The Place of Non-Groups in the Social Sciences." *Man* 3, no. 4.
   1974   *Friends of Friends: Networks, Manipulators and Coalitions*. Oxford:
          Basil Blackwell.

Bott, Elizabeth
  1957 *Family and Social Network*. London: Tavistock.
Bourdieu, Pierre
  1977 *Outline of a Theory of Practice*. Translated by Richard Nice. Cambridge: Cambridge University Press.
Brødsgaard, Kjeld Erik
  1992 "Civil Society and Democratization in China." In *From Leninism to Freedom: The Challenge of Democratization*. Boulder, Colo.: Westview.
Burgess, J. S.
  1928 *The Guilds of Beijing*. Ph.D. diss., Columbia University, New York.
Chan, Anita, and Jonathan Unger
  1982 "Grey and Black: The Hidden Economy of Rural China." *Pacific Affairs* 55 (Fall).
Chan, Anita, Richard Madsen, and Jonathan Unger
  1984 *Chen Village*. Berkeley and Los Angeles: University of California Press.
Chan Wing-tsit, ed.
  1963 *A Source Book in Chinese Philosophy*. Princeton: Princeton University Press.
Chang Kwang-Chih
  1980 "The Chinese Bronze Age: A Modern Synthesis." In *The Great Bronze Age of China*, ed. Wen Fong. New York: Alfred A. Knopf and the Metropolitan Museum of Art.
  1983 *Art, Myth, and Ritual: The Path to Political Authority in Ancient China*. Cambridge: Harvard University Press.
  1986 *The Archaeology of Ancient China*. 4th ed. New Haven: Yale University Press.
China News Analysis (CNA)
       Hong Kong. (News reports.)
Chodorow, Nancy.
  1974 "Family Structure and Feminine Personality." In *Woman, Culture, and Society*. Stanford: Stanford University Press.
  1978 *The Reproduction of Mothering*. Berkeley: University of California Press.
Chow Tse-tsung
  1960 *The May Fourth Movement: Intellectual Revolution in Modern China*. Cambridge: Harvard University Press.
Ch'u Tung-tsu
  1972 *Han Social Structure*. Seattle: University of Washington Press.
Clastres, Pierre
  1987 *Society Against the State*. Translated by Robert Hurley. Cambridge: Zone Books.
Clifford, James
  1988a "Introduction: The Pure Products Go Crazy." In *The Predicament of Culture: Twentieth-Century Ethnography, Literature, and Art*. Cambridge: Harvard University Press.

1988b "On Ethnographic Authority." In *The Predicament of Culture: Twentieth-Century Ethnography, Literature, and Art.* Cambridge: Harvard University Press.

1988c "On Orientalism." In *The Predicament of Culture: Twentieth-Century Ethnography, Literature, and Art.* Cambridge: Harvard University Press.

1990 "Notes on (Field)notes." In *Fieldnotes: The Makings of Anthropology,* ed. Roger Sanjek. Ithaca: Cornell University Press.

1992 "Traveling Cultures." In *Cultural Studies,* ed. Lawrence Grossberg, Cary Nelson, and Paula Treichler. New York: Routledge.

Clifford, James, and George E. Marcus, eds.

1986 *Writing Culture: The Poetics and Politics of Ethnography.* Berkeley and Los Angeles: University of California Press.

Cohen, Myron

1976 *House United, House Divided: The Chinese Family in Taiwan.* New York: Columbia University Press.

Cooper, Eugene

1982 "The Potlatch in Ancient China: Parallels in the Sociopolitical Structure of the Ancient Chinese and the American Indians of the Northwest Coast." *History of Religions* 22 (November): 103–28.

Creel, Herrlee G.

1964 "The Beginnings of Bureaucracy in China: The Origin of the *Hsien.*" *Journal of Asian Studies* 23, no. 2.

1970 *The Origins of Statecraft in China: The Western Chou Empire.* Chicago: University of Chicago Press.

Crissman, Lawrence

1967 "The Segmentary Structure of Urban Overseas Chinese Communities." *Man* 2, no. 2.

Dean, Kenneth, and Brian Massumi

1992 *First and Last Emperors: The Absolute State and the Body of the Despot.* Brooklyn: Autonomedia.

de Certeau, Michel

1984 *The Practice of Everyday Life.* Translated by Steven F. Rendall. Berkeley and Los Angeles: University of California Press.

1986 *Heterologies: Discourse on the Other.* Translated by Brian Massumi. Minneapolis: University of Minnesota Press.

de Lauretis, Teresa

1987 "The Technology of Gender." In *Technologies of Gender: Essays on Theory, Film, and Fiction,* 1–30. Bloomington: Indiana University Press.

Deleuze, Gilles

1983 *Nietzsche and Philosophy.* Translated by Hugh Tomlinson. New York: Columbia University Press.

Deleuze, Gilles, and Felix Guattari

1983 *Anti-Oedipus: Capitalism and Schizophrenia.* Translated by Robert Hurley. Minneapolis: University of Minnesota Press.

1987   *A Thousand Plateaus: Capitalism and Schizophrenia*. Translated by Brian Massumi. Minneapolis: University of Minnesota Press.

Dreyfus, Hubert L., and Paul Rabinow

1983   *Michel Foucault: Beyond Structuralism and Hermeneutics*. 2d ed. Chicago: University of Chicago Press.

Duara, Prasenjit

1987   "State Involution: A Study of Local Finances in North China, 1911–1935." *Comparative Studies in Society & History* 29, no. 1.

1988a   *Culture, Power and the State: Rural North China, 1900–1942*. Stanford: Stanford University Press.

1988b   "Superscribing Symbols: The Myth of Guandi, Chinese God of War." *Journal of Asian Studies* 47, no. 4: 778–95.

1991   "Knowledge and Power in the Discourse of Modernity: The Campaigns against Popular Religion in Early Twentieth-Century China." *Journal of Asian Studies* 50 (February).

1992a   "Rescuing History from the Nation-State." *Working Papers and Proceedings of the Center for Psychosocial Studies*, no. 48.

1992b   "State and Civil Society in the History of Chinese Modernity." Paper presented at the conference "China's Quest for Modernization: A Historical Approach," Fudan University, Shanghai.

1993   "Provincial Narratives of the Nation: Centralism and Federalism in Republican China." In *Cultural Nationalism in East Asia*, ed. Harumi Befu. Berkeley: Institute of East Asian Studies, University of California at Berkeley.

Dubs, H. H., trans.

1928   *The Works of Hsuntze*. London: Probsthain.

Duke, Michael S.

1985   *Blooming and Contending: Chinese Literature in the Post-Mao Era*. Bloomington: Indiana University Press.

Dumont, Louis

1970   *Homo Hierarchicus*. Chicago: University of Chicago Press.

Durkheim, Emile

1961   *The Elementary Forms of Religious Life*. Joseph Swain, trans. New York: Collier Books (1915).

Duyvendak, J.J.L., trans.

1928   *The Book of Lord Shang*. Chicago: University of Chicago Press. *See Shang Jun Shu* 1988.

Eames, Elizabeth

1992   "Navigating Nigerian Bureaucracy, or, 'Why Can't You Beg?' She Demanded." In *The Naked Anthropologist*, ed. P. R. DeVita. New York: Wadsworth.

Elvin, Mark

1985   "Between the Earth and Heaven: Conceptions of the Self in China." In *The Category of the Person*, ed. M. Carrithers, S. Collins, and S. Lukes. Cambridge: Cambridge University Press.

Eno, Robert
   1990   *The Confucian Creation of Heaven: Philosophy and the Defense of Ritual Mastering.* Albany: State University of New York Press.
Falasca-Zamponi, Simonetta
   1992   *The Aestheticization of Politics: A Study of Power in Mussolini's Fascist Italy.* Ph.D. diss., University of California at Berkeley.
Feher, Ferenc, Agnes Heller, and Gyorgy Markus
   1983   *Dictatorship over Needs: An Analysis of Soviet Societies.* Oxford: Basil Blackwell.
Fehl, Noah Edward
   1971   *Li, Rites and Propriety in Literature and Life: A Perspective for a Cultural History of Ancient China.* Hong Kong: Chinese University of Hong Kong.
Fei Hsiao-t'ung (Fei Xiaotong)
   1968   "Peasantry and Gentry: An Interpretation of Chinese Social Structure and Its Changes." In *State and Society*, ed. Reinhard Bendix et al. Berkeley and Los Angeles: University of California Press.
Fei Xiaotong
   1992   *From the Soil: The Foundations of Chinese Society (Xiangtu Zhongguo).* Translated by Gary Hamilton and Wang Zheng. Berkeley and Los Angeles: University of California Press. *See* Fei 1983.
Fingarette, Herbert
   1972   *Confucius—The Secular as Sacred.* New York: Harper & Row.
Folsom, Kenneth E.
   1968   *Friends, Guests, and Colleagues: The Mu-fu System in the Late Ch'ing Period.* Berkeley and Los Angeles: University of California Press.
Fortes, Meyer
   1949   *The Web of Kinship Among the Tallensi.* Oxford: Oxford University Press.
   1969a "The Kinship Polity." In *Kinship and the Social Order.* Chicago: Aldine.
   1969b "Kinship and the Axiom of Amity." In *Kinship and the Social Order.* Chicago: Aldine.
Foucault, Michel
   1973   *Madness and Civilization.* New York: Vintage Books.
   1979a "Governmentality." *Ideology and Consciousness*, no. 6 (Autumn).
   1979b *Discipline and Punish: The Birth of the Prison.* Translated by Alan Sheridan. New York: Vintage.
   1980   *The History of Sexuality*, vol. 1. Translated by Robert Hurley. New York: Random House.
   1983   "The Subject and Power." In *Michel Foucault: Beyond Structuralism and Hermeneutics*, by H. Dreyfus and P. Rabinow, 2d ed. Chicago: University of Chicago Press.
   1984   "Nietzsche, Genealogy, History." In *The Foucault Reader*, ed. Paul Rabinow. New York: Pantheon.
Freud, Sigmund
   1951   *Group Psychology and the Analysis of the Ego.* Translated by James Strachey. New York: Liveright. (1921.)

1960 *Jokes and their Relationship to the Unconscious.* Translated by James Strachey. New York: W. W. Norton. (1916.)

1973 "Mourning and Melancholia." In *The Standard Edition of the Complete Psychological Works of Sigmund Freud,* vol. 14. London: Hogarth Press. (1917.)

1989 "On Narcissism: An Introduction." In *The Freud Reader,* ed. Peter Gay. New York: W. W. Norton. (1914.)

Fried, Morton

1953 *The Fabric of Chinese Society.* New York: Praeger.

1983 "Tribe to State or State to Tribe in Ancient China?" In *Origins of Chinese Civilization,* 467–93. Berkeley and Los Angeles: University of California Press.

Frolic, B. Michael

1980 *Mao's People.* Cambridge: Harvard University Press.

Fujitani, Takashi

1993 "Inventing, Forgetting, Remembering: Toward a Historical Ethnography of the Nation-State." In *Cultural Nationalism in East Asia,* ed. Harumi Befu. Berkeley: Institute of East Asian Studies, University of California at Berkeley.

1994 "Crowds and Imperial Pageantry in Modern Japan: Some Thoughts on Visual Domination." In *Problems in Modernity and Japan's Emperor Systems,* ed. Takashi Fujitani and Naoki Sakai. Armonk, N.Y.: M. E. Sharpe.

Galasi, Peter

1985 "Peculiarities and Limits of the Second Economy in Socialism (The Hungarian Case)." In *The Economics of the Shadow Economy,* ed. W. Gaertner and A. Wenig. Berlin: Springer Verlag.

Gao Yuan

1987 *Born Red: A Chronicle of the Cultural Revolution.* Stanford University Press.

Geertz, Clifford

1973a "Thick Description: Toward an Interpretive Theory of Culture." In *The Interpretation of Cultures.* New York: Basic Books.

1973b "Person, Time, and Conduct in Bali." In *The Interpretation of Cultures.* New York: Basic Books.

1977 "Centers, Kings, and Charisma: Reflections on the Symbolics of Power." In *Culture and Its Creators: Essays in Honor of Edward Shils,* ed. Joseph Ben-David and Terry Nichols Clark. Chicago: University of Chicago Press.

1980 *Negara: The Theatre State in Nineteenth-Century Bali.* Princeton: Princeton University Press.

1984 "From the Native's Point of View: On the Nature of Anthropological Understanding." In *Culture Theory: Essays on Mind, Self and Emotion,* ed. Richard Shweder and Robert Levine. Cambridge: Cambridge University Press.

Gernet, Jacques
  1985   *A History of Chinese Civilization.* Translated by J. R. Foster. Cambridge: Cambridge University Press.
Giddens, Anthony
  1990   *The Consequences of Modernity.* Stanford: Stanford University Press.
  1991   *Modernity and Self-Identity: Self and Society in the Late Modern Age.* Cambridge: Polity Press.
Gilligan, Carol
  1982   *In a Different Voice: Psychological Theory and Women's Development.* Cambridge: Harvard University Press.
Gladney, Dru
  1991   *Muslim Chinese: Ethnic Nationalism in the People's Republic.* Cambridge: Harvard East Asian Monographs, 149.
Gluckman, Max
  1965   *Politics, Law and Ritual in Tribal Society.* Oxford: Blackwell.
  1965b "Stateless Societies and the Maintenance of Order." In *Politics, Law, and Ritual in Tribal Society.* Oxford: Basil Blackwell.
Gold, Thomas
  1985   "After Comradeship: Personal Relations in China since the Cultural Revolution." *The China Quarterly* 104 (December): 657–75.
  1989   "Urban Private Business in China." *Studies in Comparative Communism* 22, no. 2–3: 187–201.
Goodman, Bryna
  1990   "Urban Identity and the Question of a Public Sphere in Chinese Cities: Regional Associations in Shanghai." Paper prepared for the Center for Chinese Studies Regional Seminar, University of California at Berkeley.
Graham, A. C.
  1989   *Disputers of the Tao: Philosophical Argument in Ancient China.* LaSalle, Ill.: Open Court.
Gregory, C. A.
  1982   *Gifts and Commodities.* London: Academic Press.
Grossman, Gregory
  1977   "The 'Second Economy' of the USSR." In *Problems of Communism* 26: 5.
  1982   "The 'Shadow Economy' in the Socialist Sector of the USSR." In *The CMEA Five-Year Plans (1981–85) in a New Perspective.* Brussels: NATO Economics and Information Directorates.
Habermas, Jürgen
  1987   "Modernity's Consciousness of Time and Its Need for Self-Reassurance." In *The Philosophical Discourse of Modernity*, trans. Frederick Lawrence. Cambridge: M.I.T. Press.
  1989   *The Structural Transformation of the Public Sphere: An Inquiry into a Category of Bourgeois Society.* Translated by Thomas Burger. Cambridge: M.I.T. Press.
Hamilton, Gary
  1984   "Patriarchalism in Imperial China and Western Europe." *Theory and Society* 13, no. 3: 393–425.

1992   "Overseas Chinese Capitalism." Paper prepared for the Program in East Asian Business and Development Working Paper Series, Institute of Governmental Affairs, University of California at Davis.

Han Minzhu and Hua Sheng, eds.
1990   *Cries for Democracy: Writings and Speeches from the 1989 Chinese Democracy Movement*. Princeton: Princeton University Press.

Hankiss, Elemer
1988   "The 'Second Society': Is There an Alternative Social Model Emerging in Contemporary Hungary?" *Social Research* 55, no. 1: 13–42.

Healey, Christopher J.
1984   "Trade and Sociability: Balanced Reciprocity as Generosity in the New Guinea Highlands." *American Ethnologist* 11 (February).

Henderson, Gail, and Myron Cohen
1984   *The Chinese Hospital: A Socialist Work Unit*. New Haven: Yale University Press.

Hevia, James L.
1990   "Disposing Bodies and Configuring Space in Manchu Imperial Ritual." Paper presented at the meeting of the American Ethnological Society, Atlanta, Georgia.

Hobsbawm, Eric, and Terence Ranger
1983   *The Invention of Tradition*. Cambridge: Cambridge University Press.

Holston, James
1989   *The Modernist City: An Anthropological Critique of Brasilia*. Chicago: University of Chicago Press.

Hsiao Kung-chuan
1967   *Rural China: Imperial Control in the 19th Century*. Seattle: University of Washington Press.
1979   *A History of Chinese Political Thought*, vol. 1. Translated by F. W. Mote. Princeton: Princeton University Press.

Hsu Cho-yun
1965   *Ancient China in Transition*. Stanford: Stanford University Press.

Hsu Cho-yun and Katherine M. Linduff
1988   *Western Chou Civilization*. New Haven: Yale University Press.

Hsu Dau-lin
1970–71   "The Myth of the 'Five Human Relations' of Confucius." *Monumenta Serica*, no. 29:27–37.

Hsu, Francis L.K.
1967   *Under the Ancestors' Shadow*. Stanford: Stanford University Press.

Hu Hsien-chin
1944   "The Chinese Concept of 'Face.'" *American Anthropologist* 46.

Hubert, Henri, and Marcel Mauss
1964   *Sacrifice: Its Nature and Function*. Translated by W. D. Halls. Chicago: University of Chicago Press.

Jacobs, Bruce
1979   "A Preliminary Model of Particularistic Ties in Chinese Political Alli

ances: Kan-ch'ing and Kuan-hsi in a Rural Taiwanese Township." *China Quarterly*, no. 78 (June).

1980 *Local Politics in a Rural Chinese Cultural Setting*. Canberra: Australian National University, Contemporary China Centre.

Jakobson, Roman, and Morris Halle

1956 *Fundamentals of Language*. The Hague: Mouton.

JanMohamed, Abdul R.

1993 "Worldliness-without-World, Homelessness-as-Home: Toward a Definition of the Specular Border Intellectual." In *Edward Said: A Critical Reader*, ed. Michael Sprinker. London: Basil Blackwell.

Judd, Ellen.

1989 "Niangjia: Chinese Women and their Natal Families." *Journal of Asian Studies* 48, no. 3.

Kandel, Barbara

1978 "New Interpretations of the Han Dynasty Published During the Pi-Lin Pi-Kong Campaign." *Modern China* 4 (January): 91–120.

Keane, John, ed.

1988a *Civil Society and the State*. London: Verso.

1988b "Despotism and Democracy: The Origins and Development of the Distinction between Civil Society and the State 1750–1850." In *Civil Society and the State*, 35–72. London: Verso.

Keightley, David

1981 "The Giver and the Gift: The Western Chou State as Social Polity." (Manuscript.)

1982 "The Western Chou as Social Polity: Vassalage Without Feudalism." Paper presented at the conference for Asian Studies on the Pacific Coast, University of California at Santa Cruz, 27 June.

1983 "The Late Shang State: When, Where, and What?" In *The Origins of Chinese Civilization*, 523–64. Berkeley and Los Angeles: University of California Press.

Keller, Evelyn Fox

1983 "Feminism and Science." In *The Signs Reader: Women, Gender, and Scholarship*. Chicago: University of Chicago Press.

Kenedi, J.

1981 *Do It Yourself: Hungary's Hidden Economy*. New York: Pluto Press.

King, Ambrose Yeo-chi

1991 "Kuan-hsi and Network Building: A Sociological Interpretation." *Daedalus* 120, no. 2: 63–84.

Kligman, Gail

1990 "Reclaiming the Public: A Reflection on Creating Civil Society in Romania." *East European Politics and Societies*. 4, no. 3: 393–438.

Kondo, Dorinne

1991 *Crafting Selves*. Chicago: University of Chicago Press.

Lang, Olga

1946 *Chinese Family and Society*. New Haven: Yale University Press.

Laplanche, Jean, and J.-B. Pontalis
1973 *The Language of Psycho-Analysis.* Translated by Donald Nicholson-Smith. New York: W. W. Norton.
Lee, Leo Ou-fan
1990 "In Search of Modernity: Some Reflections on a New Mode of Consciousness in Twentieth-Century Chinese History and Literature." In *Ideas Across Cultures: Essays on Chinese Thought in Honor of Benjamin Schwartz.* Cambridge: Harvard University Press.
1991 "On the Margins of the Chinese Discourse: Some Personal Thoughts on the Cultural Meaning of the Periphery." *Daedalus* 120 (Spring): 207–26.
Lefort, Claude
1986 *The Political Forms of Modern Society: Bureaucracy, Democracy, Totalitarianism.* Edited by J. B. Thompson. Cambridge: M.I.T. Press.
Legge, James, trans.
1865 *The Shoo King (Book of Documents).* Vol. 3 of *The Chinese Classics.* Oxford: Clarendon Press.
1872 *The Ch'un Ts'ew with the Tso Chuen.* Vol. 5 of *The Chinese Classics.* Oxford: Clarendon Press.
1885 *The Li Ki (Book of Rites).* Vols. 27–28 of *The Sacred Books of the East,* ed. Max Muller. Oxford: Clarendon Press.
1961 *The Analects.* Vol. 1 of *The Chinese Classics.* Hong Kong: Hong Kong University Press.
Lévi-Strauss, Claude
1969 *The Elementary Structures of Kinship.* Tranlsated by J. H. Bell and J. R. von Sturner. Boston: Beacon Press.
Levy, Marion J.
1949 *The Family Revolution in Modern China.* Cambridge: Harvard University Press.
Lewis, Mark Edward
1990 *Sanctioned Violence in Early China.* Albany: State University of New York Press.
Li Yu-ning, ed.
1975 *The First Emperor of China.* New York: International Arts & Sciences Press.
1977 *Shang Yang's Reforms and State Control in China.* White Plains, N.Y.: M. E. Sharpe.
Liang, Heng, and Judith Shapiro
1983 *Son of the Revolution.* New York: Vintage Books.
Liao, W. K., trans.
1959 *The Complete Works of Han Fei Tzu.* Vol. 2., London: A. Probsthain.
Lin Yu-sheng
1974–75 "The Evolution of the Pre-Confucian Meaning of *Jen* and the Confucian Concept of Moral Autonomy," *Monumenta Serica* 31.
Liu, James J.Y.
1967 *The Chinese Knight-Errant.* Chicago: University of Chicago Press.

Liu, Lydia
  1991   "The Female Tradition in Modern Chinese Literature: Negotiating
         Feminisms Across East/West Boundaries." *Genders*, no. 12 (Winter).
  1993   "Translingual Practice: The Discourse of Individualism Between China
         and the West." *Positions* 1 (Spring).
  1994   "The Female Body and Nationalist Discourse: The Split National Sub-
         ject in Xiao Hong's *Field of Life and Death*." In *Scattered Hegemonies*,
         ed. Caren Kaplan and Inderpal Grewal. Minneapolis: University of
         Minnesota Press.
Liu Zheng, Song Dian et al.
  1981   *China's Population: Problems and Prospects*. Beijing: New World Press.
Loewe, Michael
  1985   "Attempts at Economic Co-ordination during the Western Han Dy-
         nasty." In *The Scope of State Power in China*, ed. Stuart R. Schram.
         London: School of Oriental and African Studies.
Lomnitz, Larissa A.
  1971   "Reciprocity of Favors in the Urban Middle Class of Chile." In *Studies
         in Economic Anthropology*, ed. George Dalton. Washington D.C.:
         American Anthropological Association.
Lyotard, Jean-François
  1984   *The Postmodern Condition: A Report on Knowledge*. Translated by
         Geoff Bennington and Brian Massumi. Minneapolis: University of Min-
         nesota Press.
Madsen, Richard
  1984   *Morality and Power in a Chinese Village*. Berkeley and Los Angeles:
         University of California Press.
Malinowski, Bronislaw
  1961   *Argonauts of the Western Pacific*. New York: E. P. Dutton.
Marcus, George E., and Michael M. J. Fischer
  1986   *Anthropology as Cultural Critique: An Experimental Moment in the
         Human Sciences*. Chicago: University of Chicago Press.
Marx, Karl
  1906   *Capital: A Critique of Political Economy*. Translated by S. Moore and
         E. Aveling. New York: The Modern Library.
Mauss, Marcel
  1967   *The Gift*. Translated by Ian Cunnison. New York: W. W. Norton.
  1985   "A Category of the Human Mind: The Notion of Person; the Notion of
         Self." In *The Category of the Person*, ed. M. Carrithers, S. Collins, and
         S. Lukes. Cambridge: Cambridge University Press.
Mayer, Adrian
  1966   "The Significance of Quasi-Groups in the Study of Complex Societies."
         In *The Social Anthropology of Complex Societies*, ed. Michael Banton.
         ASAM Monograph 4. London: Tavistock.
Meisner, Maurice
  1982   "The Cult of Mao Tse-tung." In *Marxism, Maoism, and Utopianism*.
         Madison: University of Wisconsin Press.

Moody, Peter R.
   1974   "The New Anti-Confucian Campaign in China: The First Round."
          Asian Survey 14, no. 4: 307–24.
Munro, Donald
   1969   *The Concept of Man in Early China*. Stanford: Stanford University
          Press.
Nee, Victor, and David Stark, eds.
   1989   *Remaking the Economic Institutions of Socialism: China and Eastern
          Europe*. Stanford: Stanford University Press.
Nivison, David S.
   1978   "Royal 'Virtue' in Shang Oracle Inscriptions." *Early China* 4.
Nowak, Krzysztof
   1988   "Covert Repressiveness and the Stability of a Political System: Poland
          at the End of the Seventies." *Social Research* 55, nos. 1–2: 179–208.
O'Hearn, Dennis
   1980   "The Consumer Second Economy: Size and Effects." *Soviet Studies* 32,
          no. 2.
Ong Aihwa
   1987   *Spirits of Resistance and Capitalist Discipline: Factory Women in Ma-
          laysia*. Albany: State University of New York Press.
   1994   "Engendering Cantonese Modernity: Social Imaginary and Public Cul-
          ture in Southern China." In *Gender, Social Regulation, and Economic
          Restructuring in East Asia*, ed. Diane Wolf, Cynthia Truelove and Tai-
          luk Lui (forthcoming).
Ortner, Sherry
   1973   "On Key Symbols." *American Anthropologist* 75 (October).
Parry, Jonathan
   1986   "*The Gift*, The Indian Gift and the 'Indian Gift,'" *Man* 21: 453–73.
Pelczynski, Z. A.
   1988   "Solidarity and the Rebirth of Civil Society." In *Civil Society and the
          State*, ed. John Keane. London: Verso.
Polanyi, Karl
   1944   *The Great Transformation*. New York: Rinehart.
   1957   "The Economy as Instituted Process." In *Trade and Market in Early
          Empires*, ed. Karl Polanyi and Conrad Arensberg. Glencoe, Ill.: The
          Free Press.
Potter, Sulamith, and Jack Potter
   1990   *China's Peasants: The Anthropology of a Revolution*. New York: Cam-
          bridge University Press.
Rabinow, Paul
   1986   "Representations Are Social Facts: Modernity and Post-Modernity in
          Anthropology." In *Writing Culture: The Poetics and Politics of Eth-
          nography*, ed. James Clifford and George Marcus. Berkeley and Los
          Angeles: University of California Press.
   1989   *French Modern: Norms and Forms of the Social Environment*. Cam-
          bridge: M.I.T. Press.

Rankin, Mary Backus
   1986   *Elite Activism and Political Transformation in China: Zhejiang Province, 1865–1911*. Stanford: Stanford University Press.

Rappaport, Roy A.
   1979a   "The Obvious Aspects of Ritual." In *Ecology, Meaning, Religion*. Berkeley, Calif.: North Atlantic Books.
   1979b   "Sanctity and Lies in Evolution." In *Ecology, Meaning, Religion*. Berkeley, Calif: North Atlantic Books.
   1986   "The Construction of Time and Eternity in Ritual." Lecture delivered at Indiana University, October.

Reich, Wilhelm
   1970   *The Mass Psychology of Fascism*. Translated by Vincent Carfagno. New York: The Noonday Press.

Rickels, Laurence
   1988   *Aberrations of Mourning: Writing on German Crypts*. Detroit: Wayne State University Press.

Rigby, Harry T.
   1977   "Stalinism and the Mono-Organizational Society." In *Stalinism: Essays in Historical Interpretation*, ed. Robert C. Tucker. New York: W. W. Norton.

Rofel, Lisa
   1992   "Rethinking Modernity: Space and Factory Discipline in China." *Cultural Anthropology* 7, no. 1: 93–114.

Rosaldo, Michelle Z.
   1984   "Toward an Anthropology of Self and Feeling." In *Culture Theory: Essays on Mind, Self & Emotion*. ed. Richard Shweder and Robert Levine, 137–57. Cambridge: Cambridge University Press.

Rosaldo, Renato
   1989   *Culture and Truth: The Remaking of Social Analysis*. Boston: Beacon Press.

Rosen, Stanley
   1982   *Red Guard Factionalism and the Cultural Revolution in Guangzhou*. Boulder: Westview Press.

Rousseau, Jean-Jacques
   1967   *The Social Contract and Discourse on the Origin of Inequality*. Edited by Lester G. Crocker. New York: Washington Square Press. (1762.)

Rowe, William T.
   1984   *Hankow: Commerce and Society in a Chinese City, 1796–1889*. Stanford: Stanford University Press.
   1990   "The Public Sphere in Modern China." *Modern China* 16 (July).

Rubin, Gayle
   1975   "The Traffic in Women: Notes on the Political Economy of Sex" in *Toward an Anthropology of Women*. Rayna Reiter, ed. New York: Monthly Review Press.

Sahlins, Marshall
   1972   *Stone Age Economics*. New York: Aldine.

1976   *Culture and Practical Reason*. Chicago: University of Chicago Press.
Said, Edward
    1979   *Orientalism*. New York: Random House.
    1986   "Intellectuals in the Post-Colonial World." *Salmagundi*, no. 70–71.
Sampson, Steven
    1983   "Rich Families and Poor Collectives: An Anthropological Approach to Romania's 'Second Economy,'" *Bidrag til Oststatsforskning*. (Contributions to East European Research) (Uppsala) 11, no. 1.
    1985   "The Informal Sector in Eastern Europe." *Telos*, no. 66.
Sass, Louis A.
    1987   "Schreber's Panopticism: Psychosis and the Modern Soul." *Social Research* 54 (Spring): 101–47.
Savage, William
    1985   *In the Tradition of Kings: The Gentleman in the Analects of Confucius*. Ph.D. diss., University of Michigan.
Schwartz, Benjamin
    1985   *The World of Thought in Ancient China*. Cambridge: Harvard University Press.
Scott, James
    1985   *Weapons of the Weak: Everyday Forms of Peasant Resistance*. New Haven: Yale University Press.
Shue, Vivienne
    1988   *The Reach of the State: Sketches of the Body Politic*. Stanford: Stanford University Press.
Silverman, Kaja
    1983   *The Subject of Semiotics*. New York: Oxford University Press.
Si-ma Qian
    1964   *Shi Ji* (*Records of the Grand Historian of China*), vol. 2. Translated by Burton Watson. New York: Columbia University Press. *See* Si-Ma 1972.
Siu, Helen
    1990   "Recycling Rituals." In *Unofficial China*, ed. Perry Link, Richard Madsen, and Paul Pickowicz. Boulder, Colo.: Westview Press.
    1993   "Cultural Identity and the Politics of Difference in South China." *Daedalus* (Spring).
Skinner, G. William
    1977a   "Introduction: Urban Social Structure in Ch'ing China." In *The City in Late Imperial China*, ed. G. W. Skinner. Stanford: Stanford University Press.
Skinner, G. William, ed.
    1977b   *The City in Late Imperial China*. Stanford: Stanford University Press.
Solinger, Dorothy
    1983   "Marxism and the Market in Socialist China: The Reforms of 1979–1980 in Context." In *State and Society in Contemporary China*, ed. Victor Nee and David Mozingo. Ithaca: Cornell University Press.

Southall, Aidan

1956   *Alur Society*. Cambridge: Heffer.

1965   "A Critique of the Typology of States and Political Systems." In *Political Systems and the Distribution of Power*, 113–40. A.S.A. Monographs 2. London: Tavistock.

1988   "The Segmentary State in Africa and Asia." *Comparative Study of Society and History* 30 (January): 52–82.

Stack, Carol B.

1974   *All Our Kin: Strategies for Survival in a Black Community*. New York: Harper & Row.

Strand, David

1989   *Rickshaw Beijing: City People and Politics in 1920's China*. Berkeley and Los Angeles: University of California Press.

1990   "Protest in Beijing: Civil Society and Public Sphere in China." *Problems of Communism* (May–June).

Strathern, Marilyn

1983   "Subject or Object? Women and the Circulation of Valuables in Highland New Guinea." In *Women and Property, Women as Property*, ed. R. Hirschon. London: Croom Helm.

1987   "Producing Difference: Connections and Disconnections in Two New Guinea Highland Kinship Systems." In *Gender and Kinship*, ed. J. Collier and Sylvia Yanagisako. Stanford: Stanford University Press.

1988   *The Gender of the Gift: Problems with Women and Problems with Society in Melanesia*. Berkeley and Los Angeles: University of California Press.

1990   "Partners and Consumers: Making Relations Visible." *New Literary History* 22, no. 3: 581–601.

Sun, Lung-kee

1992   "Social Psychology in the Late Qing Period." *Modern China* 18 (July): 235–62.

Szelenyi, Ivan

1982   "The Intelligentsia in the Class Structure of State-Socialist Societies." In *Marxist Inquiries*, ed. M. Burawoy and T. Skocpol. Chicago: University of Chicago Press. (Supplement to *American Journal of Sociology* 88.)

1983   *Urban Inequalities under State Socialism*. London: Oxford University Press.

Taussig, Michael

1992   *The Nervous System*. New York: Routledge.

Taylor, Charles

1990   "Invoking Civil Society." *Public Culture* 3, no. 1.

Thurston, Anne F.

1988   *Enemies of the People: The Ordeal of the Intellectuals in China's Great Cultural Revolution*. Cambridge: Harvard University Press.

Tien H. Yuan

1973   *China's Population Struggle*. Columbus: Ohio State University Press.

Tu Wei-ming
  1968 "Creative Tension between *Jen* and *Li.*" *Philosophy East and West* (January): 29–39.
  1972 "*Li* as a Process of Humanization." *Philosophy East and West* 22 (April): 187–201.
  1983 "The Idea of the Human in Mencian Thought: An Approach to Chinese Aesthetics." In *Theories of the Arts in China*. Princeton: Princeton University Press.
  1991 "Cultural China: The Periphery as the Center." *Daedalus* 120 (Spring).
van der Sprenkel, Sybille
  1977 "Urban Social Control." In *The City in Late Imperial China*, ed. G. W. Skinner. Stanford: Stanford University Press.
Van Velsen, J.
  1964 *The Politics of Kinship*. Manchester: Manchester University Press.
Verdery, Katherine
  1991 "Theorizing Socialism: A Prologue to the 'Transition.'" *American Ethnologist* 18 (August): 419–39.
Vogel, Ezra
  1965 "From Friendship to Comradeship: The Change in Personal Relations in Communist China." *China Quarterly*, no. 21: 46–60.
Wakeman, Frederic
  1988a "Policing Modern Shanghai." *The China Quarterly*, no. 115 (September): 408–40.
  1988b "Mao's Remains." In *Death Ritual in Late Imperial and Modern China*, ed. James L. Watson and Evelyn Rawski. Berkeley and Los Angeles: University of California Press.
  1989 "All the Rage in China." *The New York Review of Books*, 2 March: 19–21.
  1993 "The Civil Society and Public Sphere Debate: Western Reflections on Chinese Political Culture." *Modern China* 10 (April): 108–38.
Walder, Andrew G.
  1986 *Communist Neo-Traditionalism: Work and Authority in Chinese Industry*. Berkeley and Los Angeles: University of California Press.
Waley, Arthur, trans.
  1954 *The Book of Songs*. London: George Allen & Unwin. See *Shi Jing* 1980.
Wank, David L.
  1991 "Merchant Entrepreneurs and the Development of Civil Society: The Impact of Private Sector Expansion on State/Society Relations in a Chinese City." Paper presented at the meeting of the Association for Asian Studies, New Orleans, April.
Wasserstrom, Jeffrey.
  1989 "Manners Maketh the Class: Etiquette and Social Stratification in Ancient China." (Manuscript.)
Watson, James L.
  1982 "Chinese Kinship Reconsidered: Anthropological Perspectives on Historical Research." *China Quarterly*, no. 92.

Watson, James L., ed.
  1984   *Class and Social Stratification in Post-Revolution China.* New York: Cambridge University Press.
Watson, James L., and Evelyn Rawski, eds.
  1988   *Death Ritual in Late Imperial and Modern China.* Berkeley and Los Angeles: University of California Press.
Way, John L., trans.
  1983   *Mao Gong Ding (Mao Kung Ting).* Taipei: Yee Wen Publishing.
Weber, Max
  1958   *The Protestant Ethic and the Spirit of Capitalism.* Talcott Parsons, trans. New York: Charles Scribner's Sons.
  1968   *Economy and Society.* Berkeley and Los Angeles: University of California Press.
Webster's New Collegiate Dictionary
  1973   Springfield, Mass.: G. & C. Merriam.
Wedel, Janine
  1986   *The Private Poland: An Anthropological Look at Everyday Life.* New York: Facts on File.
White, Gordon
  1976   *The Politics of Class and Class Origin: The Case of the Cultural Revolution.* Contemporary China Papers, no. 9. Canberra: Australian National University.
Whyte, Martin K.
  1974   *Small Groups and Political Rituals in China.* Berkeley and Los Angeles: University of California Press.
  1988   "Death in the People's Republic of China." In *Death Ritual in Late Imperial and Modern China*, ed. James L. Watson and Evelyn Rawski. Berkeley and Los Angeles: University of California Press.
Whyte, Martin K., and William L. Parish
  1984   *Urban Life in Contemporary China.* Chicago: University of Chicago Press.
Wiener, Annette B.
  1992   *Inalienable Possessions: The Paradox of Keeping-While-Giving.* Berkeley and Los Angeles: University of California Press.
Wojcicki, Kazimierz
  1981   "The Reconstruction of Society." *Telos*, no. 47.
Wolf, Arthur P.
  1974   "Gods, Ghosts, and Ancestors." In *Religion and Ritual in Chinese Society*, ed. A. Wolf. Stanford: Stanford University Press.
Wolf, Eric
  1966   "Kinship, Friendship and Patron-Client Relations in Complex Societies." In *The Social Anthropology of Complex Societies*, ed. M. Banton. ASA Monograph 4. London: Tavistock.
Wu Pei-yi
  1979   "Self-Examination and Confession of Sins in Traditional China." *Harvard Journal of Asiatic Studies* 39, no. 1: 5–38.

Wuthnow, Robert, ed.
1991 *Between States and Markets: The Voluntary Sector in Comparative Perspective*. Princeton: Princeton University Press.
Xue Muqiao
1981 *China's Socialist Economy*. Beijing: Foreign Languages Press.
Yan Yunxiang
1992 "The Impact of Rural Reform on Economic and Social Stratification in a Chinese Village." *The Australian Journal of Chinese Affairs*, no. 27 (January).
Yang, C. K.
1959 "Some Characteristics of Chinese Bureaucratic Behavior." In *Confucianism in Action*, ed. Arthur Wright. Stanford: Stanford University Press.
1961 "State Control of Religion." In *Religion in Chinese Society*. Berkeley and Los Angeles: University of California Press.
Yang Lien-sheng
1957 "The Concept of Pao as a Basis for Social Relations in China." In *Chinese Thought and Institutions*, ed. John K. Fairbank. Chicago: University of Chicago Press.
Yang, Martin
1945 *A Chinese Village: Taitou, Shantung Province*. New York: Columbia University Press.
Yang, Mayfair Mei-hui
1988 "The Modernity of Power in the Chinese Socialist Order." *Cultural Anthropology* 3 (November): 408–27.
1989a "The Gift Economy and State Power in China." *Comparative Studies in Society and History* 31 (January): 25–54.
1989b "Between State and Society: The Construction of Corporateness in a Chinese Socialist Factory." *The Australian Journal of Chinese Affairs*, no. 22 (July): 31–60.
1991 "Une histoire du present: Gouvernement rituel et gouvernement d'état dans la Chine ancienne." *Annales* 5 (September–October): 1041–69.
1993 "Of Gender, State Censorship, and Overseas Capital: An Interview with Chinese Director Zhang Yimou." *Public Culture* 5 (Winter): 1–17.
1994 "Film Discussion Groups in China: State Discourse or a Plebeian Public Sphere?" *Visual Anthropology Review* 10 (Spring): 47–60.
Yates, Robin
1987 "Social Status in the Ch'in: Evidence from the Yun-meng Legal Documents. Part One: Commoners." *Harvard Journal of Asiatic Studies* 47, no. 1: 197–237.
Zito, Angela
1987 "City Gods, Filiality, and Hegemony in Late Imperial China." *Modern China* 13, no. 3: 333–71.
1993 "Bodies and Vessels: 'Centering' in Grand Sacrifice." In *The Philosophy of Body: Eastern Perspectives*, ed. T. P. Kasulis and Roger T. Ames. Binghamton: SUNY Press.
1994 "Ritualizing Li." *Positions* 1, no. 2.

Index

The Wilder House Series in
Politics, History, and Culture

Language and Power: Exploring Political Cultures in Indonesia
by Benedict R. O'G. Anderson

Bandits and Bureaucrats: The Ottoman Route to State Centralization
by Karen Barkey

*Reclaiming the Sacred: Lay Religion and Popular Politics in
Revolutionary France* by Suzanne Desan

*Divided Nations: Class, Politics, and Nationalism in the Basque Country
and Catalonia* by Juan Díez Medrano

*Manufacturing Inequality: Gender Division in the French and British
Metalworking Industries, 1914–1939* by Laura Lee Downs

*State and Society in Medieval Europe: Gwynedd and Languedoc under
Outside Rule* by James Given

New Voices in the Nation: Women and the Greek Resistance, 1941–1964
by Janet Hart

The Rise of Christian Democracy in Europe
by Stathis N. Kalyvas

The Presence of the Past: Chronicles, Politics, and Culture in Sinhala Life
by Steven Kemper

True France: The Wars over Cultural Identity, 1900–1945
by Herman Lebovics

*Unsettled States, Disputed Lands: Britain and Ireland, France and
Algeria, Israel and the West Bank–Gaza* by Ian S. Lustick

Communities of Grain: Rural Rebellion in Comparative Perspective
by Victor V. Magagna

Hausaland Divided: Colonialism and Independence in Nigeria and Niger
by William F. S. Miles

*"We Ask for British Justice": Workers and Racial Difference in Late
Imperial Britain* by Laura Tabili

Gifts, Favors, and Banquets: The Art of Social Relationships in China
by Mayfair Mei-hui Yang